Lecture Notes in Computer Science   10340

Commenced Publication in 1973
Founding and Former Series Editors:
Gerhard Goos, Juris Hartmanis, and Jan van Leeuwen

More information about this series at http://www.springer.com/series/7411

Nishanth Sastry · Sandip Chakraborty (Eds.)

Communication Systems and Networks

9th International Conference, COMSNETS 2017
Bengaluru, India, January 4–8, 2017
Revised Selected Papers and Invited Papers

 Springer

Editors
Nishanth Sastry
King's College London
London
UK

Sandip Chakraborty
IIT Kharagpur
Kharagpur, West Bengal
India

ISSN 0302-9743   ISSN 1611-3349 (electronic)
Lecture Notes in Computer Science
ISBN 978-3-319-67234-2   ISBN 978-3-319-67235-9 (eBook)
DOI 10.1007/978-3-319-67235-9

Library of Congress Control Number: 2017953435

LNCS Sublibrary: SL5 – Computer Communication Networks and Telecommunications

Printed on acid-free paper

This Springer imprint is published by Springer Nature
The registered company is Springer International Publishing AG
The registered company address is: Gewerbestrasse 11, 6330 Cham, Switzerland

Preface

Following an extremely successful ninth International Conference on Communication Systems and Networks (COMSNETS) in January 2017, this book has been published as a collection of the highlights of the conference. The conference this year had a new record of 192 submissions. Of these, 49 high-quality papers were chosen, after rigorous review by an 80-strong Program Committee, leading to 14 sessions over two parallel tracks in the program.

This book contains the best papers presented at the conference, and is divided into two parts: The first contains reviewed papers from invited speakers, who were chosen from across the world, and are well recognized leaders in the field. The second part contains selected best papers presented originally in the main technical program, but significantly extended and reviewed again for this highlight edition.

April 2017

Sandip Chakraborty
Nishanth Sastry

Contents

Invited Papers

Affordable Sensing Based Healthcare

Data-Driven Screening, Diagnosis and Therapy

Arpan Pal[✉]

TCS Research and Innovation, Tata Consultancy Services Ltd., Kolkata, India
arpan.pal@tcs.com

Abstract. In order to move from the current "illness"-driven model to a "wellness"-driven model in healthcare, one needs to build affordable, easily usable and mass deployable solutions. This is particularly true for developing countries like India. In this talk we look at early detection and screening for lifestyle diseases like coronary artery disease (CAD) and diabetes using mobile phones and low-cost attachments to mobile phones followed by signal processing and machine learning based analytics. We also look at creating an affordable tele-home-care based rehabilitation therapy solution for stroke patients using Kinect to help in diagnosis, assessment and therapy compliance. We present results on pilot studies done on patients in India and also on open datasets.

Keywords: Wellness · Affordable · Lifestyle diseases · Screening · Therapy · Rehabilitation

1 The Problem

As the medical science progresses, life expectancy in both developed and underdeveloped countries are going up. This is leading towards increasing number of independently living elderly patients, especially in developed counties, who need continuous monitoring. There are also a large number of physically challenged people who have suffered stroke or similar conditions who, in addition to continuous monitoring, need remote rehabilitation and therapy.

On the other hand lifestyle diseases like diabetes and heart blocks diseases are becoming more and more prevalent among younger generation. These diseases, if detected early, can be reversed via lifestyle changes, however most of the cases they are detected at an advanced stage where they are no more preventable and in many cases, fatal.

In developing countries like India also, the above issues are extremely prevalent. However the problem is compounded by a few more developing-country specific issues:

(a) Capacity issue – There are inadequate number of specialist doctors in both urban and rural areas. The poor doctor-patient ratio leads to doctors being overwhelmed with huge number of patients, thereby justifying the need for a patient screening system for lifestyle diseases.

© Springer International Publishing AG 2017
N. Sastry and S. Chakraborty (Eds.): COMSNETS 2017, LNCS 10340, pp. 3–6, 2017.
DOI: 10.1007/978-3-319-67235-9_1

(b) Reachability issue – Even if doctors are available in health centers and hospitals, for many rural and semi-urban scenarios, they may be located quite far-off and lack of good and comfortable transportation system leads towards patients not being able have access to the specialist doctors. This problem is further aggravated for patients like stroke survivors who already may have partial physical disabilities due to paralysis. Hence there is need for systems that can do tele-diagnosis and remote-therapy.

(c) Affordability – While tele-health systems have been built and deployed in pilot scenarios, they have never been scaled to a level where a large amount of mass population can take advantage of that. The main reason for this lack of scalability is the cost of the whole system that employs costly medical devices for sensing followed by expensive, custom-built doctor-patient tele-interaction systems. Hence there is need to have affordable sensing systems that can use IoT and Cloud technologies to create an affordable, scalable model.

Just to put things in context, the elderly population (65 years or older) in USA was 46.2 million in 2014 which is 14.5% of the U.S. population. By 2060, this number will almost double – percentage of elderly people is expected to grow to 20.2% of the population by 2050[1]. On the other hand, just focusing on tele-rehabilitation of stroke patients at Europe, the annual cost for the European economy is 798 Billion Euros, more than twice the cost of cancer[2]. More than 1 Billion people need rehabilitation services worldwide. India is facing an emerging epidemic of neurological disability affecting over 3.5 million people annually, 11,000 every day and 7 people/minute[3] - this includes traumatic brain injuries, dementia and stroke. For stroke alone, 0.6 million people gets added annually to the disabled population. Diagnosis, therapy prescription and exercise compliance analysis at hospitals today need extremely sophisticated and costly equipment like VICON[4] costing almost 200KUSD available only in few hospitals which aggravates the capacity problem and has issues with reachability and affordability.

Looking at the Lifestyle diseases, *"IHD [ischemic heart disease, also known as Coronary Artery Disease or CAD] causes more deaths and disability and incurs greater economic costs than any other illness in the developed world... [and it] is likely to become the most common cause of death worldwide by 2020"* - Antman et al., 2008[5]. In India, in 2015, among 800 Million adults (>20 years of age), there were 61.8 Million people with CAD which is almost 8% - a 32% increase from 2010. More importantly, there are approx. 8 Million new cases of CAD among people aged less than 40 years between 2010 and 2015[6]. Additionally, studies have already shown that South Asians typically have smaller coronary artery diameters that Caucasians (3.2 ± 0.56 mm vs. 5.53 ± 0.69 mm)[7]. Today, the only definitive diagnosis of CAD is Coronary Angiogram,

[1] http://www.aoa.acl.gov/Aging_Statistics/index.aspx.

[2] http://www.neuroathome.net/p/home.html.

[3] http://www.ncbi.nlm.nih.gov/pmc/articles/PMC3511929/.

[4] https://www.vicon.com/file/vicon/gait-analysis-print-ready-19082016-web-52778.pdf.

[5] https://www.atrainceu.com/course-all/coronary-artery-disease-cad-041.

[6] http://www.ncbi.nlm.nih.gov/pubmed/7743682.

[7] http://www.ncbi.nlm.nih.gov/pmc/articles/PMC1741307/pdf/v075p00463.pdf.

which is costly, harmful to body and cannot be prescribed to all people as preventive measure. The other possible device for such diagnosis is a digital stethoscope that costs approx. USD 1K – such devices also are not affordable in rural scenarios. Hence there is need for developing an extremely low-cost screening system for CAD that can even be used easily in early ages when usually there are no preventive check-ups.

Similarly there were nearly 415 Million diabetes cases worldwide in 2015 which is expected to rise to 642 Million by 2040. In Indian sub-continent itself there are 78 Million Diabetes cases - it will rise to 140 Million by 2035[8]. Diabetes resulted in 5 Million deaths in 2015 worldwide and 75% of diabetes people live in low and middle income countries. Today the basic diabetes test is invasive that requires pricking of skin – it cannot be used as a generic screening test for masses. Hence there is need for developing affordable non-invasive screening for diabetes.

2   Proposed Solution

We propose to use sensors on mobile phones and low cost attachment on sensors for creating affordable screening system for CAD and Diabetes. Smartphones are becoming all-pervasive in Indian Households and its camera can be used on fingertips to get a good estimate of blood flow (also called Photoplethysmogram or PPG). There are also Bluetooth enabled PPG devices available which are low cost. Similarly mobile phone microphones can be used for recording heart sound (Phonocardiogram of PCG). PCG and PPG can be thought of as input and output markers for the circulatory system and hence diseases like CAD and Diabetes which are manifestation of arterial blocks/hardening of arteries is expected to create specific signatures in PCG and PPG. We use real-time signal quality checker based user feedback systems for collecting noise-free signals from low cost phone sensors, which after suitable signal processing, feature engineering and machine learning can create models for screening CAD, and Diabetes patients from PCG and PPG.

For telerehab we propose to use Kinect sensor and its Skeleton model output. The Skeleton model data is processed for Gait Analysis and Single Limb Standing (SLS) Analysis. We use Kalman Filter based joint noise removal to improve on the noisy Kinect data.

For both disease screening and telerehab, a cloud based end to end system is built. For disease screening, a mobile phone app is used the patient screen for data collection using PPG and PCG. An extremely low-cost 3D printed attachment that can extend a mobile phone to a full-fledged digital stethoscope is also proposed. The mobile phone also serves as a gateway to the cloud connectivity. The screening analytics and recommendation for doctors are provided through the cloud service. In case of telerehab, Kinect is typically connected to a TV as display device along with a low-cost PC as a local gateway. Most of the Skeleton-level processing happens on the local PC whereas analytics on skeleton data for diagnosis and therapy analytics is performed on the cloud to provide doctors with a remote patient view.

---

[8] http://www.idf.org/about-diabetes/facts-figures.

3 Results

For CAD screening system, we first used open dataset from Physionet[9] (56 doctor certified CAD patients and 56 non-CAD people for PPG, ~36 doctor certified CAD patients and ~272 non-CAD people for PCG). For Physionet data we got both Sensitivity (correctly detecting diseased people) and Specificity (correctly detecting non-diseased people) above 80%. We also collected data from real patients (15 doctor certified CAD and 20 non-CAD) – here after fusing PCG and PPG analysis, we got 80%+ Sensitivity and Specificity [1, 2].

For diabetes screening system, we used data collected from 24 diabetic patients and 61 non-diabetic people. We have got a sensitivity of 78% and Specificity of 70% [3].

For Telerehab, we used data collected from 11 patients and 8 normal people. Gait analysis accuracy obtained was ~3.4 cm. Additionally, using Kinect data we could successfully segregate stroke vs. control patients and patients with fall history vs. patients without fall history from SLS duration and vibration with 100% accuracy [4].

It should be noted here that all the results presented are early research outcomes on limited number of real patients. Work is going on now for larger scale data collection trials in partnership with hospitals in India (500+ patients) with a goal to prove the system on that data. Only after success of the trials, we can think of creating a deployable solution that can be tested/used in the field.

Acknowledgment. I thank all the scientists and researchers working in TCS Research and Innovation in Health Sensing projects – the results of their combined work is presented in this paper. I also thank our doctor consultants for their involvement and support for the medical domain knowledge.

References

1. Dey, S., Biswas, S., Pal, A., Mukherjee, A., Garain, U., Mandana, K.: CAD patient classification using MIMIC-II. In: Giokas, K., Bokor, L., Hopfgartner, F. (eds.) eHealth 360°. LNICST, vol. 181, pp. 370–375. Springer, Cham (2017). doi:10.1007/978-3-319-49655-9_44
2. Banerjee, R., et al.: Time-frequency analysis of phonocardiogram for classifying heart disease. In: Computing in Cardiology (CinC), September 2016
3. Ramu Reddy, V., et al.: PerDMCS: weighted fusion of heart rate variability features for robust and efficient diabetes mellitus classification. In: HealthInf, Portugal, February 2017
4. Sinha, A., et al.: Accurate upper body rehabilitation system using Kinect. In: EMBC, Orlando, USA, August 2016

---

[9] www.physionet.org.

Interference Power Bound Analysis of a Network of Wireless Robots

Pradipta Ghosh[✉] and Bhaskar Krishnamachari

University of Southern California, Los Angeles, CA 90089, USA
{pradiptg,bkrishna}@usc.edu

Abstract. We consider a fundamental problem concerning the deployment of a wireless robotic network: to fulfill various end-to-end performance requirements, a "sufficient" number of robotic relays must be deployed to ensure that links are of acceptable quality. Prior work has not addressed how to find this number. We use the properties of Carrier Sense Multiple Access (CSMA) based wireless communication to derive an upper bound on the spacing between any transmitter-receiver pair, which directly translates to a lower bound on the number of robots to deploy. We focus on SINR-based performance requirements due to their wide applicability. Next, we show that the bound can be improved by exploiting the geometrical structure of a network, such as linearity in the case of flow-based robotic router networks. Furthermore, we also use the bound on robot count to formulate a lower bound on the number of orthogonal codes required for a high probability of interference free communication. We demonstrate and validate our proposed bounds through simulations.

1 Introduction

In the field of Robotics and Automation, one of the emerging area of research is focused on the applicability of a wireless network of robots to create a temporary communication backbone between a set of communication endpoints with no or limited connectivity [1]. In these contexts, the robots act as relay nodes to form wireless communication paths between the communication endpoints. The application of this field of research ranges from fire fighting [2] and underground mining [3] to supporting temporary increase in the communication demands or creating a secure mesh network for clandestine operations [4]. To the best of our knowledge, one of the unexplored problem in this context is to determine the number of robots to deploy such that all the links can maintain certain acceptable link qualities, such as maximum allowed bit error rate (BER) or minimum supported data rate, in presence of fading and shadowing. Interestingly, most of these link quality metrics are known to be directly related to the Signal to Interference plus Noise Ratio (SINR) of the links. Now, the SINR value of a link depends on the spacing between the transmitter and receiver of the link as well as the locations of the interfering nodes. Thus, an offline characterization of SINR values as a function of the maximum allowed inter-node distance is required to

© Springer International Publishing AG 2017
N. Sastry and S. Chakraborty (Eds.): COMSNETS 2017, LNCS 10340, pp. 7–23, 2017.
DOI: 10.1007/978-3-319-67235-9_2

properly select the number of nodes to be deployed and to properly place the nodes across a deployment region. Moreover, the presence of CSMA/CA among the robots needs to be taken into account for more practical estimation.

In our venture for a generic model to estimate the number of robots to deploy (by estimating the maximum allowed inter-node distance to maintain the target SINR), we explored the existing literature in search for a proper model of interference and SINR range analysis in a CSMA/CA based wireless network. There exist a large body of works that characterize the mean interference power distribution in CSMA networks [5,6] by employing the concepts of point process such as Poisson Point process, Matérn hard core process and Simple Sequential Inhibition [7]. *The basic idea of this class of work is to represent the locations of the interferers as spatial point processes, more specifically, hard core point processes where the nodes fulfil a criterion of being certain distance apart to take into account CSMA among themselves.* Through application of different point process properties such as thinning and superpositions, researchers [5,6,8,9] estimated the probability distributions of the mean interference powers in the presence of CSMA/CA. Interested readers are referred to [10] for a detailed survey on this class of works. Among the other class of works, the work of Hekmat and Van Mieghem [11] is the most relevant to us. They demonstrated that the interference power in the presence of CSMA is actually upper bounded and can be best estimated by use of a hexagonal lattice structure. *However, this work as well as most of the other works include some assumptions such as the receiver being located at the center of a contention region, which is only acceptable if the devices follow the 802.11 RTS/CTS standards* [12]. *Interestingly, in practice, very few commercially available products actually employ the RTS/CTS mechanism. Furthermore, the Internet of Things (IoT) and Wireless Sensor Network (WSN) standard 802.15.4, which is also a standard choice for robotic network platforms, does not use RTS/CTS mechanism, in order to avoid inefficiencies.* Thus, it is actually the transmitter that employs the CSMA and should be located at the center of the contention region, whereas, the receiver is free to be anywhere inside the transmitter's communication range. In such cases, the SINR and the interference mean values as well as the bounds for a link are, in fact, functions of the separation distance (d) between the endpoints of the link. **However, none of the existing works try to characterize the SINR or the interference as a function of the separation distance (d), which is crucial for the number of robot estimations.** In this paper, we modify the bounds proposed in [11] and flesh out details of applying the modified bounds to estimate the number of robots to be deployed to satisfy the communication performance goals. Note that, in the rest of the paper, we focus on interference limited networks and, thereby, ignore the effect of noise and focus on Signal to Interference Ratio (SIR) instead of SINR.

In this paper, we **first** explain the concepts presented in [11] (for a general dense wireless network) as well as the impracticality of the bounds, followed by our proposed modified interference and SIR bounds as functions of the distance between a transmitter and a receiver, for any network that employs CSMA/CA.

Through a set of simulation results we show that, with fading introduced in the model, we can form a stochastic bound as well, such that the probability of the real interference being higher than the bound is very low. This formulation helps any network designer to properly choose a maximum separation between the nodes and to properly place a set of nodes in any practical deployment. **Secondly,** we extend this bound one step further to determine a bound on the number of orthogonal codes to be used in order to guarantee a high probability of interference free communication. We also explore the bounds on interference power, if a fixed number of orthogonal codes are employed. **Thirdly,** we consider our application specific scenario of robotic router network to devise a better bound by applying the structure of the network. Through a set of simulation experiments we validate the bounds and show that the improved application specific bound significantly $(10\% - 45\%)$ decreases the required number of costly, resource constraint robots.

2   Problem Description

In this section, we detail our problem formulations. For compactness, we list the symbols used for base problem formulation in Table 1 and symbols related to our goals in Table 2, respectively. Say, we have a transmitter node T and a receiver node X that are placed at d distance apart, alongside with a larger number of interfering wireless nodes. Each node of this interference limited network (i.e., the interference dominates over noise) employs *Channel Sense Multiple Access with Collision Avoidance* (CSMA/CA) [13] for wireless media access and has a transmission power of P_t. The radio range of each node is subdivided into three regions, centered at the node's location: a circular **connected/contention**

Table 1. General parameters

Symbol	Description
T	Transmitter
X	Receiver
d_{ij}	Distance between node i and j
d	Distance between T and X i.e., d_{TX}
η	Path loss exponent
$\psi \sim \mathcal{N}(0, \sigma^2)$	Log normal fading noise with variance σ^2
P_t	Transmitted signal power
P_r	Received signal power
$P_{\mathcal{I}}$	Received interference power
$\mathcal{I}^C$	Interference set cover
M	Number of flows

Table 2. System parameters

Symbol	Description
SIR_{th}	The target minimum SIR
$SIR_X(d)$	Minimum achievable SIR at X for d separation
D_1	Contention region outer radius
D_2	Transition region outer radius
γ	Required probability of $SIR \geq SIR_{th}$
κ	Minimum probability of interference free communication
d_{max}	Maximum distance allowed between T and X
$N_{\mathcal{O}}$	Number of orthogonal codes
$N_{\mathcal{I}}^{max}$	Maximum number of interfering nodes

region of radius D_1, an annular **transition region** with inner radius D_1 and outer radius D_2 (including the boundaries), and a **disconnected region** which is the entire region outside the circle with radius $D_2 > D_1$; where the values of D_1 and D_2 depend on the actual RSSI thresholds of the devices used [14]. Undoubtedly, in the presence of fading, the regions are not so nicely structured, nonetheless, can be approximated by proper choice of D_1 and D_2. Now, the CSMA restricts the transmissions from the nodes in the contention region of T, while the nodes in the transition region are aware of T's transmission with very low probabilities and, therefore, are the potential interferers. However, only a subset of the nodes in the transition region can be active simultaneously, due to CSMA among themselves, which requires any two simultaneous interferers to be at least D_1 distance apart. The interference power from the nodes in the disconnected region are considered insignificant.

Definition 1. *A set of interfering nodes ($\mathcal{I}^C$) such that $D_2 \geq d_{iT} \geq D_1$ and $d_{ij} \geq D_1 \ \forall \ i,j \in \mathcal{I}^C$, is referred to as an **Interference Set Cover**.*

Now, there are four main objectives of this work as follows.

Objective 1. *Find a mapping between d and the minimum achievable SIR at X, $SIR_X(d)$.* □

Objective 2. *Find the range, $0 < d \leq d_{max}$, such that the outage probability i.e., $\mathbb{P}(SIR_X(d) < SIR_{th}) < \gamma$ where $0 \leq \gamma \leq 0.5$ is the choice of the designer.* □

Now, one can employ a set of orthogonal codes to further restrict the interference in a CSMA network. In such cases, the maximum value of interference power decreases, based on the number of codes employed, possibly leading to near zero interference. In this context, our goal is as follows.

Objective 3. *Characterize $SIR_X(d)$ as a function of the number of orthogonal codes ($N_\mathcal{O}$) employed for concurrent transmissions, and find a bound $N'_\mathcal{O}$ such that $\mathbb{P}(\mathbb{1}_{\mathcal{I}0} = 1) \geq \kappa \ \forall N_\mathcal{O} > N'_\mathcal{O}$, where the indicator function $\mathbb{1}_{\mathcal{I}0}$ refers to interference free communication and $\kappa \geq 0.5$ is a designer choice.* □

For our SIR and Interference bound analysis, we consider two different scenarios in this paper. In the **first scenario**, the node pair in focus is placed in a *"dense"* network, where a countably many *uncontrollable wireless nodes* are co-located in the area of interest. **Secondly**, we consider our target application of robotic router placement, where the goal is to place a set of robots such that they form multihop links between a set of maximum M concurrent communication end-point pairs. This application context restricts the possible configuration of the interfering nodes within a class of network formations, such as straight line formation, that voids the earlier dense network assumption. At any time instance, we associate a set of routers with each flow $i \in \{1, 2, \cdots M\}$ that form a chain between the communication endpoints. *Thus, for a fixed set of communication endpoints of a flow i, the minimum number of nodes ($N_i^\mathcal{R}$) to be allocated to flow i depends on d_{max} which in turn controls the minimum number of nodes to be deployed, $N^\mathcal{R} \geq \sum_{i=1}^{M} N_i^\mathcal{R}$.*

Objective 4. *Find a better and tighter bound on interference as well as SIR by exploiting the application specific restrictions on the network configurations. Next, analyze the improvement in the number of robots required, with this improved bound.*   □

3   Outline of the Proposed Solution

In this section, we summarize our methodologies for achieving the target objectives while the details are discussed later on.

3.1   Methodology for Mapping from d to SIR_X

For a fixed value of the separation distance d between T and X, we estimate the maximum feasible interference as well as minimum feasible SIR, by exploiting the geometry of the connectivity region and transition region. For received power modelling, we opt for the standard log normal fading model [13], where the received power is distributed log normally with mean power calculated using simple path loss model. Thus, the received power can be represented as:

$$P_r(d) = Q.P_t d^{-\eta} 10^{\frac{\psi}{10}} \tag{1}$$

where Q is some constant. Next, we introduce the following claim as our whole estimation process revolves around this claim.

Claim 1. *In presence of Independent and Identically Distributed (I.I.D) fading noise, the Interference Set Cover (see Definition 1) with maximum mean power as well as maximum number of interferers will give us better stochastic bound than any other Interference Set Cover.*

Justification. This claim is justified by the fact that, if the fading noises are I.I.D, the Interference Set Cover with maximum number of nodes will give the highest variance. Thus, the Interference Set Cover with highest mean as well as highest number of nodes will be a better bound than any other Interference Set Cover.

Now, the main steps for representing SIR_X as a function of d are as follows.

Step 1. *We first identify the **Interference Set Cover(s)** $(\mathcal{I}^C)$ that will potentially give us the best estimate of the maximum feasible mean interference power, for a fixed d, using greedy algorithm.*

Step 2. *We estimate the maximum number of nodes in any **Interference Set Cover**, $N_{\mathcal{I}}^{max}$.*

Step 3. *To get the maximum interference power, we add up the interference powers of the nodes of the Interference Set Covers selected in Step 1, according to Eq. (1). Thus the total interference power at X is a sum of log normal variables as follows.*

$$P_{\mathcal{I}^C}(d) = Q. \sum_{j \in \mathcal{I}^C} P_t d_{jX}^{-\eta} 10^{\frac{\psi}{10}} \tag{2}$$

Step 4. *We multiply the interference power estimate in Step 3 by a correction factor* $\zeta = \max\{1, \frac{N_{\mathcal{I}}^{max}}{|\mathcal{I}^C|}\}$, *where* $|.|$ *denotes the cardinality of a set, to account for the Interference Set Covers with less than* $N_{\mathcal{I}}^{max}$ *number of nodes, i.e.,* $|\mathcal{I}^C| < N_{\mathcal{I}}^{max}$. *Now, the modified interference power is:*

$$P_{\mathcal{I}^C}(d) = \zeta.Q. \sum_{j \in \mathcal{I}^C} P_t d_{jX}^{-\eta} 10^{\frac{\psi}{10}} \tag{3}$$

Step 5. *We calculate the SIR value for each of the Interference Set Covers selected in Step 1 in dB, as follows.*

$$SIR_X(d) = 10 \log_{10} \left(\frac{P_t d^{-\eta} 10^{\frac{\psi}{10}}}{\zeta. \sum_{j \in \mathcal{I}^C} P_t d_{jX}^{-\eta} 10^{\frac{\psi}{10}}} \right) \tag{4}$$

3.2   Methodology for Selecting d_{max}

In order to properly select d_{max}, first of all, we need to estimate the distribution of the $SIR_X(d)$ using Eq. (4), which is not very straightforward as it involves division and summation of a large set of log normal random variables. The traditional log normal summation methods involve sampling and filtering to fit the distribution into an approximated log normal [15]. We opt for similar approach where we collect a good number of samples, say 50000, from each of the contributing log normal distributions, for a fixed d, to generate the SIR samples ($SIR_X(d)$) and use the SIR samples to determine the mean, $\mu_{SIR_X(d)}$, the variance of the SIR, $\sigma^2_{SIR_X(d)}$ and the empirical probability distribution function (PDF) of the $SIR_X(d)$. A rigorous mathematical PDF formulation is one of our future works. *Note that in presence of fading, using simple path loss model, we can easily get the mean powers received from each interferer, which can be used to estimate* $\frac{E(P_r)}{E(P_{\mathcal{I}})}$, *but, not the mean SIR, i.e.,* $E(SIR) = E\left(\frac{P_r}{P_{\mathcal{I}}}\right) \neq \frac{E(P_r)}{E(P_{\mathcal{I}})}$.

Step 6. *To properly select* d_{max}, *we first choose an acceptable value for* SIR_{th} *and* γ. *Next, we use the samples of* $SIR_X(d)$ *to estimate the outage probability* $\Gamma(d) = \mathbb{P}(SIR_X(d) < SIR_{th})$, *for a uniformly selected values of* $d \in [0, D_1]$. *The highest value of d that satisfies* $\Gamma(d) < \gamma$ *is the estimated* d_{max}.

3.3   Orthogonal Code Bound for Interference Free Network

First of all, say, $N_\mathcal{O}$ number of orthogonal codes are used and each node chooses a code randomly (all codes are equally likely to be chosen) and independently. The new code specific interference power bound for a randomly selected Interference Set Cover ($\mathcal{I}^C$) will be:

$$P_{\mathcal{I}^C}(d|\mathcal{O}_T) = \sum_{j=1}^{|\mathcal{I}^C|} P_{\mathcal{I}^C}^j \times {}_{\{\mathcal{O}_j = \mathcal{O}_T\}} \quad \text{and} \quad \mathbb{E}(P_{\mathcal{I}^C}(d)) = \frac{1}{(N_\mathcal{O})} \sum_{j=1}^{|\mathcal{I}^C|} \mathbb{E}(P_{\mathcal{I}^C}^j) \tag{5}$$

where $\mathcal{O}_T$ is the code chosen by T, $P_{\mathcal{I}^C}^j$ denotes the interference power due to j^{th} interferer in $\mathcal{I}^C$, and the indicator function $\mathbb{1}_{\{\mathcal{O}_j=\mathcal{O}_T\}}$ denotes whether the jth interferer have chosen same code as the transmitter i.e., $\mathcal{O}_T$. **Notice that, the Interference Set Cover with maximum mean interference power will still give us the maximum mean estimated interference power in presence of orthogonal codes.**

Step 7. *We use the estimated Interference Set Cover from Step 1 to determine the new SIR bounds as follows.*

$$SIR_{\mathcal{I}^C}(d|\mathcal{O}_T) = \frac{P_t d^{-\eta} 10^{\frac{\psi}{10}}}{\varsigma \cdot \sum_{j \in \mathcal{I}^C} \left(P_t d_{jX}^{-\eta} 10^{\frac{\psi}{10}} \right) \cdot \mathbb{1}_{\{\mathcal{O}_j=\mathcal{O}_T\}}} \tag{6}$$

Now, at any time instance, maximum $N^{max} = (N_{\mathcal{I}}^{max} + 1)$ number of nodes can be active simultaneously. Given that $N_{\mathcal{O}} \geq N^{max}$, we deduce that (Refer to [16] for Proof):

$$\mathbb{P}(\mathbb{1}_{\mathcal{I}0} = 1) \geq \prod_{i=1}^{N^{max}} \left(1 - \frac{i-1}{N_{\mathcal{O}}} \right) \tag{7}$$

From Eq. (7), we can see that for $N_{\mathcal{O}} \geq N^{max}$, $\prod_{i=1}^{N^{max}} \left(1 - \frac{i-1}{N_{\mathcal{O}}} \right)$ is a strictly increasing function of $N_{\mathcal{O}}$.

Step 8. *To find the optimum value of $N_{\mathcal{O}}$, we estimate $\prod_{i=1}^{N^{max}} \left(1 - \frac{i-1}{N_{\mathcal{O}}} \right)$ for increasing value of $N_{\mathcal{O}}$ (starting from N^{max}), and select the minimum value of $N_{\mathcal{O}}$ such that $\prod_{i=1}^{N^{max}} \left(1 - \frac{i-1}{N_{\mathcal{O}}} \right) \geq \kappa$.*

4   Identification of Maximum Power Interference Set Cover

In the section, we identify the Interference Set Covers that result in the highest total interference power at a given receiver location, X, for both scenarios i.e., dense random network and robotic router network.

4.1   Dense Random Network

In [11], Hekmat and Van Mieghem showed that the mean interference power in a CSMA Network is bounded by the interferers located along the hexagonal rings centred at the receiver's location, where the ith ring with each side length equal to $i \times D_1$ contains $6 * i$ nodes. While the assumption of putting the receiver at the center is valid in the presence of RTS/CTS mechanism in CSMA, in reality, RTS/CTS mechanism is **NOT** employed in most of the enterprise wireless networks as well as Internet of Things (IoT) networks. *In such cases, the transmitter is the node to be located at the center of the rings while* *the receiver is free to be located anywhere in the connected region of T. With this modification, the maximum feasible interference can actually be higher than the bound estimated in* [11] *e.g., when X is located at the farthest point of the connected region of T. Moreover, for determining the number of nodes to deploy, we need to know the maximum separation distance (d_{max}) that can support an acceptable maximum interference level, in order to place a set of nodes in any area of deployment.* This requires us to modify the bounds to have a separation distance (d) dependency. However, hexagonal packing is known to be the densest packing in circular spaces which leads us to believe that the distance dependent interference are also bounded by the interference power of the set of interferers located at hexagonal rings (similar to [11] but in an annular ring) around the Transmitter's location. With this assumption, our focus becomes restricted to all possible sets of locations that form such hexagonal packing. *We can easily prove that, with the separation distance $d > 0$, we only need to consider two different angular orientations of such hexagonal packing, as illustrated in* Figs. 1a *and* b.

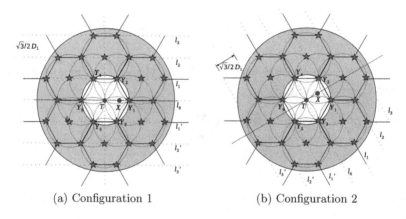

(a) Configuration 1   (b) Configuration 2

Fig. 1. Illustration of the Interference Set Covers for estimation of interference upper bound in a dense network

In the first type of configuration, which we refer to as **Configuration 1**, the closest interferer is located at the intersection of the inner boundary of the annulus and the line joining T and X (Illustrated in Fig. 1a). *This configuration is generated by taking a greedy iterative approximation approach, where we start with an empty $\mathcal{I}^C$ and, in each iteration, we select a point on the annulus that is closest to the receiver X and is not located in the connected regions of the nodes already added to $\mathcal{I}^C$.* In the second configuration, which we refer to as **Configuration 2** (illustrated in Fig. 1b), the number of closest interferers is two and they are exactly D_1 distance apart from each other as well as from the transmitter. *With this new initial condition, we can find the rest of the nodes, again, using the greedy approach.* Now, WLOG, we assume that T is located at $(0,0)$ in a 2D domain, while X is located at $(d,0)$. In this 2D domain, the positions of the interfering nodes for both of these Interference Set Covers are listed in Table 3. It can be easily shown that these two configurations form the bound of the interference power for any configuration within same class i.e., with similar relative position between nodes with hexagonal corner positioning. Next, we calculate the interference and SIR for these two configurations according to Eqs. (3) and (4). Then, we choose the maximum of these two interference estimates as our interference estimate, and minimum of these two SIR estimates as our SIR estimate. We perform this using the sampling method discussed in Sect. 3.2, where **we collect a large number of pairs of samples from these two configurations and take the highest interference power sample (or lowest SIR sample) from each pair as a sample for our estimated bounds.**

Table 3. Interference Set Cover node locations for a dense network

Line number (Illustrated in Figs. 1a and b)	Configuration 1	Configuration 2	
l_0	$\{(\pm jD_1, 0)\}$ $\forall j \in \{1, 2, \cdots, N_0+1\}$	$\{(0, \pm jD_1)\}$ $\forall j \in \{1, 2, \cdots, N_0+1\}$	$N_0 = \lfloor \frac{D_2-D_1}{D_1} \rfloor$
l_k where k is odd $\forall k \in \{1, \lfloor \frac{2D_2}{\sqrt{3}D_1} \rfloor\}$	$\{(\pm\frac{D_1(1+2\times j)}{2}, \frac{\sqrt{3}}{2}kD_1)\}$ $\forall j \in \{0, 1, \cdots, N_k\}$	$\{(\frac{\sqrt{3}}{2}kD_1, \pm\frac{D_1(1+2\times j)}{2})\}$ $\forall j \in \{0, 1, \cdots, N_k\}$	$N_k = \lfloor \frac{\left(D_2^2 - \frac{3}{4}k^2 D_1^2\right)^{\frac{1}{2}}}{D_1} \rfloor$
l'_k where k is odd $\forall k \in \{1, \lfloor \frac{2D_2}{\sqrt{3}D_1} \rfloor\}$	$\{(\pm\frac{D_1(1+2\times j)}{2}, -\frac{\sqrt{3}}{2}kD_1)\}$ $\forall j \in \{0, 1, \cdots, N_k\}$	$\{(-\frac{\sqrt{3}}{2}kD_1, \pm\frac{D_1(1+2\times j)}{2})\}$ $\forall j \in \{0, 1, \cdots, N_k\}$	$N_k = \lfloor \frac{\left(D_2^2 - \frac{3}{4}k^2 D_1^2\right)^{\frac{1}{2}}}{D_1} \rfloor$
l_k where k is even $\forall k \in \{1, \lfloor \frac{2D_2}{\sqrt{3}D_1} \rfloor\}$	$\{(\pm jD_1, \frac{\sqrt{3}}{2}kD_1)\}$ $\forall j \in \{0, 1, \cdots, N_k\}$	$\{(\frac{\sqrt{3}}{2}kD_1, \pm jD_1\}$ $\forall j \in \{0, 1, \cdots, N_k\}$	$N_k = \lfloor \frac{\left(D_2^2 - \frac{3}{4}k^2 D_1^2\right)^{\frac{1}{2}}}{D_1} \rfloor$
l'_k where k is even $\forall k \in \{1, \lfloor \frac{2D_2}{\sqrt{3}D_1} \rfloor\}$	$\{(\pm jD_1, -\frac{\sqrt{3}}{2}kD_1)\}$ $\forall j \in \{0, 1, \cdots, N_k\}$	$\{(-\frac{\sqrt{3}}{2}kD_1, \pm jD_1\}$ $\forall j \in \{0, 1, \cdots, N_k\}$	$N_k = \lfloor \frac{\left(D_2^2 - \frac{3}{4}k^2 D_1^2\right)^{\frac{1}{2}}}{D_1} \rfloor$

However, since this is an greedy solution, the resulting Interference Set Cover combination may not include the maximum number of interferer and, therefore, does not guarantee maximum possible interference power. Now say the greedy logic includes n interferes. Then according to the greedy logic, it is most likely that the top n interfering nodes of the maximum power Interference Set Cover will have less or equal interference power compared to the interference power from the greedily found Interference Set Cover. To guarantee that our estimated interference power is no less than the maximum possible interference power, we multiply our estimated interference power by a correction factors, $\zeta = \max\{1, \frac{N_\mathcal{I}^{max}}{|\mathcal{I}^C|}\}$, where $N_\mathcal{I}^{max}$ denotes the maximum number of simultaneous interferers and $|.|$ denotes the cardinality of a set. The correction factor (ζ) compensates for the cardinality of the Interference Set Cover i.e., if $|\mathcal{I}^C| < N_\mathcal{I}^{max}$. **We found that the number of interferers estimated from the hexagonal packing is in fact also $N_\mathcal{I}^{max}$ for most of the cases.** Nonetheless, we can determine the maximum number of concurrent interfering nodes ($N_\mathcal{I}^{max}$) by formulating the problem as a circle packing problem [17] as follows.

Definition 2. Pack Problem: *Maximize the number of circles with radius* $\left(\frac{D_1}{2}\right)$ *that can be packed inside an annulus with inner and outer radius:* $\left(\frac{D_1}{2}\right)$ *and* $\left(D_2 + \frac{D_1}{2}\right)$, *respectively.*

Lemma 1. *The cardinality of the solution to the Pack Problem is also the maximum cardinality of an Interference Set Cover. (Proof in [16])*   □

Note that, there exists a range of approximation solutions to the circle packing problem [17], which can be directly applied to solve this problem. In this paper, we do not present any circle packing solution. We validate the bounds via a set of simulation experiments in Sect. 5.

4.2   Interference Estimation for Robotic Router Network

In this section, we focus on the interference estimation for our application specific context of robotic wireless networks in a obstacle free environment. Before that, we make an assumption, based on two related works [1,18], as follows.

Assumption 1. *For a flow based robotic network in a obstacle free environment, if the goal is to optimize a flow's performance in terms of SIR, the best configuration of robots allocated to that flow is to stay on the straight line joining that flow's static endpoints.*

This assumption is justified by the work presented in [1] which shows that the best configuration of robots in order to optimize packet reception rate (which is directly related to SIR) of a flow based network is to evenly place them along the line segment joining the static endpoints. The work of Yan and Mostofi [18] further justify the linear arrangement of same flow nodes for Signal to Noise Ratio (SNR) based optimization goal. In our analysis, we employ Assumption 1 to restrict the feasible positions of the interfering nodes, thereby, leading to better and tighter bounds on interference. In this context, we divide the interference into two components: Intra-flow interference and Inter-flow interference. These two components refer to the interference power from the nodes in the same flow as the transmitter T and interference power from the nodes of different flows, respectively.

Intra-flow Interference. Our intra-flow interference estimation is based on the following lemma.

Lemma 2. *The maximum intra-flow interference power for a link corresponds to the sum of interference powers from nodes located at distances* $\{D_1, 2.D_1, \cdots k.D_1\}$ *from the transmitter node T along the line segment joining the flow endpoints, where* $k.D_1 \leq D_2$. *(Proof in [16])*   □

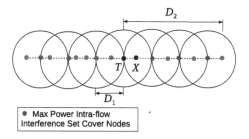

Fig. 2. Illustration of the maximum power intra-flow Interference Set Cover

Therefore, the maximum number of intra-flow interferers is $2\left(\lfloor\frac{D_2-D_1}{D_1}\rfloor+1\right)$, where the factor 2 accounts for both sides. In Fig. 2, we present an illustration of such scenario. Thus, the set of nodes that will result in the highest intra-flow interference power are located at $\{(\pm jD_1, 0)\}\ \forall j \in \{1, \cdots, \lfloor\frac{D_2-D_1}{D_1}\rfloor+1\}$ in the 2-dimensional area of interest. Interestingly, these set of locations are same as the line l_0 of **Configuration 1** discussed in Sect. 4.1.

Inter-flow Interference. In realistic scenarios, there will be more than one flows in the network where robots assigned to different flows can interfere as well. We refer to such interference as the *inter-flow interference*. Now, the interferers can be located in the annular transition region around the transmitter, while the nodes allocated to same flow stay on the straight line joining the endpoints of the respective flow (according to Assumption 1). In this section, we start the bound estimation with a two flow network, followed by a network with M flows. In this context, we make a key assumption about the maximum power Interference Set Cover for multi-flow scenario, as follows.

Assumption 2. *For any transmitter-receiver node pair of a flow, the intra-flow maximum power Interference Set Cover estimated in Sect. 4.2 is always part of the maximum power Interference Set Cover in presence of multiple flows.* □

The reason behind this assumption is mainly the fact that in practical deployments some node-pairs might not have any inter-flow interference at all (e.g., single flow network). Therefore, neglecting any of the intra-flow interfering nodes will lead to a incorrect estimate of the interference in such cases. Under the given assumption, our next step is to find another line segment that will generate the maximum inter-flow interference power, for two flow cases. In general case with M flows, we need to find $M-1$ other line segments such that carefully placed set of interferers on those segments result in the highest inter-flow interference power. Now, following the greedy approach mentioned in the Sect. 4.1, the second flow should contain Y_2 or Y_3 or both, in Fig. 3a, since they are the next closest points to X after the Intra-flow interference set cover nodes are accounted for.

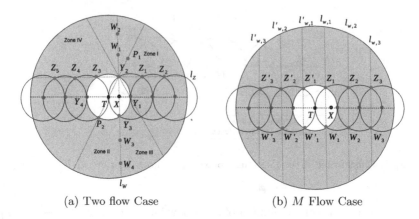

(a) Two flow Case   (b) M Flow Case

Fig. 3. Illustration of the multi flow interference estimation (Blue nodes: intra-flow interferer, Red nodes: inter-flow interferer) (Color figure online)

Lemma 3. *Among the possible line segments through Y_2 or Y_3 or both, we just need to consider l_Z and l_W in Fig. 3a for estimating the bound on the interference power for two flow case. (Proof in [16])* □

The set of nodes on l_W that will result in highest interference power should be located at $(\frac{D_1}{2}, \pm(\frac{\sqrt{3}}{2}D_1 + jD_1))\}$ $\forall j \in \{0, 1, \cdots, \lfloor \frac{\left(D_2^2 - \frac{D_1^2}{4}\right)^{\frac{1}{2}} - \frac{\sqrt{3}}{2}D_1}{D_1} \rfloor\}$. On the other hand, The maximum power interference set cover node locations on l_Z are same as the line l_1 of **Configuration 1**, listed in to Table 3. Now, the inter flow interference power is $\max\{P_{\mathcal{I}}^{l_W}(d), P_{\mathcal{I}}^{l_Z}(d)\}$, where $P_{\mathcal{I}}^{l_W}$ and $P_{\mathcal{I}}^{l_Z}$ denotes the total maximum interference power for nodes in line l_W and l_Z, respectively.

Next, we extend this concept to M flow scenario i.e., maximum $M - 1$ interfering flows. For a fixed pair of transmitter and receiver node of a flow with $M - 1$ interfering flows, we need to consider two class of configurations. The mean inter-flow interference power bound of the **first class of configurations** is calculated by summing up the total interference power of the first M' lines from the set $\{l_1, l'_1, l_2, l'_2, \cdots, l_K, l'_K\}$ in Fig. 1a, where $K = \lfloor \frac{2D_2}{\sqrt{3}D_1} \rfloor$ and $M' = \min\{M - 1, 2K\}$. Now, for the bound estimation of **second class of configurations**, we consider the line segment joining the closest pair of nodes at any point of time. More precisely, we choose M' pairs of nodes from the pairs illustrated in Fig. 3b as $\{(Z_1, W_1), (Z_2, W_2), (Z'_1, W'_1), (Z_3, W_3), \cdots, (Z'_K, W'_K)\}$ where $K = \left(\lfloor \frac{(D_2 - D_1/2)}{D_1} \rfloor + 1\right)$, $M' = \min\{M - 1, 2K\}$, and the pairs are sorted in terms of the respective distances to the receiver. Thus, the flows situated along lines $l_{W,i}$ and $l'_{W,i}$, $i \in \{1, 2, \cdots, K\}$ determine the second type of interference bound in our estimation. The respective locations of the interferers are illustrated in Table 4. Next, we compare these two bounds and take the maximum of them as the estimated interference power bound. We prove the validity of this bound through a set of MATLAB based simulation experiments, discussed in Sect. 5.

Table 4. Interference Set Cover node locations for a flow based network

Line number (Illustrated in Figs. 3b)	
$l_{W,k} \; \forall k \in \{0, \lfloor \frac{(D_2 - D_1)}{2D_1} \rfloor\}$	$\{((2k+1)\frac{D_1}{2}, \pm(\frac{\sqrt{3}}{2}D_1 + jD_1))\} \; \forall j \in \{0, 1, \cdots, N_{W,k}\}$
$l'_{W,k} \; \forall k \in \{0, \lfloor \frac{(D_2 - D_1)}{2D_1} \rfloor\}$	$\{(-(2k+1)\frac{D_1}{2}, \pm(\frac{\sqrt{3}}{2}D_1 + jD_1))\} \; \forall j \in \{0, 1, \cdots, N_{W,k}\}$
$N_{W,k} = \lfloor \frac{\left(D_2^2 - \frac{\{(2k+1)D_1\}^2}{4}\right)^{\frac{1}{2}} - \frac{\sqrt{3}}{2}D_1}{D_1} \rfloor$	

5   Simulation Results

In this section, we verify our proposed d dependent bounds on the interference and SIR, through a set of MATLAB 8.1 based experiments performed on a machine with 3.40 GHz Intel i7 processor and 12 GB RAM. For this set of experiments, we fix the values of the transmitter powers and the path loss exponent at $P_t = 1$ and $\eta = 2.2$, respectively. The value of $\eta = 2.2$ is motivated by our experiences from real outdoor experiments (from a different project). As a measure of the annular transition region area, we choose the ratio of $\frac{D_2}{D_1} = 3$ as the typical RSSI CCA thresholds are separated by 10 dB to 15 dB [14]. The absolute value of D_1 is randomly selected to be 6 m as *the major factors that controls the performance is the $\frac{D_2}{D_1}$ ratio, not the absolute values of D_1 and D_2*. With these initializations, we vary the separation distance d from 1 m to $D_1 - 1$ m with granularity of 0.1 m to plot the separation distance dependent bounds.

First, we verify the bounds for a general dense network, where the interfering nodes are uniformly distributed over the annular transition region around T. To verify the bounds, we randomly generate 1000 sets of interfering nodes, for a fixed value of d, using Algorithm 1. In Fig. 4a, we compare our estimated interference power and estimated SIR, with the interference powers and SIR of the generated $\mathcal{I}^S$ sets, for no fading scenario and $\frac{D_2}{D_1} = 3$. Figure 4a clearly validates our d dependent interference and SIR bounds for a general dense network in absence of fading. Next, we perform similar experiments but in the presence of log normal fading of variance $\sigma^2 = 4$ and $\frac{D_2}{D_1} = 3$. In this set of experiments, the estimated bounds for each value of d are some probability distributions, rather than deterministic values. In this context, we empirically collect a set of 50000 samples $(SIR(d))$ from the distributions estimated according to Eq. (4) and estimate the mean, $\mu_{SIR_X(d)}$ and the variance of the SIR, $\sigma^2_{SIR_X(d)}$. Next, we collect 50000 sample from each generated $\mathcal{I}^S$ and empirically compute the probabilities, $\mathbb{P}(SIR_{\mathcal{I}^S} < \mu_{SIR_X(d)})$, $\mathbb{P}(SIR_{\mathcal{I}^S} < \mu_{SIR_X(d)} - \sigma_{SIR_X(d)})$ and $\mathbb{P}(SIR_{\mathcal{I}^S} < \frac{\mathbb{E}(Signal)}{\mathbb{E}(Interference)})$. We plot the results in Fig. 4b which shows that the estimated SIR mean (from Eq. (4)) is higher than the actual SIR for around 25% of the cases, while $\mu_{SIR_X(d)} - \sigma_{SIR_X(d)}$ is higher than the actual SIR for only 10% of the case. Thus, if we were to choose a deterministic value for the bound rather than a distribution, $\mu_{SIR_X(d)} - \sigma_{SIR_X(d)}$ is considered as a good

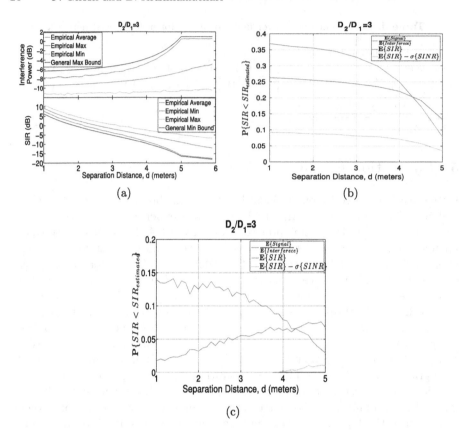

Fig. 4. (a) Validation of estimated interference power (Top) and SIR (Bottom) bounds in dB, for dense network with no fading (b) Probability that actual SIR is lower than the estimated minimum SIR with log-normal fading with variance $\sigma^2 = 4$ (c) Probability that actual SIR is lower than the estimated minimum SIR with NO fading but in presence of 10 orthogonal codes

estimate. Next, we use similar sampling method to generate the orthogonal code based SIR bounds when the number of codes used is 10, while the maximum number of simultaneously interfering node is 38 (For $D_2/D_1 = 3$). In this set of experiments, each node randomly selects a code from the code alphabet. But, we only sum up the interference powers of the interferers that select the same code as the transmitter. We apply the same method for each of the $\mathcal{I}^S$ set as well to validate our bounds and plot the probabilities $\mathbb{P}(SIR_{\mathcal{I}^S} < \mu_{SIR_X(d)})$ and $\mathbb{P}(SIR_{\mathcal{I}^S} < \mu_{SIR_X(d)} - \sigma_{SIR_X(d)})$ in Fig. 4c, for log normal fading scenario. Figure 4c shows that our proposed bound also works well in presence of orthogonal codes.

Similar to the generic dense wireless network, we perform a set of bound tests for the robotic network scenario for $\frac{D_2}{D_1} = 3$. In this case, we randomly select two pairs of endpoints (i.e., we consider a 3 flow network) along the circumference of

Algorithm 1. Generate a random set of Interferer

```
1: procedure GENERATE( )
2:     Initialize a Dense Set of Nodes: I^D
3:     Initialize I^S as a empty set
4:     while I^D is not Empty do
5:         Randomly select v ∈ I^D
6:         I^S = I^S ∪ v
7:         B_v = {i|i ∈ I^D & d_{iv} < D_1}
8:         I^D = I^D \ B_v
9:     end while
10: end procedure
```

the outer circle with radius D_2, which are the flow endpoint for two other flows. Next, we place a dense set of points along each of the randomly selected flow segments as well as the line segment joining the transmitter T and the receiver X

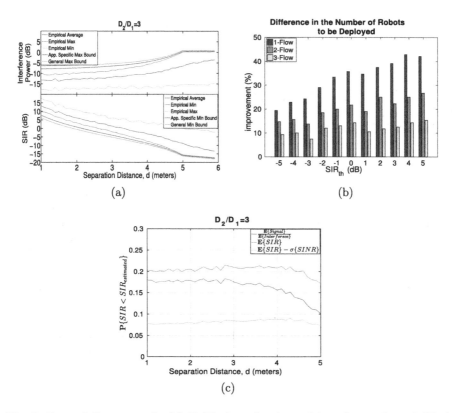

Fig. 5. For a 3 flow network: (a) Validation of estimated interference bound (Top) and SIR bound (bottom) with no fading (b) Illustration of less number of robots to be deployed with our application specific bound with no fading (c) Probability that actual SIR is lower than the estimated minimum SIR with log-normal fading with variance $\sigma^2 = 4$

to include the intra-flow interference. Then, we use Algorithm 1 to generate 1000 sets of interfering nodes for each value of d and for each of the 500 randomly generated sets of flow endpoints. In all cases, the total interference power is bounded by our proposed theoretical maximum interference power, for no fading scenario, as illustrated in Fig. 5a. This figure also shows that our application specific bounds are much tighter than the generic bound. In order to illustrate the impact of this improvement, we also plot the difference in the number of robots required to cover a distance of 100 m for different values of $SIR_{th} \in$ [−5 dB, 5 dB] in Fig. 5b for $\frac{D_2}{D_1} = \{3\}$. Figure 5b clearly illustrates that with our improved bound, the required number of robots to guarantee some target SIR requirements, is significantly lower than the generic bound based number of robots estimations, ranging from a maximum of ∼45% for single flow network to a minimum of ∼10% for a three flow network. The improvement is significant for less number of flows, as for higher number of flows (∼6 − 7 flows) the general dense network bound becomes dominant, which is quite intuitive. Next, similar to the generic bound, in Fig. 5c we compare the bounds in presence of fading to show that the estimated $\mu_{SIR_X(d)} - \sigma_{SIR_X(d)}$ is higher than the actual SIR for only 10% of the case, for $\frac{D_2}{D_1} = 3$.

6   Conclusion

In this paper, we proposed a method for estimation of the maximum interference and minimum achievable SIR for a link of length d in an unknown environment while CSMA-CA or equivalent MAC layer protocols are employed. First, we demonstrate a strong dependency of these bounds on the transmitter-receiver separation distance d. Next, by considering two different scenarios: generic dense network and robotic router network; we demonstrate that we can formulate better and tighter bounds by exploiting the network topology structure which infact improves our main goal of estimating the number of nodes to be deployed for our robotic router network in order to guarantee some network performance. We also perform a set of MATLAB based simulation experiments that validate our findings. This work is a part of our bigger project of development of a CSMA aware autonomous reconfigurable network of wireless robots, which we refer to as SWANBOT, that can adapt its configuration over time to maintain link qualities while performing some allocated task. As a part of our future work on this specific topic, we plan to develop a more formal algorithmic approach with polynomial time complexity as well as flesh out analytical details about the correctness of the bounds, if possible. Another direction of future work will be to validate this bounds with real testbed experiments.

References

1. Williams, R., Gasparri, A., Krishnamachari, B.: Route swarm: wireless network optimization through mobility. In: Proceedings of the IEEE/RSJ International Conference on Intelligent Robots and Systems (IROS) (2014)

2. Penders, J., Alboul, L., Witkowski, U., Naghsh, A., Saez-Pons, J., Herbrechtsmeier, S., El-Habbal, M.: A robot swarm assisting a human fire-fighter. Adv. Robot. **25**(1–2), 93–117 (2011)
3. Thrun, S., Thayer, S., Whittaker, W., Baker, C., Burgard, W., Ferguson, D., Hahnel, D., Montemerlo, D., Morris, A., Omohundro, Z.: Autonomous exploration and mapping of abandoned mines. IEEE Rob. Autom. Mag. **11**(4), 79–91 (2004)
4. Nguyen, H.G., Pezeshkian, N., Raymond, M., Gupta, A., Spector, J.M.: Autonomous communication relays for tactical robots. Technical report, DTIC Document (2003)
5. Haenggi, M.: Mean interference in hard-core wireless networks. IEEE Commun. Lett. **15**(8), 792–794 (2011)
6. Ganti, R.K., Haenggi, M.: Interference and outage in clustered wireless ad hoc networks. IEEE Trans. Inf. Theory **55**(9), 4067–4086 (2009)
7. Busson, A., Chelius, G.: Capacity and interference modeling of CSMA/CA networks using SSI point processes. Telecommun. Syst. **57**(1), 25–39 (2014)
8. ElSawy, H., Hossain, E.: Modeling random CSMA wireless networks in general fading environments. In: Proceedings of the IEEE International Conference on Communications (ICC). IEEE (2012)
9. Busson, A., Chelius, G.: Point processes for interference modeling in CSMA/CA ad-hoc networks. In: Proceedings of the 6th ACM Symposium on Performance Evaluation of Wireless Ad Hoc, Sensor, and Ubiquitous Networks (2009)
10. Cardieri, P.: Modeling interference in wireless ad hoc networks. IEEE Commun. Surv. Tutorials **12**(4), 551–572 (2010)
11. Hekmat, R., Van Mieghem, P.: Interference in wireless multi-hop ad-hoc networks and its effect on network capacity. Wirel. Netw. **10**(4), 389–399 (2004)
12. Bianchi, G.: Performance analysis of the IEEE 802.11 distributed coordination function. IEEE J. Sel. Areas Commun. **18**(3), 535–547 (2000)
13. Rappaport, T.S.: Wireless Communications: Principles and Practice, vol. 2. Prentice Hall PTR, New Jersey (1996)
14. Zeng, Y., Pathak, P.H., Mohapatra, P.: A first look at 802.11ac in action: energy efficiency and interference characterization. In: Proceedings of IFIP Networking Conference (2014)
15. Safak, A.: Statistical analysis of the power sum of multiple correlated log-normal components. IEEE Trans. Veh. Technol. **42**(1), 58–61 (1993)
16. Ghosh, P., Krishnamachari, B.: Interference power bound analysis of a network of wireless robots. Technical report ANRG-2016-04, arXiv:1608.08261, USC ANRG (2016)
17. Hifi, M., M'hallah, R.: A literature review on circle and sphere packing problems: models and methodologies. Adv. Oper. Res. **2009** (2009)
18. Yan, Y., Mostofi, Y.: Robotic router formation in realistic communication environments. IEEE Trans. Rob. **28**(4), 810–827 (2012)

Your Privacy Is in Your Hand: Interactive Visual Privacy Control with Tags and Gestures

Jiayu Shu[✉], Rui Zheng, and Pan Hui

Hong Kong University of Science and Technology, Kowloon, Hong Kong
{jshuaa,rzhengac,panhui}@ust.hk

Abstract. Built–in cameras on mobile and wearable devices enable a number of vision related applications, such as mobile augmented reality, continuous sensing, and life-logging systems. While wearable cameras with smaller size and higher resolution bring joy and convenience to human lives, being recorded by unreliable cameras has raised people's concerns about visual privacy, particularly the potential leak of identity. Consequently, protecting identity of people who are not willing to appear in the photo or video has become an urgent issue that has yet to be resolved. In this paper, we propose an interactive method for individuals to control their visual privacy based on privacy indicators and control rules. We design and implement a prototype on Android smartphones, which allows individuals to inform cameras of their privacy control intentions through interaction using tags, hand gestures, and their combinations. Protection measures such as blurring the face will be performed to remove individual's identifiable information according to control rules. Evaluation results of the overall performance and feedbacks from real users demonstrate the effectiveness and usability of our approach, showing potentials of interactive visual privacy control.

1 Introduction

Nowadays, the development of sensors boosts the appearance of many modern consumer devices. Among multiple sensors, camera is serving as the key functional component in devices such as Google Glass[1], LifeLogger[2], Narrative Clip 2[3], and HTC RE Camera[4] as shown in Fig. 1. These mobile and wearable devices provide platforms for cameras to collect media data anywhere and anytime in an unobtrusive way. For example, the Narrative app automatically captures pictures every 30 seconds for people to record their life moments. Moreover, with increasing computing capability and advanced computer vision techniques, captured image can be analyzed for different purposes. For instance, Theodeolite[5] is a multi-function app that overlays real-time information like position,

---

[1] http://www.google.com/glass/start.
[2] http://lifelogger.com.
[3] http://getnarrative.com.
[4] http://www.htc.com/us/re/re-camera.
[5] http://hunter.pairsite.com/theodolite.

© Springer International Publishing AG 2017
N. Sastry and S. Chakraborty (Eds.): COMSNETS 2017, LNCS 10340, pp. 24–43, 2017.
DOI: 10.1007/978-3-319-67235-9_3

Fig. 1. Ubiquitous cameras. From left to right: Google Glass, LifeLogger, Narattive Clip 2, and HTC RE Camera.

altitude, and inclination on live camera images. NameTags[6] is a facial recognition app that users can snap a picture of someone and see his or her public online information.

When these applications and devices provide services that make our lives better, there are growing privacy concerns from the public raised by ubiquitous presence of wearable cameras. People usually take photos or record videos without getting permissions from bystanders. The media data may be uploaded online afterwards, which can be accessed by everyone on the Internet, potentially infringing bystanders' privacy. Furthermore, the media data actually contain much more information than people have realized. Shaw claimed that recognition technologies link images to specific people, places, and things, thus can reveal far more information than expected, making those previously unsearchable searchable [25]. Similarly, Acquisti, Gross, and Stutzman demonstrated privacy concerns raised by the convergence of three technologies: face recognition, cloud computing and online social networks [4]. With increasing public self-disclosures and continuing improvements in face recognition and ubiquitous computing, it becomes possible not only to identify that individual, but also to infer additional and more sensitive information. In addition to indeliberate sharing of photos or videos, the device or applications are not one hundred percent reliable as some installed applications leak or misuse personal data.

All these possible consequences threaten people to have private and anonymous social lives. Their privacy concerns lead to negative attitudes towards wearable cameras. An example is Google Glass, which has been oppugned by the society since its appearance. For example, both US Congress and Privacy and Data Protection Commissioners have questioned privacy risks caused by Google Glass, such as collecting data about non-users without consent [1,2].

In this paper, we propose an interactive approach for individuals to control their visual privacy based on privacy indicators and control rules. Privacy indicators are static tags and dynamic hand gestures, that individuals can use to interact with cameras. In most of the cases, individuals may not find they are being captured, therefore we provide privacy protection tags as the basic privacy indicators. When people are aware of being recorded, they can show specific hand gestures to convey their privacy preferences as well. As hand gestures are

---

[6] http://www.nametag.ws.

proactive behaviors from individuals, they can also be used with tags to convey new privacy preferences. If any tag or gesture is detected, corresponding privacy protection actions will be performed on specific individuals according to privacy control rules to protect their identity information.

To the best of our knowledge, our work is the first investigation into protecting visual privacy with special tags, dynamic hand gestures, and their combinations. It is an in-situ visual privacy protection service for image capture. Bystanders can express their privacy wishes via privacy indicators conveniently. Recorders who capture images do not need to filter all data manually in order to respect bystanders' privacy preferences.

The remainder of the paper is organized as follows: in Sect. 2 we discuss related work; in Sect. 3 we introduce the motivation, design guidelines, and constrains; in Sect. 4 we propose the privacy indicators, control rules, and protection framework; in Sect. 5 we describe the implementation in detail; in Sect. 6 we present the evaluation results with our prototype; and finally, in Sect. 7 we conclude the paper and discuss future work.

2   Related Work

2.1   Visual Privacy Concerns

Issues about visual privacy have been studied for years, where the focus ranges from surveillance systems, life-logging systems, to recent AR, wearable camera applications [11,14,15,20].

For video surveillance, development in surveillance ubiquity and capabilities has led to questions about monitoring public places versus people's freedom of passing through public places without being monitored. Gavison discusses that people expect their actions only to be observed by those they see around them, and then people can judge how they should act [13]. For life-logging applications and smart home sensing systems, there are also worries about leak of privacy [9]. A user study shows that users want to be in control of logging the most private data due to privacy concerns [18]. For AR and perceptual applications which require access to various sensor data, it is not only the image or video itself that threatens privacy, but also the possibility of being identified [4,25]. Moreover, users' personal data is at the risk of being stolen or misused by malicious applications [22].

2.2   Protection Techniques

To address visual privacy concerns about personal identity, many privacy preserving techniques have been proposed. Some methods restrict applications' access to raw sensor data with least privilege. Users can control what visual information an app has access to through devices' cameras. For example, the Recognizer takes raw sensor data as input and exposes higher-level objects (e.g., a skeleton or a face) to AR applications [16]. The Darkly system only allows applications to receive selected parameterized information (e.g., the number of detected faces) [17]. The PrivateEye and WaveOff systems allow users to mark regions as safe to release to an app [21]. Least privilege approach works well for applications of which functionalities can be achieved with largely filtered and simplified data like skeleton. Different from this scenario, our approach aims at protecting visual privacy of bystanders, therefore we need to keep as much information as possible.

To infer who requires privacy protection, some approaches rely on visual indicators to inform devices to automatically enforce privacy policies specified by real-world objects. One representative solution uses color-based visual markers such as hats or vests to obscure faces of those who wish to remain anonymous in the video surveillance [24]. However, color-based approach is not reliable as any appearance of the assigned color will be processed. Another solution allows people to use markers such as QR code to convey privacy policies [8,23]. However, static visual markers alone can not satisfy people's privacy preferences, which may change according to the surroundings. Recently, I-pic uses broadcasted face features to locate individuals who want to be protected in an image [5]. However, the computation and communication overheads of extracting face features and matching on mobile and wearable devices will restrict its adoption. As a result, a more viable and flexible method that specifically focuses on preserving privacy of targeted individuals with finer granularity needs to be proposed.

Based on literature search, we find that despite general privacy protection framework and some specific methods, no effort takes both usability and feasibility into consideration to guarantee privacy of targeted individual threatened by ubiquitous cameras. There are gaps and opportunities for us to design and implement viable privacy protection approach with current knowledge, which also leaves sufficient potentials for further advances in computer vision techniques.

3 Motivation and Guidelines

To better understand people's concerns over potential privacy invasion, we designed an online survey. The results not only help us confirm our intuition and prediction, but also inform some significant privacy preserving principles. We then conclude our design guidelines after looking from applications' point of view as well. We further put forward practical constraints and technical challenges.

3.1 Attitude Study

We conduct an online survey to understand people's attitudes on privacy issues due to ubiquitous presence of cameras, especially wearable devices (e.g. Google Glass)[7]. The questions are asked progressively around three keywords: mobile and wearable devices with cameras, visual information collection, and privacy. Specifically, we first ask the participants if they mind the presence of wearable

---

[7] https://ust.za1.qualtrics.com/jfe/form/SV_3VLbhQJRKbN7x9H.

devices with cameras. Then we try to find the relationship between their attitudes toward wearable devices and unauthorized visual information collection. Further, we emphasize that captured visual information can disclosure personal information to see whether this is people's major concern. Finally, we ask if blurring face or the whole body satisfies those who are worried about invasion of privacy in this situation.

The online survey is mainly distributed among university students and staff. Among 162 participants who completed the survey, 88 are male and 74 are female. Apart from 112 participants from Hong Kong, 38 are from mainland China, and 12 from other nationalities. As to the age, 131 participants are between 16 and 25 years old. 13 participants age between 26 and 35, 12 between 36 and 45, and 6 are older than 45.

From the survey, we find 95% of participants mind people recording videos of them in public spaces, either intentionally or accidentally without asking for consent. There are some places people mind the most, such as hospital, restaurant, bar, and hotel. For all participants who mind visual information collection, 87% of them chose the reason of possible disclosure of their personal information, especially some are afraid that they might be doing something unpleasant, therefore do not want to get spotted. For participants who mind being recorded due to leak of personal information, 50% think blurring faces would work, while 19% more require the blurring of both face and body. The major reason for participants who are not happy with proposed blurring processing is that they think acquaintances can still recognize them even after blurring the whole body.

The results not only validate that the majority of people have paid attention to the privacy issues related to wearable devices with cameras, but also inform some valuable privacy control principles. We can infer that people are eager for restrictions on use of cameras in some sensitive places in particular. It means location plays an extremely important role in possible privacy intrusion. However, this is not the whole story. Participants' responses imply that what individuals are doing and with whom are more essential and crucial factors that determine the violation of privacy. Therefore, privacy control actions should depend on context. To inform the camera of the context, human should be involved to flexibly deliver efficient privacy control messages. In addition to the triggering of privacy preserving, how to remove sensitive information in the captured photos or videos also needs to be treated carefully, as simply blurring the face cannot satisfy half of the participants in our survey. Thus, more options to prevent privacy disclosure should be provided. We briefly conclude the principles we have learned from the attitude study as follows: privacy control with finer granularity for both privacy control triggering and action should be proposed.

3.2   Design Guidelines

Before designing our privacy control approach, we also need to think about privacy issues from the perspectives of the applications that rely on the camera, and the holders of the mobile and wearable device.

The first problem is the balance between appropriate level of privacy protection and the utility of the application. A thorough solution is to ban the use of camera in certain places. This means no camera related application can work, even if when people just want to take a picture of themselves without any bystander or sensitive object. Some improved approaches suggest to restrict the amount of information exposed to the application. For example, only the number of faces or the contour of the object will be passed to the application. However, offering largely simplified and reduced information is not applicable to all applications, since some applications totally lose their functionalities. As a result, more direct and pertinent measures should be adopted, while maintaining as much information as possible to ensure the utility of the camera. For example, only removing sensitive information so that people's privacy can be protected and the application can still work.

To achieve this goal is not easy. People may argue that users of the devices should be responsible for protecting privacy of others whose identity may leak due to their devices. Nevertheless, even people filter sensitive information manually, applications may already misuse it before user can process the data. To address this problem, we can ask device to automatically remove all sensitive information. However, it is extremely difficult for devices to isolate and identify all the objects in a single frame. Therefore, individuals themselves are required to take actions that inform the device of their privacy preferences. Then the device will distinguish these individuals from others for specific privacy preserving actions.

We summarize our design guidelines, with both voice from the public and practical considerations for camera related applications, trying our best to balance the usefulness and privacy:

- The approach should provide necessary privacy protection while keeping the most of applications' original functionalities at the same time.
- The privacy control approach should work according to the context. It is a broader concept than location, which attaches more importance to the people with their surroundings.
- Individual's proactivity can be leveraged to protect privacy actively. That is, individuals who are concerned about leak of identity can express their privacy preferences in a flexible and convenient way.
- The proposed approach should gain both feasibility and usability. In other words, we need to make sure that people are willing to accept such method for protecting their privacy, and it is allowed by current techniques and situations.

We would like to emphasize again that different from existing approaches, we try to involve human into this privacy preserving ecosystem, leveraging their proactivity to express their privacy preferences in a natural way. The proposed approach pays much attention to the individuals and the context, rather than location alone. The solution still works in a vision-based way, but takes feasibility and usability into consideration. We hope to offer an approach which is practical and easy to deploy, with finer granularity and flexibility.

3.3   Constraints and Challenges

As privacy issues cover many aspects, a simple privacy control approach cannot address privacy issues in all possible situations. Our approach explicitly focuses on protecting individual privacy that may be leaked due to unauthorized or unnoticed visual information collection by ubiquitous cameras.

We also need to elucidate the practical constraints of our privacy control approach. A useful in-device privacy protection solution must either be enforced in the operating system to guarantee the protection of privacy, or adopted by compliant users. In other words, nothing will be protected for devices that do not use our framework to take pictures. This constraint is common for most of the privacy protection approaches, as it is not completely a technical issue. What we can do is to demonstrate the possibility and benefits of our approach, and provide implications for device operators.

Apart from practical constrains, there are some technical challenges. As we mostly apply computer vision algorithms on Android smartphones to detect faces and privacy indicators which we will discuss later, the processing time and detection accuracy are core challenges. In particular, the burden for accurate detection is incredibly high for our approach, which we have to point out in advance. We will further discuss this issue in the evaluation.

4   Interactive Visual Privacy Control

In this section, we first introduce the desired user experience of our visual privacy control approach. We then explain visual privacy indicators and how they work. Finally, we describe the overall framework.

4.1   Usage Scenario and Desired Functions

We first present a scenario that our approach can be used for individuals to control their visual privacy. Imagine you go to public activities such as an exhibition, where people usually take photos or videos to record the moments that they like. Whether you are willing or not, you will get into someone's sight and appear in some pictures unavoidably. Then people who take these pictures will post them online, sharing with their friends. What is even worse is that some malicious applications installed in the device may collect visual data, sending to their servers and selling to others.

Now the activity organizers provide an image capture platform which adopts our privacy control approach. With this platform, bystanders can use tags and hand gestures to convey their privacy control messages. People that take pictures using this platform do not need to worry about bystanders' visual privacy, as the platform will automatically process the image according to the privacy indicators detected.

4.2 Privacy Indicators

As discussed in design guidelines, privacy control messages had better be sent from individuals to the device for automatic protection measures. We come up with privacy control indicators that play the role of communication and interaction between human and devices. They will be translated to commands that deliver people's intentions of whether they are willing to be captured in the view or not. They work as visual cues to inform system to take necessary privacy protection actions.

These visual clues should have the following traits to achieve our goals:

- Efficiently detectable. This is the prerequisite that determines the feasibility of the whole system.
- Uniquely identifiable. In order to locate a certain individual in real world who needs privacy protection, indicators should be distinguished from other objects that may appear in the view to avoid incorrect operations.
- Easy to use. We should not confuse or place greater burdens on people for the sake of simple implementation.
- Robust for a variety of occasions. The performance affected by changes and uncertainties such as the illumination and object occlusion should be in an acceptable level.

There are many choices for privacy control indicators such as the Quick Response (QR) code, bar code, and markers designed for AR applications [12,29]. However, they do not possess all listed traits. For example, though QR code can be quickly detected and exclusively decoded, they require to be scanned in the right place and angle. As for visual markers in AR systems, they are simple but usually occupy most of the view due to their essential functions in calibration, 3D model, etc. We find that a common limitation for QR code and AR markers is their inconvenience for the use of conveying privacy control messages in daily lives.

According to our design guidelines, instead of using sophisticated visual markers, we take advantage of simple visual cues that human can interact with device to meet the requirements: tags and hand gestures. In our prototype, we use the tags and hand gestures shown in Fig. 2. The tag can be a logo, a template, or a decorative pattern printed or stuck on clothes. The hand gesture can be a clenched fist, a victory sign, or any specified one. Figure 2(a) shows tag examples, and Fig. 2(b) are different hand gestures that can be used in our approach. They basically meet our requirements, outweighing typical makers not only in their ease of use, but also their robustness in most occasions.

Tags and hand gestures work in a complementary way. Tags help convey privacy control messages even when individuals are not aware of being photographed. More importantly, hand gestures can be used to modify tag-represented privacy preferences. According to detected privacy indicators, corresponding privacy protection will be performed to preserve bystanders' privacy. Figure 3 shows an example of privacy protection actions to be applied for different indicators.

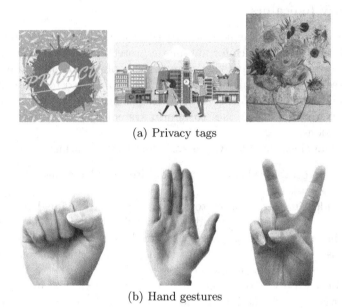

(a) Privacy tags

(b) Hand gestures

Fig. 2. Privacy control indicators: (a) three exemplary privacy tags; (b) three representative hand gestures. Different visual indicators and their combinations correspond to different privacy protection actions.

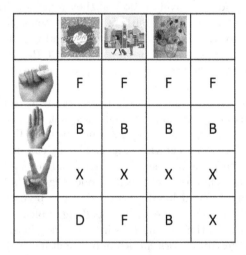

Fig. 3. Rules for determining privacy control actions. Privacy indicators can be used alone. When tag and gesture appear together, we give hand gesture higher priority as they are temporal and proactive behaviors from individuals. In this example, "F" means blurring face; "B" means removing body; "D" means deleting image; "X" means no action. The last column refers to no tag, and the last row refers to no gesture.

4.3 In-device Visual Privacy Protection Framework

Figure 4 is the preferred in-device visual privacy protection framework integrated with proposed privacy protection approach. It consists of privacy control module, visual privacy indicators and privacy control rules. Users can use privacy indicators to convey their desired privacy preferences according to the privacy control rules. The always-on privacy control module is responsible for processing raw camera data if any privacy indicator is detected. As a result, different privacy protection actions will be performed on the raw image, such as blurring the face, removing the body, or deleting the whole image.

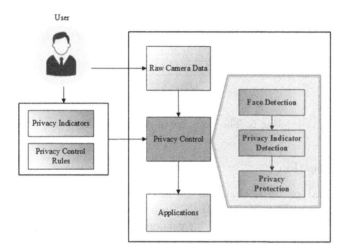

Fig. 4. In-device privacy protection framework. Users can use privacy indicators for corresponding privacy control operations to be enforced by the device. The raw image data will be processed before being used by applications.

When the camera works, raw data will first be filtered by the privacy control module according to the detected visual privacy indicators used by people who express privacy preferences. Then privacy protection actions will be performed on specific individuals to remove identity information before sending the data to any third-party application.

5 Implementation

The workflow of the proposed approach is shown in Fig. 5. We first detect all faces in the image using AdaBoost cascade classifier [27] implemented in OpenCV library [3], and further filter detected faces with skin color to reduce false positives. If there is any face detected, we will start hand detection and tag detection tasks to determine who conveys privacy control messages. Finally, privacy protection actions will be performed on specific individuals according to detected privacy indicators and control rules as described in above sections.

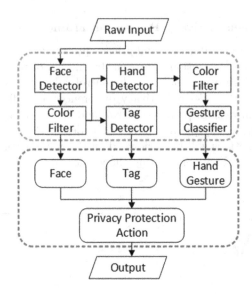

Fig. 5. The workflow of our approach.

5.1 Tag Detection

Tags are special patterns that can be stuck or printed on clothes. We use Speeded-Up Robust Features (SURF) [7] implemented in OpenCV library [3] for tag detection. It is a more speeded-up version of Scale-Invariant Feature Transform (SIFT) [19] for key point detection and description. To improve detection efficiency and reduce computational load on device, we first narrow down the tag detection region according to the detected face as shown in Fig. 6. It extends from the bottom of face region to the bottom of the image, and its width is twice of the face region.

To detect the tag in tag region, the SURF algorithm first finds interest points and calculate feature descriptors of both provided tag and the tag region. Next, descriptors are matched between the provided tag and the tag region, and the information of maximum matching will be used to locate the position of the tag in the image. As a result, texture-rich tags with distinct features are more suitable for our approach.

5.2 Hand Gesture Detection and Recognition

Similar to face detection, we can use the pre-trained hand cascade classifiers [28] to find hand regions, and apply skin color filter to filter out some false positives. The filter works on HSV space of detected regions. Hand regions whose proportion of skin-like areas lower than a certain threshold will be ignored.

For recognition of hand gestures, we apply back projection after sampling a small area of the detected hand region, followed by erosion and dilation processing to get the binary image. Finally, we get the contour and compare the shape

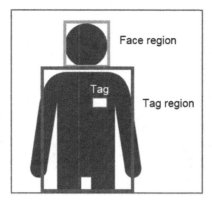

Fig. 6. Tag detection region.

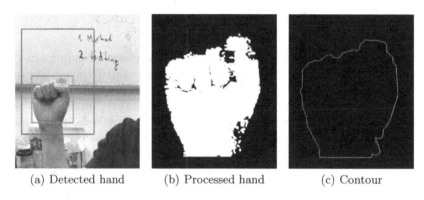

(a) Detected hand   (b) Processed hand   (c) Contour

Fig. 7. Hand gesture contour is acquired after image processing. (a) shows the detected hand with hand detection classifier; (b) shows binary image after image processing steps; (c) is the final contour used for matching and recognition.

with three templates of hand gesture. Results of each step is illustrated in Fig. 7. More advanced and accurate gesture recognition techniques can be used, which is described in [26]. We do not apply the method here because it needs to offload the image to the cloud for gesture detection. Therefore, we adopt a simple hand detection method to demonstrate how the proposed approach works, which leaves much space for further improvement.

After we recognize the hand gesture, we infer the individual who shows gestures according to the positions of detected faces and gestures. Currently, our strategy is to find the nearest face for each hand gesture.

5.3   Privacy Protection Action

The privacy protection action will be performed according to detected tags and gestures. We apply median blurring method [6] to obfuscate the determined face

(a) Using tags   (b) Using gestures

Fig. 8. Processed image applying face blurring for tags and gestures. In (a), the person on the left wearing a tag is protected. In (b), the person on the right showing gesture is protected; the person on the left use gestures to modify tag-represented privacy preferences, therefore is not protected.

region as the basic protection action. It smoothens the image by sliding a median filter across it. Every pixel's output value will be replaced with the median value of pixels located in a square neighboring around it. This blurring method is irreversible, therefore, we guarantee that once the face region is obfuscated, it cannot be recovered. Compared with other blurring methods, the result of median blur is not abrupt. The contour of the face and the hairline are mostly remained, while facial features are removed. In general, the blurring operation for face region does not affect beauty, maintaining the most of the picture without significant changes. The processed image applying median blurring as privacy protection action is shown in Fig. 8.

6   Evaluation

We evaluate our approach with the implemented prototype on Android smartphones in terms of effectiveness, overall performance, and user experience. We first explore the effectiveness of interacting with camera via tags and hand gestures under different conditions. Then we compare the overall performance of tag and hand gesture to show their strengths and weaknesses respectively. Finally we evaluate user experience of our prototype in three aspects.

6.1   Effectiveness

In the real world, many factors will influence the success ratio of our approach. For example, the image resolution determined by the sensor of the camera, the distance between the camera and people, and the relative positions of people in the picture. Therefore, we evaluate the effectiveness of our interactive privacy protection framework under different conditions. We conduct experiments with control variable method to explore how effective and robust our system is with respects to certain factors. The photos we use for effectiveness evaluation are taken with Xiaomi MI 3W. In the experiments, we use the same tag and the clenched fist hand gesture as representatives of two kinds of privacy control indicators, and we simply blur the face to illustrate if our prototype would work.

Distance, Angle, and Size. Distance, viewing angle, and size of privacy indicators affect the detection results, therefore they are crucial to the whole system performance. We record videos of the spinning tag and fist with resolution 1920×1080 at three different distances in an outdoor environment. We also record videos with tags of different sizes in an indoor environment.

The detection accuracy from different distances and viewing angles is shown in Fig. 9. Figure 9(a) illustrates four directions that we test. For the privacy tag, the accuracy declines when the distance or the angle increases as shown in Fig. 9(b). Further, the accuracy decreases faster along the distance than the angle, which indicates the tag detection accuracy is much more sensitive to the

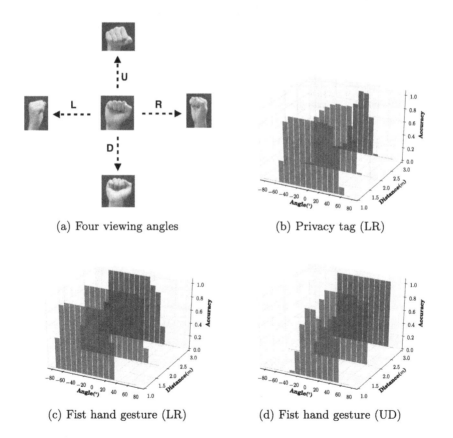

(a) Four viewing angles

(b) Privacy tag (LR)

(c) Fist hand gesture (LR)

(d) Fist hand gesture (UD)

Fig. 9. Results of detection accuracy at different distances and viewing angles.

distance than the angle. However, when the angle exceeds 40° along R direction, the accuracy decreases dramatically regardless of distance.

We then evaluate the detection accuracy of the fist hand gesture with regards to distance and angle in horizontal (L and R) and vertical (U and D) direction. Both Fig. 9(c) and (d) show that the detection accuracy decreases with increasing angle as well. As the method we use to detect the hand gesture with blob properties is robust to the distance, the accuracy does not achieve the best when the distance is the shortest. In Fig. 9(d), we also find that the effective vertical angular range for fist detection is the smallest at distance of 1 m. It results from the fact that the same movement will cause greater visual change of the fist when facing the camera at a shorter distance.

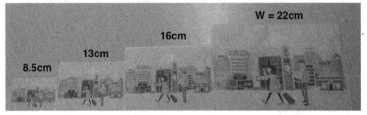

(a) Four different sizes

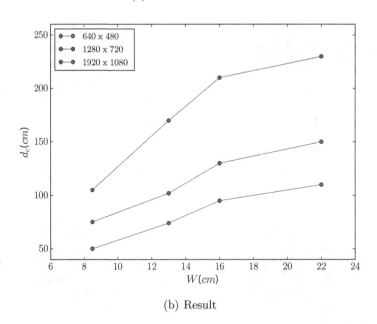

(b) Result

Fig. 10. Critical distance (d_c) for tags with 4 different sizes (W). Three colors refer to three image resolutions, and four points on the same line represent four different sizes. (Color figure online)

In general, for both the tag and fist detection, they have an effective angular range of ±60° and distance within 2 m. Moreover, the detection of tag is more sensitive to distance compared with the detection of fist, which is caused by different methods we use to detect the tag and the fist. In the case of long distance, the background in the image will generate large amounts of noisy features which affects the matching process of SURF severely. However, the classifier we use to detect the hand and face can work well at long distances.

To quantify how far the privacy tag can be detected, we define critical distance d_c as the limit of effective detection. We use four tags with different sizes W as depicted in Fig. 10(a). The image resolution is also taken into consideration.

Figure 10(b) shows a linear relation between the critical distance d_c and the tag size W for each resolution. Essentially, the number of pixels occupied by the tag in the image determines the detection accuracy. From the figure, we can see that the critical distance increases with higher resolution, and we can expect a critical distance over 5 m for high resolution taken by most current smartphones.

Occlusion. Considering that other objects in the picture may cause the occlusion of visual privacy indicators, we test if the tag can still be detected in such situations. As shown in Fig. 11, within detectable distance, our approach is quite robust to occlusion, being able to achieve a 50% occlusion limit without serious performance degradation.

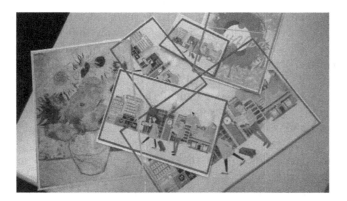

Fig. 11. Tags can still be detected with partial occlusion.

6.2 Overall Performance

To compare the computational performance of two privacy control indicators, we take around 200 high resolution images from six places, including three indoor (office, library, and corridor) and three outdoor spots. At each spot, we take about 30 images. The distance is within 5 m, and the angle is within ±60°. Each image has resolution 4208 × 3120.

Table 1 gives the recall and average processing time of each detection module. The recall refers to the fraction of indicators that are detected by the system. Most of the faces not detected are side faces. As tag detection region is determined by the face region, the recall of tag is affected by face detection recall.

The average processing time shows that using tags and hand gestures as indicators to protect visual privacy can be performed in real time, and the high ratio of successful tag detection guarantee the success of our privacy control approach. In general, the results are promising, since detection of both the tag and hand gesture can be improved.

Table 1. Performance of privacy control indicators.

Indicator	Recall (%)	Average processing time (ms)
Face	90	830
Tag	88	1088
Hand gesture	68	230

6.3 User Experience

We invite 18 participants (12 males and 6 females) from different departments in our campus. Their ages range from 20 to 31 years old with a mean of 24 years old. In this study, we first tell participants all privacy indicators they can use. Then we show them corresponding results after they try our proposed visual privacy indicators. We evaluate user experience with reference to the Technology Acceptance Model (TAM), which is developed to predict individual adoption and use of new technologies [10]. Among multiple factors described in TAM, we assess perceived usefulness (PU), perceived ease of use (PEOU), and attitude towards using (ATU) with a five-point Likert scale (1 = strongly disagree and 5 = strongly agree).

First, we ask participants to rate the statement *"I believe my personal identity could be protected with this interactive visual privacy control approach."* Participants generally agree with the sentence with a median of 4 and an average of 3.8 (SD = 1.02). Although three participants question the reliability of our vision-based approach, these ratings are encouraging since the current un-optimized prototype was generally approved by the majority of participants.

We further ask participants to rate the statement, *"It is easy to use for protecting identity information."* Participants respond they agree with the sentence with a median of 4 and an average of 4.3 (SD=0.49). Six participants choose strongly agree, and the rest choose agree. It proves the proposed interactive privacy control approach is easy to use.

We finally ask participants to rate the statement, *"I would like to use visual privacy indicators such as hand gesture and visual tag to prevent leak of my identity information."* Their general attitudes towards using it are positive, with a median of 4 and an average of 3.7 (SD = 0.83). Three participants choose strongly agree, eight choose agree, six choose neutral, and one choose disagree. P6 says, *"I hope my body can be perfectly removed from the image as if nothing is there."* P7 notes, *"I think those who want to be captured in the picture should show gestures, rather than placing burdens on those who wants to remain anonymous."* P16 comments, *"It is useful, but I don't care being recorded without my consent."* On the other hand, P1 says, *"It is fun to show a gesture then I can disappear or appear in the image."* P2 says, *"Though inferring the individual who wants to be protected with visual clues may not work sometimes, it is a good attempt to use hand gesture for inference."* P10 says, *"I really hope that I can have clothes with privacy tag when I take part in some activities."* Their responses are encouraging, which show possibilities of improving our approach, as well as new directions to protect visual privacy.

7   Conclusion and Future Work

This paper proposed an interactive visual privacy control method that enables individuals to convey privacy protection messages with tags and hand gestures. We discussed people's attitudes, design guidelines, and challenges for protecting visual privacy. The underlying technical solution of our approach builds on computer vision object detection techniques. With our privacy protection method, it offers a simple and efficient way for individuals to fight against potential infringement of privacy. The evaluation results showed that our approach has both usability and effectiveness. It is approved by a majority of participants according to our user experience study.

There are some future work. First, the vision-based approach highly relies on object detection techniques. The object detection methods we use are not optimal. Therefore, we will apply more sophisticated algorithms without placing much burden on the user or device. Moreover, inference of individual who wants to remain anonymous with only visual data may not be always reliable. We need to incorporate other useful information. For example, mobile devices carried by individuals may provide information to help decide who needs privacy protection. Finally, methods of removing identity information need to be improved. With pedestrian detection and scene reconstruction techniques, we hope body area can be removed naturally, thus more people will be willing to use it.

In summary, privacy issues are complicated that no simple method or mechanism can perfectly solve them. It is related to factors such as people's attitudes, behaviors, state-of-art technologies. We believe this paper makes a first step towards protecting visual privacy in an interactive way.

References

1. Congress's letter. http://blogs.wsj.com/digits/2013/05/16/congress-asks-google-about-glass-privacy
2. Data protection authorities' letter. https://www.priv.gc.ca/en/opc-news/news-and-announcements/2013/nr-c_130618/

3. Opencv. http://opencv.org/
4. Acquisti, A., Gross, R., Stutzman, F.: Privacy in the age of augmented reality. In: Proceedings of the National Academy of Sciences (2011)
5. Aditya, P., Sen, R., Druschel, P., Oh, S.J., Benenson, R., Fritz, M., Schiele, B., Bhattacharjee, B., Wu, T.T.: I-Pic: a platform for privacy-compliant image capture. In: Proceedings of the 14th Annual International Conference on Mobile Systems, Applications, and Services, MobiSys, vol. 16 (2016)
6. Bardyn, J., et al.: Une architecture Vlsi pour un operateur de filtrage median. In: Congres Reconnaissance des Formes et Intelligence Artificielle, vol. 1, pp. 557–566 (1984)
7. Bay, H., Tuytelaars, T., Gool, L.: SURF: speeded up robust features. In: Leonardis, A., Bischof, H., Pinz, A. (eds.) ECCV 2006. LNCS, vol. 3951, pp. 404–417. Springer, Heidelberg (2006). doi:10.1007/11744023_32
8. Bo, C., Shen, G., Liu, J., Li, X.Y., Zhang, Y., Zhao, F.: Privacy.tag: privacy concern expressed and respected. In: Proceedings of the 12th ACM Conference on Embedded Network Sensor Systems, pp. 163–176. ACM (2014)
9. Caine, K.E., Fisk, A.D., Rogers, W.A.: Benefits and privacy concerns of a home equipped with a visual sensing system: a perspective from older adults. In: Proceedings of the Human Factors and Ergonomics Society Annual Meeting, vol. 50, pp. 180–184. Sage Publications (2006)
10. Davis, F.D., Bagozzi, R.P., Warshaw, P.R.: User acceptance of computer technology: a comparison of two theoretical models. Manage. Sci. **35**(8), 982–1003 (1989)
11. Denning, T., Dehlawi, Z., Kohno, T.: In situ with bystanders of augmented reality glasses: perspectives on recording and privacy-mediating technologies. In: Proceedings of the 32nd Annual ACM Conference on Human Factors in Computing Systems, pp. 2377–2386. ACM (2014)
12. Fiala, M.: Artag, a fiducial marker system using digital techniques. In: 2005 IEEE Computer Society Conference on Computer Vision and Pattern Recognition, CVPR 2005, vol. 2, pp. 590–596. IEEE (2005)
13. Gavison, R.: Privacy and the limits of law. Yale Law J. **89**, 421–471 (1980)
14. Hoyle, R., Templeman, R., Anthony, D., Crandall, D., Kapadia, A.: Sensitive lifelogs: a privacy analysis of photos from wearable cameras. In: Proceedings of the 33rd Annual ACM Conference on Human Factors in Computing Systems, pp. 1645–1648. ACM (2015)
15. Hoyle, R., Templeman, R., Armes, S., Anthony, D., Crandall, D., Kapadia, A.: Privacy behaviors of lifeloggers using wearable cameras. In: Proceedings of the 2014 ACM International Joint Conference on Pervasive and Ubiquitous Computing, pp. 571–582. ACM (2014)
16. Jana, S., Molnar, D., Moshchuk, A., Dunn, A., Livshits, B., Wang, H.J., Ofek, E.: Enabling fine-grained permissions for augmented reality applications with recognizers. In: Presented as part of the 22nd USENIX Security Symposium (USENIX Security 2013), pp. 415–430 (2013)
17. Jana, S., Narayanan, A., Shmatikov, V.: A scanner darkly: protecting user privacy from perceptual applications. In: 2013 IEEE Symposium on Security and Privacy (SP), pp. 349–363. IEEE (2013)
18. Kärkkäinen, T., Vaittinen, T., Väänänen-Vainio-Mattila, K.: I don't mind being logged, but want to remain in control: a field study of mobile activity and context logging. In: Proceedings of the SIGCHI Conference on Human Factors in Computing Systems, pp. 163–172. ACM (2010)
19. Lowe, D.G.: Distinctive image features from scale-invariant keypoints. Int. J. Comput. Vision **60**(2), 91–110 (2004)

20. Nguyen, D.H., Bedford, A., Bretana, A.G., Hayes, G.R.: Situating the concern for information privacy through an empirical study of responses to video recording. In: Proceedings of the SIGCHI Conference on Human Factors in Computing Systems, pp. 3207–3216. ACM (2011)
21. Raval, N., Srivastava, A., Razeen, A., Lebeck, K., Machanavajjhala, A., Cox, L.P.: What you mark is what apps see. In: ACM International Conference on Mobile Systems, Applications, and Services (Mobisys) (2016)
22. Roesner, F., Kohno, T., Molnar, D.: Security and privacy for augmented reality systems. Commun. ACM **57**(4), 88–96 (2014)
23. Roesner, F., Molnar, D., Moshchuk, A., Kohno, T., Wang, H.J.: World-driven access control for continuous sensing. In: Proceedings of the 2014 ACM SIGSAC Conference on Computer and Communications Security, pp. 1169–1181. ACM (2014)
24. Schiff, J., Meingast, M., Mulligan, D.K., Sastry, S., Goldberg, K.: Respectful cameras: detecting visual markers in real-time to address privacy concerns. In: Senior, A. (ed.) Protecting Privacy in Video Surveillance, pp. 65–89. Springer, London (2009)
25. Shaw, R.: Recognition markets and visual privacy. In: UnBlinking: New Perspectives on Visual Privacy in the 21st Century (2006)
26. Shu, J., Zheng, R., Hui, P.: Demo: interactive visual privacy control with gestures. In: Proceedings of the 14th Annual International Conference on Mobile Systems, Applications, and Services Companion, p. 120. ACM (2016)
27. Viola, P., Jones, M.J.: Robust real-time face detection. Int. J. Comput. Vision **57**(2), 137–154 (2004)
28. Wachs, J., Stern, H., Edan, Y., Gillam, M., Feied, C., Smith, M., Handler, J.: A real-time hand gesture interface for medical visualization applications. In: Knowles, J., Avineri, E., Dahal, K. (eds.) Applications of Soft Computing, pp. 153–162. Springer, Heidelberg (2006)
29. Zhang, X., Fronz, S., Navab, N.: Visual marker detection and decoding in AR systems: a comparative study. In: Proceedings of the 1st International Symposium on Mixed and Augmented Reality, p. 97. IEEE Computer Society (2002)

Navigation Assistance for Individuals with Visual Impairments in Indoor Environments

Rupam Kundu$^{(\boxtimes)}$, Gopi Krishna Tummala, and Prasun Sinha

Department of Computer Science and Engineering, The Ohio State University,
Columbus, USA
{kundu.24,tummala.10,sinha.43}@osu.edu

Abstract. Canes or service dogs in indoor environments are unable to provide spatial information to the Individuals with Visual Impairments (IVIs) to make them independent. An indoor navigation assistance system can provide information on the presence of any obstacles in their vicinity, the distance of separation and their direction of motion (in case of mobile objects) w.r.t the IVIs. In this paper, we attempt to address the above objective by designing a novel time-efficient algorithm where a smart-glass is employed to spot an obstacle (stationary or mobile) in indoor environment using the inbuilt camera and inertial sensors. The system is implemented and tested extensively in indoor settings.

1 Introduction

Obtaining the spatial information around us is inevitably necessary to perform our day-to-day activities and to move around safely without colliding with other objects. However, Individuals with Visual Impairments (IVIs) are devoid of this crucial human functionality. According to WHO's announcement in 2014 [5], around 285 million people are victims of visual impairments worldwide out of which 39 million are blind and the rest suffer from low vision. Out of these 39 million (30% of world blind population), 12 million blind people in India alone [6]. So the urge to restore the vision functionality in IVIs to ensure an independent and a comfortable life, has drawn the attention of many researchers from diverse domains.

Recently, various wearable frameworks have been devised for detecting obstacles in the user's vicinity. They belong to one of the four categories stated below:

Ultrasonic Sensors: Ifukube et al. [12] used two ultrasonic sensors which gather spatial information based on reflections of the transmitted wave from various objects. Ultrasonic sensors are highly directional (resolution of 1 mm) and require mechanical movements to pinpoint obstacles in different directions [4]. Shovel et al. [17] introduced a belt, a portable computer and an array of ultrasonic sensors that scan all the signals arriving at the sensors. The hardware is bulky, and the technique requires training.

© Springer International Publishing AG 2017
N. Sastry and S. Chakraborty (Eds.): COMSNETS 2017, LNCS 10340, pp. 44–52, 2017.
DOI: 10.1007/978-3-319-67235-9_4

Infrared: An Infrared sensor can be used to compute the depth of an object by detecting the phase shift of the modulated light reflected from the target. The range of detection is 10 cm to 1.5 m with 95% accuracy [8]. However, the depth maps become noisy in presence of sunlight (since it contains infrared light) [22]. The Infrared sensors are also highly directional and require mechanical panning to detect objects in different directions.

Radar: RADAR operates similar to ultrasound navigation. Instead of acoustic waves, radio waves are employed to measure the Time-of-Flight as the signals bounce back from nearby obstacles. However, due to the high directionality of RADAR, either a mechanical movement is required or an array of such sensors need to be employed resulting in a bulky design. Moreover, commercially available RADARS and LIDARS consumes high power (nearly 8 W) [7].

Stereo: "Smart-Vision" introduced by Fernandes et al. [11] used several independent modules like GPS, RFID, Vision and Wi-Fi but it can detect only specific landmarks. Balakrishnan et al. [9] and Vimal et al. [16] proposed to identify obstacles in the user's vicinity based on stereo disparity. As the disparity is measured using pixel based operations, these processes are computationally heavy. Moreover, small depth variations for far away objects are hard to interpret using stereo disparity techniques. For a baseline of 28 mm, image sensor pixel size of 17 um, focal length of 2.8 mm and a disparity range of 5–35, Khaleghi et al. [13] showed that if an object is detected at 1 m, the error is around 20 cm. The error increases non-linearly for higher ranges. Also, commercially available long range stereo cameras consume high power (nearly 4 W) [1], while the small ones [2] have very short range (2.5 m).

RFID: Ding et al. [10] proposed the use of RFID readers on canes and RFID tags along navigation paths so that the reader can read pre-installed information from the tags. The tag installations require modification to the infrastructure and also information about moving objects cannot be captured using this technique.

Advanced positioning and tracking services can be used along with smart-glass to emulate stereo across the motion of the smart-glass. Smart-glasses, such as Google-glass and Microsoft HoloLens [19], are integrated with sensors such as camera, accelerometer, magnetometer and gyroscope. Also, they are capable of communicating with the infrastructure or a paired mobile phone using wireless technologies. However, unlike stereo, the smart-glasses are usually equipped with a single camera. Recent advancements in wireless localization and tracking techniques using wireless radio [14,23], RF-ID's [24] and camera [15,21] can achieve sub-meter level accuracies. These location-tracking techniques can be used to relate multiple frames captured at different spatial points to estimate the depth of different objects. So the key question we raise in this context is: *Can we estimate the depth of obstacles in an indoor environment using a smart-glass to provide a vision based navigation aid for IVIs?*

Fusing multiple frames across the motion trajectory of a smart-glass is challenging due to - *location errors in the trajectory, lack of information about objects in the environment, dynamic objects, limited-range* and *run-time complexity* of different multi-frame fusion algorithms. In this paper, we design a novel and time-efficient algorithm for assisting IVIs for enabling them to navigate independently in indoor settings using vision in a smart-glass framework that can be implemented in real time. The following are the contributions of this paper:

– Novel algorithms to spot an obstacle in the IVI's path (stationary or dynamic) and also to figure out the direction of motion of the dynamic object w.r.t. IVI.
– Proof of concept implementation, experiments and evaluation of modules for static object sensing and dynamic object sensing.

2   Challenges

– **Lack of Depth Information:** Video feed captured by commodity smart glass lacks - **(a)** depth information of the captured objects, **(b)** association of the observed objects with their real entities.
– **Object Uncertainty:** Neither the object's shape nor its location or mobility information (stationary or dynamic) is known. Vision-based modules are not suited for real time implementation when there are many of objects in the scene.

3   Vision Based Tracking for IVIs

3.1   Background

The *Pinhole camera model* [20] describes the geometric relationship between the 2D image-plane (i.e., pixel positions in a camera capture) and the 3D ground coordinate system. Let the image plane be the UV-plane and the camera coordinate system be the (XYZ) space. Let us assume that the perpendicular ray emanating from the center of the camera frame is along the Z-axis, V-axis is parallel to Y-axis and U-axis is parallel to X-axis (see Fig. 1). The geometrical relationship is given by,

$$\frac{u_1}{f_u} = \frac{x_1}{z_1},$$
$$\frac{v_1}{f_v} = \frac{y_1}{z_1}, \tag{1}$$

where f_u and f_v are the focal lengths of the camera.

3.2   Design

The system is implemented as a smart-glass app that uses a camera in a Google-glass framework and identifies feature points in the environment. Feature points are distinguishable points such as corners or the edges of a shirt etc., which can be tracked across consecutive image frames using optical-flow based techniques [21]. The user wearing a smart-glass walks in an indoor environment. The camera records a short video which is processed to identify feature points corresponding

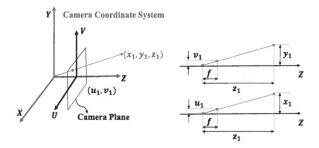

Fig. 1. Geometric relationship between image plane and the camera coordinate system. Illustration assumes $f = f_u = f_v$

to the objects across multiple video frames. Using the coordinates of the observed feature points in camera frame along with the location of the user, the location of the object can be determined. The location of the user can be obtained from any localization services such as WiFi [14], Visual Light Communication [15] or Fingerprinting [18].

To spot an obstacle in an IVI's path, we need to consider two scenarios (a) When the user is moving towards a static object, e.g., a wall, door or tables; and, (b) When the user is approaching a moving object, e.g., a human passing by. We discuss the above cases in the subsequent sections.

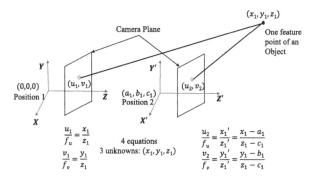

Fig. 2. Static case: set of equations over-constrained

3.3 Static Case

We consider the static case when the user is moving while the object is static as illustrated in Fig. 2. Let us assume that the user moves from Position 1 (P_1) - $(0,0,0)$ to Position 2 (P_2) - (a_1, b_1, c_1) while the feature point associated with an object (x_1, y_1, z_1) is static. For sake of simplicity, let us assume the orientation of the camera is not changing from P_1 to P_2 (later this assumption is relaxed). *All the coordinates in the rest of the paper are measured according to camera coordinate system when it is at* P_1. In particular, this coordinate system has its XY-Plane aligned with camera plane, and the Z-axis is perpendicular to the camera plane. Let P_1 and P_2 correspond to two frames in a video feed which are analyzed to sense object depths. Due to the translation, the new coordinate system at P_2 is a translated version of the coordinate system at P_1. Therefore, the coordinates of the point located at (x_1, y_1, z_1) will be $(x_1', y_1', z_1)'$ in coordinate system at position 2, where $x_1' = x_1 - a_1$, $y_1' = y_1 - b_1$ and $z_1' = z_1 - c_1$.

Following the Pinhole Camera Model, two equations can be written for each position similar to Eq. (1) as shown in Fig. 2. Analyzing a set of two frames, the change in the relative location of the object w.r.t. the user can be determined. Geometric representation of a feature point with pixel positions (u, v) represents a ray emanating from the camera. The translation of the user - (a_1, b_1, c_1) can be obtained from standard localization services. Therefore, using four equations along with the user's location, the object's position (x_1, y_1, z_1) can be determined. The intersection of two rays from P_1 and P_2 gives the location of the feature point. Essentially, this resembles stereo to compute the depth of an object.

XYZ to X'Y'Z' Coordinate System: For simplicity, we have shown in Fig. 2 that the camera plane at P_1 and P_2 are aligned. In reality, the camera orientation might change from P_1 to P_2 and the user might be moving in an arbitrary direction. We use translation of camera from P_1 to P_2 w.r.t camera coordinate system at P_1, $\mathbf{T_{12}}$ (3×1) obtained using a localization technique. The Rotation matrix from the coordinate system at P_1 to P_2, $\mathbf{R_{12}}$ (3×3) is obtained from MEMS gyroscope present in smart-glass. Using the translation and rotation, the position of the feature point in the two coordinate systems can be related as,

$$\begin{bmatrix} x_1' \\ y_1' \\ z_1' \end{bmatrix} = \mathbf{R_{12}} \times \begin{bmatrix} x_1 \\ y_1 \\ z_1 \end{bmatrix} + \mathbf{T_{12}}. \tag{2}$$

Gyroscopes are known to accumulate error, but since we are using orientation information for two closely spaced frames, the error accumulated is negligible.

3.4   Dynamic Case

We now consider a scenario in which the feature point corresponding to the object is also moving as the user holding the camera moves. In Fig. 3, the feature point of an object moves from $\mathbf{O}$-(x_1, y_1, z_1) to $\mathbf{P}$-(x_2, y_2, z_2) as the user carrying the camera moves from P_1 - $(0, 0, 0)$ to P_2 - (a_1, b_1, c_1). For the sake of simplicity, we assume that the orientation of the camera is same at P_1 and P_2. In Fig. 3 the two rays intersect at a point 'A' which is not the true current location of the obstacle. This provides an incorrect estimation to the IVI. Figure 3 shows the entire range of possible wrong solutions for different movements of the feature point.

Exploring Multiple Points Belonging to Dynamic Object: To overcome the above problem, we make use of multiple feature points. Suppose the camera

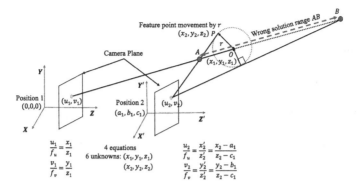

Fig. 3. Dynamic case: both the user and the object are moving

observes n feature points from a particular object at both P_1-$(0,0,0)$ and P_2-(a_1, b_1, c_1). P_1 and P_2 correspond to two different frames from the video feed. The location coordinate of the n feature points - $(x_i^j, y_i^j, z_i^j), 1 \le i \le n, \forall j \epsilon [1,2]$ at two positions have $6n$ unknowns. Using the Pinhole Camera Model, for each feature point (x_i^j, y_i^j, z_i^j) at each position, two equations can be written similar to Eq. (1). This generates $4n$ equations for two positions. Additionally, the velocity vector along x, y and z axes for all the feature points are equal since they belong to the same object providing $3.(n-1)$ equations. These equations can be written as $V_i^x = V_j^x$, $V_i^y = V_j^y$ and $V_i^z = V_j^z$ where $i, j \in [1, n]$. Moreover, since we are considering closely spaced frames, we can assume the height has not changed from P_1 to P_2 which provides one more equation since the velocity along y axis will be zero $V_i^y = V_j^y = 0$ where $i, j \in [1, n]$. Therefore, there are $6n$ unknowns and $4n + 3(n-1) + 1$ equations. For solving these sets of equations, the following relation needs to hold:

$$4n + 3(n-1) + 1 \ge 6n$$

$$\Rightarrow n \ge 2 \tag{3}$$

For sensing depth of dynamic objects at least two feature points from it must be identified and tracked across two closely spaced frames.

Object Detection Modules to Group Feature Points: To identify feature points from the same object, object boundaries need to be determined. Object detection modules like '*face detection*' are already available on Android [3]. Once the object is detected, its boundaries can be identified and the corresponding feature points within that object contour can be deduced. Here also, for simplicity, we have shown in Fig. 3 that the camera plane is aligned with the ground coordinate system and the user moves along the Z-axis. We have used the same technique as mentioned in Sect. 3.3.

4   Experiments

The system is implemented in Python which uses open source computer vision library (OpenCV) to track different future points and the static and dynamic object sensing modules are implemented in Matlab. The video is recorded using a Samsung Galaxy S6 phone and the videos are analyzed offline. With this implementation, we have performed some *Proof of Concept* experiments to test the feasibility of our design in sensing both the *Static* and *Dynamic* objects. We have also assumed perfect knowledge about the absolute location of a user. We plan to work in more real settings using an accurate indoor localization service in future extensions.

Static Case: In this case, we placed an object at different distances along a straight line, starting from 3.95 m w.r.t the user. A camera mounted on a moving cart is moved following the same straight line for a distance of 1.22 m for all the sets of experiments. The ground truths are marked with red colored markers and were documented using a different camera. A sample error measurement in sensing depth information for one of the experiments is shown in Fig. 4. The average depth estimation error vs Object depth is shown in Fig. 5.

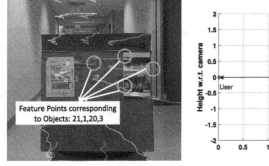
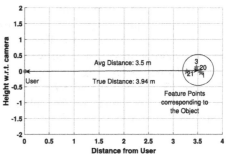

Fig. 4. Depth estimation at 3.94 m

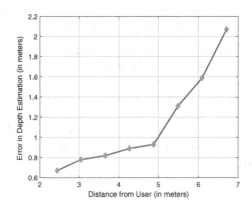

Fig. 5. Error in depth estimation in static case

Dynamic Case: In this case, a person is asked to take a step within a circle of 0.6096 m (2 ft) circle at known locations, starting from 3.95 m w.r.t. the object. A camera mounted on a moving cart is moved in a straight line for a distance of 1.22 m for all the sets of experiments. The average depth estimation error for movement at various separation distances from the user is shown in Fig. 6.

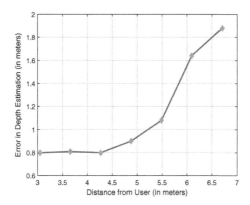

Fig. 6. Error in depth estimation in dynamic Case

Analyzing Figs. 5 and 6, we observe for closer separation distances (within 5 m), the *Static* and *Dynamic* cases provide comparable errors close to 1 m. However, as the distance increases beyond 5 m, the error shoots up due to:

- Reduction in the number of feature points.
- Feature points belonging to the edges get merged with other background objects as the feature point moves.

5   Conclusion and Future Work

We proposed a novel time-efficient solution for assisting IVIs in navigating independently in indoor scenarios. The proposed system is built on a smart-glass framework and uses it's camera to capture video of the scene in front of an IVI. Both static and dynamic obstacles can be pointed out using our technique.

References

1. Bumblebee   XP3   3D.   https://www.ptgrey.com/bumblebee-xb3-1394b-stereo-vision-camera-systems-2
2. Duo 3D Camera. https://duo3d.com/
3. Face   Detection.   https://developer.android.com/reference/android/media/FaceDetector.html
4. Ultrasonic sensors Find Direction And distance. http://www.maxbotix.com/documents/MaxBotix_Ultrasonic_Sensors_Find_Direction_and_Distance.pdf

5. Visual impairment and blindness. http://www.who.int/mediacentre/factsheets/fs282/en/
6. Visual Impairment and Blindness statistics India. http://www.sightsaversindia.in/
7. VLP 16 Specs. http://velodynelidar.com/docs/manuals/VLP-16%20User%20Manual%20and%20Programming%20Guide%2063-9243%20Rev%20A.pdf
8. Al-Fahoum, A.S., Al-Hmoud, H.B., Al-Fraihat, A.A.: A smart infrared microcontroller-based blind guidance system. Act. Passive Electron. Compon. **2013** (2013)
9. Balakrishnan, G., Sainarayanan, G., Nagarajan, R., Yaacob, S.: A stereo image processing system for visually impaired. Int. J. Inf. Commun. Eng. **2**(3), 136–145 (2006)
10. Ding, B., Yuan, H., Jiang, L., Zang, X.: The research on blind navigation system based on RFID. In: 2007 International Conference on Wireless Communications, Networking and Mobile Computing. pp. 2058–2061. IEEE (2007)
11. Fernandes, H., Costa, P., Filipe, V., Hadjileontiadis, L., Barroso, J.: Stereo vision in blind navigation assistance. In: World Automation Congress (WAC), pp. 1–6. IEEE (2010)
12. Ifukube, T., Sasaki, T., Peng, C.: A blind mobility aid modeled after echolocation of bats. IEEE Trans. Biomed. Eng. **38**(5), 461–465 (1991)
13. Khaleghi, B., Ahuja, S., Wu, Q.J.: A new miniaturized embedded stereo-vision system (MESVS-I). In: Canadian Conference on Computer and Robot Vision, CRV 2008, pp. 26–33. IEEE (2008)
14. Kumar, S., Gil, S., Katabi, D., Rus, D.: Accurate indoor localization with zero start-up cost. In: Proceedings of ACM MobiCom 2014, pp. 483–494 (2014)
15. Kuo, Y.S., Pannuto, P., Hsiao, K.J., Dutta, P.: Luxapose: indoor positioning with mobile phones and visible light. In: Proceedings of ACM MobiCom 2014, pp. 447–458 (2014)
16. Mohandas, V., Paily, R.: Stereo disparity estimation algorithm for blind assisting system. CSI Trans. ICT **1**(1), 3–8 (2013)
17. Shoval, S., Borenstein, J., Koren, Y.: The Navbelt-A computerized travel aid for the blind based on mobile robotics technology. IEEE Trans. Biomed. Eng. **45**(11), 1376–1386 (1998)
18. Shu, Y., Shin, K.G., He, T., Chen, J.: Last-mile navigation using smartphones. In: Proceedings of ACM MobiCom 2015, pp. 512–524 (2015)
19. Statt, N.: Microsoft's HoloLens Explained: How it Works and Why it's Different (2015)
20. Szeliski, R.: Computer Vision: Algorithms and Applications. Springer, Heidelberg (2010)
21. Tummala, G.K., Kundu, R., Sinha, P., Ramnath, R.: Vision-track: vision based indoor tracking in anchor-free regions. In: Proceedings of the ACM HotWireless (2016)
22. Viswanathan, P., Boger, J., Hoey, J., Mihailidis, A.: A comparison of stereovision and infrared as sensors for an anti-collision powered wheelchair for older adults with cognitive impairments. In: Proceedings of the 2nd International Conference on Technology and Aging. Citeseer (2007)
23. Xiong, J., Jamieson, K.: ArrayTrack: a fine-grained indoor location system. In: Presented as Part of USENIX NSDI 2013, pp. 71–84 (2013)
24. Yang, L., Chen, Y., Li, X.Y., Xiao, C., Li, M., Liu, Y.: Tagoram: real-time tracking of mobile RFID tags to high precision using COTS devices. In: Proceedings of the ACM MobiCom 2014, pp. 237–248 (2014)

SpectraMap: Efficiently Constructing a Spatio-temporal RF Spectrum Occupancy Map

Aditya Ahuja[1(✉)], Vinay J. Ribeiro[1], Ranveer Chandra[2], and Amit Kumar[1]

[1] Department of Computer Science and Engineering,
Indian Institute of Technology Delhi, New Delhi 110016, India
{aditya.ahuja,amitk}@cse.iitd.ac.in, vinay@iitd.ac.in
[2] Microsoft Research, Redmond, WA 98052, USA
ranveer@microsoft.com

Abstract. The RF spectrum is typically monitored from a single, or few, vantage points. A larger spatio-temporal view of spectrum occupancy, such as over a few weeks on a city-wide scale, would be beneficial for several applications, for example, spectrum inventory by regulators or spectrum monitoring by wireless carriers. However, achieving such a view requires a dense deployment of spectrum analyzers, both in space and time, which is prohibitively expensive.

In this paper, we present a novel efficient approach to obtain an accurate extrapolated spatio-temporal view of spectrum occupancy. Our method uses RSSI measurements alone and does not require a-priori information of terrain, transmitter location, transmit power or path-loss model. We present our method as an algorithmic framework, called SpectraMap, which through targeted deployment of both static and mobile spectrum analyzers, gives a view of the spectrum occupancy over both time and space. We contrast SpectraMap's accuracy with that of Kriging (an accepted well performing method of RSSI spatial extrapolation) through simulations and present RSSI map construction savings achieved through actual deployment on a large university campus. Finally, we draw a theoretical distinction between SpectraMap and relevant contemporary solutions in the fields of space-time RSSI maps and spectrum management.

Keywords: Dynamic spectrum access · Network measurements · Algorithms

1 Introduction

Spectrum is a critical resource for wireless communication. Consequently, its utilization is frequently monitored for white-spaces, coverage, and interference detection (among other reasons). The recent growth of mobile devices, and the subsequent increase in spectrum demand, has further increased the need for spectrum monitoring.

© Springer International Publishing AG 2017
N. Sastry and S. Chakraborty (Eds.): COMSNETS 2017, LNCS 10340, pp. 53–71, 2017.
DOI: 10.1007/978-3-319-67235-9_5

Spectrum monitoring typically consists of a single spectrum analyzer that captures power levels over time for a frequency range of interest. The spectrum profile is then analysed for various applications. Although this technique is extremely useful for many scenarios, such a single-point spectrum monitoring approach falls short of providing enough data for a number of applications – like dynamic spectrum access, or a spectrum inventory, or monitoring a carrier's network coverage (among others). These applications require distributed spectrum analyzers as for them a single measurement point does not provide much information about the spectrum occupancy view even a few 100 s of meters away.

Several applications require a *space-time-frequency* view of spectrum occupancy. The space might be a big city or campus, and the time might be of the order of days, while the frequency range might vary from a few MHz to several GHz depending on the application. For example, the FCC would like to have spectrum occupancy views for days over multiple GHz of spectrum [5]. The carriers might be more interested to notice any change in coverage, or interferers, in 10 s of MHz frequency range in a given area. We highlight more applications in Sect. 2.

Despite the need for (sparse) distributed spectrum monitoring, this problem has not received much attention in the research community. The optimal technique would require a dense deployment of sensors, say every meter. But little is known about approximation techniques that can provide a near-similar view at a cheaper cost, i.e. with fewer sensors. For example, at how many points in space must one measure to maintain an up-to-date spectrum map? How frequently must one measure these points? And in doing so, what is the confidence in the estimated power values at various locations for times when spectrum occupancy is not measured?

This paper attempts to answer the above questions. To the best of our knowledge it is the first paper to provide an approach to efficiently build an extrapolated spatio-temporal spectrum occupancy map within specified confidence bounds. A key distinguishing feature of our approach, called SpectraMap, from other solutions such as Radio Environmental Maps (REMs) [10] for spatio-temporal spectrum maps, is that it does not need apriori information about transmitter locations, transmit powers, or propagation models. Also, unlike Kriging [18], SpectraMap does not require the RSSI (Received Signal Strength Indicator) stochastic process to be Gaussian.

SpectraMap takes as input the region over which the spectrum occupancy is to be measured/predicted as a set of space points, and the RSS confidence levels of prediction desired. It begins with the calibration phases, which provide estimates of RSS variations over space and time and help determine practically achievable bounds on (extrapolated) RSSI at unmeasured locations at different times. These are followed by a series of tours which bound the region's RSSI using sparse measurements in space-time. SpectraMap then gives: (i) when the spectrum needs to be re-measured, (ii) which subset of space points need to be measured to quickly complete spatial extrapolation, and (iii) the approximate spectrum map at unmeasured locations through an RSS confidence set.

We evaluate our approach by quantifying SpectraMap's prediction error through simulations. We conduct real measurements on a university campus, which span over two years to construct SpectraMap's RSSI map. Our results show that SpectraMap provides accurate RSSI estimates with simultaneous savings in time taken and distance traveled to build the map.

2   The Need for Spatio-temporal Spectrum Maps

Several applications require spectrum occupancy data from a larger area over a period of time. We highlight some of them in this section.

Dynamic Spectrum Access: The TV white spaces have led the way to a new paradigm for wireless communication, that of dynamic spectrum access. If devices know that portions of the spectrum are not being used, then they could potentially operate in that spectrum as long as they do not interfere with primary users. The current approach used by the FCC is to use a modeling-based white space database [8]. However, recent research has shown that this approach is very conservative. An empirically determined spectrum occupancy approach, where the database is populated with real measurements, can allow devices to use many channels currently flagged as occupied in the modeling-based white space database [19]. Such an approach would be extremely valuable if it is possible to compute a spatio-temporal spectrum occupancy map. Furthermore, the SpectraMap approach can increase the opportunity for dynamic spectrum access in new regions, and in new bands, that until now has not been investigated.

Spectrum Inventory: The US Congress has passed the Spectrum Inventory Legislation [5], requiring the FCC to gather information on spectrum utilization throughout the country, and making it available on the Internet. The FCC has been working with the NTIA, and is investigating ways in which one could make claims about spectrum occupancy in a region, as opposed to a single measurement point [6].

Monitoring Coverage: Carriers or broadcasters often want to monitor the coverage of their network. For example, are their signals reaching all parts of a city? Are there coverage holes? Also, what is the heat map of their signals in a region – how does it compare to the modeling (and sparse measurements) done during planning? Most importantly, have there been changes in the environment (such as a new construction) because of which the heat map, and coverage has changed?

Unauthorized Transmitters: Spectrum regulators, and licensees of spectrum, often want to know if parts of their spectrum are being used by unauthorized transmitters. Currently, they react only to concerns from consumers, which is known to be inefficient. A consumer might not be knowledgeable enough to isolate interference from poor network planning, and unless the interference is severe, might not complain about it. Even if the consumer complains, it takes a long time to determine the presence of an interferer. SpectraMap can help determine such rogue transmitters proactively, instead of the current reactive approach.

3   The SpectraMap Formulation

3.1   The Framework - A Simplified View

SpectraMap provides an efficient method to create a spatio-temporal RF spectrum map with adjustible levels of precision. In this section, we introduce the terminology used throughout the paper.

Referring to Fig. 1, let us assume that we have measured the receive power $\mathcal{Z}_i^{\checkmark}(t_0)$ at a space point i at time instant t_0. The question we address is how to estimate/predict the receive power $\mathcal{Z}_i^{?}(t_2)$ at the same location i at a future time instant $t_2 \in [t_0, t_3)$, and make a similar prediction for the receive power $\mathcal{Z}_j^{?}(t_1)$ at an adjacent location j at the current time instant t_1, given $\mathcal{Z}_i^{\checkmark}(t_1)$?

SpectraMap targets this question by *establishing an upper-bound on the absolute value of the difference between the unknown $\mathcal{Z}^{?}$ and the known $\mathcal{Z}^{\checkmark}$*. We call the upper-bounds *precision factors* (as they give the size of the RSSI confidence set, with confidence equalling twice the upper-bound) and the absolute value of the difference between the unknown and the known RSS, the *RSSI-delta*. We also call $\mathcal{Z}^{\checkmark}$ the center RSSI.

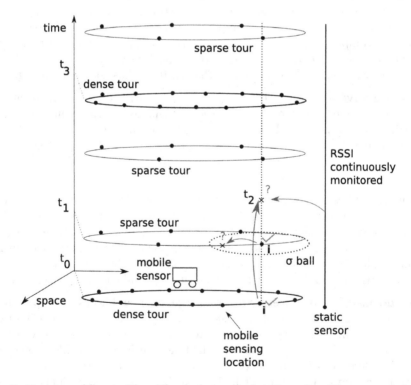

Fig. 1. Top view of SpectraMap: The deployment of static and mobile sensors to build a space-time RF map

The *Time Cover* formalization of SpectraMap bounds the RSSI over time at a given location i, that is $|\mathcal{Z}_i^?(t_2) - \mathcal{Z}_i^{\checkmark}(t_0)| \le \rho_t^*$ for future time instants $t_2 \in [t_0, t_3)$, with the intent of giving a large (weak) RSSI confidence set for space point i. This is achieved through static sensors, and a mobile sensor *dense tour* - a Hamilton cycle visiting all space points. Following our convention, we call $|\mathcal{Z}_i^?(t_2) - \mathcal{Z}_i^{\checkmark}(t_0)|$ the time RSSI-delta and ρ_t^* the time precision factor.

The *Space Cover* formalization of SpectraMap bounds the RSSI over space at unmeasured locations j using measured values at locations i at a time instant t_1 when the Time Cover holds, $|\mathcal{Z}_j^?(t_1) - \mathcal{Z}_i^{\checkmark}(t_1)| \le \rho_s^*$. This is achieved through a mobile sensor *sparse tour* - a Hamilton cycle visiting a strict subset of space points (as in our question, visiting i and skipping j). SpectraMap determines which locations to make measurements in the sparse tours. Typically the space precision factor ρ_s^* is much smaller than ρ_t^*, giving a small (strong) confidence set. Needless to say, j and i must be close to each other to achieve such a bound. Formally, j must be within a σ-ball around i, that is within radius σ of i.

SpectraMap optimizes bounds on the RF spectrum as follows. Let's say we are given precision factors ρ_t^*, ρ_s^*. After the first dense tour at time t_0, we obtain a large (weak) ρ_t^* upper-bound on the space point i receive power for a time cover period $\tau = t_3 - t_0$. When a better characterization of occupancy is needed, a sparse tour in the interim time $t_1 \in [t_0, t_3)$ is performed, giving a smaller (stronger) upper-bound ρ_s^* for space point j. After the period τ, we reinstantiate SpectraMap by performing a *Time Cover* again.

Note that the *Time Cover* RSSI-delta is obtained 'in expectation' - meaning the upper-bound is established on the expected value of the time RSSI-delta, not the on-ground value. This would be seen in Sect. 3.3.

3.2   Definitions

All arithmetic of power variables (calculating RSSI-Delta and multiplications, additions etc.) are performed on the mW scale, but the values in experiments are reported on the dBm scale.

We will first define the variables that will provide the foundation of our model.

1. ρ_t^* : the given time precision factor.
2. ρ_s^* : the given space precision factor. Always $\rho_s^* < \rho_t^*$.
3. τ : time cover period.
4. σ : space cover radius - the radius for which two road points are classified as spatially adjacent in a sparse tour.
5. s : A static sensor point.
6. $\hat{m}$: a dense and sparse tour point which is spatially close to a corresponding static s point.
7. m : a dense and sparse tour point.
8. m' : a dense tour only point, not visited in sparse tours.
9. V : set of all dense tour points.
10. $\mathbb{Z}_i(t)$: the (mW scale) RSS stochastic process for node i at time t. The corresponding realization is $z_i(t)$.

11. $B_\sigma(v) = \{u \in V : dist(u,v) \le \sigma\}$: the σ-ball.
12. $\rho_\sigma(v) = max\{|z_u(t) - z_v(t)| : u \in B_\sigma(v)\}$: per node maximum RSS distance in the ball.
13. $\lambda = \frac{|\{v \in V:\ \rho_\sigma(v) \le \rho_s^*\}|}{|V|}$: the fraction of space points with ball RSS distance less than ρ_s^*.

To establish the *Time Cover* and *Space Cover*, we also use the following stochastic processes.

1. $\mathbb{S}_i(t,u) = |\mathbb{Z}_i(t+u) - \mathbb{Z}_i(t)|$, $\forall t$: to bound the RSSI-Delta for the same node i between two different instances of time.
2. $\mathbb{D}_{i,j}(t) = |\mathbb{Z}_i(t) - \mathbb{Z}_j(t)|$, $\forall t$: to define the RSSI correlation between a tour point and a static point.
3. $q_i(t,\delta) = z_i(t+\delta) - z_i(t)$, with the corresponding process $\mathbb{Q}_i$: for establishing 'space quietness' - a notion which allows the ρ_s^* precision factor to apply for all sparse tours (see Sect. 3.3).

As SpectraMap is equally applicable to any frequency band g, the band g is suppressed in the notation. Also note that all RSSI-delta stochastic processes are assumed to be Stationary Ergodic (a similar assumption in [15]), and thus their expected values can be discerned from a sufficiently long stream of realizations (thus $\mathbf{E}[\mathbb{X}(t)] = \mathbf{E}[\mathbb{X}]$, $\forall t$).

3.3   The Map Algorithm

Time Cover. The intention behind the *Time Cover* is to find the largest time period τ, from the dense tour instant t_d, for which the time precision factor ρ_t^* holds for an $\hat{m}$ point on our tour, and then, by extension, the entire tour. This information can be deduced from RSSI realizations at $(\hat{m}, s)$ pairs. The more $(\hat{m}, s)$ pairs, the better characterization of τ (for a pessimistic view, take the minimum τ over all available $(\hat{m}, s)$ pairs).

Our aim is to maximize τ subject to $\mathbf{E}[|\mathbb{Z}_{\hat{m}}(t_d+u) - \mathbb{Z}_{\hat{m}}(t_d)|] \le \rho_t^*$, $u \in [0, \tau]$. To that end, we state the following theorem, the proof of which is given in the Appendix.

Theorem 1. *Define $\rho_t(u) := 2 \times \mathbf{E}[\mathbb{D}_{\hat{m},s}] + \mathbf{E}[\mathbb{S}_s](u)$. Then $\forall u$,*
$\mathbf{E}[|\mathbb{Z}_{\hat{m}}(t_d + u) - \mathbb{Z}_{\hat{m}}(t_d)|] \le \rho_t(u)$.

Thus our optimization problem reduces to finding the largest τ such that $\rho_t(u) \le \rho_t^*, u \in [0, \tau]$. Consequently, we have a time period τ for which a weak RSSI confidence $2\rho_t^*$ centered on $z_{\hat{m}}(t_d)$ (in expectation) exists for the tour.

Space Cover. In order to establish how sparse tours can succeed dense tours, we have the following knowledge from the dense tour. We have the dense tour instant t_d. We have two spatially adjacent road-points m and m', within the σ ball of each other. Although m is visited in the subsequent sparse tour, m' is not. t_s is the time instance of the sparse tour, with $t_s \in [t_d, t_d + \tau]$. We know

$z_m(t_d)$, $z_{m'}(t_d)$ and $z_m(t_s)$. We have, pre established, $|z_{m'}(t_d) - z_m(t_d)| \leq \rho_s^*$ for λ fraction points. We do not know $z_{m'}(t_s)$.

The intention behind the *Space Cover* is to prove that even for a unvisited point m' in a sparse tour, the dense tour established (tighter) confidence $2\rho_s^*$ holds with a different centre $z_m(t_s)$. To that end, we state the following theorem, the proof of which is in the Appendix.

Theorem 2. *Define* $q_{m,m'}^{\Delta}(t_d, t_s) := |q_{m'}(t_d, t_s - t_d) - q_m(t_d, t_s - t_d)|$, $\alpha \in [0,1], \kappa := \frac{\mathbf{E}[\mathbb{Q}_{m,m'}^{\Delta}]}{\alpha \times \rho_s^*}$. *Then,* $|z_{m'}(t_s) - z_m(t_s)| \leq q_{m,m'}^{\Delta}(t_d, t_s) + \rho_s^* \approx \rho_s^*$ *for* λ *fraction points as long as* (α, κ) *is small.*

Algorithms for Sparse Tours. We now model the set of visited road point vertices in the dense tour and possible edges taken between them as a weighted planar graph $G = (V, E)$. We find the sparse tour as a minimum-weight Hamiltonian circuit on a subset of the dense tour points. The σ-ball around this subset equals the set of dense tour points.

We are given an edge weighted graph $G = (V, E)$ on the set of points V which corresponds to the road network, and a starting vertex v_0. As G corresponds to the road network on V, we can assume that G is drawn on the plane (and hence, is planar graph), and the weight of an edge is equal to the length of the arc connecting the endpoints of this edge. Given a parameter $\sigma > 0$, our solution finds a σ-cover of V – call this set V', and constructs a closed tour on $V' \cup \{v_0\}$. The goal is to minimize the total length of the tour. We call this variant of the Travelling Salesman Problem the DiskTSP problem.

We state that the DiskTSP problem is NP-hard, and it is even hard to approximate within a small factor of approximation.

We describe our algorithms for the DiskTSP problem. Our algorithms will run in two phases. In the first phase, we shall select a subset of points V' ($\subseteq V$). In the second phase, we shall just build a tour over $V' \cup \{v_0\}$. This can be achieved by using any algorithm for TSP restricted to the set V'. Henceforth, we focus on the first phase only. We propose two algorithms – the first algorithm, $\mathcal{A}_1$ is a natural greedy algorithm, and the second one, $\mathcal{A}_2$ is based on the results in [9].

Algorithm $\mathcal{A}_1$: Here, we greedily pick the set V' as follows. Initially, V' is empty, and we will iteratively add vertices to the set V'. Given a set of vertices V', let uncover(V') denote the set of vertices in V which do not lie within Euclidean distance σ of any vertex in V'. Our algorithm picks the vertex v for which the cardinality of uncover(V') $\cap B_\sigma(v)$ is highest, i.e., the vertex which is able to cover the maximum number of uncovered vertices within its ball of radius σ. This vertex gets added to V'. This process continues till uncover(V') becomes empty.

Algorithm $\mathcal{A}_2$: It is similar to the one in $\mathcal{A}_1$, but one can prove that it achieves constant factor approximation algorithm. Initially, V' is empty. The algorithm performs the following steps as long as possible: while there is a vertex $v \notin V'$ such that dist(v, V') $> \sigma$, add v to V'. Here dist(v, V') denotes the closest Euclidean distance between v and a vertex of V'.

3.4   The Map Entropy

In this sub-section, we give the approximate SpectraMap entropy to identify the factors contributing to the precision of our proposed RSSI-map.

Let a denote the minimum (best) achievable resolution bandwidth of the spectrum analyzer. Let S denote the set of static analyzers deployed adjacent to the dense tour set V. Let $\hat{M}$ be a set of points in V which are adjacent to S. So $|\hat{M}| = |S|$, and $z_{\hat{m}} \approx z_s$ for adjacent $(\hat{m}, s)$. Note that due to calibration (Sect. 4), we almost always have z_s. For all space points $m \in V \setminus \hat{M}$, we have $|z_m - \xi| \le \rho^*$. Thus, $\forall m, z_m \in [\xi - \rho^*, \xi + \rho^*]$.

One maximum entropy distribution for our map, is the uniform distribution on the (discrete) set $[\xi - \rho^*, \xi + \rho^*]$ with a step size a. Using this, we have the Shannon entropy h_m for a space point $m \in V \setminus \hat{M}$ as $h_m = \log(\frac{2\rho^*}{a} + 1)$ and approximately zero for space points in $\hat{M}$.

Theorem 3. *Given the shannon entropy h_i for a space point i as above, the map entropy H for SpectraMap with all space points equi-weighted is $H = \frac{1}{|V|} \times \sum_i h_i \approx (1 - \frac{|S|}{|V|}) \times \log(\frac{2\rho^*}{a} + 1)$.*

Theorem 3 shows that the precision factor ρ^* is aptly named: it gives the uncertainty of the spectrum characterization provided by SpectraMap, as H functionally depends on it. Also the map entropy is a linearly decreasing function in $|S|$.

3.5   Certain Use Cases

In this sub-section, we give examples of applying SpectraMap for some of our motivating problems. Note that ξ will denote the center RSSI.

White-Space Prediction for DSA. Let's say for a particular band g, we intend to detect a white-space at time instant t_w for a duration τ_w. Also assume we have established a *Time Cover* with parameters $(t_d, \tau, \xi_t, \rho_t^*)$. We can safely say that a white-space exists in band g, if the following hold

1. $t_w \in [t_d, t_d + \tau]$
2. $t_w + \tau_w \le t_d + \tau$
3. $\xi_t + \rho_t^*$ is below the noise floor of g.

Rogue Transmitter Detection. Assume for a band g we want to detect the presence of a rogue transmitter at time instant t_r (at which point the power should be at the noise floor). If the *Time Cover* parameters $(t_d, \tau, \xi_t, \rho_t^*)$ hold and we perform a *Space Cover* at t_r to get (ξ_s, ρ_s^*), then there is a rogue transmitter operating if

1. $t_r \in [t_d, t_d + \tau]$
2. $\xi_s - \rho_s^*$ is above the noise floor of g.

4   Deploying SpectraMap

SpectraMap works in the following four (uncoupled) phases, to characterize ρ_t^* and maintain ρ_s^* across sparse tours.

*Phase 1 - **C1** (Calibration)*: In this phase the static analyzers are used to collect spectrum measurements for large periods of time and these are used to estimate the correlation of the RSSI stochastic process over time-shifts at these static locations - and thus help establish $\mathbf{E}[\mathbb{S}_s](u)$.

*Phase 2 - **C2** (Calibration)*: Here static analyzers are deployed along with sensors at a few locations in their vicinity which are on the mobile tour. These simultaneously measure spectrum for large periods of time and the correlation in time between static points and the chosen tour points - and so help find $\mathbf{E}[\mathbb{D}_{\hat{m},s}]$. (**C2** duration requirement is significantly less than that of **C1**.)

*Phase 3 - **T-Q** (Space Quietness Determination)*: This phase is used to determine how spectrum measurements are correlated in two adjacent tour points by determining $\mathbf{E}[\mathbb{Q}_{m,m'}^{\Delta}]$. It helps prove that the ρ_s^* upper-bound also holds for sparse tours.

*Phase 4 - **Tour***: This phase consists of dense and sparse tours as defined in the framework. More formally, a dense tour consists of visiting all the tour points V of the geographic area in a (min-weight) Hamilton cycle. A sparse tour consists of visiting a subset V' of the tour points (again in a min-weight Hamilton cycle) such that, for a given space cover radius σ, $B_\sigma(V') = V$.

Note that one invocation of SpectraMap consists of a single dense tour followed by a sequence of sparse tours. The moment τ expires, or $q_{m,m'}^{\Delta}(t_d, t_s)$ becomes comparable to ρ_s^*, we reinstantiate SpectraMap after refreshing the parameters.

4.1   Band Usage Stability and Multipath Management

In order to establish the RSS periodicity of a particular band of interest g, the system administrator can choose to profile the band for a reasonable time period (say 1–2 days) before the calibration phases begin. This can be achieved through the same deployment of static analyzers to identify RSSI patterns in g and time periods when these patterns repeat. This would characterize the stability conditions of band g usage.

Also, during the calibration phases **C1** and **C2**, the deployed analyzers can weed out RSSI spikes that significantly deviate from legitimate band usage as determined in the band profile. Thus the calculation of expected values of stochastic processes $\mathbb{S}_s$ and $\mathbb{D}_{\hat{m},s}$ would be free from multipath effects and would result in small (strong) RSS confidence sets.

5   Evaluating SpectraMap

5.1   Prediction Accuracy

We conducted multiple rounds of NS-3 simulations with different wireless scenarios to obtain complete spatio-temporal true-RSSI maps for the participating nodes. We present an RSSI prediction error comparison from one such scenario. We configure a 8×8 node grid with a 5 m separation. The nodes are on an 802.11b physical layer, with 802.11b NICs in ad-hoc mode. One node on a corner of the grid sends one packet of 1000 application octets to the diagonally opposite node with an inter-packet interval of 1 s. The outermost square of 28 nodes makes up our dense tour V, constituting the set of nodes for which we present the error in prediction. The largest square inside the outermost square, of 24 nodes, makes up the set of nodes from which we pick our static analyzers preferentially as the set S. We use this topology, as it induces an asymmetry in the received power at the non-transmitting nodes. Our *Time Cover* period lasts 180 tours, the first of which is the dense tour (and the remaining sparse).

Error in Time Cover. We define the Time-Cover error to be the maximum distance of the true RSS from the dense-tour predicted RSS set for the *Time Cover* period. Kriging error is defined to be the absolute value of the difference between the predicted (Kriged) RSS and true RSS. In Fig. 2, we compare the Time-Cover error, which is a function of the spectrum analyzers deployed, to the Kriging error.

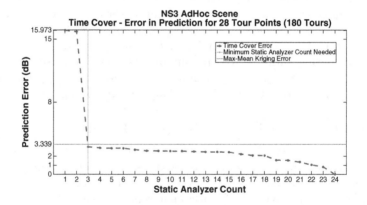

Fig. 2. SpectraMap Time-Cover error vs. Kriging error

To calculate the Time-Cover error with static analyzer count $|S|$, we chose the best static analyzer prediction, from the worst (in prediction) $|S|$-size static analyzer subset, of the 24-size available set.

For Kriging, we used the exponential variogram model. For a tour point i, we applied Ordinary Kriging (OK) to obtain the weights of the remaining 27 RSS values on the tour. Of course this still remains a convex combination of all 28 points, with a zero weight to the RSS at point i (to keep the space point i prediction independent of it's true RSS). Using these OK weights we predicted the RSS for each point i, and then the mean Kriging error per tour. Overall,

Kriging performed very well and the Kriging error reported is the maximum of the mean Kriging error per tour.

From Fig. 2 it is evident that given a minimum number of static analyzers (in this case 10.71% of dense tour points), Time-Cover error is comparable to, if not better than the Kriging error. This comparison is legitimate as we have seen in many instances that set sizes are small (like 3.6 dB) and so a 'distance from RSS set' estimate degenerates to a point distance estimate. [7,18] establish that Kriging accuracy is better than that of path-loss model predictions. Since these simulations reveal that SpectraMap accuracy is in the same space as that of Kriging, we can conclude that SpectraMap should perform better than path-loss model based estimates.

Also, given the calibration phases are over (Sect. 4), the number of power samples required for Kriging prediction is more than that need for establishing the *Time Cover*. To see this claim, consider the following approximate counting argument. Let's say we are given that the time-cover period τ corresponds to $\mu(\tau)$ tours. Kriging requires $\mu(\tau) \times |V|$ samples, which is greater than $|V|$ samples - the amount needed by SpectraMap's *Time Cover* (only one dense tour gives temporal extrapolation for a period τ). Also note that, amortized over time, the cost of calibrating for ρ_t^* would be less than the total number of RSS samples needed by Kriging.

Finally we would like to state that in the formulation (Sect. 3.3), we had established the ρ_t^* upper-bound on $\mathbf{E}[|\mathbb{Z}_{\hat{m}}(t_d + u) - \mathbb{Z}_{\hat{m}}(t_d)|]$ and not the realization of $\mathbb{S}_{\hat{m}}(t_d, u)$. These simulation results show that we can substitute $|z_{\hat{m}}(t_d + u) - z_{\hat{m}}(t_d)|$ for $\mathbf{E}[|\mathbb{Z}_{\hat{m}}(t_d + u) - \mathbb{Z}_{\hat{m}}(t_d)|]$ without any significant loss in accuracy.

Checking Space-Quietness. We chose ρ_s^* as 63% of ρ_t^* and achieved $\lambda = 0.82$ (82% compliance) for $\sigma = 6$ m. Two Pareto-optimal sets of space-quietness factor (α, κ) observed are shown in Fig. 3. As t_s moved further away from t_d, $q_{m,m'}^{\Delta}(t_d, t_s)$ grew. But ρ_s^* should dominate $q_{m,m'}^{\Delta}(t_d, t_s)$.

5.2   Map Construction Savings

The mapped geographic area spans the entire road network of the 325 acre IIT Delhi campus. The measurement setup included the 'RF Explorer' hand-held spectrum analyzer which scanned the 240–960 MHz frequency band with a resolution bandwidth of 178.6 kHz. We also employed a GPS receiver to record the Latitude-Longitude per RSSI sense instant (Fig. 4).

Data Collection. We conducted seven rounds of mobile tours, four rounds of static receiver deployments, two rounds of static mobile correlation measurements, and one round of space quietness factor determination. For each of the rounds, we considered normal scale averaged RSSI values in prominent bands of interest, for instance the TV band (510–518 MHz), or the CDMA band (890–960 MHz).

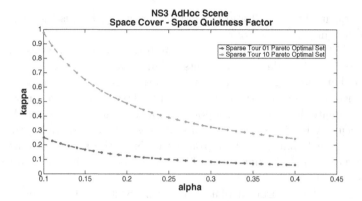

Fig. 3. SpectraMap space-cover quietness-factor

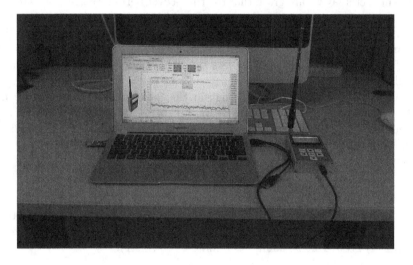

Fig. 4. Measurement setup - RF explorer with a GPS receiver

In order to see the spatial power distribution and establish patterns, we plotted several heat maps for different bands. One particular heat map for the 510–518 MHz band over the campus is given in Fig. 5.

In order to observe the temporal variation, we set up the spectrum analyzers at strategic locations to continuously scan the scope band 240–960 MHz for 2–3 days uninterrupted. An example temporal plot for one such location is given in Fig. 6.

Evaluating Time and Space Cover. In order to validate our model, we applied our algorithmic framework to a high-activity, highly-variable receive power band 942–960 MHz. We did analyze a series of sub-bands of 240–960 MHz

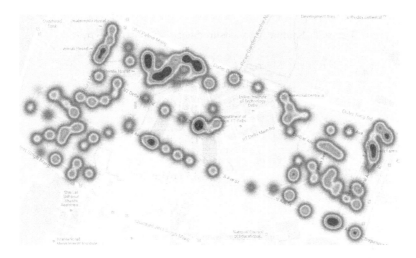

Fig. 5. IITD TV band heat map (RSSI between −106.93 and −89.50 dBm)

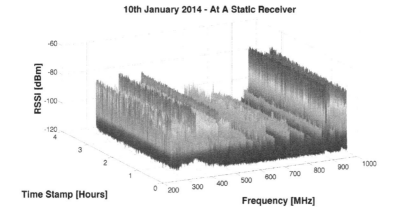

Fig. 6. Static receiver deployed at a vantage point

but present results of the mentioned scope band (the band of interest) on account of it's high variation over both space and time (Table 1).

Thus, for a particular center RSSI, we obtained a large (weak) RSSI bound ρ_t^* (reported in dBm) for a period of 15.4 h. This could have extended to a day or more considering the variation of the underlying stochastic processes was less. Using a space cover radius of $\sigma = 20$ m, we were able to classify $\lambda = 72\%$ of points with the tighter confidence $2\rho_s^*$.

For three disjoint RF bands, we observed the fraction of points correctly classified with a space precision factor $\rho_s^* = -100$ dBm as a function of space cover radius σ. It is seen that the 420–440 MHz band has behavior similar to the 890–960 MHz band in the space cover phase (Fig. 7).

Table 1. Evaluating measurements' Time/Space cover

Metric	Value
Scope band	942–960 MHz
Peak RSSI	−71.22 dBm
τ	15.4 h
ρ_t^*	−71.52 dBm
ρ_s^*/ρ_t^*	0.6
ρ_s^*	−73.74 dBm

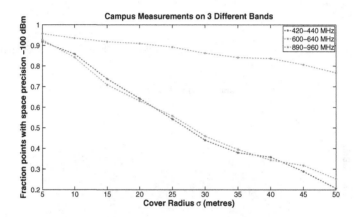

Fig. 7. Percent of points with space precision factor −100 dBm as a function of σ in different bands.

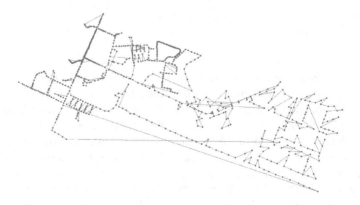

Fig. 8. Approx TSP tour of the (complete) IITD road graph

Sparse Tour Savings. We will now mention the tour size savings obtained for certain values of σ associated with ρ_s^*. Our campus road graph consists of 762 vertices/road points (Fig. 8). For the mobile spectrum analyzer, we take a stop and scan time of 37 s. We assume a vehicle speed of 10 kmph.

For a generous space cover $\sigma = 80$ m, which could be applicable to bands of the nature of TV bands, $\mathcal{A}_1$ gives a vertex cover of 73 vertices while $\mathcal{A}_2$ gives a cover of 95 vertices.

Sense Cost: We compared the sense cost incurred of a complete approx-TSP tour with the $\mathcal{A}_1$ and $\mathcal{A}_2$ vertex cover approx-TSP tours. For the complete tour, the sense time required was 10.95 h. For a $\mathcal{A}_1$ vertex cover tour, the sense-time required was 2.52 h. For an $\mathcal{A}_2$ cover, the corresponding time was 2.75 h.

Tour savings: The full TSP tour spanned 31.26 km. We saved 13.6 km in tour distance between the complete road graph and the $\mathcal{A}_1$ vertex covered road graph. Similarly, using $\mathcal{A}_2$, we saved 13.58 km.

We even observed that the $\mathcal{A}_1$ vertex cover gave better tour time savings as compared to the $\mathcal{A}_2$ cover (Fig. 9).

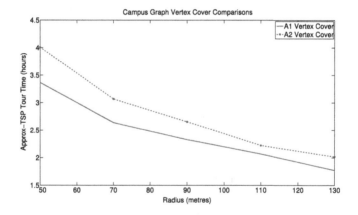

Fig. 9. Approx TSP tour time of the vertex covered road graph

6 Related Work

The primary form of network support used till date for opportunistic spectrum access is the notion of a Radio Environment Map (REM) [10] (simplified introductions in [3,13]). It provides information of the radio territory (primarily for cognitive radios to leverage) such as spectral regulation, location-specific policy, geographic information, radio equipment profile, and the RF environment. With this information, REMs provide situation awareness to the cognition cycle of Cognitive Radios (CRs) [20,23]. Seminal contribution in REMs and their utility was given by Youping Zhao [21]. This work investigated the role of REMs in CR development from a networking perspective. It also covers designing/populating REMs, using CE algorithms to mine REMs and evaluating cognitive radio performance. Additionally, it applies REMs to WLANs and WRANs, and validates REM enabled CCL (cognitive cooperative learning) and CKL (case and knowledge based learning) algorithms (work also in [11,22]). However, one drawback of the REM is that unlike SpectraMap, it requires multilayer information (like geographic information, service regulation, policy, radio equipment, etc.) to build it's consolidated RSS database. Also, like SpectraMap's map-entropy, Wei et al. [16] have established that REM error is a decreasing convex function of the measurement count.

Roy et al. [18] quantified prediction errors of DBA models and Kriging. They also applied Kriging to TV band measurement data. Mahonen et al. [7] concluded for multi-transmitter networks on TVWS, the summing of output power does not give an accurate RSS prediction. They also study based on measurement data the prediction error of standard propagation models and Kriging. Both these works conclude that path-loss models are significantly inaccurate in many instances and that Kriging outperforms path-loss models.

Nekovee [14] stated that although US and UK are adopting regulatory frameworks for secondary TVWS utilization, high precision spectrum sensing is the major challenge.

A recent program on Advanced RF Mapping by DARPA under Dr. John Chapin [1] intends to provide a real-time visualization of RF spectrum use over space and time for defence purposes.

Other approaches to predict occupancy have included works which model spectrum usage through random fields and point processes [17] and the use of cyclo-stationary signal analysis in finding hidden PHY layer signal repeating patterns which form signatures [12].

7   Conclusion and Future Work

In this paper, we have introduced a new paradigm for generating RF spectrum receive power maps through SpectraMap. We believe we are the first to extrapolate RSSI measurements *over time* in a way that is sufficient to model spectrum occupancy for our motivating problems. The precision of our map, given a minimum number of static analyzers, is comparable (using a smaller set of deployed spectrum analyzers) with that of Kriging, which is the most accepted RSS spatial only extrapolation technique. We believe that our theoretical and experimental comparisons establish that SpectraMap can coexist alongside contemporary solutions like REMs and Kriging databases. We also see that, on an actual real world deployment, SpectraMap achieves significant RSSI-map construction savings as compared to dense measurements.

In the future, we wish to investigate two different directions. First, we would like to establish a probability distribution over SpectraMap's predicted RSSI set per space point, in order to identify the most 'expected' RSSI realization for that point. Second, we would like to build an online service (similar to Microsoft's spectrum observatory [2] and the spectrum observatory of the University of

Washington [4]) which displays spectrum occupancy over space instead of a single measurement point. Of course, building such a map is challenging, and requires manual effort. However, our hope is that SpectraMap will help reduce the manual effort, and make it feasible to create such a space-time spectrum occupancy map.

Acknowledgements. This work was partially supported by project RP02565 titled "SPARC: Spectrum Aware Rural Connectivity" at IIT Delhi funded by the Ministry of Electronics and Information Technology, Government of India. The authors would also like to thank Himanshu Varshney and Sanoj Kumar for contributing to the spectrum measurement setup.

Appendix

Proof of Theorem 1 (Time Cover bound):
Our aim is to find an upper-bound for $\mathbf{E}[|\mathbb{Z}_{\hat{m}}(t_d + u) - \mathbb{Z}_{\hat{m}}(t_d)|]$.
    To that end, consider the following derivation (through arithmetic):

$$\mathbf{E}[|\mathbb{Z}_{\hat{m}}(t_d + u) - \mathbb{Z}_{\hat{m}}(t_d)|]$$

$$= \mathbf{E}[|\mathbb{Z}_{\hat{m}}(t_d + u) - \mathbb{Z}_s(t_d + u) + \mathbb{Z}_s(t_d + u) - \mathbb{Z}_{\hat{m}}(t_d)|]$$
$$\{\text{introducing} \mathbb{Z}_s(t_d + u)\}$$

$$= \mathbf{E}[|(\mathbb{Z}_{\hat{m}}(t_d + u) - \mathbb{Z}_s(t_d + u)) - (\mathbb{Z}_{\hat{m}}(t_d) - \mathbb{Z}_s(t_d)) + (\mathbb{Z}_s(t_d + u) - \mathbb{Z}_s(t_d))|]$$
$$\{\text{introducing} \mathbb{Z}_s(t_d) \text{and re-arranging}\}$$

$$\leq \mathbf{E}[|\mathbb{Z}_{\hat{m}}(t_d + u) - \mathbb{Z}_s(t_d + u)|] + \mathbf{E}[|\mathbb{Z}_{\hat{m}}(t_d) - \mathbb{Z}_s(t_d)|] + \mathbf{E}[|\mathbb{Z}_s(t_d + u) - \mathbb{Z}_s(t_d))|]$$
$$\{\text{subadditivity}\}$$

$$= \mathbf{E}[\mathbb{D}_{\hat{m},s}(t_d + u)] + \mathbf{E}[\mathbb{D}_{\hat{m},s}(t_d)] + \mathbf{E}[\mathbb{S}_s(t_d, u)]$$
$$\{\text{from the definitions}\}$$

$$= 2 \times \mathbf{E}[\mathbb{D}_{\hat{m},s}] + \mathbf{E}[\mathbb{S}_s](u)$$
$$\{\text{from the definitions}\}$$

$$:= \rho_t(u).$$

Proof of Theorem 2 (Space Cover bound):
    We need to find an upper-bound for $|z_{m'}(t_s) - z_m(t_s)|$. It is as follows:

$$|z_{m'}(t_s) - z_m(t_s)|$$

$$= |(z_{m'}(t_s) - z_{m'}(t_d)) - (z_m(t_s) - z_m(t_d)) + (z_{m'}(t_d) - z_m(t_d))|$$
$$\{\text{introducing} z_{m'}(t_d), z_m(t_d) \text{and re-arranging}\}$$

$$= |q_{m'}(t_d, t_s - t_d) - q_m(t_d, t_s - t_d) + (z_{m'}(t_d) - z_m(t_d))|$$
$$\{\text{introducing } q\}$$

$$\leq |q_{m'}(t_d, t_s - t_d) - q_m(t_d, t_s - t_d)| + |z_{m'}(t_d) - z_m(t_d)|$$

$$\{\text{subadditivity}\}$$

$$\leq |q_{m'}(t_d, t_s - t_d) - q_m(t_d, t_s - t_d)| + \rho_s^*$$

$$\{\text{introducing } \rho_s^*, \text{for fraction } \lambda\}$$

$$= q_{m,m'}^{\Delta}(t_d, t_s) + \rho_s^*$$

$$\{\text{from the definition}\}$$

$$\approx \rho_s^*$$

The final approximation can be justified by Markov's Inequality. Let $\alpha \in [0, 1]$. Then, $Pr[\mathbb{Q}_{m,m'}^{\Delta} \geq \alpha \times \rho_s^*] \leq \frac{\mathbb{E}[\mathbb{Q}_{m,m'}^{\Delta}]}{\alpha \times \rho_s^*} := \kappa$.

Now, the smaller the 'space-quietness factor' (α, κ), the more ρ_s^* dominates $q_{m,m'}^{\Delta}(t_d, t_s)$.

References

1. Darpa strategic technology office radiomap program. http://www.darpa.mil/Our_Work/STO/Programs/Advanced_RF_Mapping_(Radio_Map).aspx
2. The microsoft spectrum observatory. https://observatory.microsoftspectrum.com
3. Radio environmental maps (rems): A cognitive tool for environmental awareness. http://www-syscom.univ-mlv.fr/~najim/gdr-ecoradio/sayrac.pdf
4. The university of washington spectrum observatory. http://specobs.ee.washington.edu
5. The radio-spectrum inventory act (2010). https://www.govtrack.us/congress/bills/111/hr3125/text
6. Ntia spectrum sharing (2015). http://www.ntia.doc.gov/category/spectrum-sharing
7. Achtzehn, A., et al.: Improving coverage prediction for primary multi-transmitter networks operating in the TV whitespaces. In: 2012 9th Annual IEEE Communications Society Conference on Sensor, Mesh and Ad Hoc Communications and Networks (SECON), pp. 623–631. IEEE (2012)
8. Baykas, T., et al.: Overview of TV white spaces: current regulations, standards and coexistence between secondary users. In: 2010 IEEE 21st International Symposium on Personal, Indoor and Mobile Radio Communications Workshops (PIMRC Workshops), pp. 38–43. IEEE (2010)
9. Elbassioni, K., Fishkin, A.V., Mustafa, N.H., Sitters, R.: Approximation algorithms for euclidean group TSP. In: Caires, L., Italiano, G.F., Monteiro, L., Palamidessi, C., Yung, M. (eds.) ICALP 2005. LNCS, vol. 3580, pp. 1115–1126. Springer, Heidelberg (2005). doi:10.1007/11523468_90
10. Fette, B.A.: Cognitive radio technology. Academic Press, New York (2009)
11. Gaeddert, J., et al.: Radio environment map enabled situation-aware cognitive radio learning algorithms. In: Software Defined Radio Forum (SDRF) Technical Conference (2006)
12. Hong, S.S., Katti, S.R.: DOF: a local wireless information plane. In: ACM SIGCOMM Computer Communication Review, vol. 41, pp. 230–241. ACM (2011)
13. Lunnamo, S.: Radio Environment Maps: Capabilities and challenges

14. Nekovee, M.: A survey of cognitive radio access to TV white spaces. In: 2009 International Conference on Ultra Modern Telecommunications and Workshops, pp. 1–8. IEEE (2009)
15. Vogel, C., et al.: An Analysis of a Low-Complexity Received Signal Strength Indicator for Wireless Applications (2004)
16. Wei, Z., Zhang, Q., Feng, Z., Li, W., Gulliver, T.A.: On the construction of radio environment maps for cognitive radio networks. In: 2013 IEEE Wireless Communications and Networking Conference (WCNC), pp. 4504–4509. IEEE (2013)
17. Wellens, M., Riihijärvi, J., Mähönen, P.: Spatial statistics and models of spectrum use. Comput. Commun. **32**(18), 1998–2011 (2009)
18. Ying, X., et al.: Revisiting TV coverage estimation with measurement-based statistical interpolation. In: 2015 7th International Conference on Communication Systems and Networks (COMSNETS), pp. 1–8. IEEE (2015)
19. Zhang, T., et al.: A vehicle-based measurement framework for enhancing whitespace spectrum databases. In: Proceedings of the 20th Annual International Conference on Mobile Computing and Networking, pp. 17–28. ACM (2014)
20. Zhao, Y., Reed, J.: Radio Environment Map Design and Exploitation. MPRG Technical (2005)
21. Zhao, Y.: Enabling cognitive radios through radio environment maps (2007)
22. Zhao, Y., et al.: Applying radio environment maps to cognitive wireless regional area networks. In: 2007 2nd IEEE International Symposium on New Frontiers in Dynamic Spectrum Access Networks, pp. 115–118. IEEE (2007)
23. Zhao, Y., et al.: Development of radio environment map enabled case-and knowledge-based learning algorithms for IEEE 802.22 WRAN cognitive engines. In: 2007 2nd International Conference on Cognitive Radio Oriented Wireless Networks and Communications, pp. 44–49. IEEE (2007)

Activity Signatures in Smart IoT Environments

Ravi Kokku[✉]

IBM T.J. Watson Research Center, Yorktown Heights, USA
`ravi.kokku@acm.org`

Abstract. IoT enabled smart environments typically include large number of simple sensors that are designed to detect specific events. In many environments, however, not one but combinations of sensor events represent activities of interest (such as activities of daily living of a patient in a smarthome). Detecting and monitoring these activities of interest result in both application-specific benefits and operational benefits. However, human activities often overlap, thereby making activity detection from the collected sensor events a challenging problem. In this paper, we first present the various benefits of such materialization of sensor events into activities, and then discuss the challenges in detecting diverse activities taken up by humans. More interestingly, the diversity of human activities and the time-variability of a given activity by the same human, makes reliable detection of activities even harder, and open up interesting avenues for future research.

1 Introduction

[1]IoT (Internet of Things) enabled smart environments have been a rapidly growing area of interest, with a number of commercial applications such as assisted living for elderly [1] and post-operative patient care, wellness monitoring, home security, safety, energy efficiency, etc. By 2020, it is estimated that there will be more than 20 billion devices in a variety of IoT environments [2,3], and the total number of connectable things via the Internet will grow by 50% and will be used for smart living [4]. In today's market there already exist several smart home initiatives and products like Google Nest, Apple Home Kit, Samsung smart home [5], which comprises various lifestyle applications and promises to improve inhabitant's lifestyle by providing home systems up to their comfort level.

2 Activity Signatures

Interestingly, many physical world activities of interest in the emerging application domains (such as assisted living, safety and wellness monitoring and edu-

---

[1] This document derives largely from joint work with several colleagues over the last three years, including Palanivel Kodeswaran, Sayandeep Sen and Uma Devi of IBM Research – India, Payel Das, Satya Nitta, Sharad Sundararajan and Mudhakar Srivatsa of IBM T.J. Watson Research Center - USA, and Madhumita Mallick of IIT-Kharagpur.

© Springer International Publishing AG 2017
N. Sastry and S. Chakraborty (Eds.): COMSNETS 2017, LNCS 10340, pp. 72–76, 2017.
DOI: 10.1007/978-3-319-67235-9_6

cational settings) are often complex patterns that can only be detected by multiple sensors; i.e. an activity is characterized by a combination of a variety of heterogeneous sensors triggering over a period of time. For instance, a recent study [6] shows that more than 70% of activities in smart homes in several data sets involved the triggering of 5 or more sensors. Further, 70% of the sensors contribute to 5 or more activities in a home.

In the healthcare domain, family caregivers of patients with Alzheimer's disease rank tracking and identifying such Activities of Daily Living of the patient at the top of their list of needs for health assistance [7]. Prior work [8] has shown that for people with mild cognitive impairment(MCI), walking speed varies in the different stages of their disease, and it is important to observe and understand the underlying events in an activity to properly measure user's characteristics that would improvise health monitoring in clinical assessment. Similarly, sensors measuring some physical phenomenon may contribute to detecting mutiple activities that are happening simultaneously. For instance, in an elderly care scenario, a remote family member may want to ensure that an elderly lady is cooking and eating, and doing the daily chores regularly. A cooking activity may involve various sequences of events such as switching-on a gas burner, taking vegetables out from a refrigerator, opening one or more kitchen cabinets several times, using the microwave for a sub-task, etc. As a result of the complexity of human activities, a single sensor may not be able to conclusively say that a cooking activity is occurring in a given home, unless video monitoring that covers the entire kitchen is used for monitoring over a period of time[2].

In child education and safety contexts, there has been growing interest in approaches to identify children with specific exceptional abilities [9], support for monitoring children with learning disabilities and autism spectrum disorders [10], etc. One of the compelling applications of technological advancements involves being able to monitor various sensors deployed around the child (either worn by the child or in the proximity) and identify patterns of interest. For instance, monitoring autistic children is a challenging task since they may not by themselves have a fear of dangers, may not display sensitivity to pain, may show inappropriate attachment to objects, and inappropriate response to any sounds, thereby having increased susceptibility of being situations that can hurt them [10].

In the context of exceptional abilities identification, observations by able humans (including teachers and parents) are needed today over a sustained period of time to identify children with such abilities [9]; at least a part of these observations can be made automatically by IoT-enabled environments that sense the various behaviors of the children and identify unique and interesting patterns of giftedness. Timely identification of such abilities (at scale, potentially across the world) may result in boosting confidence in children of their unique abilities, which in turn results in them leveraging and honing their strengths.

---

[2] The possibilities and challenges of using video monitoring is a topic by itself due to its apparent intrusiveness, issues with privacy and reservations people may have, and the overhead of continuous visual monitoring needed by the remote member.

To this end, a number of research efforts have focused on identifying activities of daily living [11–16]. For instance, Kasteren et al. [15] propose using hidden markov models for activity recognition while incorporating duration of activities as a feature for classification. Roy et al. [16] propose techniques for ADL recognition in multi-inhabitant environments by combining infrastructure sensors and smartphone sensors and learning spatio-temporal patterns. The eventual goal of all these efforts is to be able to tag a sequence of sensor events with specific activities taken up by a human during her daily routine. To do so, they use the notion of activity signatures—that represent a co-occuring pattern of sensor combinations, time-of-day and durations—to label training data and then use them to classify the occurrence of activities on sensor events at run-time. Using activity signatures, our recent work also demonstrated an approach for efficient failure management in IoT-enabled smart environments [17]. We show that the time-before-repair in a smart environment for any sensor can be significantly increased based on the specific activities of daily living the sensor contributes to, and the inherent redundancy in sensor deployments for detecting various activities in the environment.

3   Challenges and Avenues for Future Work

Despite significant past research, detecting human activities in smart IoT environments with multiple sensors remains a non-trivial task and requires a number of complex steps involving signature generation, labeling, run-time signature detection while accounting for variations in activity patterns by humans on different times of day, and graceful degradation in identification of activities in the presence of sensor failures.

Signature generation and labeling involves understanding and finding patterns/invariants in a given activity, while incorporating the possibility of variations inherent in human behaviors. For instance, a cooking activity may involve different order of using appliances on different days, different set of appliances (e.g. stove vs. microwave), different amount of time depending on what is cooked, etc. Similarly, a refrigerator door may be opened before cooking, or everytime a person would like to take a drink, or when picking a snack or a medicine. While several labeled datasets have been generated from data captured in different smart homes, this task remains an important activity for each new smart environment and due to diversity in each instance of the environments, and will involve effective combination of manual labeling and transfer learning (from labelled data from other similar environments). For instance, what are the signatures of dangerous behavior when monitoring a child? what are the signatures of children with gifted abilities? etc.

Run-time activity detection from a combination of sensor triggers has an interesting tradeoff to strike: when a variation of an activity (in terms of the set of sensors and the sequence in which they are triggered, and the duration for which they are triggered) happens, should a system still be able to detect the activity by allowing for the variation, or should the system tag it as deviation from expected behavior (i.e., that a given activity such as cooking did not take place). This detection is exacerbated by temporally overlapping activities either by a single resident or multiple residents in a home. Further, in scenarios where real-time detection is required (such as monitoring a post-operative care patient or a child for potential dangerous situations), the system may need to maintain multiple hypotheses of activities that could be occuring, and generate a confidence of which activity is actually taking place as more data arrives. Finally, if there is a deviation in sensor pattern usage and activity detection suffers, is it to be interpreted as failed sensors or change in human patterns? Alternately, if the inhabitant of a smart environment changes his pattern of activity or if a new set of sensors are introduced into the environment, how should a system detect the change and re-trigger signature generation and labeling?

In summary, as IoT enabled smart environments proliferate, successful operation of them would require us to address the above problems through a combination of effective characterization of the activities the environments need to monitor, methods for accurate run-time detection and robustness to failures and variations inherent in these deployments.

References

1. Using sensor technology to lower elder care costs. http://deloitte.wsj.com/cio/2014/07/28/using-sensor-technology-to-lower-elder-care-costs/
2. The internet of things: sizing up the opportunity. http://www.mckinsey.com/industries/high-tech/our-insights/the-internet-of-things-sizing-up-the-opportunity
3. Gartner says 6.4 billion connected
4. When will your home be a smart home? http://www.howtogeek.com/207607/when-will-your-home-be-a-
5. Smart home: how apple, google and samsung will take over your home. http://www.trustedreviews.com/opinions/home-automation-how-apple-google-and-samsung-will-take-over-your-home
6. Kodeswaran, P., Kokku, R., Mallick, M., Sen, S.: Demultiplexing activities of daily living in IoT enabled smarthomes. In: IEEE Infocom (2016)
7. Rialle, V., Ollivet, C., Guigui, C., Herv, C.: What do family caregivers of Alzheimer's disease patients desire in smart home technologies? Methods Inf. Med. **47**, 63–69 (2008)
8. Dodge, H., Mattek, N., Austin, D., Hayes, T., Kaye, J.: In-home walking speeds and variability trajectories associated with mild cognitive impairment. Neurology **78**(24), 1946–1952 (2012)
9. National association for gifted children: gifted children identification. https://www.nagc.org/resources-publications/gifted-education-practices/identification
10. Keeping your autistic kids safe. https://www.safety.com/p/autism-safety/
11. Acampora, G.: A survey on ambient intelligence in healthcare. Proc. IEEE **101**(12), 2470–2494 (2013)
12. Chen, C., Das, B., Cook, D.: A data mining framework for activity recognition in smart environments. In: 2010 Sixth International Conference on Intelligent Environments (IE), pp. 80–83, July 2010

13. Nazerfard, E., Rashidi, P., Cook, D.J.: Using association rule mining to discover temporal relations of daily activities. In: Proceedings of the 9th International Conference on Toward Useful Services for Elderly and People with Disabilities: Smart Homes and Health Telematics, Ser., ICOST 2011, pp. 49–56. Springer, Heidelberg (2011). http://dl.acm.org/citation.cfm?id=2026187.2026195

14. Rashidi, P., Cook, D.J., Holder, L.B., Schmitter-Edgecombe, M.: Discovering activities to recognize and track in a smart environment. IEEE Trans. Knowl. Data Eng. **23**(4), 527–539 (2011)

15. Van Kasteren, T., Englebienne, G., Kröse, B.J.: Activity recognition using semi-Markov models on real world smart home datasets. J. Ambient Intell. Smart Environ. **2**(3), 311–325 (2010)

16. Roy, N., Misra, A., Cook, D.J.: Infrastructure-assisted smartphone-based ADL recognition in multi-inhabitant smart environments. In: 2013 IEEE International Conference on Pervasive Computing and Communications, PerCom 2013, San Diego, CA, USA, 18–22 March 2013, pp. 38–46 (2013)

17. Kodeswaran, P.A., Kokku, R., Sen, S., Srivatsa, M.: Idea: a system for efficient failure management in smart IoT environments. In: Proceedings of the 14th Annual International Conference on Mobile Systems, Applications, and Services (MobiSys), pp. 43–56 (2016). ACM, New York. http://doi.acm.org/10.1145/2906388.2906406

Integrating GLONASS with GPS for Drone Orientation Tracking

Mahanth Gowda[1(✉)], Justin Manweiler[2], Ashutosh Dhekne[1],
Romit Roy Choudhury[1], and Justin D. Weisz[2]

[1] University of Illinois at Urbana-Champaign, Urbana, IL, USA
gowda2@illinois.edu
[2] IBM Research, Yorktown Heights, NY, USA

Abstract. In addition to position sensing, GPS receivers can be leveraged for orientation sensing too. We place multiple GPS receivers on drones and translate their relative positions into orientation. Such an orthogonal mode of orientation sensing provides failsafe under Inertial sensor failures – a primary cause of drone crashes today. This paper integrates GLONASS satellite measurements with GPS for enhancing the orientation accuracy.

Accurate estimate of orientation depends upon high precision relative positioning of the GPS receivers. While GPS carrier phases provide high precision ranging data, the phases are noisy and wrap after every wavelength which introduces ambiguity. Moreover, GPS signals experience poor SNR and loss of satellite locks under aggressive flights. This can severely limit both the accuracy and the amount of carrier phase data available. Fortunately, integrating the ubiquitously available Russian GLONASS satellites with GPS can double the amount of observations and substantially improve the robustness of orientation estimates. However, the fusion is non-trivial because of the operational difference between FDMA based GLONASS and CDMA based GPS. This paper proposes a temporal differencing scheme for fusion of GLONASS and GPS measurements, through a system called *SafetyNet*. Results from 11 sessions of 5–7 min flights report median orientation accuracies of 2° even under overcast weather conditions.

1 Introduction

Multiple GPS receivers can be used for tracking drone orientation. A rigid body is formed by placing 3 or more GPS receivers on the body of a drone. The orientation of the drone is a simple function of relative positions of the GPS receivers on the rigid body. While inertial sensors (IMU) like accelerometers, gyroscopes and compasses are conventionally used for orientation tracking, they can fail – leading to crashes [1,2,4,8,33]. Many of the failures are correlated from common sources of engine vibration and on-board electromagnetic interference [18,21,22,26,31]. Hence, it is not possible to cope with such failures by having redundant sensors. Since GPS provides a completely orthogonal modality of orientation sensing, it can serve as a failsafe for IMU failures.

© Springer International Publishing AG 2017
N. Sastry and S. Chakraborty (Eds.): COMSNETS 2017, LNCS 10340, pp. 77–92, 2017.
DOI: 10.1007/978-3-319-67235-9_7

Achieving an orientation accuracy of 2° with GPS requires the relative positions between the GPS receivers to be known to an accuracy of 2 cm. Moreover, the accuracy needs to be upheld constantly over time, especially during periods of aggressive maneuvers, where the SNR is poor, locks with satellites break and other errors manifest. This is a challenging task since a basic GPS location is only 3 m accurate.

Even the best differential GPS technique only provides a relative positioning accuracy of 15 cm [14,15]. They leverage carrier phase data, which is a precise estimate of range from satellites, but polluted by ambiguity due to phase wrapping. Our recent Mobicom paper [10] shows how carrier phase data can be differenced over time and space and fused using an augmented particle filter framework. This results in accurate orientation estimate with a median accuracy of 2° and 95th percentile accuracy of 8°.

In this paper, we expand the GPS/GLONASS integration component of SafetyNet, which is a critical factor in achieving a high accuracy. Under aggressive flights, the carrier phase data is not only noisy, but also sparse in number because of poor SNR and loss of satellite locks. Fortunately, integrating the ubiquitously available GLONASS (GLObal NAvigation Satellite System – [19]) satellite measurements with GPS doubles the number of measurements and enhances the robustness of orientation estimates. However, the fusion is non trivial since GLONASS operates on FDMA whereas GPS uses CDMA.

In the rest of the paper, we first provide a background of GPS, GLONASS and the basics of satellite positioning systems. We then revisit the math behind orientation sensing from [10]. We derive orientation as a function of various differences of carrier phases over, receivers, satellites and time. Finally, we integrate GLONASS measurements into our model. Evaluation results show substantial gains from the integration, especially in eliminating errors in the tail.

2   GPS Foundations

We present GPS foundations from first principles and end with discussions on modern techniques. As a result, this section is long. However, given that this paper builds over core GPS algorithms, the material is necessary. We also believe the material is easy to follow.

2.1   Global Navigation Satellite System (GNSS)

GNSS is the generic name given to satellite systems that provide localization services to receiver's on earth. The Global Positioning System (GPS) [24] is one example of a GNSS, developed by the US Government during 1970–1980s. GPS consists of a constellation of 31 satellites orbiting the earth at a height of 20,000 km. The satellites are continuously transmitting unique pseudo-random noise (PRN) sequences using CDMA at 2 different frequencies –1575.42 (L1) and 1227.60 MHz (L2). They also broadcast ephemeris data using which the (satellite) position and time of transmission can be calculated. A GPS receiver on the ground localizes itself by trilateration, i.e., measuring and combining the time-of-flight (ToF) from different satellites. Velocity is computed from the doppler shifts from various satellites.

GLObal NAvigation Satellite System (GLONASS) is another GNSS system launched by Russia in the 1980's [19]. GLONASS has 24 operational satellites. Unlike GPS which uses CDMA for multiplexing, GLONASS uses a 15 channel FDMA with a center frequency of 1602 MHz and an inter-channel separation of 0.5625 MHz. Since, there are only 15 channels, but 24 operational satellites, those satellites that are antipodal (on opposite side of earth), reuse the same frequency, such that they are not simultaneously visible to a GPS receiver. Similarly, GALILEO [3] is an European GNSS system currently under development. Many GNSS receivers are capable of decoding signals from multiple GNSS systems, providing increased accuracy. This paper will also use such receivers and exploit the advantages of satellite diversity.

2.2   GPS Localization and Error Sources

A GNSS receiver on the ground can compute its 3D location, time, and velocity. The key idea is to measure various attributes of the arriving signal (e.g., time of flight, phase, etc.), and then apply statistical algorithms to estimate the errors and ambiguities in measurements. We give an overview of the techniques that underpin GPS; other GNSS systems are similar.

Pseudorange

When a satellite transmits a signal, it includes the starting time of the transmission (obtained from its atomic clock). The ground receiver records the time of reception also using its less accurate local clock. The time-of-flight (ToF) is the difference between these timestamps. When multiplied by the speed of light, the result gives the *rough* distance to the satellite, called *pseudorange*.

$$\text{Pseudorange} = \text{ToF} * (\text{speed of light})$$

Of course, the measured ToF is inaccurate because the clock of a typical GPS receiver is not synchronized to the GPS satellites. The resulting error can be up to 300 km. In addition, when the GPS signal enters the Earth's atmosphere, it can get delayed due to refractions in the Ionosphere and Troposphere. A signal also passes through a multipath channel, adding more errors. Assuming the true range between a satellite s and receiver i is ρ_i^s, the measured Pseudorange P_i^s, inclusive of all error sources, can be modeled as

$$P_i^s = \rho_i^s + ct_i - ct^s + A + M_i + \epsilon_i^s \tag{1}$$

Here, t_i and t^s are receiver and satellite clock biases, respectively, with respect to true time. A represents the range error due to refractions in the atmosphere. M_i^s denotes Multipath, ϵ_i^s is receiver's hardware noise and c is the speed of light. In today's systems, the satellite clock error t^s is small[1], and ct_i proves to be the

---

[1] Satellites estimate the errors themselves from mutually exchanged signals as well as from ground sources.

major source of error. Hence, ct_i is modeled as an unknown, and ρ_i^s is written as a function of the *unknown* 3D receiver location ρ_i and the *known* 3D satellite position ρ^s. This results in a total of 4 unknowns. Once we have a lock with 4 satellites, the time bias and the 3D locations can be jointly estimated resulting in a position fix. The ignored error sources, i.e., t^s, A, M, and ϵ, could contribute to an error of 1–4 m, depending upon the environmental conditions.

GPS receivers on phones and car dashboards use the above techniques. However, higher accuracy applications such as 3D orientation tracking require better performance. To this end, modern GPS research has leveraged the *phase* of the arriving signals, as detailed next.

Carrier Phase

Once a satellite lock is acquired, the phase of the arriving signal, ϕ_i^s, is constantly tracked by a *phase lock loop* (PLL). The true range between the satellite and the receiver, ρ_i^s, can be expressed in terms of wavelength λ.

$$\rho_i^s = \lambda N_i^s + \lambda \phi_i^s \tag{2}$$

N_i^s is an unknown integer, meaning that the PLL measurement of ϕ_i^s only captures the fractional part of the range. However, due to atmospheric effects, multipath, and clock issues, the above equation can be updated:

$$\lambda \phi_i^s = \rho_i^s + ct_i - ct^s + A + M_i + \epsilon_i - \lambda N_i^s \tag{3}$$

Estimating N_i^s is non-trivial and several algorithms exist [20, 32].

One advantage of carrier phase is that *its changes over time* can be tracked reliably by utilizing the doppler shift in the signal [16]. Hence, $\phi_i^s(t_2)$ takes the same mathematical form as Eq. 3. Thus, if the initial value of N_i^s can somehow be estimated, the tracking thereafter can be good. We now explain how today's systems like Differential GPS (DGPS) with this integer ambiguity, N_i^s, and other error sources.

2.3 Computing Differentials

Environmental error sources in Eq. 3 are correlated over short time periods and within small geographical areas (200 km). Thus, two GPS measurements across time can be subtracted (or differenced) to eliminate some of these factors. Similarly, simultaneous measurements from multiple GPS receivers can also be differenced. Differential GPS (DGPS) [25] performs such operations on *pseudoranges*, while Real-Time Kinematic (RTK) [23] applies differentials to *carrier phase*. For our purpose of precise orientation tracking, the latter is more relevant. To this end, we outline 4 kinds of carrier phase differentials.

(1) Single Differentials Across Receivers (SD_{ij})

Consider the carrier phase equations for two GPS receivers i and j from the same satellite s. We ignore multipath and noise in the rest of the equations.

$$\lambda\phi_i^s = \rho_i^s + ct_i - ct^s + A^s - \lambda N_i^s \tag{4}$$
$$\lambda\phi_j^s = \rho_j^s + ct_j - ct^s + A^s - \lambda N_j^s \tag{5}$$

Differencing the above two equations yields the relative position between i and j with fewer error terms. Correlated error sources of atmospheric delays and satellite clock biases disappear.

$$\lambda\Delta\phi_{ij}^s = \Delta\rho_{ij}^s + c\Delta t_{ij} - \lambda\Delta N_{ij}^s \tag{6}$$

Figure 1 illustrates the scenario. Assuming that the satellite is far away, $\Delta\rho_{ij}^s$ can be approximated as $\rho_{ij}Cos\theta$, where ρ_{ij} is the true relative position between i and j (called **baseline** vector). Replacing $\rho_{ij}Cos\theta$ as a vectorial projection of ρ_{ij} on to the line of sight unit-vector $\hat{l}_s$ of satellite s, we have:

$$\lambda\Delta\phi_{ij}^s = \rho_{ij}.\hat{l}_s + c\Delta t_{ij} - \lambda\Delta N_{ij}^s \tag{7}$$

While some errors have disappeared[2], a function of the clock bias errors, $c\Delta t_{ij}$ still remains, motivating the need for double differentials.

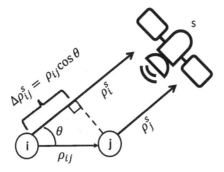

Fig. 1. $\rho_i^s - \rho_j^s = \Delta\rho_{ij}^s = \rho_{ij}.\hat{l}_s$

(2) Double Differentials Across Receivers and Satellites (DD_{ij}^{sk})

Given multiple satellites in range, the GPS ground receivers i and j can perform the same measurements with satellite k. Equation 7 can then be rewritten as:

$$\lambda\Delta\phi_{ij}^k = \rho_{ij}.\hat{l}_k + c\Delta t_{ij} - \lambda\Delta N_{ij}^k \tag{8}$$

---

[2] We are aware that differentials can amplify noise and multipath, however, since carrier phase noise is in the granularity of few mm [7], we ignore noise in the rest of the paper. We also assume multipath is not excessive, such as the drone flying low in Manhattan-like areas.

Subtracting the single differential Eqs. 7 and 8, we have a double differential (DD) as follows:

$$\lambda \nabla \Delta \phi_{ij}^{sk} = \rho_{ij}.(\hat{l}_s - \hat{l}_k) - \lambda \nabla \Delta N_{ij}^{sk} \tag{9}$$

The double differential (DD) eliminates the clock biases and the residue is only the integer ambiguity terms. More details on integer ambiguity resolution is done in [10], but assuming that the ambiguities are magically fixed, this provides us a reasonably precise estimate of relative positions (called baselines) between receiver pairs. Ignored factors, including multipath, noise, and antenna phase center errors, add up to a few centimeters of error. Thus, if one of the receiver's absolute position is known in the granularity of millimeters, the absolute position of the other receiver can be estimated precisely as well. Real Time Kinematics (RTK) technology operates exactly as above – *it uses the accurately known location of the reference receiver to calculate the location of the other.* Figure 2 shows the relative distance between two receivers placed roughly 45 cm apart. Differencing techniques convincingly outperform naive subtraction of 3D GPS positions.

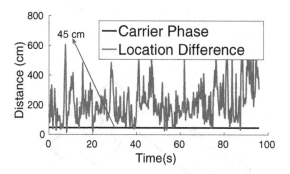

Fig. 2. Relative positioning using carrier phase and double differentials is an order of magnitude more accurate than naïve location differencing. Here, a 45 cm baseline is correct within a few cm.

(3) Double Differentials Across Receivers and Time ($DD_{ij}^{t_{12}}$)

Our final double differential combines receivers and time. We compute the single differential between receivers ij from Eq. 7 but write them for consecutive time points t_1 and t_2.

$$\lambda \Delta \phi_{ij}^s(t_1) = \rho_{ij}(t_1).\hat{l}_s + c\Delta t_{ij}(t_1) + \lambda \Delta N_{ij}^s(t_1) \tag{10}$$

$$\lambda \Delta \phi_{ij}^s(t_2) = \rho_{ij}(t_2).\hat{l}_s + c\Delta t_{ij}(t_2) + \lambda \Delta N_{ij}^s(t_2) \tag{11}$$

Assuming no cycle slips (we will relax this assumption later), $\Delta N_{ij}^s(t_2) = \Delta N_{ij}^s(t_1)$, hence subtracting the above two equations eliminates integer ambiguity:

$$\lambda \nabla \Delta \phi_{ij}^s(t_{12}) = (\rho_{ij}(t_1) - \rho_{ij}(t_2)).\hat{l}_s + c.\Delta t_{ij}(t_{12}) \tag{12}$$

One may physically interpret this equation as the subtraction of two vectors, where the first vector is a drone baseline at time t_1 and the second vector is the same baseline at t_2. In other words, this captures the relative motion of the drone across time.

2.4   The Bigger Picture

We take-away 2 key points from the discussion on the differentials:

- The double differentials across receivers and satellites (DD_{ij}^{sk}) yields the drone's baseline vectors at any given time point (Eq. 9). However, this estimate is still polluted by integer ambiguity.
- The double differential across receivers and time $(DD_{ij}^{t_{12}})$ yields the drone's *relative change* in the baseline vectors during flight (Eq. 12). Importantly, this relative estimate is free of the integer ambiguities.

Thus, we now have *two* separate estimates of the drone's 3D baseline vectors, each with different error properties. SafetyNet recognizes the opportunity of combining these two noisy estimates to precisely track the drone baselines, ultimately tracking orientation.

3   System Model

SafetyNet will model orientation tracking as a state estimation problem, where the state is defined as 3D orientation. We formally define "3D orientation" first and then design the model.

Figure 3 pretends 4 GPS receivers have been placed on a drone – their locations denoted as ρ_1, ρ_2, ρ_3 and ρ_4. The baseline vectors joining one of the receivers (say ρ_4) to the others can be defined as $\rho_{ij} = \rho_i - \rho_j$. When the "baselines" are aligned with the North-East reference axes, the baseline matrix B_o can be written as:

$$B_o = [\rho_{41} \; \rho_{42} \; \rho_{43}] \tag{13}$$

Assuming that the magnitude of the baseline vectors are d_1 and d_2, we can expand B_o as:

$$B_o = \begin{bmatrix} d_1 & 0 & d_1 \\ 0 & d_2 & d_2 \\ 0 & 0 & 0 \end{bmatrix} \tag{14}$$

Figure 3 also shows the rotation conventions of the 3 Euler angles – *pitch, roll and yaw*. Applying these rotations on B_o will obviously yield the new baseline matrix, B. For all our results, we will express rotations in terms of the Euler angles (i.e., degrees), which are intuitive to understand. However, for the purpose of mathematical efficiency, we will use *quaternion mathematics*, an alternative representation to Euler angles. Briefly, the baselines at an arbitrary orientation,

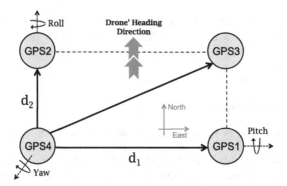

Fig. 3. The drone baseline vectors ρ_{41} and ρ_{42} aligned with Earth's reference frame.

called quaternion q, can be expressed in terms of the initial orientation q_o (aligned with reference axes), as below:

$$\rho_{ij}(q) = A(q)'\rho_{ij}(q_o) \tag{15}$$

Here $A(q)$ is the *rotation matrix* associated with the orientation quaternion q. Similarly, extending the effect of rotations to the entire baseline matrix, we have:

$$B(q) = A(q)'B_o \tag{16}$$

Effectively, orientation is about estimating the rotation matrix $A(q)$ using projected measurements of $B(q)$ on various satellite directions. Details on conversion between quaternions, Euler angles and rotation matrices can be found in [9]. Regardless of these mathematical conversions, *the core conceptual question still pertains to estimating the matrix B at any given time.*

4   System Design: Phase 1

We adopt a Bayesian filtering approach for tracking drone orientation. Figure 4 shows the model: (1) A state transition function, derived from the incremental changes in orientation ($DD_{ij}^{t_{12}}$), models the next state of the drone. Recall that these changes are affected by the hardware noise and multipath errors. (2) A measurement function, (DD_{ij}^{sk}), reflects the absolute orientation of the drone at any given time. Of course, this measurement is polluted by integer ambiguity. We adopt a Kalman Filter to combine the uncertainties from the transition and measurement functions, and track the most likely state of the system through time. We describe this basic design first. Then we focus on resolving the error sources (such as integer ambiguity, cycle slips, and missing data), and redesign the framework to accommodate these optimizations. Our final design is an "adjusted" particle filter algorithm that tracks drone orientation with consistent accuracy.

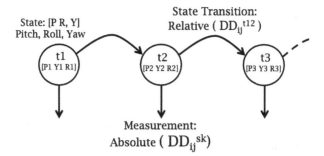

Fig. 4. Bayesian filtering approach to tracking orientation state over time.

4.1   State Transition Model

The relative baseline changes over time are directly obtained from Eq. 12, copied for convenience:

$$\lambda \nabla \Delta \phi_{ij}^s(t_{12}) = (\rho_{ij}(t_1) - \rho_{ij}(t_2)).\hat{l}_s + c.\Delta t_{ij}(t_{12}) \tag{17}$$

Omitting details, we rewrite with quaternions:

$$\lambda \nabla \Delta \phi_{ij}^s(t_{12}) = \rho_{ij}(q_o) \lfloor A(q_1).\hat{l}_{s\times} \rfloor \delta\theta + c.\Delta t_{ij}(t_{12}) \tag{18}$$

where, q_1 is the orientation quaternion at time t_1, $\delta\theta$ is the rotation vector [5] associated with quaternion δq. $\lfloor \times \rfloor$ is the vector cross operator [6]. We now solve Eq. 18 for various satellites s and GPS receiver-pairs ij using least-squares estimation. The result yields an estimate of the rotation vector $\delta\theta$ (hence δq) between two time points t_1 and t_2. We can thus estimate the new orientation quaternion q_2 as:

$$q_2 = \delta q \otimes q_1 \tag{19}$$

Here, $\otimes$ is the quaternion multiplication operator. When translated back to Euler angles, the result is the relative orientation change – pitch, yaw, and roll – from one state to the next. As mentioned earlier, this estimate is polluted by hardware noise and multipath.

4.2   Absolute Orientation Measurement

Equation 9 showed that double differentials across receivers and satellites (DD_{ij}^{sk}) are estimates of the *absolute* baseline vectors of the drone. While they cancel out clock bias errors, they leave the integer ambiguities as follows:

$$\lambda \nabla \Delta \phi_{ij}^{sk} = \rho_{ij}.(\hat{l}_s - \hat{l}_k) + \lambda \nabla \Delta N_{ij}^{sk} \tag{20}$$

Translating to quaternions again, using very similar conventions as described earlier, we have:

$$\lambda \nabla \Delta \phi_{ij}^{sk} - \rho_{ij}(q_o).A(q_n).(\hat{l}_s - \hat{l}_k) =$$
$$\rho_{i,j}(q_o).\lfloor A(q_n).(\hat{l}_s - \hat{l}_k)_\times \rfloor \delta\theta + \lambda.\nabla \Delta N_{ij}^{sk} \tag{21}$$

For now, let's assume the integer ambiguities are resolved (details in [10]) – then, we are left with a set of linear equations over different satellite pairs sk and baselines ij. By solving them using standard Least Squares Estimation (LSE), the rotation vector $\delta\theta$ and associated quaternion δq can be obtained. Hence the orientation q is.

$$q = \delta q \otimes q_n \tag{22}$$

Here q_n is an initial orientation estimate for the purposes of linearization of Eq. 21 (usually comes from the transition model). Note that this estimate q is absolute in the earth's reference frame, since the satellite locations sk are both known in that reference frame.

4.3 Filtered Orientation Estimation

We combine the state transition and absolute measurement models from the previous two subsections using an Augmented Particle Filter (APF) framework. Details are elaborated in [10].

4.4 Boosting Transition Function Reliability: GLONASS

Unlike GPS satellites, GLONASS uses FDMA and the satellites transmit in different frequencies. Hence, the *Double Differentials across Receivers and Satellites* (DD_{ij}^{sk}) equations of GLONASS have integer ambiguities that are more complex to resolve compared to GPS. Let us rewrite Eqs. 7 and 8 for two GLONASS satellites s and k

$$\lambda^s \Delta \phi_{ij}^s = \Delta \rho_{ij}.\hat{l}_s + c\Delta t_{ij} + \lambda^s \Delta N_{ij}^s \tag{23}$$
$$\lambda^k \Delta \phi_{ij}^k = \Delta \rho_{ij}.\hat{l}_k + c\Delta t_{ij} + \lambda^k \Delta N_{ij}^k \tag{24}$$

Here, λ^s and λ^k are wavelengths of two GLONASS satellites. Differencing the two equations above similar to the derivation of Eq. 9 results in

$$\lambda^s \Delta \phi_{ij}^s - \lambda^k \Delta \phi_{ij}^k =$$
$$\Delta \rho_{ij}.(\hat{l}_s - \hat{l}_k) + \lambda^s \Delta N_{ij}^s - \lambda^k \Delta N_{ij}^k \tag{25}$$

The ambiguity terms do not group themselves into a single integer. This makes it difficult to use the GLONASS DD_{ij}^{sk} equation above towards derivation of absolute drone orientation, as outlined in Sect. 4.2.

As discussed in Sect. 6, it might be possible to use finer integer ambiguity resolution effectively in both integers, but it would be expensive. Alternatively, it might be possible to use two satellites with adjacent channels and assume a common frequency, but it would be inaccurate for our purposes. Hence, we take a completely alternative approach and use temporal differencing instead. Equation 12 in Sect. 2 has only one term with a wavelength factor. It gives relative changes in the geometry over time, which can be easily exploited for computing the transition function in Sect. 4.1. This will not only add more confidence to the transition function, but also helps in quickly converging on the set of outliers caused due to cycle slips.

5 Evaluation

We conduct all experimentation using a 3DR X-8 octocopter (8-rotor), pictured in Fig. 5. "X" implies 4 arms with unequal spacing – yielding greater stability of roll angle versus pitch (recall that pitch is the dominant motion when an airplane takes off or lands, roll is dominant when the plane makes a left/right turn). Two rotors attach to each arm: one above, one below. To the X-8, we mounted 4 u-Blox NEO-M8T multi-GNSS receivers, adjacent to the top motor of each arm. We also mounted a Raspberry Pi 2 near the drone's center of mass – the GPS receivers transfer the data to the Pi via USB at 5 Hz. IMU data at 10 Hz is recovered as binary logs from the X-8's USB interface.[3]

A GoPro camera, affixed to the underbelly of the airframe, points vertically downwards. The GoPro captures video at 30 fps with a fast shutter (to minimize motion blur and rolling shutter effects). We use ffmpeg to sample the video into stills at 7.5 fps (every fourth frame). We post-process the images using *Pix4D*:

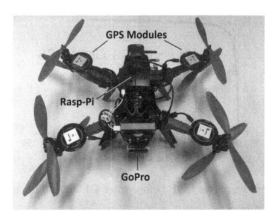

Fig. 5. Description of our drone platform

---

[3] Experiments were conducted as per FAA regulations. Operator trained by a general aviation pilot, over relatively vacant fields, with flight height not exceeding 45 m.

advanced commercial photogrammetry software that uses *structure from motion* (SfM) to perform 3D registration of each frame. From Pix4D's outputs, we can recover a high-precision estimate of drone attitude (accuracy ≈0.05° [13,28]). Note: structure from motion would not be practical as a realtime IMU replacement – each 5–7 min flight requires several hours of processing on a server of 16 CPU cores, 32 GB RAM, and CUDA on a high-end NVIDIA GRID K2 GPU.

We refer to *pitch/roll* angles together as *tilt* angles and the *yaw* angle as the *heading* angle. Figures 6 and 7 show the distribution of tilt and heading orientation errors before and after incorporation of GLONASS satellite measurements. Median errors before and after GLONASS integration is 2.26° and 1.79° respectively. The corresponding 95th percentile errors are 26° and 7° respectively. Evidently, GLONASS measurements increase the accuracy substantially, and more importantly towards the tail of the distribution. Cutting down the tail errors will enhance the reliability of SafetyNet.

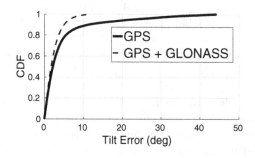

Fig. 6. Tilt error CDF before/after GLONASS integration

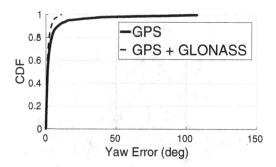

Fig. 7. Heading error CDF before/after GLONASS integration

Figure 8(a), (b) gives a break up of the 95th percentile and median errors of tilt orientation angles over several flights conducted under varying weather conditions. Flights 7–11 were conducted in fog. As evident, GLONASS integration contributes to an error reduction of 3.5x at the 95th percentile and 27% at the median. Similarly, Fig. 9(a), (b) gives a break of the 95th and median errors for the yaw angle. GLONASS integration is contributing to a gain of $11x$ at the 95th percentile and 37% at the median. Substantial boost in orientation estimation accuracy by GLONASS would increase the reliability of *SafetyNet* to serve as IMU failsafe.

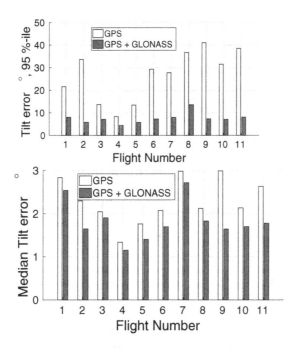

Fig. 8. GLONASS integration dramatically cuts down the tail tilt errors (a) 95th percentile tilt errors with/without GLONASS (b) Median tilt errors with/without GLONASS

6   Related Work

Resolving Integer ambiguities in GLONASS is challenging because the satellites operate at different frequencies. We summarize the main techniques in literature which attempt to solve this problem.

Common Clock: The second term in single differencing Eq. 7 represents the clock bias difference between the two receivers whose phases are being differenced. If we connect the two receivers with a common clock, this bias term is completely eliminated. Works in [11,17] exploit this opportunity for integrating GLONASS with GPS. Since there is no differencing performed across satellites, the wavelength difference will not matter. Such an approach however requires tight synchronization between receivers with a common clock. This increases the hardware complexity, whereas SafetyNet doesn't have this requirement.

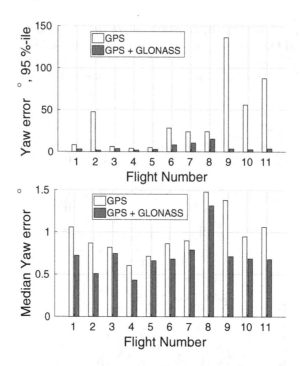

Fig. 9. GLONASS integration dramatically cuts down the tail heading errors (a) 95th percentile heading errors with/without GLONASS (b) Median heading errors with/without GLONASS

Search: Work in [29] follows an extensive searching and optimization techniques for resolving single differenced (SD_{ij}) and double differenced integer ambiguities (DD_{ij}^{sk}). Such an approach increases the complexity especially under heavy cycle slip rate during aggressive flights. Work in [30] also uses an extensive search procedure with a resolution of 64 um which becomes impractical under low SNR and heavy cycle slip rate.

Pseudorange: Works in [12, 27] use pseudoranges for resolving integer ambiguities. However, pseudorange data is low in precision (30 cm), hence not suitable for integer ambiguity resolution for drone orientation estimate which needs an accuracy of around 2 cm.

7   Discussion

Energy Consumption: GPS receivers are known to be power hungry. While this is a concern for smart-phone like applications, a flying drone consumes 1000 times higher power than GPS. Therefore supporting GPS receivers constantly is feasible.

Cost: Commercial drones already use multiple GPS receivers for redundancy. Moreover, the need for safety is higher for bigger drones carrying heavier payloads. Given the cost of GPS receivers is negligible relative to the cost of such drones, we believe the additional cost of GPS receivers is justifiable.

8 Conclusion

GPS sensors offer substantial promise in orientation sensing, a desirable feature for serving as failsafe for IMU failures. Augmenting GPS with GLONASS measurements can offer enormous gain in the orientation accuracy, particularly in cutting down the tail of the error distribution and thereby enhancing the robustness. While integrating FDMA based GLONASS with CDMA based GPS is non-trivial, we show that incorporating time differenced GLONASS carrier phase data with GPS provides effective fusion.

References

1. Diydrones.   http://diydrones.com/forum/topics/problem-quad-copter-spins-around-itself
2. Drone crash survey. https://docs.google.com/forms/d/1R4MaX8iZWRoyzKJ6rKr 0U-p3x-6j0ZVm5a0p83hHty0/viewanalytics
3. Galileo. https://en.wikipedia.org/wiki/Galileo_(satellite_navigation)
4. Google forum. https://groups.google.com/forum/#!msg/drones-discuss/fnWYM 48pGys/kwPL_q_qv0QJ
5. Rotation vectors. http://farside.ph.utexas.edu/teaching/301/lectures/node100. html
6. Vector cross product. http://soe.rutgers.edu/~meer/GRAD561/ADD/antisymm. pdf
7. Blewitt, G.: Basics of the GPS technique: observation equations. In: Johnson. B. (ed.) Geodetic Applications of GPS, pp. 10–54. Nordic Geodetic Commission, Gothenburg (1997)
8. De Pasquale, G., Somà, A.: Reliability testing procedure for MEMS IMUs applied to vibrating environments. Sensors 10(1), 456–474 (2010)
9. Diebel, J.: Representing attitude: Euler angles, unit quaternions, and rotation vectors. Matrix 58(15–16), 1–35 (2006)
10. Gowda, M., Manweiler, J., Dhekne, A., Choudhury, R.R., Weisz, J.D.: Tracking drone orientation with multiple GPS receivers. In: Mobicom. ACM, New York (2016)
11. Han, K.J., Gerard, L.: Determining Heading and Pitch Using a Single Difference GPS/GLONASS Approach. University of Calgary, Canada (1999)
12. Han, S., Dai, L., Rizos, C.: A new data processing strategy for combined GPS/GLONASS carrier phase-based positioning. In: Proceedings of the ION GPS 1999, pp. 1619–1627 (1999)
13. Harwin, S., Lucieer, A.: Assessing the accuracy of georeferenced point clouds produced via multi-view stereopsis from Unmanned Aerial Vehicle (UAV) imagery. Remote Sens. 4(6), 1573–1599 (2012)
14. Hedgecock, W., et al.: Regtrack: a differential relative GPS tracking solution. In: Proceedings of the 11th Annual International Conference on Mobile Systems, Applications, and Services - MOBISYS 2013 (2013)

15. Hedgecock, W., Maroti, M., Ledeczi, A., Volgyesi, P., Banalagay, R.: Accurate real-time relative localization using single-frequency GPS. In: Proceedings of the 12th ACM Conference on Embedded Network Sensor Systems - SENSYS 2014, pp. 206–220. ACM (2014)
16. Kaplan, E., Hegarty, C.: Understanding GPS: Principles and Applications. Artech House, Boston (2005)
17. Keong, J.: GPS/GLONASS attitude determination with a common clock using a single difference approach. In: ION GPS 1999 Conference, Nashville, pp. 14–17 (1999)
18. Lai, Y.-C., Jan, S.-S.: Attitude estimation based on fusion of gyroscopes and single antenna GPS for small UAVs under the influence of vibration. GPS Solut. 15(1), 67–77 (2011)
19. Langley, R.B.: GLONASS: review and update. GPS World 8(7), 46–51 (1997)
20. Laurichesse, D., Mercier, F., Berthias, J.-P., Broca, P., Cerri, L.: Integer ambiguity resolution on undifferenced GPS phase measurements and its application to PPP and satellite precise orbit determination. Navigation 56(2), 135–149 (2009)
21. Liu, X., Randall, R.: Blind source separation of internal combustion engine piston slap from other measured vibration signals. Mech. Syst. Signal Process. 19(6), 1196–1208 (2005)
22. Malyavej, V., Torteeka, P., Wongkharn, S., Wiangtong, T.: Pose estimation of unmanned ground vehicle based on dead-reckoning/GPS sensor fusion by unscented Kalman filter. In: 6th International Conference on Electrical Engineering/Electronics, Computer, Telecommunications and Information Technology, ECTI-CON 2009, vol. 1, pp. 395–398. IEEE (2009)
23. Mekik, C., Arslanoglu, M.: Investigation on accuracies of real time kinematic GPS for GIS applications. Remote Sens. 1(1), 22–35 (2009)
24. Misra, P., Enge, P.: Global Positioning System: Signals, Measurements and Performance, 2nd edn. Ganga-Jamuna Press, Lincoln (2006)
25. Parkinson, B.W., Enge, P.K.: Differential GPS. Glob. Position. Syst. Theor. Appl. 2, 3–50 (1996)
26. Suh, Y.S.: Attitude estimation by multiple-mode Kalman filters. IEEE Trans. Industr. Electron. 53(4), 1386–1389 (2006)
27. Tsujii, T., Harigae, M., Inagaki, T., Kanai, T.: Flight tests of GPS/GLONASS precise positioning versus dual frequency KGPS profile. Earth, Planets Space 52(10), 825–829 (2000)
28. Vallet, J., Panissod, F., Strecha, C., Tracol, M.: Photogrammetric performance of an ultra light weight swinglet UAV. In: UAV-g, no. EPFL-CONF-169252 (2011)
29. Wang, J.: An approach to GLONASS ambiguity resolution. J. Geodesy 74(5), 421–430 (2000)
30. Wang, J., Rizos, C., Stewart, M.P., Leick, A.: GPS and GLONASS integration: modeling and ambiguity resolution issues. GPS Solut. 5(1), 55–64 (2001)
31. Wells, M.: Attenuating magnetic interference in a UAV system. Ph.D. thesis, Carleton University, Ottawa (2008)
32. Zhang, B., Teunissen, P.J., Odijk, D.: A novel un-differenced PPP-RTK concept. J. Navig. 64(S1), S180–S191 (2011)
33. Zhang, Y., Chamseddine, A., Rabbath, C., Gordon, B., Su, C.-Y., Rakheja, S., Fulford, C., Apkarian, J., Gosselin, P.: Development of advanced FDD and FTC techniques with application to an unmanned quadrotor helicopter testbed. J. Franklin Inst. 350(9), 2396–2422 (2013)

Edge Computing in the Extreme
for Sustainability

Suman Banerjee, Neil Klingensmith, Peng Liu$^{(\boxtimes)}$,
and Anantharaghavan Sridhar

Department of Computer Sciences, University of Wisconsin-Madison,
Madison, WI 53706, USA
{suman,klingens,pengliu,anantharaghavan}@cs.wisc.edu

Abstract. The notion of edge computing introduces new computing
functions away from centralized locations and closer to the network edge,
thus facilitating new applications and services. This enhanced computing paradigm provides new opportunities to applications developers, not
available otherwise. In this paper, we will discuss why placing computation functions at the extreme edge of a network infrastructure, i.e.,
in wireless Access Points and home set-top boxes, is particularly beneficial for a large class of emerging applications. We will discuss a specific
approach, called ParaDrop, to implement such edge computing functionalities. Based on the ParaDrop platform, we have implemented two smart
home applications for sustainability: environment control and water quality management, to demonstrate the advantages of edge computing. The
implementations of the two applications on the ParaDrop platform have
advantages including high privacy, reliability, and efficiency. The process
to build them demonstrates the flexibility of ParaDrop to implement
edge applications and cloud-edge hybrid applications. In addition, the
API and tools provided by the ParaDrop platform make the application
deployment process transparent to end users.

1   Introduction

Cloud computing platforms are being widely used to deploy services accessible
by various devices. Popular examples of such platforms include Amazon EC2,
Microsoft Azure, and Google App Engine. These platforms are reliable, always-
on, robust, and globally accessible. They are also more economically efficient in
comparison to running private, dedicated servers because tenants can share the
hardware resources. However, deploying services in the cloud necessitates off-
site computation and storage, and despite increased geo-distribution—the end-
user perceived latency is still higher than local servers in many cases [19]. Web
applications based on HTTP protocol are well suited to such a service model,
but there are an increasing number of applications requiring reduced latency.
Additionally, many other applications prefer to have computation and storage
resources close to the client devices in order to provide a better user experience or more efficient use of network bandwidth. In the recent decade, keeping
the aforementioned requirements in mind, many researchers have studied the

© Springer International Publishing AG 2017
N. Sastry and S. Chakraborty (Eds.): COMSNETS 2017, LNCS 10340, pp. 93–109, 2017.
DOI: 10.1007/978-3-319-67235-9_8

need and benefits of edge computing approaches that put resources close to the client devices, with Cyber Foraging [17], Cloudlets [35], and more recently Fog Computing [18] to name a few.

This paper presents a specific edge computing platform, *ParaDrop*, and describes two edge computing applications built, and deployed on that platform. ParaDrop is implemented on Wi-Fi Access Points (APs), which are ubiquitous in homes and offices, and are always "on". These APs also sit in the data path between the Internet and client devices, making them the ideal location to deploy an edge computing platform. By providing a framework to manage resources on Wi-Fi APs, ParaDrop allows third-party developers to bring computational functions into homes and enterprises, ergo closer to the client devices. In order to provide an isolated multi-tenant environment, ParaDrop uses a lightweight virtualization solution through which third-party developers can create, deploy, and revoke their services in different APs. ParaDrop allows user state to be gathered by services hosted in containers. Additionally, ParaDrop can migrate the states for the users as they change their points of attachment. ParaDrop also recognizes that Wi-Fi APs are likely to be resource constrained for many different types of applications, and hence implements a policy framework to control resource utilization.

The ParaDrop framework has three key components[1]: (i) a virtualization substrate in the Wi-Fi APs that hosts third-party computations in isolated containers (which we call *chutes*, short for parachutes); (ii) a cloud backend through which all of the ParaDrop APs and the third-party containers are dynamically installed, instantiated, and revoked; and (iii) a developer API through which developers can manage the resources of the platform and monitor the running status of APs and chutes [30]. To elaborate, ParaDrop uses more efficient virtualization technology based on Linux containers [9] rather than the heavier Virtual Machines (VMs). This implies that the platform can provide more resources per service, with the given hardware. The backend server manages the gateways through a real-time messaging protocol, Web Application Messaging Protocol (WAMP) [16], which guarantees very low latency in service deployment and monitoring.

ParaDrop, which can provide distributed computational resources for applications that would otherwise use cloud-based services, is a good fit as a backend platform for Internet of Things (IoT) applications. In this work, we study the smart home, which is one of many popular IoT applications flooding the marketplace today. Combining smart sensors in buildings or houses and cloud applications in datacenters, these smart home applications collect real-time data from people's living environment, process them in the cloud, and then make intelligent decisions to optimize people's comfort, reduce power/materials consumption, etc. However, most of the computing tasks of these types of applications can be done locally with a modest hardware platform. Generally speaking, information

---

[1] The history and detailed design of the ParaDrop platform are out of the scope of this paper. They were introduced in [30,37]. This paper uses some contents previous appeared in [30,37] for completeness.

collected in smart home and other IoT applications is only used locally—for example, your neighbor's smart thermostat does not need to know the temperature of your living room to function. Cloud-based architectures, popular in many IoT applications, typically concentrate data archiving and control functionality on a central computing platform. The cloud-based architecture potentially exposes users to unnecessary security and privacy risks in addition to overconsuming network, storage, and computation resources.

Using ParaDrop to implement such an application under the edge computing paradigm, we can reduce the network traffic significantly because a large portion of data from the sensors is processed locally (an additional privacy benefit). Additionally, the systems are more reliable (and available) because they can continue working even if the access network to the Internet is broken. Furthermore, the cloud services provider does not need to invest heavily in computational capacity (i.e. high-performance servers, etc.) because the data processing and archiving functionality is distributed among users.

To summarize, ParaDrop is a promising computing platform to deploy applications (such as smart home applications) at the extreme network edge. ParaDrop provides the tools to provision resources and monitor them in realtime. It is flexible as developers can choose diverse programming languages, and frameworks convenient to them to implement applications. ParaDrop is built upon a lightweight virtualization technology, and it provides an isolated and controlled execution environment for applications with very low overhead. It provides an on-demand deployment feature to end users, which means the system

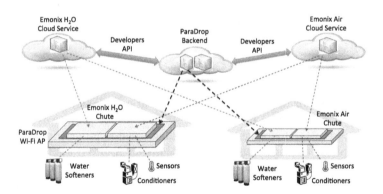

Fig. 1. Emonix Air and Emonix H_2O edge computing services deployed on the ParaDrop platform. On the ParaDrop platform, we call an edge computing service a chute. Chutes can be managed by developers through the ParaDrop API. Users can also control the chute directly through the web frontend of the ParaDrop platform. A chute's internal implementation is orthogonal to the ParaDrop platform, Developers can use the same programming language and framework as the ones on cloud computing platform. Thus it is fairly easy to port a part of cloud computing service to ParaDrop platform. The popularity of microservice architecture [32], in which a system is composed of some loosely integrated small services, makes the porting work straightforward.

can choose to deploy the chute on demand when applications require. We have deployed two such applications leveraging the power of ParaDrop: Emonix Air [27,29] and Emonix H_2O [2,28]. Based on our experience, ParaDrop provides a highly efficient framework to deploy these services and convenient tools to manage these services for both end users and developers. Figure 1 illustrates the high-level architecture of the system implementation on the ParaDrop platform.

The remainder of the paper is structured as follows. Section 2 contains an overview of the ParaDrop platform. Section 3 discusses the applications developed for ParaDrop. We proceed to introduce the requirements of the two smart home applications we built, and discuss the benefits to implementing them on ParaDrop in Sect. 4. Section 5 presents the implementation and deployment details of the earlier discussed applications. Section 6 discussed related works, and we conclude the paper and discuss future work in Sect. 7.

2   ParaDrop Overview

The goal of ParaDrop is providing a flexible edge computing platform composed of ubiquitous devices residing in the proximity of end users. A decade or two ago, the desktop computer was the primary ubiquitous platform used by users. However, mobile devices, such as smartphones and tablets, have gone on to deprecate the desktop computers. The Wi-Fi Access Point (or router) is one such ubiquitous device that provides the required user proximity, and most off-the-shelf Wi-Fi APs have the capabilities developers require for their services. Moreover, Wi-Fi AP operate in an always on mode. These decisions motivated us to choose Wi-Fi APs as the platform to build ParaDrop.

2.1   ParaDrop Design

A critical requirement of ParaDrop is the isolated execution environment provided through virtualization. We ignored the isolation primitives offered by the process abstraction provided by operating systems as the primitives offered by virtualization were far more generic, providing greater programming flexibility. For example, if an edge computing service is an Android application, then developers need to use the Android SDK to develop it. As a result, the service will bind to the Android operating system, forcing the developers to handle the version compatibility. Instead, in ParaDrop, edge computing services are similar to the services deployed in the cloud. Developers can choose programming languages and frameworks based on their skills and preferences so that they have the highest possible flexibility to develop services. Such a high degree of flexibility is a very important feature required to attract third-party developers to implement diverse edge computing services for the ParaDrop platform. As we will show in Sect. 3.2, it is relatively straightforward to implement "hybrid" services (a combination of cloud computing components and edge computing components) because we can use the same programming environment on both cloud computing and edge computing platforms.

In order to provide an isolated environment for services on a relatively low-performance hardware platform, we leverage lightweight virtualization—the Linux container, specifically Docker. ParaDrop is primarily geared at deploying services. Hence, we do not need to provide bulky virtual machines to users and developers. Docker has features such as layered imaging and NAT, which ease the development, management, and deployment of chutes. Docker also effectively solves the dependency problem when developers migrate software tested in a development environment to a deployment environment [31].

Along with the distributed substrate atop Wi-Fi routers, ParaDrop has a cloud backend. The ParaDrop backend has three responsibilities, namely it: (i) monitors and manages the resources on the Wi-Fi routers in a centralized approach, (ii) stores the metadata of edge computing services, and launch or shut down services on the extreme edge—Wi-Fi routers, and (iii) provides an API for developers and users to view the system status and control the whole system, e.g. add new Wi-Fi routers to the system, change configurations of the Wi-Fi routers, create new edge computing services, start/stop a service on specified Wi-Fi routers, etc.

Services deployed into the Wi-Fi routers can be handled by the end users themselves—if they possess the required skills, or can be delegated to the developers. In the latter case, developers can use the RESTful API of ParaDrop to achieve smooth and transparent chute deployment for users if they grant the permissions to developers to do so.

2.2   ParaDrop Implementation

We chose the low-cost, single-board "PC Engines apu1d" [12] to build the ParaDrop routers, and the backend server was deployed in an Ubuntu 14.04 LTS VM in the cloud. We chose Ubuntu Core, also known as Snappy [15], as the operating system for the ParaDrop routers, as Ubuntu Core is more lightweight in comparison to other distributions. Additionally, compared to embedded Linux distributions, such as OpenWrt [22], Ubuntu Core provides a better package management system and extensive tools. We chose an off-the-shelf operating system as we strongly believe that the efficiency of a customized Linux distribution (with tools like buildroot [5] or yocto [34]) does not justify the maintenance cost.

The key component of the ParaDrop platform is the ParaDrop agent which runs atop the router. This agent is implemented with the Python twisted framework. Figure 2 illustrates the software architecture of a ParaDrop router and the major components.

We install a Docker engine on the router to manage Docker images and containers. The ParaDrop agent tracks the chutes installed on the routers. It parses the chute configuration files, creates local environments for the Docker containers, and exposes context information to the containers. It maintains a network connection to the backend server to receive commands from the backend, and also sends command feedback and status reports to the backend.

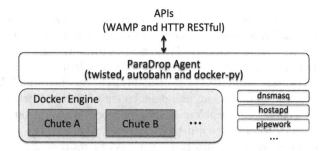

Fig. 2. Major software components on a ParaDrop gateway. All the components are snappy packages. We implemented the ParaDrop agent with Python from scratch. And we made the snappy packages for dnsmasq and hostapd based on the corresponding open source projects. The Docker engine is packaged by Ubuntu. All the snappy packages can be securely and transactionally updated over-the-air if required.

Since ParaDrop routers are deployed in the wild, we need to provide a robust software maintenance scheme to make sure the software running on the routers can be managed from the cloud. An important difference between ParaDrop routers in the wild and servers in datacenters is accessibility. Due to firewalls, NATs, and other middleboxes, we do not have direct access to the Wi-Fi routers in deployment. A real-time messaging protocol is needed to transmit notifications between the ParaDrop backend and routers. We chose WAMP [16] for that purpose.

The backend server is implemented with the "MEAN" stack (MongoDB, Express, Angular, and Node.js) [20]. It provides both web frontend to users and administrators, and also a RESTful API for developers. Through the web interfaces, users and administrators can add new routers to the platform, configure the routers with permissions, and manage the services on the routers. Third-party developers can use the RESTful API to manage the chutes on the ParaDrop platform transparently to end users.

3 Develop Applications for ParaDrop

In this section, we will first illustrate the structure of a ParaDrop application. We proceed to discuss how one can develop applications for ParaDrop. Finally, we will explain how to use the ParaDrop API to deploy a service at the network edge.

3.1 ParaDrop Application Overview

First and foremost, applications need to be in the proximity of mobile devices, sensors, or actuators to take advantage of the ParaDrop platform. ParaDrop applications have a well-defined structure—including config files, application source code, and binaries. In this paper, we use two specific IoT applications as examples for our discussion. These applications use sensors to collect data from a user's environment, and actuators to carry out commands to interact with the user's environment.

Very similar to the applications deployed on the cloud platform, a ParaDrop application also operates with a split architecture—it has a web/mobile-based frontend, and a backend. Depending on the requirements, the backend can solely reside on the ParaDrop platform, or can be split between the ParaDrop router and the cloud. We only briefly discuss the application frontend, as it is not the primary focus of this paper. However, we discuss the backend part (chute) of ParaDrop applications in greater detail.

Consider IoT applications, where the chute connects to sensors and actuators. Such applications are required to provide APIs to end users in the form of a web frontend or a mobile application so that users can change the settings, and view the real-time status if users have direct access to the ParaDrop router. The chute will also have to connect to the service backend in the cloud if the application needs to provide global access to users. At a high level, we categorize the applications as follows: (i) Pure edge computing applications, and (ii) Cloud-edge hybrid applications. The pure edge applications are similar to the applications installed on smart routers and do not have any backend. Users can only view system status and change system settings locally. Users of the cloud-edge hybrid applications, however, can manage the applications if they have Internet access.

3.2 Developing Applications for ParaDrop

A chute is primarily a Dockerfile defining the container image, a configuration file describing the environment for the container, and service logic. We can choose various programming languages and frameworks to implement the service, including Python, Go, Node.js, etc. Developers need not master a dedicated programming language or framework for ParaDrop in order to develop applications for it. Additionally, ParaDrop provides local context, for example, sensors, actuators, and wireless networks—to enhance the developmental procedure.

The edge computing application can process data, cache/store data, and take actions. These operations can be done with very low latency. The applications can be more reliably because the Internet access interruption will not break the system completely.

In Sect. 4, we will give two concrete examples to illustrate the details of developing ParaDrop applications.

3.3 Deploying Applications (Chutes) on ParaDrop

For pure edge applications, users can use the web frontend to deploy the chutes. ParaDrop provides the interfaces to configure the chutes during deployment, and the application can provide interfaces by itself to change the settings on the fly.

For the cloud-edge hybrid applications, users can either deploy the chutes themselves, or delegate that task to application developers by granting them the permissions to install/remove chutes on their ParaDrop routers. ParaDrop provides a RESTful API that application developers can use to deploy chutes on-demand.

4   Applications for Sustainability

In this section, we outline two sustainability applications for which the ParaDrop platform is ideally suited. Our sustainability applications are building automation systems—those that control resource consumption within buildings with the goal of improving efficiency and user comfort. We have implemented both of them based on cloud computing platform [27,28]. Thanks to the flexibility of the ParaDrop platform, we can easily push the computation tasks from the cloud to the edge, so that the system can take advantages of edge computing. In this paper, we only focus on the discussion about migrating core components of these systems from the cloud to the extreme edge. But we do not discuss the detailed implementation and evaluation of these applications[2].

4.1   Emonix Air

Emonix Air is an automation system for heating and cooling control within the home. Its main goal is to provide fine-grained temperature control in different regions of the home independently based on user comfort preferences. Emonix air has two principal components: (i) a collection of smart vents and heaters deployed throughout the home equipped with network-connected embedded computer systems that can track local temperatures and make local temperature adjustments and (ii) a controller backend that communicates with frontend computers to control the temperature at setpoints based on user's input.

Why Is Emonix Air Needed? Forced-air heating and cooling systems often have poor efficiency in multi-story homes, in terms of both energy and comfort. One of the reasons for this is the duct network inside such homes often results in poor airflow in rooms that are far from the heater or air-conditioner. For a given temperature setpoint, the desired temperature is only achieved in the room where the thermostat is located and there is a significant variation in the temperature across different rooms. Consequently, a user in a second-floor room might set the thermostat in the basement (say) to either way below or above the desired temperature so that the room on the second floor is maintained at the desired temperature. This leads to excessive energy consumption by the heating or air-conditioning system.

One solution to this problem is to use zoned heating/cooling systems [1,21,39]. However, these solutions are both expensive and difficult to retrofit in many existing homes. We propose a much simpler solution that is easy to retrofit: the Emonix Air SmartVents and Space Heaters.

---

[2] We use some contents previous appeared in [27,28] for completeness.

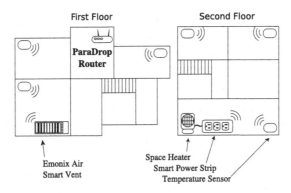

Fig. 3. An example architecture of an Emonix Air powered home. The figure shows distributed temperature sensors, smart vents and space heaters as they would be deployed. The optional backend server in the cloud is omitted here.

The Emonix Air system (Fig. 3) leverages distributed wireless temperature sensors and provides room-level personalized temperature control [27]. The temperature control is effected by using smart power strips to manage the space heaters and smart vents to manage the airflow from forced air systems.

What Does Emonix Air Need for Deployment? To manage this spread of distributed resources, we require a network connected computational entity that has the following capabilities:

- The ability to provide an interface to the users to interact with the system
- The ability to connect with the distributed resources over a network
- The computational power to manage the distributed resources (temperature sensors, smart vents, space heaters) for maximizing user comfort and energy efficiency

The Wi-Fi router, being the central connectivity hub inside a home, is a natural choice for this computational entity. Modern Wi-Fi routers are able to meet all three requirements listed above. However, they lack the flexibility to host and deploy custom applications.

ParaDrop is a flexible edge computing platform to deploy such a computational entity. Since the router is already connected to the distributed wireless resources by nature and no additional infrastructure is required, retrofitting the Emonix Air System in an existing home is a transparent and simple process.

4.2 Emonix H_2O

Emonix H_2O [2] is a feedback control system for water softeners. A water softener is a building system that is used to remove minerals from water to prevent scale buildup on fixtures and appliances. Existing water softener control systems do not have closed-loop controllers, meaning that they do not measure the quality or mineral concentration of the water that they treat. Consequently, most water softeners operate inefficiently, which costs building owners money and creates unnecessary pollution.

Why Is Emonix H_2O Needed? Water Softeners are the primary sources of Chloride ion pollution in effluent sewage systems. Water Softeners are used to stop lime buildup in pipes and equipment by removing dissolved minerals (Calcium and Magnesium ions) from the municipal water supply. To achieve this, the Softener contains a resin tank which exchanges the Calcium and Magnesium ions with Sodium ions. Consequently, the Softeners need to undergo a periodic regeneration process to maintain their softening power. The regeneration process involves the following:

- Purchase of concentrated salt to create the concentrated salt brine
- Flushing the resin tank inside the softener with the brine, thereby replenishing the resin tank with Sodium ions
- The regeneration process is triggered by a water flow based open-loop controller built with a safety margin

The safety margin results in the water softener being regenerated at a higher frequency than necessary. This leads to the following concerns:

- Wastage of water caused by frequent regenerations
- Increase in Chloride ion pollution in effluent sewage systems caused by frequent regenerations
- Hard water is common in many areas in the US (Fig. 4) and Water Softeners are a necessity in all these areas. Consequently, the impact of the Chloride ion pollution has a massive scale that could affect water tables and other endpoints that receive the effluent discharge.

The Emonix H_2O system (Fig. 5) [2] leverages Calcium-ion sensors to detect water hardness at the output of the Softener and optimally regenerates the Water Softener when the water demand is low while maximally utilizing the capacity of the Water Softener [28].

What Does Emonix H_2O Need for Deployment? To manage the water softener regeneration effectively, we require a network connected computational entity that has the following capabilities:

- The ability to provide an interface to users to interact with the system
- The ability to connect with the network-connected sensor node at the Water Softener
- The ability to sense occupancy, predict water consumption and demand
- The computational power to execute optimization and inference algorithms to minimize the frequency of Water Softener regeneration while protecting building equipment from hard water

Concentration of Water Hardness in Grains Per Gallon

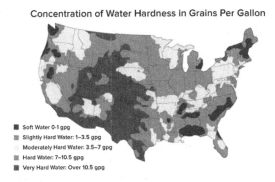

Fig. 4. The map of the U.S. indicates areas with hard water. Red is the worst while blue is best [3]. (Color figure online)

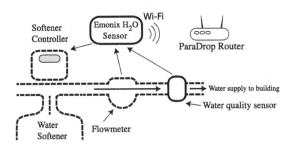

Fig. 5. Schematic of an Emonix H_2O deployment. The figure shows the connections between the Emonix H_2O system and existing components of Water Softener Systems. The optional backend server in the cloud is omitted here.

The ParaDrop router features a 1 GHz x86 processor that is easily capable of handling the computational load for this application. The Emonix H_2O sensor node is already connected to the router inside a home, which results in a minimal infrastructural change to install the Emonix H_2O system. Additionally, the ParaDrop router would also interface with other smart home devices (Nest thermostat, Smart Light Bulbs etc.) which help connected in-home systems to take advantage of multiple sensor modalities to improve their functions or performance and behave as a cohesive unit. For example, in the case of Emonix H_2O, the Nest thermostat provides valuable information about occupancy patterns which is used to predict the optimal time to regenerate the Softener. Such integrated services are extremely easy to deploy using ParaDrop APIs for containerized applications that run on ParaDrop.

5 Application Implementations—from Smart Homes to Sustainable Homes

Our primary objective is to realize sustainable homes which employ the power of the ParaDrop platform for the collaborative performance of smart home services. As we discussed in Sect. 3, we can implement both pure edge computing applications, and cloud-edge hybrid applications for ParaDrop. We chose to develop cloud-edge hybrid applications for Emonix Air and Emonix H_2O for the following two reasons: (i) we want to provide global access dashboards for users to view the real-time status of the system and change the system settings, and (ii) we can reuse the earlier designed system architecture, and the components for logistics, e.g. user account management, history data storage, web user interfaces, etc.

5.1 Implementing Emonix Air on ParaDrop

The Emonix Air SmartVents are motorized vents that are interfaced to a Wireless Sensor Node (WSN). The Space Heaters are connected to smart power strips which also contain a Wireless Sensor Node. The WSN carries a small Linux computer running Ubuntu, a 16-bit temperature sensor, and a Wi-Fi interface. A typical functional sequence of the SmartVent system is described below.

- The sensor nodes run an adaptive sampling algorithm that decides the interval until the next temperature sample (at most 15 min) and sleep in the intervening period to conserve energy.
- When a temperature sample is measured, the sensor nodes send it to the master application (a ParaDrop chute) running on the ParaDrop router.
- The master application records the measurement from the temperature sensors (which is specific to a particular room in the building) and logs them into a local MySQL database.
- The master application communicates an action back to each wireless nodes in the house (either the SmartVents or the Space Heaters).
- The action is identified based on the temperature setpoint for the room, setpoint schedule, predicted room occupancy and energy consumption.
- The master application also supports a web interface that the user can access to adjust the setpoints and setpoint schedules for every room in the house.

It is intuitive as to how the entire system can achieve its goals locally without access to the cloud. We note that reusing the implementation for the cloud computing platform required minimal effort. We did, however, require an additional module responsible for data synchronization between the cloud and the edge. With the edge computing architecture, the intelligent entity of the system can get data from the sensors and dispatch commands to actuators with lower latency. The local data processing in such a paradigm also reduces network traffic.

5.2   Implementing Emonix H_2O on ParaDrop

The Emonix H_2O smart modules for water softeners also contain a Wireless Sensor Node (WSN) [28]. The WSN carries a small Linux computer running Ubuntu, a Wi-Fi interface, a separate water pipe system to sample the water output from the softener and a Calcium-ion sensor. A typical functional sequence of the system is described below.

- The sensor node runs an adaptive sampling algorithm for water hardness in order to minimize the water consumed for sampling.
- When a water hardness sample is measured, the sensor node sends it to the master application running on a ParaDrop router.
- The master application records the measurement from the Emonix H_2O sensor and records it into a MySQL database.
- The master application communicates a regenerate softener command (if appropriate) back to the Emonix H_2O sensor node.
- The regeneration instant is determined by an optimization algorithm based on forecasted water hardness and forecasted water usage.

Very similar to Emonix Air, we also moved the intelligent entity of the system which was running in the cloud to a ParaDrop router.

5.3   Transparent Deployment of Edge Computing Service with ParaDrop

With the original implementation in the cloud, users of Emonix Air and Emonix H_2O could access the system to view the status and change settings anywhere if they had Internet access. Since the intelligent entities were deployed in the cloud, users did not need to worry about software installations and configurations. However, with ParaDrop, the intelligent entities (chutes) need to be installed into the ParaDrop routers at the user's premise, and they need to be configured correctly. ParaDrop provides an API that developers can use to ask for users' permissions and deploy chutes to users' Wi-Fi APs transparently if the permissions were given.

6   Related Work

Edge Computing. Many researchers have explored the advantages of edge computing and proposed different approaches to using them. Balan et al. proposed cyber foraging: a mechanism to augment the computational and storage capabilities of mobile devices [17]. Satyanarayanan et al. proposed cloudlet, a trusted, resource-rich computer or cluster of computers that is well-connected to the Internet and available for use by nearby mobile devices [35]. Bonomi et al. discussed Fog Computing, which brings data processing, networking, storage and analytics closer to mobile devices [18].

Some applications were built to leverage the advantages of edge computing architecture. MOCHA is a mobile-cloudlet-cloud architecture that partitions tasks from mobile devices to the cloud and distribute compute load among cloud servers (cloudlet) to minimize the response time [36]. Ha et al. describe the architecture and prototype implementation of an assistive system based on Google Glass devices [25]. Zhang et al. built Vigil, a real-time distributed wireless surveillance system that leverage edge computing to support real-time tracking and surveillance in different scenarios [38]. They use very powerful machines to build the cloudlet. However, ParaDrop uses the hardware platform with medium resources because it has different goals. The targeting applications of ParaDrop are those requiring low latency and resource always on and available.

Smart Wi-Fi Routers. As the performance of Wi-Fi routers keeps increasing, many companies are interested in building smart routers that can be managed and monitored with mobile Apps [10,13]. Users can even install third-party applications on some of them [8]. Their goal is to optimize the experience of mobile devices users, whereas ParaDrop's goal is to push services from datacenters to the network edge.

Smart Home Platforms. Other than smart Wi-Fi routers, Companies are building other devices for smart home applications, for example, Amazon Echo [6], Apple HomeKit on Apple TV [14], and Google Home [7]. Companies are trying to build their smart home ecosystems around these smart devices. Unlike these companies trying to build ecosystems, ParaDrop provides a flexible edge computing platform that developers can implement and deploy diverse services at the extreme edge.

Sustainability Applications. Network-connected controllers for residential heating, ventilation, and air conditioning (HVAC) systems have been introduced in various forms. The Nest Learning Thermostat [11] and the Bay Web Thermostat [4] are both commercial examples of so-called "smart thermostats". Unlike Emonix Air, both of these devices use a single point of measurement and a single point of control for the HVAC system without providing fine-grained control on a room-by-room basis.

There are many other pieces of research on smart water systems focusing on reducing water consumption [23,26], optimizing hot water distributions [24,33]. Emonix H_2O addresses issues in a different area—water treatment systems.

7   Conclusion and Future Work

In this paper, we briefly introduce ParaDrop - an edge computing platform built with Wi-Fi routers. ParaDrop provides the framework and tools to deploy intelligent entities at the extreme network edge. Developers can easily migrate services from the cloud to the ParaDrop platform because of the virtualization solution in ParaDrop's implementation. We discuss two types of edge computing applications that can be developed for the ParaDrop platform, and give two concrete example applications for sustainability - Emonix Air and Emonix H_2O. With the ParaDrop platform, developers can deploy the intelligent entities of the systems into users' premise transparently to users. And provide reliable services to users with very low latency. These two example applications show the feasibility to implement both user and developer friendly edge computing applications with ParaDrop.

ParaDrop is still an ongoing research work. We are working on the implementation of ParaDrop on more hardware devices, for example, IoT gateways. And we plan to expose more information to the chutes deployed on the routers, for instance, Wi-Fi signal interferences. More edge computing applications based on ParaDrop are under development, and we will continue polishing the API for developers.

Acknowledgements. All authors are supported in part by the US National Science Foundation through awards CNS-1555426, CNS-1525586, CNS-1405667, CNS-1345293, CNS-1343363, CNS-1629833, and CNS-1647152.

References

1. Carrier infinity zone control. http://www.utcccs-cdn.com/hvac/docs/1010/Public/0A/01-TSTAT-022-25.pdf. Accessed 14 Oct 2016
2. Emonix H_2O. http://www.emonix.io
3. Areas most affected by hard water (2016). https://akwamag.com/areas-most-affected-by-hard-water/
4. Bay web thermostat (2016). http://www.bayweb.com
5. Buildroot making embedded Linux easy (2016). https://buildroot.org/
6. Echo & Echo Dot, Build voice experiences for Echo and Echo Dot with the Alexa skills kit (2016). https://developer.amazon.com/echo
7. Google home (2016). https://madeby.google.com/home/
8. HiWiFi apps (2016). http://www.hiwifi.com/j3-func
9. Linuxcontainers.org: Infrastructure for container projects (2016). https://linuxcontainers.org/
10. Meet OnHub: A new type of router for the new way to Wi-Fi. (2016). https://on.google.com/hub/
11. Nest learning thermostat (2016). https://store.nest.com/product/thermostat/
12. PC Engines apu platform (2016). http://www.pcengines.ch/apu.htm
13. Smart wifi app center (2016). http://www.linksys.com/us/smart_wifi_center
14. The smart home just got smarter (2016). http://www.apple.com/ios/home/
15. Ubuntu for the Internet of Things (2016). https://www.ubuntu.com/internet-of-things
16. WAMP: the web application messaging protocol (2016). https://www.ubuntu.com/internet-of-things
17. Balan, R., Flinn, J., Satyanarayanan, M., Sinnamohideen, S., Yang, H.I.: The case for cyber foraging. In: Proceedings of the 10th Workshop on ACM SIGOPS European Workshop, pp. 87–92. ACM (2002)

18. Bonomi, F., Milito, R., Zhu, J., Addepalli, S.: Fog computing and its role in the Internet of Things. In: Proceedings of the 1st Edition of the MCC Workshop on Mobile Cloud Computing, pp. 13–16. ACM (2012)
19. Choy, S., Wong, B., Simon, G., Rosenberg, C.: The brewing storm in cloud gaming: a measurement study on cloud to end-user latency. In: Proceedings of the 11th Annual Workshop on Network and Systems Support for Games, p. 2. IEEE Press (2012)
20. Dickey, J.: Write modern web apps with the MEAN stack: Mongo, Express, AngularJS, and Node.js. Pearson Education, San Francisco (2014)
21. Dounis, A., Caraiscos, C.: Advanced control systems engineering for energy and comfort management in a building environment a review. Renew. Sustain. Energy Rev. **13**(67), 1246–1261 (2009). http://www.sciencedirect.com/science/article/pii/S1364032108001457
22. Fainelli, F.: The OpenWrt embedded development framework. In: Proceedings of the Free and Open Source Software Developers European Meeting (2008)
23. Froehlich, J.E., Larson, E., Campbell, T., Haggerty, C., Fogarty, J., Patel, S.N.: HydroSense: infrastructure-mediated single-point sensing of whole-home water activity. In: Proceedings of the 11th International Conference on Ubiquitous Computing, pp. 235–244. ACM (2009)
24. Frye, A., Goraczko, M., Liu, J., Prodhan, A., Whitehouse, K.: Circulo: saving energy with just-in-time hot water recirculation. In: Proceedings of the 5th ACM Workshop on Embedded Systems For Energy-Efficient Buildings, pp. 1–8. ACM (2013)
25. Ha, K., Chen, Z., Hu, W., Richter, W., Pillai, P., Satyanarayanan, M.: Towards wearable cognitive assistance. In: Proceedings of the 12th Annual International Conference on Mobile Systems, Applications, and Services, pp. 68–81. ACM (2014)
26. Kim, Y., Schmid, T., Charbiwala, Z.M., Friedman, J., Srivastava, M.B.: NAWMS: Nonintrusive Autonomous Water Monitoring System. In: Proceedings of the 6th ACM Conference on Embedded Network Sensor Systems, pp. 309–322. ACM (2008)
27. Klingensmith, N., Bomber, J., Banerjee, S.: Hot, cold and in between: enabling fine-grained environmental control in homes for efficiency and comfort. In: Proceedings of the 5th International Conference on Future Energy Systems, pp. 123–132. ACM (2014)
28. Klingensmith, N., Sridhar, A., LaVallee, Z., Banerjee, S.: Water or slime? A platform for automating water treatment systems. In: Proceedings of the 2Nd ACM International Conference on Embedded Systems for Energy-Efficient Built Environments, BuildSys 2015, NY, USA, pp. 75–84. ACM, New York (2015). http://doi.acm.org/10.1145/2821650.2821652
29. Klingensmith, N., Willis, D., Banerjee, S.: A distributed energy monitoring and analytics platform and its use cases. In: Proceedings of the 5th ACM Workshop on Embedded Systems For Energy-Efficient Buildings, BuildSys 2013, NY, USA, pp. 36:1–36:2. ACM, New York (2013). http://doi.acm.org/10.1145/2528282.2534156
30. Liu, P., Willis, D., Banerjee, S.: ParaDrop: enabling lightweight multi-tenancy at the networks extreme edge. In: Proceedings of The First IEEE/ACM Symposium on Edge Computing. IEEE (2016)
31. Merkel, D.: Docker: lightweight Linux containers for consistent development and deployment. Linux J. **2014**(239), 2 (2014)
32. Newman, S.: Building Microservices. O'Reilly Media, Inc., Sebastopol (2015)
33. Prodhan, M.A., Whitehouse, K.: Hot water DJ: saving energy by pre-mixing hot water. In: Proceedings of the Fourth ACM Workshop on Embedded Sensing Systems for Energy-Efficiency in Buildings, pp. 91–98. ACM (2012)

34. Salvador, O., Angolini, D.: Embedded Linux Development with Yocto Project. Packt Publishing Ltd., Birmingham (2014)
35. Satyanarayanan, M., Bahl, P., Caceres, R., Davies, N.: The case for VM-based cloudlets in mobile computing. IEEE Pervasive Comput. **8**(4), 14–23 (2009)
36. Soyata, T., Muraleedharan, R., Funai, C., Kwon, M., Heinzelman, W.: Cloud-vision: real-time face recognition using a mobile-cloudlet-cloud acceleration architecture. In: 2012 IEEE Symposium on Computers and Communications (ISCC), pp. 000059–000066. IEEE (2012)
37. Willis, D., Dasgupta, A., Banerjee, S.: ParaDrop: a multi-tenant platform to dynamically install third party services on wireless gateways. In: Proceedings of the 9th ACM Workshop on Mobility in the Evolving Internet Architecture, pp. 43–48. ACM (2014)
38. Zhang, T., Chowdhery, A., Bahl, P.V., Jamieson, K., Banerjee, S.: The design and implementation of a wireless video surveillance system. In: Proceedings of the 21st Annual International Conference on Mobile Computing and Networking, pp. 426–438. ACM (2015)
39. Zhao, P., Suryanarayanan, S., Simoes, M.G.: An energy management system for building structures using a multi-agent decision-making control methodology. IEEE Trans. Ind. Appl. **49**(1), 322–330 (2013)

Unleashing the Potential of Data-Driven Networking

Junchen Jiang[1(✉)], Vyas Sekar[1], Ion Stoica[2,3,4], and Hui Zhang[1,3]

[1] CMU, Pittsburgh, USA
junchenj@cs.cmu.edu
[2] UC Berkeley, Berkeley, USA
[3] Conviva, New York City, USA
[4] Databricks, San Francisco, USA

Abstract. The last few years have witnessed the coming of age of data-driven paradigm in various aspects of computing (partly) empowered by advances in distributed system research (cloud computing, MapReduce, etc.). In this paper, we observe that the benefits can flow the opposite direction: the design and management of networked systems can be improved by data-driven paradigm. To this end, we present DDN, a new design framework for network protocols based on data-driven paradigm. We argue that DDN has the potential to significantly achieve better performance through harnessing more data than one single flow. Furthermore, we systematize existing instantiations of DDN by creating a unified framework for DDN, and use the framework to shed light on the common challenges and reusable design principles. We believe that by systematizing this paradigm as a broader community, we can unleash the unharnessed potential of DDN.

1   Introduction

Ask not what networking can do for data;
Ask what data can do for networking!

Most networked applications require some form of control and adaptation logic to respond to changing network conditions. Traditionally, such control and adaptation strategies in application and transport protocols have come to rely on a *per-session*[1] *view* and using *manually designed* strategies. For instance, TCP congestion control relies on many human-picked constants (e.g., init_cwnd, AIMD parameters) and is driven by feedback (e.g., acks, ECN) observed within the current flow. In some sense, this de-facto design template has been passed down across generations of designers as a form of conventional wisdom drawn from lessons (e.g., end-to-end principles [50], congestion collapse [28]) from the early days of the Internet.

---

[1] A session could be an application session (e.g., video session, web session), or a transport session (e.g., TCP session).

© Springer International Publishing AG 2017
N. Sastry and S. Chakraborty (Eds.): COMSNETS 2017, LNCS 10340, pp. 110–126, 2017.
DOI: 10.1007/978-3-319-67235-9_9

While this conventional wisdom has indeed served us well for decades, today we face a confluence of use case "pulls" that increasingly make such approaches ineffective:

- First, we see *growing expectations* of user-perceived Quality of Experience (QoE) [31]. Thus, conventional approaches that worked well for a "best effort" mentality are no longer good enough!
- Second, we observe a *growing decision space* of potential control decisions to optimize application quality. Consequently, trial-and-error strategies driven by single-session feedback are fundamentally inefficient and slow in exploring the decision space and reacting to changes. For instance, it takes a video player several chunks (roughly 10 s of seconds) to converge to an optimal combination of CDN and bitrate [7].
- Third, we see an *increasing heterogeneity* in operating conditions, each requiring different control logic and parameters. For instance, TCP parameters such as initial congestion window and AIMD parameters could be tweaked to work better in different operating conditions [20,57].

Tackling these challenges requires us to radically rethink the design of the control plane of network protocols. In this context, we observe an opportunity for a new paradigm, which we refer to as *Data-Driven Networking or DDN*, inspired in part by the successes in other aspects of computing driven by the ability to collect and extract insights from large corpus of data [16,25]. DDN transforms the design of the "control plane" of network protocols by the availability of massive data from millions of endpoints and devices. This is orthogonal to recent efforts to optimize the "data planes", such as ICN [29]. More specifically, a DDN-based control loop is driven by real-time *multi-session* (not single-session) view of *in-situ quality* [23] measurement (not active measurements or indirect metrics), and *automatically* tuned actuation algorithms based on data-driven insights with little to no manual tuning. For instance, to apply the concept of DDN to optimize quality for video streaming, one can think of a controller that takes as input the quality measurements of millions concurrent and history video clients, and use such data to automatically learn the best configuration such as server/CDN/cache, bitrate, and network path for each client.

In parallel to the use-case pulls described above, we also observe that DDN fortuitously has key technology "pushes" that are suitably aligned. Specifically, many application providers today have widely deployed client-side instrumentation to collect real-time performance data [23], and "big data" processing capabilities are finally a reality [6].

We are already seeing point evidence of this paradigm shift starting to reach the shores of many networked applications. This includes work in optimizing Internet video streaming (e.g., [24,32]), Internet telephony (e.g., [30]), cloud service availability (e.g., [39]), data center scheduling (e.g., [56]), congestion control (e.g., [18,51,57]), and network management (e.g., [15]), as well as industrial initiatives (e.g., [2,8]).

To fully unleash the potential of DDN, however, we identify key challenges spanning a wide spectrum: (1) algorithms and machine learning (e.g., tackling high dimensionality, data sparsity, and exploration-exploitation trade-offs), (2) system design (e.g., balancing scalability, responsiveness and stale-ness), and (3) broader architectural questions (e.g., stability and interactions with other possibly competing control loops). Unfortunately, the aforementioned early DDN efforts suffer fundamental shortcomings that ultimately undermines the full potential of this paradigm:

- First, each of these efforts offers point solutions tackling a small subset of DDN challenges (tied to specific workload assumptions) and as such does not focus on *generalizable* algorithmic or system-design insights for future DDN-based deployments. For instance, can these primitives (e.g., quality-determining features learned by CFA [32] + split control plane from C3 [24] + exploration-exploration strategy from VIA [30]) be composed and if so how? Are these missing any hidden aspects; e.g., how to ensure control stability or handle flash crowds?
- Second, they present techniques under application-specific assumptions and it is unclear if, why, and by how much they could benefit other applications. For instance, CFA assumes that video quality-determining features are persistent, while VIA assumes that VoIP quality distribution between the same source and destination ASes depends only on relay servers, and it is not obvious if these are necessary or sufficient, or how much the benefit would be if we relax these assumptions.

Rather than develop yet-another point solution to a narrow application, this paper takes a *first-principles* approach to help democratize the potential benefits of the DDN paradigm to a broader spectrum of use cases. To that end, this paper makes two contributions:

1. **Formalizing DDN (Sect. 2).** We define key features that distance DDN from alternatives, provide illustrative examples of when DDN benefits, and generalize the design space as well as the use cases of DDN.
2. **Common building blocks (Sect. 3).** We sketch a common platform for socializing the benefits of DDN by developing key building blocks. We artic-ulate four high-level technical challenges, which are still open: how to extrap-olate potential benefits of DDN, infer optimal decisions with sparse data, implement real-time feedback loops at scale, and stabilize DDN control behav-iors. We also see an opportunity of adapting abstractions and techniques from machine learning and control theory, and we offer promising prescrip-tive roadmap to address the challenges.

2   Formalizing DDN

In this section, we give a conceptual overview of DDN, contrasting it to tradi-tional approaches. We present early evidence from prior work on the case for DDN. We end this section by identifying key factors that can impact the poten-tial benefits of DDN.

2.1   What Is DDN?

DDN is a new paradigm for designing the control plane of network protocols. It consists of two components: (a) the *client-side instrumentation* integrates with the client-side application[2] to measure client-perceived quality and apply decisions made by DDN; and (b) the *DDN controller* runs two loosely coupled steps:

1. Aggregate quality measurement from client-side instrumentation into a *multi-session view* – a representation for summarizing the performance of similar sessions.
2. Make control decisions based on the multi-session views, and send them to client-side instrumentation.

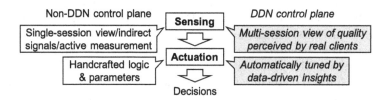

Fig. 1. DDN control plane is fundamentally different to non-DDN ones on both sensing and actuation.

To understand the contrast between DDN and traditional control planes, it is useful to revisit the two logical steps in the workflow of *any* control plane (Fig. 1): *sensing*, which gives the feedback data to control plane, and *actuation*, which turns the feedback data to control decisions. DDN radically departs from non-DDN designs on both fronts with three definitive features. (Table 1 provides some examples to contrast between DDN and non-DDN designs.)

- **Multi-session view:** Sensing of DDN is based on multiple sessions, rather than single session. By extending the spatial scope of sensing to many sessions, DDN can predict the quality of a decision even before a session actually uses it, as long as the decision has been used by some similar sessions.
- **In-situ quality:** In DDN, what to be "sensed" is exactly what to be optimized, i.e., quality perceived by all historical and ongoing sessions; not indirect signals on quality (e.g., acks [28] or bandwidth [37]), or active probes from a handful of vantage points (e.g., iPlane [42]). While in-situ quality data may compromise on the fidelity of individual measurement, they are far more efficient than alternatives in obtaining a panoramic and representative view of client-perceived quality from growingly diverse platforms [23]. Relying solely on in-situ quality data also serves pragmatic purposes as many application providers today already have a vested interest in measuring user-perceived quality for various reasons [1,36,40].

---

[2] We use "client" to denote where a session is actually run.

Table 1. Difference of DDN to non-DDN strategies.

	Sensing		Actuation
	Multi-session	In-situ quality	Auto-tuned
DDN	✓	✓	✓
TCP AIMD [28]	×	×	×
PCC [18]	×	✓	✓
OSPF, BwE [37]	✓	×	×
iPlane [42]	✓	×	NA
RemyCC [57]	×	×	✓

– **Automatically tuned control logic:** To take full advantage of the enriched sensing data, actuation algorithms of DDN should be dynamically tuned by data-driven insights with little to no manual configuration. Unlike today's protocols where handpicked constants are used as key parameters (e.g., init_cwnd and initial video bitrate), DDN picks parameters [57] and control logic [54] based on quality feedback which indicates what suit the current operating condition the best. Meanwhile, the DDN control logic also needs to handle the *downside* of having more data (e.g., lack of fidelity in client-side measurement, and whether the data source is trustworthy) by harnessing the "unreasonable effectiveness of data" [25].

2.2 Early Promise of DDN

Several early applications of DDN from prior work have shown tremendous promise of this new paradigm. They showcase how DDN can be adapted to various use cases to exploit their potential benefits (depicted in Fig. 2).

CDN/bitrate selection for video: The first example shows how a global view of video quality can optimize CDN and bitrate selection for individual video sessions. Video players today have the flexibility of streaming content from one of multiple CDNs and bitrates. However, with only information on a single session, the current protocols always start with a default CDN and fixed (and conservative) bitrate, and gradually converge to a better bitrate and CDN by local trial-and-error strategies. Given both performance of CDNs and client-side bandwidth have a substantial spatial diversity and temporal variability [40], there is a remarkable room for improvement by dynamically mapping a session to the optimal CDN and bitrate with no trial-and-errors. Prior work [24,32,54] exploits this opportunity by mapping a video session to the CDN and bitrate that has the best quality on similar sessions (e.g., those in the same AS and watching the same video content); and it can reduce the session duration spent on re-buffering by 50% without lowering bitrates.

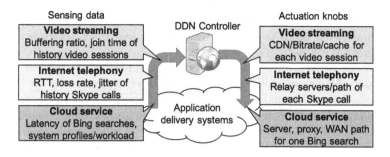

Fig. 2. Examples of DDN from prior work.

Relay selection for Internet telephony: The second example shows how VoIP quality can be improved by a controller that selects relay servers judiciously. VoIP applications (e.g., Hangout and Skype) use relay servers for NAT traversal, where the selection of relay servers has traditionally been agnostic to real-time network conditions. But recent work has shown a substantial room for improvement on call quality by selecting optimal relay servers for each call [26]. For instance, recent work [30] shows that one can select near-optimal relay servers for individual Skype calls by identifying which relay has the best quality for similar calls (e.g., those between the same source and destination ASes on the same date); compared to non-relayed paths, this can alleviate 42% of Skype calls whose quality is impacted by high packet loss rate (>1.2%).

Online service cluster selection: The last example shows how the quality of online services (e.g., search engines) can be improved by a centralized control platform, which selects optimal proxies by consolidating quality data of multiple applications and profiles of the infrastructure. Recent work [39] takes the stance of a company who has the visibility and controllability over multiple applications as well as key infrastructure building blocks. By measuring end-to-end quality from clients and dynamically modeling the workload of network paths and servers, it can select proxies that reduce mean latency by 60% and carry 2× more traffic, compared with a baseline that finds proxies by Anycast.

2.3   When Is DDN Beneficial?

A natural question that these case studies raise is the following: When is DDN beneficial? That is, what properties of an application allow it to benefit significantly from DDN. Drawing from this prior work, we highlight key features that impact the potential reward of using DDN.

- **Heterogeneity of decision space:** DDN has great room for improvement, when (1) the quality of each decision has substantial spatial diversity or temporal variability (e.g., same Skype relay cluster has significantly different performance depending on where the caller and callee are and when the call happens [30]); (2) the decision space is fine-grained (e.g., server selection has more room for improvement on video quality than CDN selection [24]); and (3) each decision needs to be probed separately (e.g., each server is reached by different WAN path [39]).

- **Usefulness of feedback data:** How useful the feedback data is in driving DDN control logic depends on whether there are enough sessions for DDN to reliably estimate the quality of candidate decisions. This happens when we have enough data to gain statistical significance and/or measurement noise is low. For instance, network latency naturally is more stable than packet loss rate, so less sessions are needed to find the server with low latency than needed to find the server with low loss rate.

- **Tail vs. median performance:** One of the key takeaways from prior work is that DDN has greater benefits on the tail than on the median, possibly because most applications have been heavily optimized for the "common" clients. For instance, the median buffering ratio (fraction of time spent on buffering per session) of most video providers is zero, while at least 10% sessions suffer from high (>1%) buffering ratio. It is worth noting that the sessions on the tail are not widely scattered; rather they often represent some groups of users (e.g., from the same small ASes [32]), which makes tail improvement more relevant and critical.

Example of new use case: Now, we apply these features to a new use case where DDN is expected to have a great advantage. Crowdsourced live streaming [5,9] faces not only the challenges of traditional live streaming, but low delay for interactivity and the need to multicast from any user at any time. It makes a perfect case for DDN, because it has (1) a heterogeneous decision space: performance of different caches and codec servers varies significant across viewers and sources and over time [14]; and (2) useful feedback data: a streaming event typically has over hundreds of viewers, which can be used to explore various decisions.

3   Key Challenges and Opportunities

In this section, we articulate four high-level challenges that are key to unleashing the full potential of DDN. For a provider, the fundamental questions are: (1) how much will I actually benefit from DDN; (2) are there existing algorithms; (3) how to build the system at scale; and (4) how will it interact with other parts of the Internet. For each challenge, we identify *opportunities* to address them using techniques from machine learning and control theory (Table 2). However, we also observe that it is not a straightforward application of existing techniques from these communities and it requires care to adapt them to handle network- and domain-specific issues (e.g., load effects) as well as to exploit domain-specific opportunities to enable simple-yet-effective designs.

In the interest of clarity, we focus on a specific DDN design point (as in [24, 30, 32]): single-provider, logically centralized, with control logic updated in real time. However, these challenges and opportunities manifest themselves in other forms of DDN as well (Sect. 4.1).

Table 2. Summary of key challenges and opportunities

Challenges	Opportunities
What-if analysis	Doubly robust estimator [19]
High dimensionality vs. data sparsity	Contextual multi-armed bandit [41]
Scale, responsiveness vs. data freshness	Regressograms and localized control logic [49]
Control stability	Benevolent feedback delay [12]

3.1 "What-If" Analysis

Problem statement: The first question for any application provider (e.g., Netflix) is that before implementing DDN, "can I quantify how much DDN would actually improve my application's quality (e.g., video quality)?"

Limitations of strawmen: Simulation is known to be unrealistic for evaluating wide-area network performance [22]. Small-scale emulation (e.g., Emulab [3]) is more realistic, but lacks the scale needed to reveal the real benefits of DDN. Finally, A/B tests may be used but require that each DDN strategy be evaluated on substantial amount of real clients, which application providers are often reluctant to do [36].

Now, the fact that application providers today have already collected massive amount of quality measurements opens an opportunity for data-driven evaluation, also known as *off-policy evaluation* [44]: given the quality of many sessions whose decisions were driven by some control logic, can we evaluate the quality of a different control logic? This is, however, not straightforward and simple solutions may have either *bias* (due to hidden factors) or high *variance* (when data is too sparse) or both. Suppose the dataset was collected by assigning wireless users to Akamai and cable users to Limelight, any method will falsely claim Akamai has worse quality than Limelight, if the last-mile connection is hidden.

These are not merely theoretical concerns; Fig. 3 shows how these manifest in real-world datasets for some seemingly natural solutions. We use a dataset of video quality in four ASes. For each AS, we randomly split it into two subsets, and show the difference between the actual quality of one subset and the extrapolation made by two standard off-policy evaluation methods based on the other subset. On one hand, the direct method (e.g., [35]) has low variance, but is vulnerable to bias of hidden features. The inverse propensity score (IPS) (e.g., used in [32,38]), on the other hand, focuses on the sessions for which DDN makes the same decision as in the dataset, so we know their actual quality, but IPS has high variance when such overlapping is rare. As shown in Fig. 3, we see that both direct method and IPS suffer from high evaluation error, due to high bias or variance. Furthermore, it is not easy to check when and where these will fail (e.g., existence of hidden features cannot be easily verified).

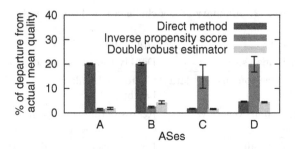

Fig. 3. Strawman data-driven evaluation methods have significant evaluation error. Direct method is biased by hidden features (AS A and B), and IPS method has high variance with sparse data (AS C and D). In contrast, the DR estimator achieves the best of two methods.

Opportunity: Doubly robust estimator. A promising alternative is the recently proposed *doubly robust* (DR) estimator [13,19], which combines the best of the direct and IPS methods described above. It is unbiased and has low variance, when *either* we know all confounding factors (i.e., suitable for direct method) *or* DDN makes overlapping decisions with the dataset on many sessions (i.e., suitable for IPS). More importantly, we do not need to explicitly know when and which assumption holds, and thus it naturally achieves the best of two methods (e.g., as shown in Fig. 3).

While the DR estimator is a promising starting point for reliable data-driven evaluation, there are network-specific factors it does not consider. For instance, the DR estimator will not identify quality degradation due to server overload, if such overload never happens in the dataset. This can be handled by simple techniques (e.g., a load-dependent discount).

3.2   High Dimensionality vs. Data Sparsity

Problem statement: In many use cases of DDN, we see *high-dimensional* relationships between session features and quality. The problem with such high dimensional structures is a classic curse of dimensionality. On one hand, as we combine many features, we will intrinsically have a *limited* number of sessions to infer the best decisions. On the other hand, as quality measurement could be different across similar sessions due to intrinsic noise [43], we will need as many sessions as possible to achieve enough statistical confidence. For instance, video quality is impacted by combinational effect; e.g., bad quality happens for a specific ISP-city-CDN combination [32]. Suppose there are 100 ISPs, 1000 cities, then probing 10 CDNs, each with only one session, requires one million sessions, which is more than what ESPN has per hour (418M/month [4]).

Table 3 shows how such data sparsity manifests in three large video providers, under even a simple model. We assume their sessions are evenly spread over time and from all US cities in proportion to the population of each city [10]. We see

Table 3. Data sparsity manifest in even large application providers. A large fraction (highlighted) of sessions has 10 or less neighboring sessions in the same city every minute.

	US sessions Sept 2012 [11]	% cities with 10 or less sessions/minute	% sessions in these cities
Netflix	382M	99%	76.6%
Hulu	694M	98%	65.2%
YouTube	16B	83%	11.8%
YouTube (Illinois)	973M	90%	22.6%

that most cities have even less than 10 sessions per minute, and the sessions from these cities amount to a significant fraction (highlighted column), which suggests that failing to handle this issue would render DDN ineffective for a large portion of users.

Limitations of strawmen: Prior work has attempted to bridge the gap between high dimensionality and data sparsity, but it is unclear whether these solutions or application-specific insights can be generalized. One approach (e.g., [32]) identifies enough similar sessions to predict the quality of one single decision by focusing on critical features, but this does not always provide enough sessions to explore a large decision space where *each* decision needs to be predicted with enough sessions. Another approach (e.g., [30]) seeks to reduce the decision space, which may not be generalizable to where data sparsity results from skewed session distributions and high dimensional models (e.g., video streaming).

Opportunity: Contextual multi-armed bandits: We see an opportunity of casting DDN control logic as a *contextual multi-armed bandits* (CMAB) problem in machine learning [41]. CMAB techniques face a very similar setting to DDN; it needs to balance exploration and exploitation under sparse data and potentially complex reward function, which in our case, is the hidden function that determines application quality of a pair of session and decision (or "context").

However, CMAB techniques are no panacea, especially in a networking context. They often make too strict assumptions about the reward function; e.g., similar contexts always yield similar rewards [53], but in network applications, two sessions, who match on all feature except one, can still have very different network performance. They also assume that the reward function is fixed, but in network applications, sending too many sessions to the same resource can cause overload and congestion, thus altering the reward function.

We conjecture that CMAB techniques can be adapted with insights from prior work of DDN and standard networking techniques. For instance, instead of using generic similarity metrics, DDN can define similarity between video sessions by whether they match on critical features [32].

3.3   Scale, Responsiveness and Freshness

Problem statement: DDN raises challenges on the algorithmic front, as well as the architectural front. Even with a desirable CMAB algorithm, we still need an architecture for DDN controller that is *scalable* (i.e., scale to tens of millions of concurrent sessions per second [11]), *responsive* (i.e., respond to every client request within at most tens of milliseconds [24]), and able to make decisions based on *fresh* data. The required data freshness depends on how long a client can tolerate a suboptimal decision before DDN reacts, which, depending on application, is typically on the scale of seconds (e.g., live video has a buffer of 5–10 s).

Limitations of strawmen: From a pragmatic view, since application providers often store client provided data in widely distributed front-end clusters [45], a pure centralized controller (e.g., [16]) that gathers data to a central cluster is not favorable for DDN in most cases. A split control architecture (e.g., [24]) is the most promising strawman. It essentially trades data freshness for scalability and responsiveness, assuming that only single-session view has to be fresh while the multi-session view can tolerate several minutes of staleness. It is a reasonable tradeoff under stable workload where best decisions do not change so often, but during sudden events such as flash crowd, it will (temporarily) fall back to traditional local adaptation, at exactly the time when multi-session view is needed the most to spot the optimal decisions and maintain desirable quality and stability. Finally, recent work on distributed analytics studies a closely related problem, but it assumes either that data can be efficiently gathered to where the analytics happens [46] or that analytics results per cluster can be efficiently collected during the analytics [45]. Both assumptions are not (at least obviously) plausible, given millions of updates and requests that DDN needs to handle at scale. In short, we see a CAP-like conjecture that it is hard for DDN to simultaneously achieve scalability, responsiveness and data freshness. Thus, a tradeoff is needed, but what is a "good" tradeoff?

Opportunity: Regressograms. The key to strike a good tradeoff is the *scale of aggregation* in which DDN control loop must be real-time. Our insight, built on the machine learning concept of *regressogram* [49], is that the decision-making of a session depends only on a small group of "similar" sessions (e.g., the best server of a session can be inferred by just looking at "neighboring" sessions who use same WAN path to each server), and each group is much smaller than the global view but large enough to avoid data sparsity. Now, if all operations (data collection, storage, and control logic) for a group are *localized* to one front-end cluster close to the sessions in the group, we will simultaneously achieve scalability, responsiveness, and limited yet *sufficient* data freshness.

The idea of regressogram can be implemented on top of existing systems [24] with two changes: (a) a learning algorithm run by the backend cluster to periodically partition sessions into groups on a relatively coarse timescale; and (b) a redirection service that forwards the updates and requests of the same group to the same frontend cluster. The resulting architecture is similar to Social Hash [52] used in social networks to optimize hit rate of data retrieval. More broadly, we see a natural *synergy* between the algorithmic and architectural aspects of DDN, and the potential of a joint design for DDN controller.

3.4   Control Stability

Problem statement: As in other time-delayed control systems [48], *feedback delay* will cause unstable behaviors in DDN, which negatively impact quality. Figure 4 uses trace-driven simulation to show how feedback delay coupled with load effect leads to oscillations. We consider two CDNs whose quality is extrapolated by real-world dataset and will degrade when overloaded [40]. Suppose DDN initially assigns most sessions to CDN1 and, due to feedback delay, DDN will react only after CDN1 is overloaded, and then switch sessions to CDN2, which again will be overloaded before DDN reacts, causing self-inflicted flash crowds and oscillations. Note that simple tricks like setting cap per CDN does not help, because DDN cannot identify if quality degradation is caused by its own decisions or not. Many causes can trigger this pathological phenomenon; e.g., when sessions arrive as flash crowd, and when multiple DDN instances run by different applications [31] or network layers [27,33] simultaneously shift traffic between resources.

Though stability has been studied in many traditional network systems (e.g., [21,47]), control stability has rarely been systematically studied in prior work of DDN.

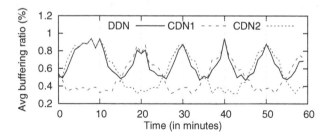

Fig. 4. Unstable control due to feedback delay. DDN observes degraded quality only after the CDN is overloaded (at each gray line), and oscillates between two CDNs.

Opportunity: "Benevolent" feedback delay. While the feedback delay in DDN is inevitable (e.g., to reliably measure packet loss rate at least takes several seconds), it is still possible to achieve stability despite of the feedback delay. One of the findings in control theory is that introducing positive random delay could sometimes *benefit* stability [12], which has found its early applications in network settings (e.g., [33]). We postulate that similar techniques can also help to stabilize DDN. Finally, to react to flash crowd in real time, DDN can "bypass" the quality measurement delay by simply monitoring the global workload (e.g., how many sessions are from each city) and available resources (e.g., how many sessions a CDN can handle).

4   Discussion

We end the paper by generalizing DDN design space, and revisiting epidemic problems in other DDN-like systems, such as single point of failure and data-driven bias.

4.1   Generalizing DDN Design Space

The earlier examples of DDN in Sect. 2.2 follow a specific deployment model: a logically centralized architecture within a single application provider (i.e., the data source and control system are in the same administrative entity). Now, we broaden the design space along two dimensions.

Degree of federation: Besides the single-provider model that we have seen, DDN can also be applied to a federated environment, where the DDN controller consolidates quality of sessions from different providers of the same application (e.g., small video sites use quality of YouTube sessions) or even of different applications or services (e.g., video providers informed by a CDN's internal server selection strategy [31]). Though DDN might benefit from having more data sources, it is not always feasible for application providers to share data with necessary fidelity or freshness. An exception, however, is where one company owns multiple applications and can effectively build a federated DDN within its borders [39]; e.g., Microsoft can use Bing query latency to infer WAN performance and optimize relay selection for Skype.

Degree of centralization: DDN controller can take a spectrum of degrees of centralization, spanning from physically centralized (i.e., in a single backend cluster), logically centralized (i.e., in globally distributed clusters with control logic driven by a potentially global view [24]), partially decentralized (i.e., in globally distributed clusters with control logic driven by a partial view of a subset of sessions, such as per edge AS [51]), as well as purely decentralized (e.g., each client runs a local control logic that can be updated based on a multi-session view on a coarse timescale [54]).

The challenges and opportunities outlined in Sect. 3 also manifest themselves in these design points to various degrees. What-if analysis in federated DDN is still challenging, but with more insights from other providers, the DR estimator might have fewer hidden features and less modeling bias. With more visibility and controllability, centralized and federated designs of DDN have less data sparsity and are relatively easier to be stabilized [40], but it will be more challenging for them to scale up and use fresh data. In addition, the control logic of federated DDN, like in any federated systems, must tolerate the uncertainties such as noise and error in the data shared by other providers [15,31].

4.2   Open Issues

Fault tolerance: In a logically centralized architecture, the DDN controller becomes a single point of failure. First, it is plausible that clients can (possibly unintentionally) launch a DDoS attack on the DDN backend by flooding control requests or quality updates. To address it, we can borrow from techniques of other centralized control platforms (e.g., SDN [34]). Second, a client may loose connection with the DDN controller due to firewall. Note that putting the controller in a highly available cloud will not address this issue. A promising alternative is the DDN client-side instrumentation automatically falls back to the control logic built into the client-side application (e.g., local bitrate adaptation of video players [24]) to achieve graceful quality degradation.

Algorithmic bias: Like any data-driven decision-making systems, DDN may suffer from algorithmic bias. To optimize the overall quality, DDN may use a small ISP, whose sessions have small room for improvement, to explore suboptimal decisions, while allowing Comcast clients to exploit the optimal decisions, because they have greater room for improvement or simply because they have paid, which leads to a *reverse* network neutrality violation, where application providers discriminate ISPs! Preventing such bias is hard as data-driven algorithms are often "black box". These pitfalls make one wonder whether DDN will systematically hurt part of users. Fortunately, security and machine learning communities have started to shed light on these issues (e.g., [17,55]), which could inspire ideas to prevent bias in DDN.

Acknowledgments. This research is supported in part by NSF award CNS-1345305 and NSF CISE Expeditions Award CCF-1139158, DOE Award SN10040 DE-SC0012463, and DARPA XData Award FA8750-12-2-0331, and gifts from Amazon Web Services, Google, IBM, SAP, The Thomas and Stacey Siebel Foundation, Adatao, Adobe, Apple Inc., Blue Goji, Bosch, Cisco, Cray, Cloudera, Ericsson, Facebook, Fujitsu, Guavus, HP, Huawei, Intel, Microsoft, Pivotal, Samsung, Schlumberger, Splunk, State Farm, Virdata and VMware. Junchen Jiang was supported in part by Juniper Networks Fellowship.

References

1. ACM SIGCOMM Workshop on QoE-Based Analysis and Management of Data Communication Networks (Internet-QoE 2016). http://conferences.sigcomm.org/sigcomm/2016/qoe.php
2. Bringing Data-Driven SDN to the Network Edge. https://www.sdxcentral.com/articles/contributed/network-edge-bringing-data-driven-sdn-to-the-network-edge-nick-kephart/2015/03/
3. Emulab. https://www.emulab.net/
4. ESPN, Inc., Fact Sheet. http://espnmediazone.com/us/espn-inc-fact-sheet/
5. Periscope. https://www.periscope.tv/
6. Spark. http://spark.incubator.apache.org/
7. Technical note on the CFA algorithm. https://www.cs.cmu.edu/dda_technote.pdf
8. The Data-Driven Approach to Network Management: Innovation Delivered. http://www.research.att.com/articles/featured_stories/2010_05/201005_networkmain2_article.html
9. Twitch.tv. https://www.twitch.tv/
10. US Census: City and Town Totals. http://www.census.gov/popest/data/cities/totals/2015/files/SUB-EST2015_ALL.csv

11. U.S. online video platforms in September 2012. http://www.statista.com/statistics/271607/video-platforms-in-the-us-by-number-of-video-streams/
12. Abdallah, C.T., Byrne, R., Benites-Read, J., Dorato, P.: Delayed positive feedback can stabilize oscillatory systems. In: Proceedings of ACC (American control conference) (1993)
13. Agarwal, A., Bird, S., Cozowicz, M., Hoang, L., Langford, J., Lee, S., Li, J., Melamed, D., Oshri, G., Ribas, O., et al.: A multiworld testing decision service. arXiv preprint arXiv:1606.03966 (2016)
14. Chen, F., Zhang, C., Wang, F., Liu, J.: Crowdsourced live streaming over the cloud. In: INFOCOM (2015)
15. Clark, D.D., Partridge, C., Ramming, J.C., Wroclawski, J.T.: A knowledge plane for the internet. In: ACM SIGCOMM 2003
16. Crankshaw, D., Bailis, P., Gonzalez, J.E., Li, H., Zhang, Z., Franklin, M.J., Ghodsi, A., Jordan, M.I.: The missing piece in complex analytics: low latency, scalable model management and serving with velox. In: Conference on Innovative Data Systems Research (CIDR) (2015)
17. Datta, A., Sen, S., Zick, Y.: Algorithmic transparency via quantitative input influence. In: Proceedings of 37th IEEE Symposium on Security and Privacy (2016)
18. Dong, M., Li, Q., Zarchy, D., Godfrey, P.B., Schapira, M.: PCC: re-architecting congestion control for consistent high performance. In: Proceedings of NSDI (2015)
19. Dudík, M., Langford, J., Li, L.: Doubly robust policy evaluation and learning. In: Proceedings of International Conference on Machine Learning (2011)
20. Dukkipati, N., Refice, T., Cheng, Y., Chu, J., Herbert, T., Agarwal, A., Jain, A., Sutin, N.: An argument for increasing TCP's initial congestion window. ACM SIGCOMM CCR **40**, 27–33 (2010)
21. Floyd, S., Jacobson, V.: Random early detection gateways for congestion avoidance. IEEE/ACM Trans. Netw. **1**(4), 397–413 (1993)
22. Floyd, S., Paxson, V.: Difficulties in simulating the internet. IEEE/ACM Trans. Netw. (ToN) **9**(4), 392–403 (2001)
23. Ganjam, A., Sekar, V., Zhang, H.: In-situ quality of experience monitoring: the case for prioritizing coverage over fidelity
24. Ganjam, A., Siddiqi, F., Zhan, J., Stoica, I., Jiang, J., Sekar, V., Zhang, H.: C3: internet-scale control plane for video quality optimization. In: NSDI. USENIX (2015)
25. Halevy, A., Norvig, P., Pereira, F.: The unreasonable effectiveness of data. IEEE Intell. Syst. **24**(2), 8–12 (2009)
26. Haq, O., Dogar, F.R.: Leveraging the power of cloud for reliable wide area communication. In: ACM Workshop on Hot Topics in Networks (2015)
27. Huang, T.-Y., Handigol, N., Heller, B., McKeown, N., Johari, R.: Confused, timid, and unstable: picking a video streaming rate is hard. In: Proceedings of SIGCOMM IMC (2012)
28. Jacobson, V.: Congestion avoidance and control. ACM SIGCOMM Comput. Commun. Rev. **18**, 314–329 (1988). ACM
29. Jacobson, V., Smetters, D.K., Thornton, J.D., Plass, M.F., Briggs, N.H., Braynard, R.L.: Networking named content. In: Proceedings of CoNext (2009)
30. Jiang, J., Das, R., Anathanarayanan, G., Chou, P., Padmanabhan, V., Sekar, V., Dominique, E., Goliszewski, M., Kukoleca, D., Vafin, R., Zhang, H.: VIA: improving internet telephony call quality using predictive relay selection. To Appear in Proceedings of SIGCOMM (2016)
31. Jiang, J., Liu, X., Sekar, V., Stoica, I., Zhang, H.: EONA: Experience-Oriented Network Architecture. In: ACM HotNets (2014)

32. Jiang, J., Sekar, V., Milner, H., Shepherd, D., Stoica, I., Zhang, H.: CFA: a practical prediction system for video QoE optimization. In Proceedings of NSDI (2016)
33. Jiang, J., Sekar, V., Zhang, H.: Improving fairness, efficiency, and stability in HTTP-based adaptive streaming with festive. In: ACM CoNEXT 2012
34. Kandoi, R., Antikainen, M.: Denial-of-service attacks in OpenFlow SDN networks. In: 2015 IFIP/IEEE International Symposium on Integrated Network Management (IM), pp. 1322-1326. IEEE (2015)
35. Krishnan, S., Sitaraman, R.: Video stream quality impacts viewer behavior: inferring causality using quasi-experimental designs (2012)
36. Krishnan, S.S., Sitaraman, R.K.: Video stream quality impacts viewer behavior: inferring causality using quasi-experimental designs. IEEE/ACM Trans. Netw. **21**(6), 2001-2014 (2013)
37. Kumar, A., Jain, S., Naik, U., Raghuraman, A., Kasinadhuni, N., Zermeno, E.C., Gunn, C.S., Ai, J., Carlin, B., Amarandei-Stavila, M., et al.: BwE: flexible, hierarchical bandwidth allocation for WAN distributed computing. In: Proceedings of SIGCOMM (2015)
38. Li, L., Chu, W., Langford, J., Schapire, R.E.: A contextual-bandit approach to personalized news article recommendation. In: Proceedings of the 19th International Conference on World Wide Web, pp. 661-670. ACM (2010)
39. Liu, H.H., Viswanathan, R., Calder, M., Akella, A., Mahajan, R., Padhye, J., Zhang, M.: Efficiently delivering online services over integrated infrastructure. In: Proceedings of NSDI (2016)
40. Liu, X., Dobrian, F., Milner, H., Jiang, J., Sekar, V., Stoica, I., Zhang, H.: A case for a coordinated internet video control plane. In: ACM SIGCOMM, pp. 359-370. ACM (2012)
41. Lu, T., Pál, D., Pál, M.: Contextual multi-armed bandits. In: AISTATS, pp. 485-492 (2010)
42. Madhyastha, H.V., Isdal, T., Piatek, M., Dixon, C., Anderson, T., Krishnamurthy, A., Venkataramani, A.: iPlane: an information plane for distributed services. In: USENIX OSDI 2006
43. Pelsser, C., Cittadini, L., Vissicchio, S., Bush, R.: From Paris to Tokyo: on the suitability of ping to measure latency. In: Proceedings of the 2013 Conference on Internet Measurement Conference, pp. 427-432. ACM (2013)
44. Precup, D., Sutton, R.S., Singh, S.: Eligibility traces for off-policy policy evaluation. In: Proceedings of the Seventeenth International Conference on Machine Learning (2000)
45. Pu, Q., Ananthanarayanan, G., Bodik, P., Kandula, S., Akella, A., Bahl, P., Stoica, I.: Low latency geo-distributed data analytics. In: Proceedings of SIGCOMM (2015)
46. Rabkin, A., Arye, M., Sen, S., Pai, V.S., Freedman, M.J.: Aggregation and degradation in JetStream: streaming analytics in the wide area. In: Proceedings of NSDI (2014)
47. Rexford, J., Wang, J., Xiao, Z., Zhang, Y.: BGP routing stability of popular destinations. In: Proceedings of SIGCOMM IMW (2002)
48. Richard, J.-P.: Time-delay systems: an overview of some recent advances and open problems. Automatica **39**(10), 1667-1694 (2003)
49. Rigollet, P., Zeevi, A.: Nonparametric bandits with covariates. In: Proceedings of the Conference on Learning Theory (2010)
50. Saltzer, J.H., Reed, D.P., Clark, D.D.: End-to-end arguments in system design. ACM Trans. Comput. Syst. (TOCS) **2**(4), 277-288 (1984)

51. Seshan, S., Stemm, M., Katz, R.H.: SPAND: shared passive network performance discovery. In: USENIX Symposium on Internet Technologies and Systems, pp. 1–13 (1997)
52. Shalita, A., Karrer, B., Kabiljo, I., Sharma, A., Presta, A., Adcock, A., Kllapi, H., Stumm, M.: Social hash: an assignment framework for optimizing distributed systems operations on social networks. In: Proceedings of NSDI (2016)
53. Slivkins, A.: Contextual bandits with similarity information. J. Mach. Learn. Res. **15**(1), 2533–2568 (2014)
54. Sun, Y., Yin, X., Jiang, J., Sekar, V., Lin, F., Wang, N., Liu, T., Sinopoli, B.: CS2P: improving video bitrate selection and adaptation with data-driven throughput prediction. To Appear in Proceedings of SIGCOMM (2016)
55. Vellido, A., Martin-Guerroro, J., Lisboa, P.: Making machine learning models interpretable. In: Proceedings of the 20th European Symposium on Artificial Neural Networks, Computational Intelligence and Machine Learning (ESANN), Bruges, Belgium, pp. 163–172 (2012)
56. Venkataraman, S., Yang, Z., Franklin, M., Recht, B., Stoica, I.: Ernest: efficient performance prediction for large-scale advanced analytics. In: Proceedings of NSDI (2016)
57. Winstein, K., Balakrishnan, H.: TCP ex Machina: computer-generated congestion control. In: Proceedings of SIGCOMM (2013)

Selected Best Papers

Dual-Hop Decode-and-Forward Relaying in the Combined Presence of CEE and RFI: Performance Analysis and Comparison

Anoop Kumar Mishra$^{(\boxtimes)}$, Debmalya Mallick, Mareesh Issar, and Poonam Singh

Department of Electronics and Communication Engineering,
National Institute of Techonology Rourkela, Rourkela, Odisha, India
anoop1mishra@gmail.com

Abstract. In this paper, we look into the performance of decode-and-forward (DF) relaying system in the presence of both channel estimation error (CEE) and radio frequency impairments (RFI). We have sub-divided the analysis into different cases based on the presence of RFI at the relay, source and destination. First, the end-to-end signal-to-noise-plus-distortion-and-error ratio (SNDER) expression is derived, followed by an exact closed-form outage probability (OP) expression for Nakagami-m fading channel. As a special case, the OP analysis for Rayleigh fading channel is also provided. From the derived expressions, the relation amongst CEE and RFI is analyzed. For a complete study, the high SNR analysis of the derived equations is also carried out. The analytical results have been verified using the Monte Carlo simulations. Intriguing results are presented with the help of plots shown in the numerical analysis. Here, we have presented plots which deal with different channel conditions. Further, plots comparing symmetric and asymmetric channels are also presented.

Keywords: Decode-and-forward · Channel Estimation Error (CEE) · Radio Frequency Impairments (RFI) · Outage Probability (OP) · High Signal-to-Noise Ratio (SNR) analysis

1 Introduction

Wireless relaying systems are now gaining immense attention in the research community [9,16] and the industry [11] due to their numerous applications in practical scenarios. They are used to extend the coverage area, improve link reliability, reduce power consumption and enhance the quality-of-service (QoS) in order to efficiently combat the issues of fading impairments [25,27]. Due to the scarcity of resources such as power and bandwidth, the idea of relaying is

Part of this paper was presented at IEEE Conference on Communication Systems & Networks (COMSNETS), Bangalore, India, January 4–8 2017 [23].

© Springer International Publishing AG 2017
N. Sastry and S. Chakraborty (Eds.): COMSNETS 2017, LNCS 10340, pp. 129–149, 2017.
DOI: 10.1007/978-3-319-67235-9_10

significant for providing a better QoS, especially at the cell periphery. These characteristics make them a suitable choice for the emerging markets.

The two most marked methods of wireless relaying are amplify-and-forward (AF) or non-regenerative relaying and decode-and-forward (DF) or regenerative relaying [27]. Under AF relaying scheme, the relay receives the signal, amplifies it and then re-transmits it towards the destination, whereas, in the case of DF relaying, the received information is first fully decoded at the relay and then re-encoded before it is sent to the destination [16, 21].

Several practical systems, use a pilot-based scheme to gather the channel state information (CSI). In such systems, the transmitter transmits the information signal comprising of both pilot and data [10]. This information is then retrieved at the destination with the help of CSI acquired from the pilot. Hence CSI plays a pivotal role in order to completely reap the benefits of relaying scheme. DF relaying scheme assuming perfect CSI is investigated in [7, 12]. But, in practice, according to [13, 32] channel estimation performed by pilots is mostly inaccurate due to the limited power of pilot symbols and channel uncertainties. This often leads to erroneous retrieval of information and thus gives rise to the problem of channel estimation error (CEE). The quality of channel estimates inescapably affect the overall performance of a relay assisted communication system and tends to become the performance hindering factor [13]. In [12, 14, 20, 32], the authors have extensively studied the topics of inaccurate CSI or CEE. But, these papers did not take into consideration another very critical problem of radio frequency impairments (RFI). Now, this assumption is too idealistic for practical relaying systems, as the transceiver front-end suffers from several types of radio frequency impairments (RFI) such as, in-phase quadrature-phase imbalance (IQI), high power amplifier (HPA) non-linearities, phase noise (PN) and quantization error [3, 26]. These impairments create a mismatch between the intended transmit signal and actual emitted signal along with distortions of received signal during the reception process [2]. The impact of RFI is much more pronounced in the case of high rate systems especially those operating with inexpensive hardware [26]. The effect of such impairments is usually mitigated by the use of analog and digital signal processing algorithms [26]. However even after using such algorithms, there is still some residual impairment which is left due to the randomness created by different types of noises. The authors in [26, 28] characterized and verified experimentally that the distortion caused by these impairments behave as additive and independent Gaussian noise. This behavior can be understood by central limit theorem, where the distortions from several dissimilar and independent sources add together. In particular if the input is Gaussian, we can explain the above observation using the Bussgang Theorem [4].

There are some recent works [5, 6], which have also analyzed the end-to-end performance of dual-hop DF relaying system in the presence of two practical problems of RFI and co-channel interference (CCI). In a more recent study [24], the joint effect of RFI and CEE is investigated for fixed-gain AF relaying systems. Also, the study in [22] looks into the combined effect of hardware impairments and imperfect CSI in the context of TWRN and OWRN systems. From these papers, we find that both RFI and CEE are of grave concern in practical relaying scenarios and neglecting the effect of either of these leads to an incomplete study. The combined study of both these problems becomes more important after knowing the fact that RFI not only distorts the data signals but also affects the pilot signal, which in turn deteriorates the quality of channel estimation. Keeping this in mind, we analyzed the aggregated impact of imperfect channel estimation and hardware impairment on the performance of DF relaying systems in [23]. In that study, we had considered the hardware impairment in all the operating nodes.

But, in general, the source and destination are very sophisticated nodes (generally Base stations) with considerably less RFI than the relay node. Hence, to extend and complete the study of the impact of RFI and CEE on DF relaying, in this paper, we investigate and compare all the possible scenarios that can be present in a real world case. The cases that we study here are DF relaying systems with: (i) perfect CSI and ideal RF front-end (ii) Imperfect CSI with only relay node suffering from RFI (iii) imperfect CSI with all nodes (Source, relay, destination) having RFI. We bring out the SNDER and outage probability expressions for each of these cases. In the numerical result section, we compare the outage performance of these systems. Taking into consideration the channel conditions, we have also compared the performance of DF relaying system with RFI and CEE in symmetric and asymmetric channels.

The paper is organized in the following way. Section 2 describes the system and channel model. It has further sub-sections for the different cases as mentioned above. Section 3 presents the analytical study of the outage probability, which has been further divided into Sects. 3.1 and 3.2 for exact and asymptotic outage analysis. Numerical and simulation results bringing out some interesting outcomes are presented in Sect. 4 of this paper. Finally, we conclude the paper with Sect. 5.

2   System and Channel Model

As depicted in Fig. 1, we revisit the long-established conventional dual-hop relaying system model, where the information is transmitted from the source to the destination using a relay. The use of a relay in such case is justified by the absence of a direct link (due to heavy shadowing or heavy blockage). All the nodes in the system are equipped with a single antenna and follow half duplex mode of communication. In contrast to previous works pertaining to the assumption of perfect CSI or ideal RF front-end, here we consider a more generalized system model with (a) Only Relay node suffering from RFI in the presence of CEE; and (b) All nodes (Relay, Source and Destination) suffering from RFI in presence of CEE.

2.1   Ideal RF Hardware with no CEE

Consider the dual-hop relaying scenario shown in Fig. 1. Here, the parameters related to hop-1 (relay link) have subscript 1 whereas those related to the hop-2

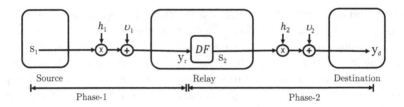

Fig. 1. Dual-hop DF relaying system with Ideal hardware and perfect CSI

(access link) have subscript 2. The transmitted signal, s_1, having average power $P_1 = \mathrm{E}_{s_1}\{|s_1|^2\}$, is transmitted from the source over an independent but non-identically distributed Nakagami-m fading channel, h_1, in the presence of an additive white Gaussian noise (AWGN), $v_1 \sim \mathbb{CN}(0, N_1)$. The received signal at the relay is conventionally modeled as

$$y_r = h_1 s_1 + v_1, \tag{1}$$

Upon successful reception of the received signal y_r it is decoded at the relay node and is then re-encoded as s_2, having average power $P_2 = \mathrm{E}_{s_2}\{|s_2|^2\}$, and is sent to the destination through the independent but non-identically distributed Nakagami-m fading channel h_2, having an AWGN noise $v_2 \sim \mathbb{CN}(0, N_2)$. The received signal at the destination is modeled as

$$y_d = h_2 s_2 + v_2, \tag{2}$$

Under the DF relaying scheme, ideally the transmitted signal s_2 at the relay should equal the original intended signal s_1. This is possible only if the relay is able to decode the signal properly. Thus, the instantaneous equivalent end-to-end SNR is the minimum of the SNR between (1) the source and the relay; and (2) the relay and the destination. With ideal hardware as given by Eqs. (1) and (2) the instantaneous equivalent end-to-end SNR becomes [16]

$$\varUpsilon_{e2e}^{id} = \min\left(\varUpsilon_1^{id}, \varUpsilon_2^{id}\right), \tag{3}$$

where, $\varUpsilon_1^{id} = \frac{P_1 \phi_1}{N_1}$ and $\varUpsilon_2^{id} = \frac{P_2 \phi_2}{N_2}$ represent the individual SNRs for hop-1 and hop-2 respectively. Instantaneous channel gain of individual hops $\phi_i = |h_i|^2$ for $i = \{1, 2\}$ are distributed as $|h_i|^2 \sim Gamma(\alpha_i, \beta_i)$. Here, $\alpha_i \geq 1$ denotes the integer shape parameters and $\beta_i > 0$ are the arbitrary scale parameters. The average SNR for Nakagami-m fading distribution is defined as

$$\bar{\varUpsilon}_i = \frac{P_i \mathrm{E}_{\phi_i}\{\phi_i\}}{N_i}, \qquad i = 1, 2 \tag{4}$$

where $\mathrm{E}_{\phi_i}\{\phi_i\} = \alpha_i \beta_i$, is the average fading power under Nakagami-m distribution.

2.2 Only Relay Node Suffering from RFI in the Presence of CEE

Unlike the sophisticated source or destination node, relay node is generally of lower-cost and lower-quality. This feature advocates for its ease of deployment and helps in increasing the network agility. But due to these features, the relay node also becomes prone to RFI (Fig. 2).

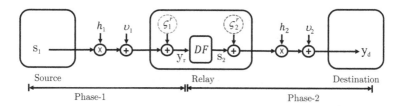

Fig. 2. Dual-hop DF relaying system with Non-Ideal Relay and CEE

In order to model this scenario, we have considered the relay node to be RF impaired while the RF front-ends of both the source and destination nodes are assumed to be ideal.

The distorted received signal at the relay is given by

$$y_r = h_1 s_1 + \upsilon_1 + \varsigma_1^r, \tag{5}$$

where, ς_1^r denotes the hardware distortion noise[1] (at relay front-end while receiving) which is modeled as $\varsigma_1^r \sim \mathbb{CN}(0, (\mu_1^r)^2 P_1 |h_1|^2)$.

The distorted signal received at the destination is given by

$$y_d = h_2 (s_2 + \varsigma_2^r) + \upsilon_2, \tag{6}$$

where, ς_2^r follows the distribution $\varsigma_2^r \sim \mathbb{CN}(0, (\mu_2^r)^2 P_2)$. Hardware design parameters μ_1^r, $\mu_2^r \geq 0$ determine the severity of RFI at the relay terminal. The estimated channel fading coefficients which follow the same distribution as $|h_i|$, are denoted by $|\tilde{h}_i|$ $(i = 1, 2)$. Assuming h_i and $\tilde{h}_i$ to be jointly ergodic processes we have,

$$h_i = \tilde{h}_i + e_{h_i}, \tag{7}$$

[19], where, e_{h_i} represents the CEE which is orthogonal to the channel estimate and is assumed to follow a zero mean complex Gaussian distribution [15,30] having variance,

$$\sigma_{i_{ni}}^2 = \Omega_i - \mathrm{E}\{|\tilde{h}_i|^2\} = \frac{1}{T_p \tilde{\Upsilon}_{i_p}^{ni\_Re} + 1}, \tag{8}$$

---

[1] An important property of the distortion noise caused at an antenna is that, it is proportional to the signal power at the antenna (i.e. it is a modification of the transmitted signal whereas the traditional noise at the receiver is modeled as random fluctuations in the circuits at the receiver).

where, $\Omega_i = \mathrm{E}\{|h_i|^2\}$, T_{i_p} is the length of training symbols and $\bar{\Upsilon}_{i_p}^{ni-Re} = \mathrm{E}\{\Upsilon_{i_p}^{ni-Re}\} = P_{i_p}\Omega_i/N_i$ represents the average SNR of training symbols for the ith hop under the presence of RFI. Here, P_{i_p} is the power of the pilot symbols and N_i is the noise variance of the ith hop. Since the training symbols are heavily damaged by RFI, we can re-write $\bar{\Upsilon}_{i_p}^{ni-Re}$ in terms of average SNR of the training symbols with system having ideal hardware ($\bar{\Upsilon}_{i_p}^{id}$) as, $\bar{\Upsilon}_{i_p}^{ni-Re} = \bar{\Upsilon}_{i_p}^{id}/(\bar{\Upsilon}_{i_p}^{id}(\mu_{i_p}^r)^2 + 1)$, where, $\mu_{i_p}^r$ signifies the error vector magnitudes[2] (EVM) ς_1^r and ς_2^r parameters affecting the training symbols of ith hop. Substituting $\bar{\Upsilon}_{i_p}^{ni-Re}$ in (8) we obtain,

$$\sigma_{i_{ni}}^2 \simeq \frac{1 + (\mu_{i_p}^r)^2 \bar{\Upsilon}_{i_p}^{id}}{1 + (T_{i_p} + (\mu_{i_p}^r)^2)\bar{\Upsilon}_{i_p}^{id}}, \tag{9}$$

where, $\sigma_{i_{ni}}^2$ reflects the quality of channel estimation and is known as linear minimum mean square error (LMMSE).

The instantaneous equivalent end-to-end SNDER for this case is expressed as

$$\tilde{\Upsilon}_{e2e}^{ni-Re} = \min\left(\tilde{\Upsilon}_1^{ni-Re}, \tilde{\Upsilon}_2^{ni-Re}\right), \tag{10}$$

where, $\tilde{\Upsilon}_1^{ni-Re} = \dfrac{P_1\tilde{\phi}_1}{P_1\tilde{\phi}_1(\mu_1^r)^2 + P_1\sigma_{1_{ni}}^2(1+(\mu_1^r)^2) + N_1}$ and $\tilde{\Upsilon}_2^{ni-Re} = \dfrac{P_2\tilde{\phi}_2}{P_2\tilde{\phi}_2(\mu_2^r)^2 + P_2\sigma_{2_{ni}}^2(1+(\mu_2^r)^2) + N_2}$ represent the individual SNDERs for hop-1 and hop-2 respectively. Expression (10) is a generalized form of [2, Eq. (17)], where only RFI was considered. It is also a generalization of [17, Eq. (1)], [2, Eq. (18)],which assumes ideal hardware as well as no CEE.

2.3   All Nodes (Relay, Source and Destination) Suffering from RFI in Presence of CEE

In order to gain more insight and to develop a generalized model, all the communicating nodes are taken to be RF impaired. The distorted received information at the relay, y_r is given by (Fig. 3),

$$y_r = h_1(s_1 + \varsigma_1^s) + v_1 + \varsigma_1^r, \tag{11}$$

and the distorted received information at the destination y_d is,

$$y_d = h_2(s_2 + \varsigma_2^r) + v_2 + \varsigma_2^d, \tag{12}$$

where, the hardware distortion noise present at the source and the destination are denoted by ς_1^s and ς_2^d respectively having distributions $\varsigma_1^s \sim \mathcal{CN}(0, (\mu_1^s)^2 P_1)$ and $\varsigma_2^d \sim \mathcal{CN}(0, (\mu_2^d)^2 P_2|h_2|^2)$. To increase the tractability, we denote the aggregated

---

[2] EVM is a common quality measure of RF transceivers and is the ratio of the average distortion magnitude to the average signal magnitude. 3GPP LTE has EVM requirements in the range [0.08, 0.175] [2].

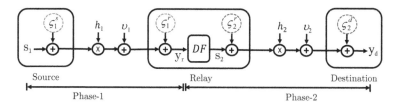

Fig. 3. Generalized Dual-hop DF relaying system with RF impairments and CEE.

distortion noise of hop-1 as $\varsigma_1 \overset{\Delta}{=} (h_1\varsigma_1^s + \varsigma_1^r) \sim \mathcal{CN}(0, ((\mu_1^s)^2 + (\mu_1^r)^2)P_1 |h_1|^2)$ and hop-2 as $\varsigma_2 \overset{\Delta}{=} (\varsigma_2^r + \varsigma_2^d/h_2) \sim \mathcal{CN}\left(0, ((\mu_2^r)^2 + (\mu_2^d)^2)P_2\right)$. In our analysis, we have assumed that these parameters are constant as they do not cross the dynamic range of the hardware. Upon violation, their value rises rapidly ([3] and references therein).

In this case, when all the nodes are suffering from RFI then the estimated error variances for both the hops are represented by,

$$\sigma_{1_{ni}}^2 = \Omega_1 - \mathrm{E}\{|\tilde{h}_1|^2\} = \frac{1}{T_{1_p}\bar{\Upsilon}_{1_p}^{ni\_All} + 1}, \tag{13a}$$

$$\sigma_{2_{ni}}^2 = \Omega_2 - \mathrm{E}\{|\tilde{h}_2|^2\} = \frac{1}{T_{2_p}\bar{\Upsilon}_{2_p}^{ni\_All} + 1} \tag{13b}$$

where, $\Omega_i = \mathrm{E}\{|h_i|^2\}$, T_{i_p} $(i = 1,2)$ is the length of training symbols and $\bar{\Upsilon}_{i_p}^{ni\_All} = \mathrm{E}\{\Upsilon_{i_p}^{ni\_All}\} = P_{i_p}\Omega_i/N_i$ represents the average SNR of training symbols for the ith hop in the presence of RFI. Here, P_{i_p} is the power of the pilot symbols and N_i is the noise variance of the ith hop. Since the training symbols are heavily damaged by RFI, we can re-write $\bar{\Upsilon}_{i_p}^{ni\_All}$ in terms of average SNR of the training symbols with system having ideal hardware ($\bar{\Upsilon}_{i_p}^{ni\_All}$) as,

$$\bar{\Upsilon}_{1_p}^{ni\_All} = \frac{\bar{\Upsilon}_{1_p}^{id}}{\bar{\Upsilon}_{1_p}^{id}\left((\mu_{1_p}^s)^2 + (\mu_{1_p}^r)^2\right) + 1}, \tag{14a}$$

$$\bar{\Upsilon}_{2_p}^{ni\_All} = \frac{\bar{\Upsilon}_{1_p}^{id}}{\bar{\Upsilon}_{1_p}^{id}\left((\mu_{2_p}^r)^2 + (\mu_{2_p}^d)^2\right) + 1}, \tag{14b}$$

where, $\mu_{1_p}^s$, $\mu_{1_p}^r$, $\mu_{2_p}^r$, $\mu_{2_p}^d \geq 0$ represent the level of RFI for training symbols at the source, relay receiver, relay transmitter and destination respectively. Substituting $\bar{\Upsilon}_{1_p}^{ni\_All}$ and $\bar{\Upsilon}_{2_p}^{ni\_All}$ in (13a) and (13b) respectively we obtain,

$$\sigma_{1_{ni}}^2 \simeq \frac{1 + ((\mu_1^s)^2 + (\mu_1^r)^2)\,\bar{\Upsilon}_{1_p}^{id}}{1 + (T_{1_p} + ((\mu_1^s)^2 + (\mu_1^r)^2))\bar{\Upsilon}_{1_p}^{id}}, \tag{15a}$$

$$\sigma_{2_{ni}}^2 \simeq \frac{1 + ((\mu_2^r)^2 + (\mu_2^d)^2)\,\bar{\Upsilon}_{2_p}^{id}}{1 + (T_{2_p} + ((\mu_2^r)^2 + (\mu_2^d)^2))\bar{\Upsilon}_{1_p}^{id}}, \tag{15b}$$

where, $\sigma_{1_{ni}}^2$ and $\sigma_{2_{ni}}^2$ reflect the quality of channel estimation of individual hops and is known as linear minimum mean square error (LMMSE) [30].

The instantaneous equivalent end-to-end SNDER for this case is given as

$$\tilde{\Upsilon}_{e2e}^{ni\_All} = \min\left(\tilde{\Upsilon}_1^{ni\_All},\ \tilde{\Upsilon}_2^{ni\_All}\right), \tag{16}$$

where, $\tilde{\Upsilon}_1^{ni\_All} = \dfrac{P_1\tilde{\phi}_1}{P_1\tilde{\phi}_1\left(\mu_1^s\right)^2 + P_1\tilde{\phi}_1\left(\mu_1^r\right)^2 + P_1\sigma_{1_{ni}}^2 + P_1\sigma_{1_{ni}}^2\left(\mu_1^s\right)^2 + P_1\sigma_{1_{ni}}^2\left(\mu_1^r\right)^2 + N_1}$ and

$\tilde{\Upsilon}_2^{ni\_All} = \dfrac{P_2\tilde{\phi}_2}{P_2\tilde{\phi}_2\left(\mu_2^r\right)^2 + P_2\tilde{\phi}_2\left(\mu_2^d\right)^2 + P_2\sigma_{2_{ni}}^2 + P_2\sigma_{2_{ni}}^2\left(\mu_2^r\right)^2 + P_2\sigma_{2_{ni}}^2\left(\mu_2^d\right)^2 + N_2}$ represent the

individual SNDERs for hop-1 and hop-2 respectively. Expression (16) is a generalized form of [2, Eq. (17)], where only RFI was considered. It is also a generalization of [18, Eq. (1)], [2, Eq. (18)], which assumes ideal hardware as well as no CEE.

3   Analytical Study of Outage Probability

This section derives the exact as well as the asymptotic OP expressions for a DF relaying system for the case (1) Ideal RF Hardware with no CEE; (2) Only Relay node suffering from RFI in the presence of CEE; and (3) All nodes (Relay, Source and Destination) suffering from RFI in presence of CEE. The OP, $\mathcal{P}_{out}(x)$ is defined as the probability that the instantaneous equivalent end-to-end SNR (or SNDER), $(\tilde{\Upsilon}_{e2e})$ falls below a particular acceptable threshold x. Mathematically, we can write [31],

$$
\begin{aligned}
\mathcal{P}_{out}(x) &\overset{\Delta}{=} \Pr\{\tilde{\Upsilon}_{e2e}^l \le x\} = F_{\tilde{\Upsilon}_{e2e}^l}(x) \\
&= \Pr\left\{\min\left(\tilde{\gamma}_1^l, \tilde{\gamma}_2^l\right) \le x\right\} \\
&= 1 - \Pr\left\{\min\left(\tilde{\gamma}_1^l, \tilde{\gamma}_2^l\right) > x\right\} \\
&= 1 - \Pr\left\{\tilde{\gamma}_1^l > x, \tilde{\gamma}_2^l > x\right\} \\
&= 1 - \left(1 - \Pr\left\{\tilde{\gamma}_1^l \le x\right\}\right)\left(1 - \Pr\left\{\tilde{\gamma}_2^l \le x\right\}\right) \\
&= 1 - \left(1 - F_{\tilde{\gamma}_1^l}(x)\right)\left(1 - F_{\tilde{\gamma}_2^l}(x)\right)
\end{aligned}
\tag{17}
$$

where $l \in (id, ni\_Re, ni\_All)$ and $\Pr\{\cdot\}$ denotes probability.

3.1   Exact Outage Behavior

In this subsection, we derive new analytical closed form expressions for the exact OP in the presence of accurate and inaccurate CSI considering different cases of RFI.

3.1.1   Ideal RF Hardware with No CEE

In the case of Nakagami-m fading channel for perfect CSI with ideal RF front-end, the OP for $\tilde{\Upsilon}_{e2e}^{id}$ is given by

$$F_{\tilde{\Upsilon}_{e2e}^{id}}(x) = 1 - \left(1 - F_{\tilde{\phi}_1}\left(\tfrac{N_1 x}{\beta_1 P_1}\right)\right)\left(1 - F_{\tilde{\phi}_2}\left(\tfrac{N_2 x}{\beta_2 P_2}\right)\right) \tag{18}$$

where, $F_{\tilde{\phi}_1}\left(\frac{N_1 x}{\beta_1 P_1}\right) = 1 - \exp\left(-\frac{N_1 x}{\beta_1 P_1}\right)\sum_{j=0}^{\alpha_1-1}\frac{1}{j!}\left(-\frac{N_1 x}{\beta_1 P_1}\right)^j$ and

$$F_{\tilde{\phi}_2}\left(\frac{N_2 x}{\beta_2 P_2}\right) = 1 - \exp\left(-\frac{N_2 x}{\beta_2 P_2}\right)\sum_{j=0}^{\alpha_2-1}\frac{1}{j!}\left(-\frac{N_2 x}{\beta_2 P_2}\right)^j.$$

3.1.2 Only Relay Node Suffering from RFI in the Presence of CEE:

For the case of Nakagami-m fading channel having imperfect CSI along with non-ideal relay node, the OP for $\tilde{\Upsilon}_{e2e}^{ni-Re}$ is given by the following theorem.

Theorem 1: Assuming $\tilde{\phi}_1, \tilde{\phi}_2$ to be non-negative independent random variables, where, $\tilde{\phi}_i \sim Gamma\left(\alpha_i, \beta_i\right)$ with integer shape parameter $\alpha_i \geq 1$ and real valued scale parameter $\beta_i > 0$, the expression for OP is given by,

$$F_{\tilde{\Upsilon}_{e2e}^{ni-Re}}(x) = 1 - \left[\left(\exp\left(-\frac{\left(\sigma_{1ni}^2\left(1+(\mu_1^r)^2\right)+\frac{N_1}{P_1}\right)x}{\beta_1\left(1-(\mu_1^r)^2 x\right)}\right)\sum_{j=0}^{\alpha_1-1}\frac{1}{j!}\left(\frac{\left(\sigma_{1ni}^2\left(1+(\mu_1^r)^2\right)+\frac{N_1}{P_1}\right)x}{\beta_1\left(1-(\mu_1^r)^2 x\right)}\right)^j\right)\right.$$
$$\left.\times \left(\exp\left(-\frac{\left(\sigma_{2ni}^2\left(1+(\mu_2^r)^2\right)+\frac{N_2}{P_2}\right)x}{\beta_2\left(1-(\mu_2^r)^2 x\right)}\right)\sum_{j=0}^{\alpha_2-1}\frac{1}{j!}\left(\frac{\left(\sigma_{2ni}^2\left(1+(\mu_2^r)^2\right)+\frac{N_2}{P_2}\right)x}{\beta_2\left(1-(\mu_2^r)^2 x\right)}\right)^j\right)\right],$$
$$(19)$$

for $x < \frac{1}{\delta}$ where, $\delta \stackrel{\Delta}{=} \max((\mu_1^r)^2, (\mu_2^r)^2)$ and $F_{\tilde{\Upsilon}_{e2e}^{ni-Re}}(x) = 1$ for $x \geq \frac{1}{\delta}$.

Proof: We can see from (17) that $P_{out}(x)$ depends on $\tilde{\Upsilon}_{e2e}^{ni-Re}$. Now, from (10), we further note that $\tilde{\Upsilon}_{e2e}^{ni-Re}$ has a functional relationship with the two independent random variables namely, $\tilde{\phi}_1$ and $\tilde{\phi}_2$. Hence,

$$F_{\tilde{\Upsilon}_{e2e}^{ni-Re}}(x) = 1 - \left(1 - F_{\tilde{\phi}_1}(x)\right)\left(1 - F_{\tilde{\phi}_2}(x)\right), \qquad (20)$$

where,

$$F_{\tilde{\phi}_1}(x) = \begin{cases} \Pr\left\{\tilde{\phi}_1 \leq \frac{\left(\sigma_{1ni}^2\left(1+(\mu_1^r)^2\right)+\frac{N_1}{P_1}\right)x}{\left(1-(\mu_1^r)^2 x\right)}\right\}, & x < 1/\delta \\ 1, & x \geq 1/\delta \end{cases} \qquad (21)$$

$$F_{\tilde{\phi}_2}(x) = \begin{cases} \Pr\left\{\tilde{\phi}_2 \leq \frac{\left(\sigma_{2ni}^2\left(1+(\mu_2^r)^2\right)+\frac{N_2}{P_2}\right)x}{\left(1-(\mu_2^r)^2 x\right)}\right\}, & x < 1/\delta \\ 1, & x \geq 1/\delta \end{cases} \qquad (22)$$

Now substituting (21) and (22) in (20) we get,

$$F_{\tilde{\Upsilon}_{e2e}^{ni-Re}}(x) =$$
$$\begin{cases} 1 - \left(1 - F_{\tilde{\phi}_1}\left(\frac{\left(\sigma_{1ni}^2\left(1+(\mu_1^r)^2\right)+\frac{N_1}{P_1}\right)x}{\left(1-(\mu_1^r)^2 x\right)}\right)\right)\left(1 - F_{\tilde{\phi}_2}\left(\frac{\left(\sigma_{2ni}^2\left(1+(\mu_2^r)^2\right)+\frac{N_2}{P_2}\right)x}{\left(1-(\mu_2^r)^2 x\right)}\right)\right), \\ \qquad\qquad\qquad\qquad\qquad\qquad\qquad\qquad\qquad\qquad x < 1/\delta \\ 1, \qquad\qquad\qquad\qquad\qquad\qquad\qquad\qquad\qquad\qquad x \geq 1/\delta. \end{cases}$$
$$(23)$$

Using the cumulative distribution function (CDF) of Gamma distributed random variable $\tilde{\phi}_i$ in (23), we get (19).

3.1.3   All Nodes (Relay, Source and Destination) Suffering from RFI in Presence of CEE:

For the case of Nakagami-m fading channel, a generalized equation for the OP $\tilde{\Upsilon}_{e2e}$ for a DF relaying system having imperfect CSI as well as non-ideal RF front-end (all nodes) is given by the following theorem.

Theorem 2: Assuming $\tilde{\phi}_1$, $\tilde{\phi}_2$ to be non-negative independent random variables, where, $\tilde{\phi}_i \sim Gamma\,(\alpha_i,\,\beta_i)$ with integer shape parameter $\alpha_i \geq 1$ and real valued scale parameter $\beta_i > 0$, the expression for OP is given by,

$$
\begin{aligned}
F_{\tilde{\Upsilon}_{e2e}^{ni}\_All}\,(x) = 1- \\
\left[\left(\exp\left(-\frac{\left(\sigma_{1_{ni}}^2\left(1+(\mu_1^s)^2+(\mu_1^r)^2\right)+\frac{N_1}{P_1}\right)x}{\beta_1\left(1-(\mu_1^s)^2 x-(\mu_1^r)^2 x\right)} \right) \sum_{j=0}^{\alpha_1-1} \frac{1}{j!} \left(\frac{\left(\sigma_{1_{ni}}^2\left(1+(\mu_1^s)^2+(\mu_1^r)^2\right)+\frac{N_1}{P_1}\right)x}{\beta_1\left(1-(\mu_1^s)^2 x-(\mu_1^r)^2 x\right)} \right)^j \right) \right. \\
\left. \times \left(\exp\left(-\frac{\left(\sigma_{2_{ni}}^2\left(1+(\mu_2^r)^2+(\mu_2^d)^2\right)+\frac{N_2}{P_2}\right)x}{\beta_2\left(1-(\mu_2^r)^2 x-(\mu_2^d)^2 x\right)} \right) \sum_{j=0}^{\alpha_2-1} \frac{1}{j!} \left(\frac{\left(\sigma_{2_{ni}}^2\left(1+(\mu_2^r)^2+(\mu_2^d)^2\right)+\frac{N_2}{P_2}\right)x}{\beta_2\left(1-(\mu_2^r)^2 x-(\mu_2^d)^2 x\right)} \right)^j \right) \right],
\end{aligned}
\tag{24}
$$

for $x < \frac{1}{\delta}$ where, $\delta \overset{\Delta}{=} \max\big(\big((\mu_1^s)^2 + (\mu_1^r)^2\big),\ \big((\mu_2^r)^2 + (\mu_2^d)^2\big)\big)$ and $F_{\tilde{\Upsilon}_{e2e}^{ni}\_All}(x) = 1$ for $x \geq \frac{1}{\delta}$.

Proof: We can see from (17) that $P_{out}\,(x)$ depends on $\tilde{\Upsilon}_{e2e}^{ni}\_All$. Now, from (16), we further note that $\tilde{\Upsilon}_{e2e}^{ni}\_All$ has a functional relationship with the two independent random variables namely, $\tilde{\phi}_1$ and $\tilde{\phi}_2$. Hence,

$$
F_{\tilde{\Upsilon}_{e2e}^{ni}\_All}\,(x) = 1 - \left(1 - F_{\tilde{\phi}_1}\,(x)\right)\left(1 - F_{\tilde{\phi}_2}\,(x)\right),
\tag{25}
$$

where,

$$
F_{\tilde{\phi}_1}\,(x) = \begin{cases} \Pr\left\{ \tilde{\phi}_1 \leq \frac{\left(\sigma_{1_{ni}}^2\left(1+(\mu_1^s)^2+(\mu_1^r)^2\right)+\frac{N_1}{P_1}\right)x}{\left(1-(\mu_1^s)^2 x-(\mu_1^r)^2 x\right)} \right\}, & x < 1/\delta \\ 1, & x \geq 1/\delta \end{cases}
\tag{26}
$$

$$
F_{\tilde{\phi}_2}\,(x) = \begin{cases} \Pr\left\{ \tilde{\phi}_2 \leq \frac{\left(\sigma_{2_{ni}}^2\left(1+(\mu_2^r)^2+(\mu_2^d)^2\right)+\frac{N_2}{P_2}\right)x}{\left(1-(\mu_2^r)^2 x-(\mu_2^d)^2 x\right)} \right\}, & x < 1/\delta \\ 1, & x \geq 1/\delta \end{cases}
\tag{27}
$$

Now substituting (26) and (27) in (25) we get,

$$
F_{\tilde{\Upsilon}_{e2e}^{ni}\_All}\,(x) = \begin{cases} 1 - \left(1 - F_{\tilde{\phi}_1}\left(\frac{\left(\sigma_{1_{ni}}^2\left(1+(\mu_1^s)^2+(\mu_1^r)^2\right)+\frac{N_1}{P_1}\right)x}{\left(1-(\mu_1^s)^2 x-(\mu_1^r)^2 x\right)} \right)\right)\left(1 - F_{\tilde{\phi}_2}\left(\frac{\left(\sigma_{2_{ni}}^2\left(1+(\mu_2^r)^2+(\mu_2^d)^2\right)+\frac{N_2}{P_2}\right)x}{\left(1-(\mu_2^r)^2 x-(\mu_2^d)^2 x\right)} \right)\right), \\ \hspace{9cm} x < 1/\delta \\ 1, \hspace{8.5cm} x \geq 1/\delta. \end{cases}
\tag{28}
$$

Using the cumulative distribution function (CDF) of Gamma distributed random variable $\tilde{\phi}_i$ in (28), we get (24).

Theorem 2 provides a tractable and generalized closed-form OP expression for DF relaying system that handles both CEE and RFI. The derived OP expression is a generalization of [2, Eq. (30)], where only hardware impairment is considered ignoring the effects of CEE. We can verify this by substituting $\sigma^2_{1_{ni}} = \sigma^2_{2_{ni}} = 0$ in (24). Theorem 2 can easily be extended for a multi-hop DF relaying systems (with Z hops) by simply varying i from 1 to Z instead of varying it from 1 to 2.

Corollary 1: *OP for this system in the absence of RFI:* By putting $\mu^s_1 = \mu^r_1 = \mu^r_2 = \mu^d_2 = 0$ in (24), the required expression is obtained as follows,

$$
F_{\tilde{\gamma}^{ni}_{e2e}-All}(x) = 1 - \left(\exp\left(-\frac{\left(\sigma^2_{1_{id}}+\frac{N_1}{P_1}\right)x}{\beta_1} \right) \sum_{j=0}^{\alpha_1-1} \frac{1}{j!} \left(\frac{\left(\sigma^2_{1_{id}}+\frac{N_1}{P_1}\right)x}{\beta_1} \right)^j \right)
$$
$$
\times \left(\exp\left(-\frac{\left(\sigma^2_{2_{id}}+\frac{N_2}{P_2}\right)x}{\beta_2} \right) \sum_{j=0}^{\alpha_2-1} \frac{1}{j!} \left(\frac{\left(\sigma^2_{2_{id}}+\frac{N_2}{P_2}\right)x}{\beta_2} \right)^j \right),
$$
(29)

for $0 \le x < \infty$.

The above written corollary provides the closed-form expression for outage performance considering only CEE, where the RF hardware is assumed to be ideal. Here, channel estimation accuracy parameter $\sigma^2_{i_{id}} = 1/(T_{i_p}\tilde{\gamma}_{i_{idp}}+1)$ is the inverse function of pilot symbol power, which is in contrast to non-ideal hardware case. Now, due to the limited power pilot symbols, $\sigma^2_{i_{id}}$ will never be zero even when the data signal power is very high. This in turn leads to occurrence of outage floor at high average SNR values.

Corollary 2: *OP for this system over Rayleigh fading channel:* After substituting $\alpha_i = 1$, $\beta_i = \Omega_i$, in (24) and further simplification, we get the required expression as,

$$
F_{\tilde{\gamma}^{ni}_{e2e}-All}(x) = 1 - \exp\left(-\frac{\left(\sigma^2_{1_{ni}}\left(1+(\mu^s_1)^2+(\mu^r_1)^2\right)+\frac{N_1}{P_1}\right)x}{\Omega_1\left(1-(\mu^s_1)^2x-(\mu^r_1)^2x\right)} \right)
$$
$$
\times \exp\left(-\frac{\left(\sigma^2_{2_{ni}}\left(1+(\mu^r_2)^2+(\mu^d_2)^2\right)+\frac{N_2}{P_2}\right)x}{\Omega_2\left(1-(\mu^r_2)^2x-(\mu^d_2)^2x\right)} \right),
$$
(30)

for $x < \frac{1}{\delta}$ where, $\delta \overset{\Delta}{=} \max(((\mu^s_1)^2 + (\mu^r_1)^2), ((\mu^r_2)^2 + (\mu^d_2)^2))$ and $F_{\tilde{\gamma}_{e2e}}(x) = 1$ for $x \ge \frac{1}{\delta}$.

This corollary finds immense application in the analysis of practical DF relaying systems with CEE and RFI in rich scattering environment, where Rayleigh fading distribution is the appropriate model. This corollary generalizes [2, Eq. (31)] which has been obtained for Rayleigh fading channel by taking perfect channel estimation. This can also be expressed as a generalization of the classical result presented in [8, Eq. (28)], which finds OP expression of DF relaying system assuming perfect channel estimation and ideal hardware.

3.2 Asymptotic Outage Behavior

To obtain some more insights on the fundamental impacts of CEE and RFI, in this section we now focus our attention to the asymptotic outage behavior of DF system in which all nodes (Source, Relay and Destination). The hardware design parameter μ_i has a direct relation with the SNR [1,29]. In order to analyze this, we have considered an arbitrary fixed value of the SNR (or SNDER) and thus μ_i can be taken as a constant. Here we have considered the transmitted power $P_1 = P_2 = P$ to be very large. It is found that the SNDER expression (16) becomes,

$$\tilde{\Upsilon}_{e2e}^{ni\_All} \Big|_{P_1, P_2 \to \infty} = \min\left(\tilde{\Upsilon}_1^\infty, \tilde{\Upsilon}_2^\infty\right) \tag{31}$$

where $\quad \tilde{\Upsilon}_1^\infty = \dfrac{\tilde{\phi}_1}{\tilde{\phi}_1(\mu_1^s)^2 + \tilde{\phi}_1(\mu_1^r)^2 + \sigma_{1_{ni}}^2\left(1+(\mu_1^s)^2+(\mu_1^r)^2\right)}\quad$ and $\quad \tilde{\Upsilon}_2^\infty =$

$\dfrac{\tilde{\phi}_2}{\tilde{\phi}_1(\mu_2^r)^2 + \tilde{\phi}_1(\mu_2^d)^2 + \sigma_{1_{ni}}^2\left(1+(\mu_2^r)^2+(\mu_2^d)^2\right)}$ represent the individual SNDERs at very

high transmit power for hop-1 and hop-2 respectively.

During this analysis, we also find that $\sigma_{1_{ni}}^2$ and $\sigma_{2_{ni}}^2$ reduces to,

$$^\infty\sigma_{1_{ni}}^2 = \sigma_{1_{ni}}^2 \Big|_{P_{1_{id_p}} \to \infty} \simeq \frac{(\mu_{1_p}^s)^2 + (\mu_{1_p}^r)^2}{T_{1_p} + (\mu_{1_p}^s)^2 + (\mu_{1_p}^r)^2} \approx \frac{(\mu_{1_p}^s)^2 + (\mu_{1_p}^r)^2}{T_{1_p}}, \tag{32a}$$

$$^\infty\sigma_{2_{ni}}^2 = \sigma_{2_{ni}}^2 \Big|_{P_{2_{id_p}} \to \infty} \simeq \frac{(\mu_{2_p}^r)^2 + (\mu_{2_p}^d)^2}{T_{2_p} + (\mu_{2_p}^r)^2 + (\mu_{2_p}^d)^2} \approx \frac{(\mu_{2_p}^r)^2 + (\mu_{2_p}^d)^2}{T_{2_p}}, \tag{32b}$$

where, $(\mu_{1_p}^s)^2 + (\mu_{1_p}^r)^2 \ll T_{1_p}$ and $(\mu_{2_p}^r)^2 + (\mu_{2_p}^d)^2 \ll T_{2_p}$.

In the case of ideal hardware, the error variance becomes zero at very high power. But, expressions (32a) and (32b) show that the value of error variance is non-zero even at very high transmit power and is directly influenced by the degree of hardware impairment. Another inference which can be drawn from the expressions (32a) and (32b) is that, the number of training symbols cannot be decreased below a particular level, as it leads to unavoidable increase in the error variance.

Theorem 3: *OP for DF relaying systems having CEE and RFI at high SNR:* It can be obtained by putting $P_1 = P_2 = P \to \infty$ in (16) as,

$$F_{\tilde{\Upsilon}_{e2e}^{ni\_All}}^\infty (x) = 1 - \left(\exp\left(-\frac{^\infty\sigma_{1_{ni}}^2\left(1+(\mu_1^s)^2+(\mu_1^r)^2\right)x}{\beta_1\left(1-(\mu_1^s)^2 x-(\mu_1^r)^2 x\right)}\right) \sum_{j=0}^{\alpha_1-1} \frac{1}{j!} \left(\frac{^\infty\sigma_{1_{ni}}^2\left(1+(\mu_1^s)^2+(\mu_1^r)^2\right)x}{\beta_1\left(1-(\mu_1^s)^2 x-(\mu_1^r)^2 x\right)}\right)^j\right)$$
$$\times \left(\exp\left(-\frac{^\infty\sigma_{2_{ni}}^2\left(1+(\mu_2^r)^2+(\mu_2^d)^2\right)x}{\beta_1\left(1-(\mu_2^r)^2 x-(\mu_2^d)^2 x\right)}\right) \sum_{j=0}^{\alpha_2-1} \frac{1}{j!} \left(\frac{^\infty\sigma_{2_{ni}}^2\left(1+(\mu_2^r)^2+(\mu_2^d)^2\right)x}{\beta_2\left(1-(\mu_2^r)^2 x-(\mu_2^d)^2 x\right)}\right)^j\right)$$

$$\tag{33}$$

for $x < \frac{1}{\delta}$ where $\delta \overset{\Delta}{=} \max\left((\mu_1^s)^2 + (\mu_1^r)^2, (\mu_2^r)^2 + (\mu_2^d)^2\right)$ and $F_{\tilde{\Upsilon}_{e2e}^{ni\_All}}^\infty (x) = 1$ for $x \geq \frac{1}{\delta}$.

Proof: Similar to Theorem 2, by using (31) instead of (16).

Theorem 3 gives a generalized OP expression for dual-hop DF relaying at high SNR with Nakagami-m fading channel. From this theorem, we can see that the outage floor obtained at high SNR depends not only on CEE but also on RFI. The studies in paper [13,32] did not consider RFI in their analysis. Hence, this paper brings out the indirect contribution of RFI on the outage floor through its effect on CEE.

Corollary 3: *High SNR analysis in case of only Non-Ideal Relay with CEE:* It can be obtained by putting $P_1 = P_2 = P \to \infty$ in (10) as,

$$F^\infty_{\tilde{r}^{ni}_{e2e}-Re}(x) = 1 - \left(\exp\left(-\frac{\infty\sigma^2_{1_{ni}}(1+(\mu^r_1)^2)x}{\beta_1(1-(\mu^r_1)^2 x)}\right)\sum_{j=0}^{\alpha_1-1}\frac{1}{j!}\left(\frac{\infty\sigma^2_{i_{ni}}(1+(\mu^r_1)^2)x}{\beta_1(1-(\mu^r_1)^2 x)}\right)^j\right)$$
$$\times\left(\exp\left(-\frac{\infty\sigma^2_{2_{ni}}(1+(\mu^r_2)^2)x}{\beta_2(1-(\mu^r_2)^2 x)}\right)\sum_{j=0}^{\alpha_2-1}\frac{1}{j!}\left(\frac{\infty\sigma^2_{2_{ni}}(1+(\mu^r_2)^2)x}{\beta_2(1-(\mu^r_2)^2 x)}\right)^j\right)$$

$$\tag{34}$$

for $x < \frac{1}{\delta}$ where $\delta \triangleq \max\left((\mu^r_1)^2, (\mu^r_2)^2\right)$ and $F^\infty_{\tilde{r}^{ni}_{e2e}-Re}(x) = 1$ for $x \geq \frac{1}{\delta}$.

Corollary 4: *High SNR analysis in case of Non-ideal Hardware without CEE:*

$$F^\infty_{r^{id}_{e2e}}(x) = \begin{cases} 0, & x < \frac{1}{\delta} \\ 1, & x > \frac{1}{\delta} \end{cases} \tag{35}$$

where $\delta \triangleq \max\left((\mu^s_1)^2 + (\mu^r_1)^2, (\mu^r_2)^2 + (\mu^d_2)^2\right)$. Hence it can be observed that beyond a certain value of threshold the system is in complete outage. This corollary concludes that just the presence of RFI creates an SNDER ceiling which significantly limits the performance of the system.

Corollary 5: *High SNR analysis in case of Rayleigh Fading:* By putting $\alpha_i = 1, \beta_i = \Omega_i$ in (33) and simplifying, the OP for high SNR in the case of Rayleigh fading channel is found to be,

$$F^\infty_{\tilde{r}^{ni}_{e2e}-All}(x) = 1 - \exp\left(-\frac{\infty\sigma^2_{1_{ni}}(1+(\mu^s_1)^2+(\mu^r_1)^2)x}{\Omega_1(1-(\mu^s_1)^2 x-(\mu^r_1)^2 x)}\right)\exp\left(-\frac{\infty\sigma^2_{2_{ni}}(1+(\mu^s_1)^2+(\mu^r_1)^2)x}{\Omega_2(1-(\mu^r_2)^2 x-(\mu^d_2)^2 x)}\right), \tag{36}$$

for $x < \frac{1}{\delta}$ where $\delta \triangleq \max\left((\mu^s_1)^2 + (\mu^r_1)^2, (\mu^r_2)^2 + (\mu^d_2)^2\right)$ and $F^\infty_{\tilde{r}^{ni}_{e2e}-All}(x) = 1$ for $x \geq \frac{1}{\delta}$.

Here, the combined effect of CEE and RFI are responsible for creating an outage floor in the Rayleigh fading scenario.

4   Numerical and Simulation Results

This section presents set of numerical results demonstrating the performance of the above analyzed DF relaying models. To validate the theoretical results, Monte-Carlo simulations are performed considering 10^6 channel realizations. Here, we have assumed that $\mu_1^s = \mu_1^r = \mu_2^r = \mu_2^d = \mu$, $\sigma_{1ni}^2 = \sigma_{2ni}^2 = \sigma^2$. In Figs. 4, 5, 6, 7 and 8, the values of shape and scale parameters are $\alpha_1 = \alpha_2 = \alpha = 2$ and $\beta_1 = \beta_2 = \beta = 1$ respectively. In Figs. 9 and 10, we have taken $\mu = 0.12$ and $\sigma^2 = 0.006$.

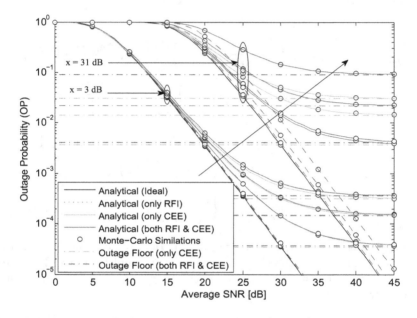

Fig. 4. Comparison of OP vs. average SNR (in dB) for different cases: (i) varying $\mu \in \{0, 0.04, 0.08, 0.12\}$ and $\sigma^2 = 0$ (ii) varying $\sigma^2 \in \{0, 0.002, 0.004, 0.006\}$ and $\mu = 0$ and (iii) varying μ and varying σ^2, $(\mu, \sigma^2) \in \{(0, 0), (0.04, 0.002), (0.08, 0.004), (0.12, 0.006)\}$.

Figure 4 depicts the OP vs. average SNR values for the case of CEE with non-ideal relay, source and destination, in accordance to (24). It is to be noted that a relay assisted communication system uses two time slots, therefore, we write $x = 2^{2R} - 1$ where, R represents transmission rate and x represents SNDER threshold. Corresponding to two different SNDER threshold values $x = 3\,\mathrm{dB}$ and $x = 31\,\mathrm{dB}$ representing transmission rates of 1 and 2.5 bits/sec/Hz respectively, we get two sets of plots. It is clearly evident that the curves with only CEE as well as those with both CEE and RFI have outage floors at high SNR region. An important notable observation is that, the curve with the combined effect of CEE and RFI has a higher outage floor than the one with only CEE. We know that

RFI alone cannot produce any outage floor, yet it increases the effect of CEE in terms of elevating the outage floor and hence has a significant impact on CEE. This can be attributed to the fact that at high power regime, $^\infty\sigma_{i_{n_i}}^2 \approx \mu_{i_p}^2/T_{i_p}$ as found in (29). Another point worth noting is that the elevation of outage floor is much greater in case of high rate systems. This shows that high rate systems are more vulnerable to the combined presence of RFI and CEE.

Figure 5 shows OP against SNDER threshold for two different average SNR values of 15 dB and 40 dB. Initially the curve with CEE (only) dominates the curve with RFI (only). But, as the SNDER threshold increases, the RFI starts to dominate over CEE after a particular SNDER threshold for both the average SNR values. Further, we observe that there is an SNDER ceiling for the OP curves, i.e., for a particular average SNR value, there is a certain SNDER threshold beyond which the OP value will always remain 1.

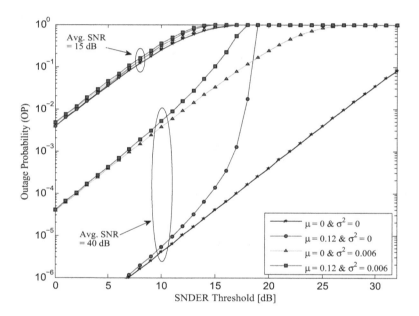

Fig. 5. OP vs. SNDER threshold (in dB) at average SNR values of 15 dB and 40 dB.

Figure 6 shows the comparison of the OP vs. Average SNR plots for the DF relaying models studied above, namely: (i) Ideal Hardware without CEE (ii) Non-ideal Relay with CEE (iii) Non-ideal Relay and Destination with CEE (iv) Non-ideal source, relay and destination with CEE, for two different SNDER threshold values of 3 dB and 31 dB corresponding to transmission rates of 1 and 2.5 bits/sec/Hz respectively. We can see that, as we add RFI to the destination, there is a huge deviation of OP from the only non-ideal relay case. But, subsequent addition of RFI in the source impacts the performance to a very little extent. This shows that if there is a non-ideal relay in presence of ICSI, then the performance of the DF relaying systems vary only slightly for the case of one non-ideal destination/source and the case of both non-ideal source and destination nodes.

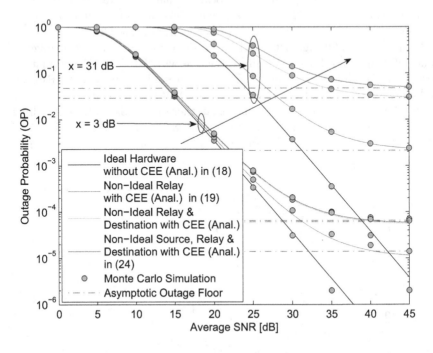

Fig. 6. Comparison of OP vs. average SNR (in dB) for different scenarios.

In Fig. 7, we have plotted the comparison of the OP vs. SNDER threshold values of the above mentioned models for two different avg. SNR values of 15 dB and 40 dB. We can see that, at lower value of average SNR, the plots for the different cases are very close to each other, whereas, at higher average SNR value, they deviate a lot from each other. This shows that at higher avg. SNR, the effect of RFI in the source as well as the destination is much more prominent than at lower values of SNR.

Figure 8 displays and compares the performance of two relaying methods: (a) fixed-gain (FG) AF relaying [24] and (b) DF relaying. For both the scenarios, the average SNR is taken to be 20 dB, $\mu = 0.10$ and $\sigma^2 = 0.01$. The first thing that the comparison reveals is that, DF relaying performs much better than FG AF relaying in the combined presence of RFI and CEE. Another observation is that, in case of DF relaying, CEE dominates the RFI for a larger range of transmission rates than it does for FG AF relaying. It is evident from the crossing points of CEE and RFI curves in both sets of plots. With the above mentioned parameter values, we can see that for FG AF relaying, only CEE curve dominates the only

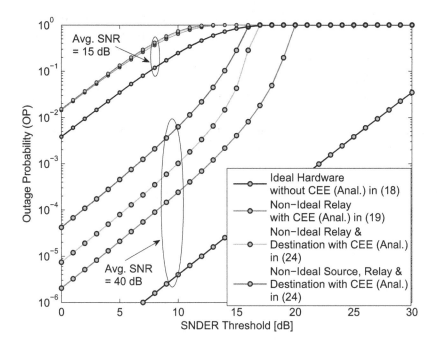

Fig. 7. Comparison of OP vs. SNDER threshold (in dB) for different scenarios.

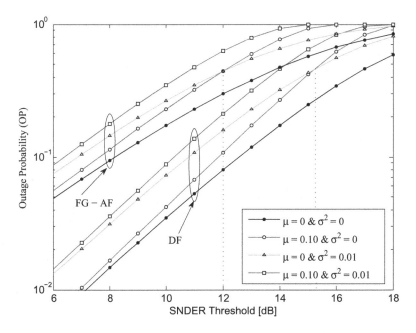

Fig. 8. Outage Probabilities for (a) fixed-gain AF relaying and (b) DF relaying for average SNR of 20 dB.

RFI curve till the transmission rate of 1.85 bits/sec/Hz (corresponding to $x = 12\,dB$), whereas, for DF relaying, only CEE curve dominates the only RFI curve till the transmission rate of 2.00 bits/sec/Hz (corresponding to $x = 15.2\,dB$).

In Fig. 9, OP vs. average SNR is plotted for different values of the shape parameter α. It is evident that, as the channel condition improves with increasing α, the OP performance improves. But the rate at which it improves at higher transmission rate is much slower than the rate at which it improves at lower transmission rate. Hence, we can infer that high rate systems are much more susceptible to the combined effects of CEE and RFI than low rate systems.

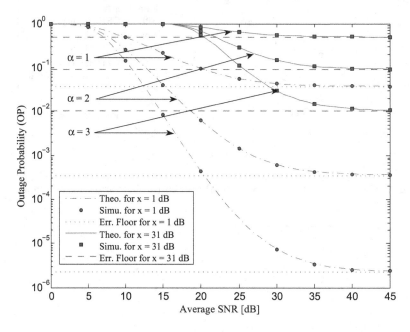

Fig. 9. OP vs. average SNR for different values of shape parameter α taking $\mu = 0.12$ and $\sigma^2 = 0.006$.

In Fig. 10, we compare the performance of DF relaying systems suffering with RFI and CEE in symmetric and asymmetric channel fading conditions. Here, we have taken $\beta_1 = \beta_2 = \beta$ to be 1. From the plot, we can see that, at both the transmission rates, the performance of the system is better when $\alpha_1 = 2$ and $\alpha_2 = 1$ (green curves) than when $\alpha_1 = 1$ and $\alpha_2 = 2$ (red curves). This shows that if the channel fading condition of hop-1 is superior to the hop-2, then the system performance is better, especially for mid-range average SNR values.

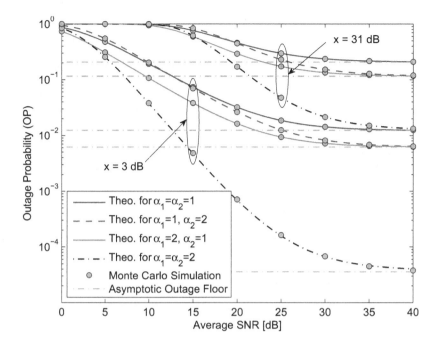

Fig. 10. OP vs. average SNR for symmetric and asymmetric channels taking $\mu = 0.12$ and $\sigma^2 = 0.006$.

5 Conclusions

In this paper, we evaluate the performance of dual-hop DF relaying systems in the presence of both CEE and RFI. The exact and asymptotic closed-form expressions for the OP are derived. Simplified asymptotic results in the high SNR regime show that, RFI alone has no role in the production of an outage floor, yet it enhances the effect of CEE in terms of elevating the outage floor further. We observe that the effect of CEE is much more pronounced in the case of DF relaying system at low-to-medium average SNR. It is also found that the combined effect of both CEE and RFI on high rate DF relaying systems is greater than that on low rate DF relaying systems. We also found out that, the performance of DF relaying systems with such problems is better if the channel fading condition of hop-1 is superior to hop-2 rather than the other way around.

References

1. Björnson, E., Jorswieck, E., et al.: Optimal resource allocation in coordinated multi-cell systems. Found. Trends Commun. Inf. Theor. **9**(2–3), 113–381 (2013)
2. Bjornson, E., Matthaiou, M., Debbah, M.: A new look at dual-hop relaying: Performance limits with hardware impairments. IEEE Trans. Commun. **61**(11), 4512–4525 (2013)

3. Bjornson, E., Papadogiannis, A., Matthaiou, M., Debbah, M.: On the impact of transceiver impairments on AF relaying. In: Proceedings of the IEEE ICASSP13, Vancouver, Canada, pp. 4948–4952, May 2013
4. Bussgang, J.: Crosscorrelation functions of amplitude-distorted Gaussian signals. Research Laboratory of Electronics (1952)
5. Duy, T., Duong, T.Q., da Costa, D.B., Bao, V., Elkashlan, M.: Proactive relay selection with joint impact of hardware impairment and co-channel interference. IEEE Trans. Commun. 63(5), 1594–1606 (2015)
6. Duy, T.T., Trang, C.N., Bao, V.N.Q., Hanh, T.: Joint impact of hardware impairment and co-channel interference on multi-hop relaying. In: International Conference on Advanced Technologies for Communications (ATC), pp. 88–92. IEEE, October 2015
7. Gao, F., Cui, T., Nallanathan, A.: Optimal training design for channel estimation in decode-and-forward relay networks with individual and total power constraints. IEEE Trans. Sig. Process. 56(12), 5937–5949 (2008)
8. Hasna, M.O., Alouini, M.S.: End-to-end performance of transmission systems with relays over Rayleigh-fading channels. IEEE Trans. Wirel. Commun. 2(6), 1126–1131 (2003)
9. Hasna, M., Alouini, M.S.: A performance study of dual-hop transmissions with fixed gain relays. IEEE Trans. Wirel. Commun. 3(6), 1963–1968 (2004)
10. Hassibi, B., Hochwald, B.M.: How much training is needed in multiple-antenna wireless links? IEEE Trans. Inf. Theor. 49(4), 951–963 (2003)
11. Hua, Y., Bliss, D.W., Gazor, S., Rong, Y., Sung, Y.: Theories and methods for advanced wireless relays-Issue I. IEEE J. Sel. Areas Commun. 30(8), 1297–1303 (2012)
12. Ikki, S., Ahmed, M.H.: Performance of decode-and-forward cooperative diversity networks over Nakagami-m fading channels. In: Proceedings of the IEEE GLOBECOM, pp. 4328–4333, November 2007
13. Ikki, S.S.: Performance analysis of cooperative diversity networks with imperfect channel estimation over Rician fading channels. IET Sign. Process. 6(6), 577–583 (2012)
14. Ikki, S.S., Amin, O., Uysal, M.: Performance analysis of cooperative diversity networks with imperfect channel estimation. In: Proceedings of the IEEE ICC, pp. 1–5, June 2010
15. Kay, S.M.: Fundamentals of Statistical Signal Processing: Estimation Theory. Prentice Hall, Englewood Cliffs (1993)
16. Laneman, J.N., Tse, D.N., Wornell, G.W.: Cooperative diversity in wireless networks: efficient protocols and outage behavior. IEEE Trans. Inf. Theor. 50(12), 3062–3080 (2004)
17. Lee, S., Han, M., Hong, D.: Average SNR and ergodic capacity analysis for proactive and reactive DF relaying over Rayleigh fading channels. In: IEEE 69th VTC Spring 2009, pp. 1–5. IEEE, April 2009
18. Lee, S., Han, M., Hong, D.: Average SNR and ergodic capacity analysis for opportunistic DF relaying with outage over Rayleigh fading channels. IEEE Trans. Wirel. Commun. 8(6), 2807–2812 (2009)
19. Li, J., Ge, J., Zhang, C., Shi, J., Rui, Y., Guizani, M.: Impact of channel estimation error on bidirectional MABC-AF relaying with asymmetric traffic requirements. IEEE Trans. Veh. Technol. 62(4), 1755–1769 (2013)
20. Medard, M.: The effect upon channel capacity in wireless communications of perfect and imperfect knowledge of the channel. IEEE Trans. Inf. Theor. 46(3), 933–946 (2000)

21. Mheidat, H., Uysal, M.: Impact of receive diversity on the performance of amplify-and-forward relaying under APS and IPS power constraints. IEEE Commun. Lett. **10**(6), 468–470 (2006)
22. Mishra, A.K., Gowda, S.C.M., Singh, P.: Impact of hardware impairments on TWRN and OWRN AF relaying systems with imperfect channel estimates. In: Proceedings of the IEEE WCNC, March 2017
23. Mishra, A.K., Mallick, D., Issar, M., Singh, P.: Performance analysis of dual-hop DF relaying systems in the combined presence of CEE and RFI. In: Proceedings of the IEEE COMSNETS, pp. 354–359, January 2017
24. Mishra, A.K., Mallick, D., Singh, P.: Combined effect of RF impairment and CEE on the performance of dual-hop fixed-gain AF relaying. IEEE Commun. Lett. **20**(9), 1725–1728 (2016)
25. Pabst, R., Walke, B.H., Schultz, D.C., Herhold, P., Yanikomeroglu, H., Mukherjee, S., Viswanathan, H., Lott, M., Zirwas, W., Dohler, M., et al.: Relay-based deployment concepts for wireless and mobile broadband radio. IEEE Commun. Mag. **42**(9), 80–89 (2004)
26. Schenk, T.: RF Imperfections in High-Rate Wireless Systems: Impact and Digital Compensation. Springer, Heidelberg (2008)
27. Soldani, D., Dixit, S.: Wireless relays for broadband access. IEEE Commun. Mag. **46**(3), 58–66 (2008)
28. Studer, C., Wenk, M., Burg, A.: MIMO transmission with residual transmit-RF impairments. In: IGT/IEEE WSA, pp. 189–196 (2010)
29. Studer, C., Wenk, M., Burg, A.: System-level implications of residual transmit-RF impairments in MIMO systems. In: Proceedings of the 5th European Conference on Antennas and Propagation, pp. 2686–2689. IEEE (2011)
30. Wang, L., Cai, Y., Yang, W.: On the finite-SNR DMT of two-way AF relaying with imperfect CSI. IEEE Wirel. Commun. Lett. **1**(3), 161–164 (2012)
31. Xu, X., Cai, Y., Cai, C., Yang, W.: Overall outage probability of two-way amplify-and-forward relaying in nakagami-m fading channels. In: IEEE WCSP, pp. 1–4, November 2011
32. Yang, C., Wang, W., Zhao, S., Peng, M.: Performance of decode-and-forward opportunistic cooperation with channel estimation errors. In: Proceedings of the IEEE PIMRC, pp. 1967–1971, September 2010

Defending Cyber-Physical Systems from Sensor Attacks

Bharadwaj Satchidanandan$^{(\boxtimes)}$ and P.R. Kumar

Texas A&M University, College Station, USA
bharadwaj.s1990@gmail.com

Abstract. We address the problem of security of cyber-physical systems where some sensors may be malicious. We consider a multiple-input, multiple-output stochastic linear dynamical system controlled over a network of communication and computational nodes which contains (i) a controller that computes the inputs to be applied to the physical plant, (ii) actuators that apply these inputs to the plant, and (iii) sensors which measure the outputs of the plant. Some of these sensors, however, may be malicious. The malicious sensors do not report the true measurements to the controller. Rather, they report false measurements that they fabricate, possibly strategically, so as to achieve any objective that they may have, such as destabilizing the closed-loop system or increasing its running cost. Recently, it was shown that under certain conditions, an approach of "dynamic watermarking" can secure such a stochastic linear dynamical system in the sense that either the presence of malicious sensors in the system is detected, or the malicious sensors are constrained to adding a distortion that can only be of zero power to the noise already entering the system. The first contribution of this paper is to generalize this result to partially observed MIMO systems with both process and observation noises, a model which encompasses some of the previous models for which dynamic watermarking was established to guarantee security. This result, similar to the prior ones, is shown to hold when the controller subjects the reported sequence of measurements to two particular tests of veracity. The second contribution of this paper is in showing, via counterexamples, that both of these tests are needed in order to secure the control system in the sense that if any one of these two tests of sensor veracity is dropped, then the above guarantee does not hold. Finally, a survey of recent results in Dynamic Watermarking is presented, along with a laboratory demonstration in securing a prototypical intelligent transportation system. The proposed approach has several potential applications, including in smart grids, automated transportation, and process control.

This material is based upon work partially supported by NSF under Contract Nos. ECCS-1547075, CNS-1646449, CCF-1619085 and Science & Technology Center Grant CCF-0939370, the U.S. Army Research Office under Contract No. W911NF-15-1-0279, and NPRP grant NPRP 8-1531-2-651 from the Qatar National Research Fund, a member of Qatar Foundation.

P.R. Kumar—*Fellow, IEEE.*

© Springer International Publishing AG 2017
N. Sastry and S. Chakraborty (Eds.): COMSNETS 2017, LNCS 10340, pp. 150–176, 2017.
DOI: 10.1007/978-3-319-67235-9_11

1   Introduction

A major concern that has risen to the fore with the advent of societal scale cyber-physical systems (CPS) capable of meeting global challenges in areas such as energy, water, healthcare, and transportation, is their increased vulnerability to security breaches. Many recent attacks on industrial-grade control systems reinforce this concern. In the year 2010, a computer worm known as Stuxnet subverted the computers controlling the centrifuges in Iran's uranium enrichment facility and issued control commands that caused them to spin at abnormal speeds and tear themselves apart [1]. In order to ensure that the human operators in the facility did not come to know of the attack, Stuxnet recorded sensor measurements under normal operating conditions prior to each attack, and replayed those measurements in the control room in a loop during the attack. This attack is referred to as the replay attack in the literature [2,3]. Another example is the attack on Davis-Besse nuclear power plant in Ohio, where the computers controlling the safety display systems were infected by the Slammer worm, causing them to shut down [4]. While the Slammer worm was not designed to target the power plant, the use of commodity IT solutions in computers controlling the power plant resulted in their vulnerability to generic cyber attacks. Owing to the many advantages that commodity IT solutions bring to Industrial Control Systems (ICS), such as rapid deployability and scalability, their use in ICS, and consequently the latter's vulnerability to cyber attacks, is only expected to increase in the coming years. While the aforementioned attacks originated from security breaches in the cyber layer, and could in principle be addressed by advanced network and information security mechanisms, the following incident illustrates the inadequacy of such an approach in which only the cyber layer is secured in order to secure the cyber-physical system. In the year 2000, a disgruntled employee of a sewage treatment facility in Maroochy-Shire, Australia, issued malicious control commands resulting in $800,000$ litres of raw sewage spilling out [5]. Since this attack was carried out by an insider who had valid authentication credentials and access control, network or information security mechanisms could not have prevented this security breach. This shows the need to fundamentally secure a cyber-physical system from attacks that fall entirely within the domain of the physical layer, i.e., attacks on the plant's physical signals that can be carried out via attacks on its sensors, controllers, etc. It is this topic that is addressed in this paper. Specifically, we extend to partially observed MIMO systems the approach of Dynamic Watermarking [2,6] which secures the physical layer of a cyber-physical system.

Consider a multiple-input, multiple-output partially observed stochastic linear dynamical system controlled over a network of communication and computational nodes. Figure 1 illustrates the architecture of such a system. At the heart of the system is a physical plant actuated by m actuators and whose outputs are measured by n sensors. Some of these sensors may be malicious. The malicious sensors may not report their measurements truthfully to the controller. Rather, they may report false measurements that are fabricated so as to achieve some malicious objective that they may have, such as destabilizing the closed-loop

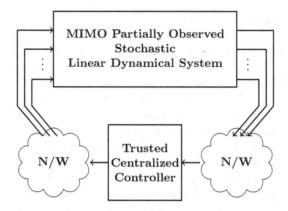

Fig. 1. A networked cyber-physical system

system or increasing its running cost. A trusted centralized controller receives measurements from the sensors, and based on these measurements and a specified control policy, computes the inputs to be applied by the actuators. The controller then communicates this information to the actuators which ultimately apply the inputs. The actuators are assumed to have minimal or no computational capabilities, so that they can be assumed as being honest. All the communication may take place over an underlying communication network such as the Internet. If the communication network is assumed to be secured using a combination of traditional approaches such as cryptography, and more recent ideas such as those reported in [7,8], then one may abstract the communication network as a set of secure, reliable, delay-guaranteed bit pipes between all pairs of nodes in the system. However, it is worth noting that the results reported in this paper also apply to the scenario where only the communication links between the controller and the actuators are secure if they are not collocated, while the other links in the communication network may not be so. We show that for such a system, under certain conditions, dynamic watermarking ensures that the malicious sensors are restricted to adding a distortion to the system's innovations process, the only information required by the controller for controlling the system, that can only be of zero power. This is the fundamental security guarantee provided by dynamic watermarking. It follows that for the class of systems that are open-loop stable, the above result is sufficient to ensure that the malicious sensors cannot destabilize the system, or under a nominal linear control law, cause a quadratic cost of the system to deviate from its optimal value.

The rest of the paper is organized as follows. Section 2 provides an account of related work in this area. Section 3 describes Dynamic Watermarking in the context of a simple first-order linear dynamical system where the core principles are easily illustrated. Section 4 extends the results of the prior section to the more general case of partially observed MIMO linear dynamical systems. It establishes (i) The fundamental security guarantee provided by dynamic watermarking for these systems, and (ii) The minimality of the two particular tests of sensor veracity that are used. Section 5 presents simulation results. The bulk of Sects. 4 and 5 is based on the results presented in COMSNETS 2017 [9]. Section 6 provides a synopsis of some additional results on dynamic watermarking already obtained. This includes the fundamental security guarantee provided by Dynamic Watermarking in the context of (i) ARMAX systems with colored noise and arbitrary delay, a model that is frequently encountered in process control, and (ii) A nonlinear advanced transportation system, along with a laboratory demonstration.

2   Related Work

Initial work on secure CPS involved defining the objective of secure control and identifying distinctive features that make it different from fields such as network and information security [10,11]. Certain key operational goals are identified such as closed-loop stability, and it is proposed that secure control constitutes the maintenance of these key operational goals even under attack, or in the case of cost functions, their graceful degradation. A model for two well-known attacks, viz., the Denial-of-Service (DoS) attack and the deception attack, are presented in [11]. Reference [12] addresses the problem of optimal control under DoS attack.

A standard detection algorithm employed in SCADA systems is the bad data detection (BDD) algorithm [13]. An unobservable attack is defined in [14] as an attack that cannot be detected by a BDD. In order to assess the vulnerability of a given system to unobservable attacks, [15] defines an index termed as "security index". Computation of this index is in general NP-hard, and a method for its efficient, approximate computation is presented in [16].

A particular attack strategy called the packet reordering integrity attack is studied in [17]. In this attack model, the adversary is assumed to have subverted the underlying communication network. The adversary then reorders the sequence of innovations process that the sensors send to the controller, so that the statistical properties of the reported innovations sequence are no different from that of the actual innovations sequence. This ensures that the residue-based anomaly detection algorithms that may be employed in the system do not detect the attack. The effect of packet reordering attack on the state estimation error is then analyzed, and the optimal packet reordering strategy which maximizes the state estimation error is derived.

Reference [18] considers the setup where the adversary has the capability to read and modify all sensor measurements. It restricts the adversary to be linear, i.e., the reported measurement is some linear transformation of the actual data observed by the sensors, and determines linear attack strategy which maximizes the state estimation error subject to the constraint that the attack is not detected by a residue-based detection algorithm.

The disclosure resources of an attacker denote those resources that enable the attacker to gather certain real-time system data. For example, a subverted

communication link through which a sensor transmits its measurements constitutes a disclosure resource since it enables the adversary to gather real-time sensor measurements. Similarly, the disruption resources of an attacker are defined
as those resources that enable the attacker to inject malicious signals into the
system. Based on the attacker's (i) system knowledge, (ii) disclosure resources,
and (iii) disruption resources, an attack space is defined in [19], and commonly
known attacks such as DoS attack, replay attack, zero-dynamics attack, etc., are
mapped into the attack space and analyzed.

At a high level, the aforementioned papers analyze the security vulnerability of CPS, mathematically model known attacks for CPS, present novel attack
strategies on CPS, and analyze their consequences. A parallel body of research
focuses on defending a CPS from such attacks. One of the fundamental problems
encountered is that of attack detection. Fundamental limits of attack detection
and identification for three classes of detectors, viz., static, dynamic, and active,
are presented in [20]. Here, attack detection refers to detection of the presence
of adversarial nodes in the system, whereas attack identification refers to determining the identity of malicious nodes in the system. A static monitor refers to
a detection algorithm that does not exploit system dynamics. A typical example
of a static monitor is the Bad Data Detector [13]. A dynamic monitor, on the
other hand, processes a time series of measurements and uses its knowledge of
the system dynamics to determine whether or not the system is under attack. An
active monitor is a dynamic monitor which also excites the system using inputs
unknown to other entities in the system. The approach of dynamic watermarking
falls in this category.

The resilience of state estimation in CPS to malicious sensors is characterized in [21,22], and for the case when the number of malicious sensors is lesser
than or equal to an appropriate measure of resiliency, an algorithm for optimal
state estimation is developed. Attacks that cannot be detected using the system's inputs and outputs are termed as zero-dynamics attacks. An approach of
perturbing system parameters to detect zero-dynamics attacks is presented in
[23]. A data verification framework for detection and removal of malicious measurements from a wireless sensor network is presented in [24]. The basic idea is
to exploit correlations between the measurements of different sensors to identify
malicious reports.

Qualitatively, the aforementioned defense mechanisms can be classified as
passive defense mechanisms. By and large, this is the approach that has domi-
nated the literature thus far. An alternate paradigm to securing cyber-physical
systems, called "Physical Watermarking" in [25], is that of active defense, where
the controller injects a certain random signal into the system in addition to the
control policy-specified input. We term this random signal the controller's "private excitation." The actual realization of the private excitation is unknown to
other nodes in the system. This private excitation which is applied by the actuators evokes a particular response from the sensors in the system in accordance
with the system dynamics. Therefore, by subjecting the reported sequence of
measurements to some carefully designed tests, one can check if the reported

measurements are appropriately correlated with the private excitation. This in turn can reveal the presence of malicious sensors in the system. The papers [2,3,26] were the first, to our knowledge, to investigate this idea of active defense, and used it to detect replay attacks. The idea was then extended in [25] to detect more intelligent attack strategies. However, a common aspect of these papers is that the reported sequence of measurements are subjected to only one test of sensor veracity, essentially Test 1 described in this paper. While this may ensure that certain *specific* attack policies don't pass the test and are hence detected, it need not be effective in the face of *arbitrary* attack policies. In Sect. 4, we construct an explicit attack policy that causes significant performance degradation to the control system, but nevertheless passes the above test. In [6,27], it has been shown that by subjecting the reported sequence of sensor measurements to an additional test of sensor veracity, one can in fact ensure that even malicious sensors employing *arbitrary* attack strategies are constrained to adding a distortion that can only be of zero power to the process noise already entering the system. This is the fundamental security guarantee provided by this method that is called "dynamic watermarking" in [6]. In this paper, we generalize this result to a more general case of partially observed MIMO systems. We also show that both of the tests are needed in our approach in the sense that neither of them can be dropped from the set if the aforementioned result is to hold.

3   Dynamic Watermarking for First-Order SISO Systems

Consider a first-order single-input-single-output linear dynamical system described by

$$y[t] = ay[t-1] + bu[t-1] + w[t], \tag{1}$$

where $y[t]$ is the output of the system at time t, $u[t]$ is the input to the system at time t, and $w[t] \sim \mathcal{N}(0, \sigma_w^2)$ is the process noise affecting the system at time t. The process noise sequence $\{w\}$ is assumed to be independent and identically distributed (i.i.d) across time, and $a, b, \sigma_w^2 \in \mathbb{R}$ are parameters of the system that are assumed to be known.

Throughout this paper, we assume that a known, possibly history-dependent control policy $\{g_t\}$ is in place which the controller uses to compute the control inputs, i.e., the controller is honest. We assume in this section that the controller is collocated with the actuator. The control input that is supposed to be applied at time t is $g_t(y^t) =: u^g[t]$, where $y^t := (y[0], y[1], ...y[t])$. However, the sensor measurements used in the control law may possibly have been reported erroneously by the sensor.

Owing to the possibility that the sensor may be malicious, we denote by $z[t]$ the measurement *reported* by the sensor at time t. If the sensor is honest, we would have $z \equiv y$. However, if the sensor is malicious, this need not be the case. Since the actuator has access to only the reported measurements $\{z\}$, it computes the input to the plant at time t as $g_t(z^t)$. As described in the previous section, the actuator does not apply this input as such to the plant. Rather, it superimposes on $g_t(z^t)$ a small random signal $e[t]$, called the actuator node's private excitation. As we shall see, this private excitation can serve as a defense against a malicious sensor. Consequently, the net input applied to the system is

$$u[t] = g_t(z^t) + e[t].$$ (2)

Here, $e[t] \sim \mathcal{N}(0, \sigma_e^2)$ for all t, and the sequence $\{e\}$ is chosen by the actuator in an i.i.d fashion across time, (i.e., $\mathbb{E}(e[t]e[t+\tau]) = \sigma_e^2 \delta(\tau)$, where $\delta(\cdot)$ denotes the Kronecker delta function). The value of σ_e^2 is made public, so that the adversary has knowledge of its value. However, the actual realization $e[t]$ is known only to the honest actuator.

The system described in (1) evolves in closed-loop according to

$$y[t+1] = ay[t] + bg_t(z^t) + be[t] + w[t+1].$$ (3)

In order to check if the sensor is malicious or not, the reported sensor measurements $\{z\}$ are subjected to the following two tests performed by the actuator (or finite-time statistically based approximations thereof). If the reported measurements fail either of these tests, the actuator declares the sensor as being malicious, and consequently disables closed-loop control.

Test 1: Check if the reported measurements $\{z\}$ satisfy

$$\lim_{T \to \infty} \frac{1}{T} \sum_{k=1}^{T} (z[k] - az[k-1] - bg_{k-1}(z^{k-1}) - be[k-1])^2 = \sigma_w^2.$$ (4)

Test 2: Check if the reported measurements $\{z\}$ satisfy

$$\lim_{T \to \infty} \frac{1}{T} \sum_{k=1}^{T} e[k-1](z[k] - az[k-1] - bg_{k-1}(z^{k-1}) - be[k-1]) = 0.$$ (5)

Note that (i) the tests are based only upon the information accessible to the actuator, thereby rendering it capable of performing them, and (ii) the true measurements $\{y\}$ would pass both the tests almost surely, so that if the sensor were honest, it would pass the tests almost surely.

The following theorem, which we term the fundamental security guarantee of Dynamic Watermarking, shows that if the sensor passes the above two tests, thereby remaining undetected, then, the malicious sensor is restricted to either reporting the measurements truthfully or adding a distortion to the process noise that can only be of zero power.

Theorem 1. *Define $v[t] := z[t] - az[t-1] - bu^g[t-1] - be[t-1] - w[t]$, so that $v \equiv 0$ for an honest sensor. If the sensor satisfies the above tests (5) and (4), then*

$$\lim_{T \to \infty} \frac{1}{T} \sum_{k=1}^{T} v^2[k] = 0.$$ (6)

Proof. Since $\{z\}$ satisfies (5), we have,

$$\lim_{T \to \infty} \frac{1}{T} \sum_{k=1}^{T} (v[k] + w[k])e[k-1] = 0. \tag{7}$$

Since $e[k-1]$ and $w[k]$ are independent, the above becomes

$$\lim_{T \to \infty} \frac{1}{T} \sum_{k=1}^{T} e[k-1]v[k] = 0. \tag{8}$$

Since the reported sequence also satisfies (4), we have

$$\lim_{T \to \infty} \frac{1}{T} \sum_{k=1}^{T} v^2[k] + 2v[k]w[k-1] + w^2[k-1] = \sigma_w^2.$$

Since $\lim_{T \to \infty} \frac{1}{T} \sum_{k=1}^{T} w^2[k-1] = E\{w^2[k-1]\} = \sigma_w^2$, we have

$$\lim_{T \to \infty} \frac{1}{T} \sum_{k=1}^{T} v^2[k] + \lim_{T \to \infty} \frac{1}{T} \sum_{k=1}^{T} 2v[k]w[k-1] = 0. \tag{9}$$

Equation (8) implies that the quantity $v[k]$ introduced by the sensor is empirically uncorrelated with the actuator's private excitation $e[k-1]$. Now, since the sensor can observe only the sum $be[k-1] + w[k]$ at each time k, and not the random variables $e[k-1]$ and $w[k]$ separately, it is reasonable to hypothesize that if $v[k]$ is uncorrelated with $e[k-1]$ it must also be uncorrelated with $w[k]$. In what follows, we establish this rigorously. The desired result follows by substituting this in (9).

Define the $\sigma-$algebra $\mathcal{S}_{k+1} := \sigma(y^{k+1}, z^{k+1}, e^{k-1})$, and $\widehat{w}[k+1] := E[w[k+1]|\mathcal{S}_{k+1}]$. Since the sequence of observations is i.i.d. Gaussian, the conditional mean estimate of $w[k+1]$ based on observing $be[k] + w[k+1]$ is [28]

$$\widehat{w}[k+1] = \frac{\sigma_w^2}{b^2 \sigma_e^2 + \sigma_w^2} (be[k] + w[k+1]) = \beta(be[k] + w[k+1]),$$

where $\beta := \frac{\sigma_w^2}{b^2 \sigma_e^2 + \sigma_w^2} < 1$. This can be written as

$$\widehat{w}[k+1] = \alpha e[k] + \beta w[k+1], \tag{10}$$

where $\alpha := b\beta$. Let $\widetilde{w}[k+1] := w[k+1] - \widehat{w}[k+1]$. Then, $\widetilde{w}[k+1]$ is a martingale difference sequence with respect to the filtration $\{\mathcal{S}_{k+2}\}$. This is because $\widetilde{w}[k+1] \in \mathcal{S}_{k+2}$ and $E[\widetilde{w}[k+2]|\mathcal{S}_{k+2}] = 0$. Also, we have $v[k] = z[k] - az[k-1] - (y[k] - ay[k-1])$. Therefore, $v[k] \in \mathcal{S}_k$. The Martingale Stability Theorem (MST) [29] applies, and we have

$$\sum_{k=1}^{T} v[k]\widetilde{w}[k] = o(\sum_{k=1}^{T} v^2[k]) + O(1). \tag{11}$$

Hence,

$$\sum_{k=1}^{T} v[k]w[k] = \sum_{k=1}^{T} v[k](\widehat{w}[k] + \widetilde{w}[k]) = \sum_{k=1}^{T} v[k]\widehat{w}[k] + o(\sum_{k=1}^{T} v^2[k]) + O(1).$$

Substituting for the estimate from (10) in the above equation yields,

$$\sum_{k=1}^{T} v[k]w[k] = \alpha \sum_{k=1}^{T} v[k]e[k-1] + \beta \sum_{k=1}^{T} v[k]w[k] + o(\sum_{k=1}^{T} v^2[k]) + O(1).$$

Simplifying,

$$\sum_{k=1}^{T} v[k]w[k] = \frac{\alpha}{1-\beta} \sum_{k=1}^{T} v[k]e[k-1] + o(\sum_{k=1}^{T} v^2[k]) + O(1).$$

From (8), we have $\sum_{k=1}^{T} v[k]e[k-1] = o(T)$. It follows that

$$\sum_{k=1}^{T} v[k]w[k] = o(\sum_{k=1}^{T} v^2[k]) + o(T) + O(1). \tag{12}$$

So,

$$\sum_{k=1}^{T} v^2[k] + \sum_{k=1}^{T} 2v[k]w[k] = (1 + o(1))(\sum_{k=1}^{T} v^2[k]) + O(1)$$

Dividing the above equation by T, taking the limit as $T \to \infty$, and invoking (9) completes the proof. □

Remark 1: The only uncertainties in the system are the initial state of the system $y[0]$ and the noise realization $\{w[1], w[2], w[3], \cdots\}$. Since the actuator can compute $z[t+1] - az[t] - bg_t(z^t) - be[t]$, which will be equal to the process noise if the sensor reports measurements truthfully, the sensor reporting the sequence $\{z\}$ is equivalent to it reporting the sequence of process noise. From the definition of $v[t]$, we have

$$z[t+1] - az[t] - bg_t(z^t) - be[t] = w[t] + v[t+1].$$

Note that the above can be computed by the actuator. i.e., it can compute the sequence $\{w + v\}$. Hence, the above theorem essentially states that a malicious sensor cannot distort the noise realization $\{w[1], w[2], w[3], \cdots\}$ beyond adding a zero-power sequence to it. As shown in a more general setting in Sect. 4, this leads to preservation of stability and performance for open-loop stable systems (Theorem 3).

4   Dynamic Watermarking: The Case of Partially Observed MIMO Systems

Consider a pth order $m \times n$ partially observed MIMO stochastic linear dynamical system described by

$$\begin{aligned}
\mathbf{x}[t+1] &= A\mathbf{x}[t] + B\mathbf{u}[t] + \mathbf{w}[t+1], \\
\mathbf{y}[t+1] &= C\mathbf{x}[t+1] + \mathbf{n}[t+1],
\end{aligned} \tag{13}$$

where $\mathbf{x}[t] \in \mathbb{R}^p$ is the system's state at time t, $\mathbf{u}[t] \in \mathbb{R}^m$ and $\mathbf{y}[t] \in \mathbb{R}^n$ are respectively the system's input and output at time t, $\mathbf{w}[t] \sim \mathcal{N}(0, Q)$ and $\mathbf{n}[t] \sim \mathcal{N}(0, R)$ with $R > 0$ are respectively the process and observation noises at time t, and A, B, C are known matrices of appropriate dimensions which specify the system dynamics. We assume that the random processes $\{\mathbf{w}\}$ and $\{\mathbf{n}\}$ are independent, and also that each of them is i.i.d. across time.

As before, we denote by $\mathbf{z}[t]$ the measurements reported by the sensors at time t to the controller, and assume the existence of a general history-dependent control policy $\{g_t\}$ according to which the controller computes the input that the actuators should apply at each time t. In order to secure the system from malicious sensors, the controller commands the actuators to superimpose a private excitation sequence $\{\mathbf{e}\}$ on the sequence of control policy-specified inputs. Hence, the net input applied to the system at time t is given by $u[t] = g_t(\mathbf{z}^t) + \mathbf{e}[t]$, where $\mathbf{e}[t] \sim \mathcal{N}(0, \sigma_e^2 I)$, i.i.d across time, is the controller's private excitation, and $\mathbf{z}^t := (\mathbf{z}[0], \mathbf{z}[1], ..., \mathbf{z}[t])$ denotes the past values of $\{\mathbf{z}\}$. Consequently, the system evolves as

$$\begin{aligned}
\mathbf{x}[t+1] &= A\mathbf{x}[t] + Bg_t(\mathbf{z}^t) + B\mathbf{e}[t] + \mathbf{w}[t+1], \\
\mathbf{y}[t+1] &= C\mathbf{x}[t+1] + \mathbf{n}[t+1],
\end{aligned} \tag{14}$$

where $g_t(\mathbf{z}^t) := [g_t^1(\mathbf{z}^t), g_t^2(\mathbf{z}^t), ..., g_t^m(\mathbf{z}^t)]^T$.

Assume that (A, C) is observable, and $(A, Q^{\frac{1}{2}})$ is reachable. The controller performs Kalman filtering on the reported sequence of measurements as follows. Let $\mathbf{x}_F(k|k)$ denote the estimate of the state $\mathbf{x}[k]$ given the information upto time k, i.e., $(\mathbf{z}^k, \mathbf{e}^{k-1})$, and $\mathbf{x}_F(k|k-1)$ denote the estimate given the information upto time $k-1$. They are given by the Kalman filtering equations:

$$\mathbf{x}_F(k+1|k+1) = A\mathbf{x}_F(k|k) + Bg_k(\mathbf{z}^k) + B\mathbf{e}[k] + K_{k+1}\nu_F[k+1], \tag{15}$$

where $\nu_F[k+1] := \mathbf{z}[k+1] - C\mathbf{x}_F(k+1|k)$. We note that if the sensors were truthful, the estimates above would be the conditional mean estimates, and $\nu[t+1]$ would be the innovations process [30] at time t. However, the sensor may be malicious, and so we refer to $\nu_F[t+1]$ as the "false innovations" at time $t+1$. For the purpose of analysis, we also define the "true" Kalman filter which operates on $\{\mathbf{y}\}$:

$$\mathbf{x}_T(k+1|k+1) = A\mathbf{x}_T(k|k) + Bg_k(\mathbf{z}^k) + B\mathbf{e}[k] + K_{k+1}\nu_T[k+1], \tag{16}$$

where $\boldsymbol{\nu}_T[k+1] := \mathbf{y}[k+1] - C\mathbf{x}_T(k+1|k)$ is the "true innovations" at time $k+1$. We suppose that the Kalman filters are initialized with the Kalman gain K_0 set to its steady-state value K so that they behave as time-invariant filters [28].

The dynamic watermarking tests we employ are based on the following two observations that hold for the true Kalman filter:

1. $\mathbf{e}[k]$ is independent of $K\boldsymbol{\nu}_T[k+1]$, and
2. the sequence of conditional estimates $\{\mathbf{x}_T(k|k)\}$ satisfies

$$\{\mathbf{x}_T(k+1|k+1) - A\mathbf{x}_T(k|k) - Bg_k(\mathbf{y}^k) - B\mathbf{e}[k]\} \sim \mathcal{N}(0, K\Sigma K^T),$$

where

$$K = PC^T(CPC^T + R)^{-1} \tag{17}$$

is the steady-state Kalman gain of the Kalman filter,

$$\Sigma = CPC^T + R \tag{18}$$

is the steady-state covariance matrix of the true innovations process, and P is the unique nonnegative definite solution of the discrete algebraic Riccati equation $P = APA^T + Q - APC^T(CPC^T + R)^{-1}CPA^T$. The unique nonnegative definite solution P is guaranteed to exist for the above Riccati equation since (A, C) is observable, $(A, Q^{\frac{1}{2}})$ is reachable, and $R > 0$ [28]. The matrix P has the interpretation of the covariance matrix of the one-step ahead state prediction error of the Kalman filter [28].

The controller therefore performs the following two tests on the reported sequence of observations $\{\mathbf{z}\}$:

1. **Controller Test 1:** Check if the sequence of reported measurements satisfies

$$\lim_{T \to \infty} \frac{1}{T} \sum_{k=0}^{T-1} (\mathbf{x}_F(k+1|k+1) - A\mathbf{x}_F(k|k) - Bg_k(\mathbf{z}^k) - B\mathbf{e}[k])$$
$$(\mathbf{x}_F(k+1|k+1) - A\mathbf{x}_F(k|k) - Bg_k(\mathbf{z}^k) - B\mathbf{e}[k])^T = K\Sigma K^T. \tag{19}$$

2. **Controller Test 2:** Check if the sequence of reported observations satisfies

$$\lim_{T \to \infty} \frac{1}{T} \sum_{k=0}^{T-1} \mathbf{e}[k](\mathbf{x}_F(k+1|k+1) - A\mathbf{x}_F(k|k) - Bg_k(\mathbf{z}^k) - B\mathbf{e}[k])^T = 0. \tag{20}$$

The above tests are equivalent to the tests proposed in [6]. In particular, the second test above can be shown, via straightforward algebraic manipulations, to be equivalent to the corresponding test for first-order SISO systems considered in [6]. We define

$$\mathbf{v}[k+1] := \mathbf{x}_F(k+1|k+1) - A\mathbf{x}_F(k|k) - Bg_k(\mathbf{z}^k) - B\mathbf{e}[k] - K\boldsymbol{\nu}_T[k+1], \tag{21}$$

and note that if there are no malicious sensors in the system, $\mathbf{v} \equiv 0$. We will call the quantity

$$\lim_{T \to \infty} \frac{1}{T} \sum_{k=1}^{T} \|\mathbf{v}[k]\|^2$$

as the *additive distortion power* of the malicious sensors, for reasons explained later in the paper.

The following theorem, which is a generalization of the results in [6], establishes the fundamental security guarantee provided by dynamic watermarking.

Theorem 2. *Suppose that (A, C) is observable, $(A, Q^{\frac{1}{2}})$ is reachable, and $R > 0$. Further suppose that the matrix CB is of rank n. Then, if the reported measurements $\{\mathbf{z}\}$ pass both (20) and (19), it can be guaranteed that the additive distortion is of zero power, i.e.,*

$$\lim_{T \to \infty} \frac{1}{T} \sum_{k=1}^{T} \|\mathbf{v}[k]\|^2 = 0. \tag{22}$$

Proof. We appeal to the following lemma.

Lemma 1: Define $M := \Sigma(\Sigma + \sigma_e^2 CBB^T C^T)^{-1}$. If CB is of rank n, then, $(I - M)^{-1}$ exists.   □

Proof.

$$I - M = I - \Sigma[\Sigma + \sigma_e^2 CBB^T C^T]^{-1}. \tag{23}$$

In the above, $[\Sigma + \sigma_e^2 CBB^T C^T]^{-1}$ is guaranteed to exist since $\Sigma > 0$ (because $R > 0$). Its inverse is

$$(I - M)^{-1} = I + \Sigma(\sigma_e^2 CBB^T C^T)^{-1}, \tag{24}$$

since $(\sigma_e^2 CBB^T C^T)^{-1}$ exists because CB has rank n.   □

Since the reported measurements pass (20), we have using (21),

$$\lim_{T \to \infty} \frac{1}{T} \sum_{k=0}^{T-1} \mathbf{e}[k](K\boldsymbol{\nu}_T[k+1] + \mathbf{v}[k+1])^T = 0.$$

Since $\mathbf{e}[k]$ is independent of the innovations $\boldsymbol{\nu}_T[k+1]$, the above simplifies to

$$\lim_{T \to \infty} \frac{1}{T} \sum_{k=0}^{T-1} \mathbf{e}[k]\mathbf{v}^T[k+1] = 0. \tag{25}$$

Since the reported measurements also pass (19), we have using (21),

$$\lim_{T \to \infty} \frac{1}{T} \sum_{k=0}^{T-1} (K\boldsymbol{\nu}_T[k+1] + \mathbf{v}[k+1])(K\boldsymbol{\nu}_T[k+1] + \mathbf{v}[k+1])^T = K\Sigma K^T.$$

Simplifying the above gives

$$\lim_{T \to \infty} \frac{1}{T} \sum_{k=0}^{T-1} K\boldsymbol{\nu}_T[k+1]\mathbf{v}^T[k+1] + (K\boldsymbol{\nu}_T[k+1]\mathbf{v}^T[k+1])^T$$

$$+\mathbf{v}[k+1]\mathbf{v}^T[k+1] = 0. \qquad (26)$$

Define the σ-algebra

$$\mathcal{S}_{k+1} := \sigma(\mathbf{y}^{k+1}, \mathbf{z}^{k+1}, \mathbf{e}^{k-1}, \mathbf{x}_T^{k|k}),$$

where $\mathbf{x}_T^{k|k} := (\mathbf{x}_T(0|0), \mathbf{x}_T(1|1), ..., \mathbf{x}_T(k|k))$. We also define $\widehat{\boldsymbol{\nu}}_T[k] := \mathbb{E}[\boldsymbol{\nu}_T[k]|\mathcal{S}_k]$, and $\widetilde{\boldsymbol{\nu}}_T[k] := \boldsymbol{\nu}_T[k] - \widehat{\boldsymbol{\nu}}_T[k]$. Then, from the definition of the innovations at time $k+1$, we have

$$\boldsymbol{\nu}_T[k+1] := \mathbf{y}[k+1] - C\mathbf{x}_T(k+1|k) = \mathbf{y}[k+1] - CA\mathbf{x}_T(k|k) - CBg_k(\mathbf{z}^k) - CB\mathbf{e}[k]. \qquad (27)$$

From the above, it follows that

$$(\mathbf{y}^k, \mathbf{e}^{k-1}, \mathbf{x}_T^{k-1|k-1}) \to (\mathbf{x}_T(k|k), \mathbf{y}[k+1], \mathbf{z}^{k+1}) \to \boldsymbol{\nu}_T[k+1]$$

forms a Markov chain. Therefore,

$$\widehat{\boldsymbol{\nu}}_T[k+1] := \mathbb{E}[\boldsymbol{\nu}_T[k+1]\big|\sigma(\mathbf{y}^{k+1}, \mathbf{z}^{k+1}, \mathbf{e}^{k-1}, \mathbf{x}_T^{k|k})]$$

$$= \mathbb{E}[\boldsymbol{\nu}_T[k+1]\big|\sigma(\mathbf{x}_T(k|k), \mathbf{y}[k+1], \mathbf{z}^{k+1})].$$

Combining the above with (27), we have the MMSE estimate as [28, Chap. 7, Lemma 2.5]

$$\widehat{\boldsymbol{\nu}}_T[k+1] = M(CB\mathbf{e}[k] + \boldsymbol{\nu}_T[k+1]). \qquad (28)$$

Hence,

$$\boldsymbol{\nu}_T[k+1] = \widehat{\boldsymbol{\nu}}_T[k+1] + \widetilde{\boldsymbol{\nu}}_T[k+1] = MCB\mathbf{e}[k] + M\boldsymbol{\nu}_T[k+1] + \widetilde{\boldsymbol{\nu}}_T[k+1]$$

Rearranging and using Lemma 1, we have

$$\boldsymbol{\nu}_T[k+1] = (I-M)^{-1}MCB\mathbf{e}[k] + (I-M)^{-1}\widetilde{\boldsymbol{\nu}}_T[k+1]. \qquad (29)$$

Now, the RHS of (27), and hence $\boldsymbol{\nu}_T[k+1]$, is measurable with respect to $\mathcal{S}_{k+2}$. Also, since $\widehat{\boldsymbol{\nu}}_T[k+1] \in \mathcal{S}_{k+1} \subset \mathcal{S}_{k+2}$, it follows that $\widetilde{\boldsymbol{\nu}}_T[k+1] \in \mathcal{S}_{k+2}$. Clearly, $\mathbb{E}[\widetilde{\boldsymbol{\nu}}_T[k+2]|\mathcal{S}_{k+2}] = 0$. Hence, we have that $(\widetilde{\boldsymbol{\nu}}_T[k+1], \mathcal{S}_{k+2})$ is a martingale difference sequence. Moreover, since $\mathbf{v}[k+1]$, after some algebra, can be expressed as $K(\mathbf{z}[k+1] - \mathbf{y}[k+1]) - KCA(\mathbf{x}_F(k|k) - \mathbf{x}_T(k|k))$, we have $\mathbf{v}[k+1] \in \mathcal{S}_{k+1}$. Hence, Martingale Stability Theorem (MST) [29, Lemma 2(iii)] holds, and we have

$$\sum_{k=0}^{T-1} \widetilde{\boldsymbol{\nu}}_T[k+1]\mathbf{v}^T[k+1] =$$

$$\begin{bmatrix} o(\sum_{k=1}^T v_1^2[k]) & \cdots & o(\sum_{k=1}^T v_p^2[k]) \\ \vdots & \vdots & \vdots \\ o(\sum_{k=1}^T v_1^2[k]) & \cdots & o(\sum_{k=1}^T v_p^2[k]) \end{bmatrix} + [O(1)]_{p \times p}, \qquad (30)$$

where $[O(1)]_{p \times p}$ denotes a $p \times p$ matrix all of whose entries are $O(1)$. Substituting (29) in (26) and using (25) and (30) yields

$$\sum_{k=1}^{T} \mathbf{v}[k] \mathbf{v}^{T}[k] + \begin{bmatrix} o(T) & \cdots & o(T) \\ \vdots & \vdots & \vdots \\ o(T) & \cdots & o(T) \end{bmatrix} + \begin{bmatrix} o(\sum_{k=1}^{T} v_1^2[k]) & \cdots & o(\sum_{k=1}^{T} v_p^2[k]) \\ \vdots & & \vdots \\ o(\sum_{k=1}^{T} v_1^2[k]) & \cdots & o(\sum_{k=1}^{T} v_p^2[k]) \end{bmatrix}$$

$$+ \begin{bmatrix} o(\sum_{k=1}^{T} v_1^2[k]) & \cdots & o(\sum_{k=1}^{T} v_1^2[k]) \\ \vdots & \vdots & \vdots \\ o(\sum_{k=1}^{T} v_p^2[k]) & \cdots & o(\sum_{k=1}^{T} v_p^2[k]) \end{bmatrix} = o(T). \quad (31)$$

Dividing the above by T, equating the trace, and letting $T \to \infty$ completes the proof. □

We now show that if one drops either of the two controller tests (20) or (19), then the guarantee does not hold. We do so by explicitly constructing two attack strategies, each of which passes exactly each one of the tests, and yet, $\lim_{T \to \infty} \frac{1}{T} \sum_{k=1}^{T} \|\mathbf{v}[k]\|^2 \neq 0$ for both the attacks.

Consider a special case of system (13), viz., a SISO first-order perfectly observed system ($p = m = n = C = 1, R = 0, Q = \sigma_w^2 \in \mathbb{R}_+$). In that case, $\mathbf{x}_F(k|k)$ reduces to $z[k]$, $\boldsymbol{\nu}_T[k]$ to $w[k]$, K to 1, and Σ to σ_w^2. Consequently, tests (19) and (20) reduce respectively to

1. **Test 1:** Check if the reported sequence of measurements $\{z\}$ satisfies

$$\lim_{T \to \infty} \frac{1}{T} \sum_{k=1}^{T} (z[k+1] - Az[k] - Bg_k(z^k) - Be[k])^2 = \sigma_w^2, \quad (32)$$

2. **Test 2:** Check if the reported sequence of measurements $\{z\}$ satisfies

$$\lim_{T \to \infty} \frac{1}{T} \sum_{k=1}^{T} e[k](z[k+1] - Az[k] - Bg_k(z^k) - Be[k]) = 0, \quad (33)$$

and $v[t+1] = z[t+1] - Az[t] - Bg_t(z^t) - Be[t] - w[t+1]$.

Counterexample showing Controller Test 1 alone is not sufficient: Suppose that the reported measurements are subjected to (32) alone, the first test. To show that this is not sufficient to guarantee zero additive distortion power by the malicious sensor, consider the following attack.

Suppose that the malicious sensor reports measurements $\{z\}$ generated as

$$z[k+1] = Az[k] + Bg_k(z^k) + \left(\frac{B^2 \sigma_e^2 - \sigma_w^2}{B^2 \sigma_e^2 + \sigma_w^2}\right)(y[k+1] - Ay[k] - Bg_k(z^k)). \quad (34)$$

We now show that the sequence $\{z\}$ so generated passes (32), the first test.

Define $\gamma[k] := z[k] - Az[k-1] - Bu^g[k-1] - Be[k-1]$, the quantity whose second moment is being empirically tested in (32). Then, we have

$$\gamma[k] = z[k] - Az[k-1] - Bg_{k-1}(z^{k-1}) - Be[k-1]$$

$$= (\frac{B^2\sigma_e^2 - \sigma_w^2}{B^2\sigma_e^2 + \sigma_w^2})(y[k] - Ay[k-1] - Bg_{k-1}(z^{k-1}) - Be[k-1])$$

$$= (\frac{B^2\sigma_e^2 - \sigma_w^2}{B^2\sigma_e^2 + \sigma_w^2})(Be[k-1] + w[k]) - Be[k-1]$$

$$= -\frac{2\sigma_w^2}{B^2\sigma_e^2 + \sigma_w^2}Be[k-1] + (\frac{B^2\sigma_e^2 - \sigma_w^2}{B^2\sigma_e^2 + \sigma_w^2})w[k]. \tag{35}$$

From the above, it is clear that $\lim_{T\to\infty} \frac{1}{T}\sum_{k=1}^{T} \gamma^2[k]$ of (32) is simply the variance of the RHS of the above, given by

$$(\frac{-2\sigma_w^2 B}{B^2\sigma_e^2 + \sigma_w^2})^2 + (\frac{B^2\sigma_e^2 - \sigma_w^2}{B^2\sigma_e^2 + \sigma_w^2})^2.$$

This simplifies to σ_w^2, and hence, this attack passes Test 1.

Finally, for the above attack, it is easy to see that $v[k+1] = \gamma[k+1] - w[k+1] = -\frac{2\sigma_w^2}{B^2\sigma_e^2 + \sigma_w^2}(Be[k] + w[k+1])$, and hence, $\lim_{T\to\infty} \frac{1}{T}\sum_{k=1}^{T} v^2[k] = \frac{4\sigma_w^4}{B^2\sigma_e^2 + \sigma_w^2} \neq 0.\square$

Counterexample showing Controller Test 2 alone is not sufficient: Now suppose that the reported measurements are subjected to (33) alone. To show that this is not sufficient to guarantee zero additive distortion power by the malicious sensor, consider the following attack. The sensor reports measurements $\{z\}$ generated as

$$z[k+1] = Az[k] + Bg_k(z^k) + (y[k+1] - Ay[k] - Bg_k(z^k) + \lambda[k+1]), \tag{36}$$

where $\lambda[k+1] \sim \mathcal{N}(0, \sigma_\lambda^2)$ is chosen by the sensor in an i.i.d. fashion across time, and also independently of all random variables that it has observed till then.

To show that the sequence $\{z\}$ so generated passes (33), the second test, note that

$$\lim_{T\to\infty} \frac{1}{T}\sum_{k=0}^{T-1} e[k](z[k+1] - Az[k] - Bg_k(z^k) - Be[k])$$

$$= \lim_{T\to\infty} \frac{1}{T}\sum_{k=0}^{T-1} e[k](y[k+1] - Ay[k] - Bg_k(z^k) + \lambda[k+1] - Be[k])$$

$$= \lim_{T\to\infty} \frac{1}{T}\sum_{k=0}^{T-1} e[k](w[k+1] + \lambda[k+1]).$$

Since $w[k+1]$ and $\lambda[k+1]$ are independent of $e[k]$, the above reduces to 0, thereby passing (33), and hence, (20).

However, for the above attack, it is easy to see that $v[k+1] = \lambda[k+1]$, and hence, $\lim_{T\to\infty} \frac{1}{T}\sum_{k=1}^{T} v^2[k] = E[\lambda^2[k]] = \sigma_\lambda^2 \neq 0.$ $\square$

Remark: It is well known that the innovations process of a stochastic process is a causal and causally invertible transformation of the stochastic process with the property that it is uncorrelated across time [30]. Hence, the innovations at time t can be thought of as summarizing all the "new" information provided by the sensors at time t, information that could not have been predicted from the past. Therefore, one can think of the honest sensors' purpose as being to report the innovations at each time t. Now, from (21), we have $\mathbf{x}_F(k+1|k+1) - A\mathbf{x}_F(k|k) - Bg_k(\mathbf{z}^k) - B\mathbf{e}[k] = K\boldsymbol{\nu}_T[k+1] + \mathbf{v}[k+1]$. The LHS of the above can be computed by the controller. Hence, $\mathbf{v}[k+1]$ has a physical interpretation as the distortion added by the malicious sensors to the true innovations at time $k+1$ (hence the nomenclature for additive distortion power). What the above theorem says is that the malicious sensors cannot distort the true innovations process beyond adding a zero-power sequence to it if they wish to remain undetected.

We now consider linear control designs that provide some guarantee on the quadratic state tracking error. The design need not be an optimal LQG design, but one that merely aims at providing some upper bound on the aforementioned quantity. The following theorem shows that for stable systems, guaranteeing that any additive distortion is of power zero is sufficient to ensure that the malicious sensors do not increase the quadratic cost of the state from its design value in the case of linear designs.

Theorem 3. *Suppose that the system (13) is open-loop stable, i.e., A has all its eigenvalues in the open left half-plane, and define*

$$\mathbf{d}[k] := \mathbf{x}_F(k|k) - \mathbf{x}_T(k|k). \tag{37}$$

If the reported measurements pass (20) and (19), then,

1.

$$\lim_{T \to \infty} \frac{1}{T} \sum_{k=0}^{T-1} \|\mathbf{d}[k]\|^2 = 0. \tag{38}$$

2. Suppose that the control policy is a linear feedback policy $g_t(\mathbf{z}^t) = F\mathbf{x}_F(t|t)$, and a control objective is quadratic regulation. Then, the true quadratic regulation performance $\lim_{T \to \infty} \frac{1}{T} \sum_{k=0}^{T-1} \|\mathbf{x}_T(k|k)\|^2$ of the system is no different from what the controller thinks it is, in the sense that

$$\lim_{T \to \infty} \frac{1}{T} \sum_{k=0}^{T-1} \|\mathbf{x}_F(k|k)\|^2 = \lim_{T \to \infty} \frac{1}{T} \sum_{k=0}^{T-1} \|\mathbf{x}_T(k|k)\|^2 \tag{39}$$

3. Under the same conditions as (2) above, the malicious sensors cannot increase the quadratic regulation cost of the system $\lim_{T \to \infty} \frac{1}{T} \sum_{k=0}^{T-1} \|\mathbf{x}_T(k|k)\|^2$ from the value that would be obtained if all the sensors were honest.

Proof. Subtracting (16) from (15), we have $\mathbf{d}[k+1] = A\mathbf{d}[k] + K(\boldsymbol{\nu}_F[k+1] - \boldsymbol{\nu}_T[k+1])$. From (15), we have $K\boldsymbol{\nu}_F[k+1] = \mathbf{x}_F(k+1|k+1) - A\mathbf{x}_F(k|k) -$

$Bg_k(\mathbf{z}^k) - Be[k]$. Combining this with (21) gives $K(\boldsymbol{\nu}_F[k+1] - \boldsymbol{\nu}_T[k+1]) = \mathbf{v}[k+1]$. Substituting this in the above equation gives $\mathbf{d}[k+1] = A\mathbf{d}[k] + \mathbf{v}[k+1]$. Since $\{\mathbf{v}\}$ is of zero power and A is stable, result (1) follows.

Now, from (37), we have $\mathbf{x}_F(k|k) = \mathbf{x}_T(k|k) + \mathbf{d}[k]$. By triangular inequality, we have $\|\mathbf{x}_F(k|k)\| \leq \|\mathbf{x}_T(k|k)\| + \|\mathbf{d}[k]\|$. Hence, $\|\mathbf{x}_F(k|k)\|^2 \leq \|\mathbf{x}_T(k|k)\|^2 + \|\mathbf{d}[k]\|^2 + 2\|\gamma\mathbf{x}_T(k|k)\|\|\gamma^{-1}\mathbf{d}[k]\|$ for all $\gamma > 0$. Since $2\|\gamma\mathbf{x}_T(k|k)\|\|\gamma^{-1}\mathbf{d}[k]\| \leq \|\gamma\mathbf{x}_T(k|k)\|^2 + \|\gamma^{-1}\mathbf{d}[k]\|^2$, substituting this in the above yields $\|\mathbf{x}_F(k|k)\|^2 \leq (1+\gamma^2)\|\mathbf{x}_T(k|k)\|^2 + (1+\gamma^{-2})\|\mathbf{d}[k]\|^2$. Hence,

$$\lim_{T\to\infty} \frac{1}{T} \sum_{k=0}^{T-1} \|\mathbf{x}_F(k|k)\|^2 \leq \lim_{T\to\infty} \frac{1}{T} \sum_{k=0}^{T-1} (1+\gamma^2)\|\mathbf{x}_T(k|k)\|^2$$
$$+ \lim_{T\to\infty} \frac{1}{T} \sum_{k=0}^{T-1} (1+\gamma^{-2})\|\mathbf{d}[k]\|^2$$

The second term reduces to zero from the previous result. Since the above is true for all $\gamma > 0$, taking $\gamma \to 0$ gives

$$\lim_{T\to\infty} \frac{1}{T} \sum_{k=0}^{T-1} \|\mathbf{x}_F(k|k)\|^2 \leq \lim_{T\to\infty} \frac{1}{T} \sum_{k=0}^{T-1} \|\mathbf{x}_T(k|k)\|^2. \tag{40}$$

Similarly, from (37), we have $\mathbf{x}_T(k|k) = \mathbf{x}_F(k|k) - \mathbf{d}[k]$. Hence, $\|\mathbf{x}_T(k|k)\| = \|\mathbf{x}_F(k|k) - \mathbf{d}[k]\| \leq \|\mathbf{x}_F(k|k)\| + \|\mathbf{d}[k]\|$. Continuing as above, we arrive at

$$\lim_{T\to\infty} \frac{1}{T} \sum_{k=0}^{T-1} \|\mathbf{x}_T(k|k)\|^2 \leq \lim_{T\to\infty} \frac{1}{T} \sum_{k=0}^{T-1} \|\mathbf{x}_F(k|k)\|^2. \tag{41}$$

Combining the above with (40) gives the second result.

It follows from the above result that even though the controller does not have access to the true measurements $\{\mathbf{y}\}$, it can empirically compute the true quadratic regulation cost $\mathbb{E}[\|\mathbf{x}_T(k|k)\|^2]$ of the system. It follows that the malicious sensors cannot increase the true quadratic regulation cost of the system from its design value without exposing their presence.   □

5   Simulation Results

This section presents the simulation results of the attacks presented in the previous section. The attacks are simulated for system parameters $A = 0.5, B = 1, \sigma_w^2 = 2$, and with $\sigma_e^2 = 1$, $g_k(\mathbf{z}^k) = -0.1z[k]$.

We first present the results for the attack that passes Test 1 alone. We call this "Attack 1." Fig. 2 plots $\delta_1[t] := \frac{1}{t} \sum_{k=1}^{t} \gamma^2[k]$ as a function of t, where $\gamma[k]$ is computed using the measurements generated using (34). It can be seen that it approaches the value of σ_w^2, thereby passing Test 1.

Also,   for   Attack   1,   we   have   the   additive   distortion power $\lim_{T\to\infty} \frac{1}{T} \sum_{k=1}^{T} v^2[k] = \frac{4\sigma_w^4}{B^2\sigma_e^2 + \sigma_w^2} = \frac{16}{3}$. Figure 3 plots $\frac{1}{t} \sum_{k=1}^{t} v^2[k]$ as

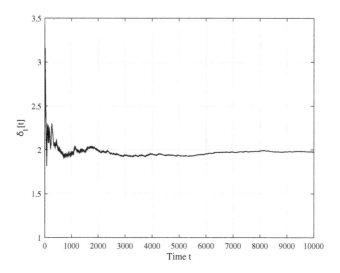

Fig. 2. Test statistic of Test 1 vs. time

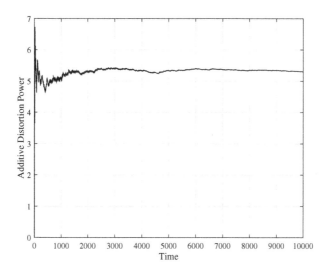

Fig. 3. Additive distortion power of Attack 1 vs. time

a function of t, and it can be seen that it indeed approaches $\frac{16}{3} = 5.3$, showing that the additive distortion power is not equal to zero. This shows that Test 1 alone is not sufficient to guard against Attack 1.

Next, we present analogous results for the attack passing Test 2 alone. We call this "Attack 2". The adversary is simulated with $\sigma_\lambda^2 = 4$. Figure 4 plots $\delta_2[t] := \frac{1}{t}\sum_{k=1}^{t} e[k](z[k+1] - Az[k] - Bg_k(z^k) - Be[k])$ as a function of t,

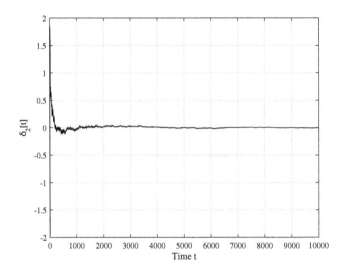

Fig. 4. Test statistic of Test 2 vs. time

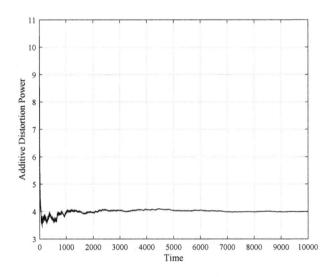

Fig. 5. Additive distortion power of Attack 2 vs. time

where $\{z\}$ is computed using (36). It can be seen that it approaches the value of 0, thereby passing Test 2.

Finally, for Attack 2, the additive distortion power $\lim_{T \to \infty} \frac{1}{T} \sum_{k=1}^{T} v^2[k] = \sigma_\lambda^2 = 4$. Figure 5 plots $\frac{1}{t} \sum_{k=1}^{t} v^2[k]$ as a function of t, and it can be seen that it indeed approaches the value of 4, showing that the additive distortion power is not equal to zero. This shows that Test 2 alone is not sufficient to guard against Attack 2.

6 Extensions to ARMAX and Nonlinear Models

The system models considered in the previous sections are among the simplest that lend themselves to analytical tractability. While many real-world systems do not obey these models, they serve as natural starting points to analyze or evaluate a new theory or methodology, which in our case is Dynamic Watermarking. The insights gained through the analysis of such systems often extend to more complex system models that one encounters in practice. The Auto-Regressive Moving Average Input (ARMAX) system model is one such model that is frequently encountered in process control. Another such model that is of interest in vehicular cyber-physical systems is a nonlinear kinematic model. In this section, we present a synopsis of our results reported in [6,27,31] on the application and demonstration of Dynamic Watermarking in securing these systems.

6.1 ARMAX Systems with Arbitrary Delay

An ARMAX system with finite but arbitrary delay l is described by the following dynamics.

$$y[t] = -\sum_{k=1}^{p} a_k y[t-k] + \sum_{k=0}^{h} b_k u[t-l-k] + \sum_{k=0}^{r} c_k w[t-k]. \tag{42}$$

We assume with no loss of generality that $c_0 = 1$. Let q^{-1} be the backward shift operator, and $a_0 := 1$, $A(q^{-1}) := a_0 + a_1 q^{-1} + ... + a_p q^{-p}$, $B(q^{-1}) := b_0 + b_1 q^{-1} + ... + b_h q^{-h}$, $C(q^{-1}) := c_0 + c_1 q^{-1} + ... + c_r q^{-r}$. We assume $B(q^{-1})$ and $C(q^{-1})$ to be strictly minimum phase, i.e., all roots of $B(q^{-1}) = 0$ and $C(q^{-1}) = 0$ satisfy $|q| > 1$.

As before, the actuator is assumed to be honest, and the sensor may be malicious. In order to secure the system, the actuator applies the control

$$u[t] = u^g[t] + B^{-1}(q^{-1})C(q^{-1})e[t], \tag{43}$$

where $u^g[t]$ is the control policy-specified input, and $\{e\}$ is a sequence of i.i.d Gaussian random variables with distribution $\mathcal{N}(0, \sigma_e^2)$, denoting the actuator node's private excitation. The above is a stable generation of control inputs since $B(q^{-1})$ is minimum phase.

As usual, let $z[t]$ denote the measurements reported by the sensor at time t. These reported measurements are subjected to the following tests [6] to detect whether or not the sensor is indeed malicious. The fundamental idea behind the tests is to compute the prediction-error of the reported sequence $\{z\}$, and check if it has the appropriate statistics. Towards this, the actuator filters the reported measurements with the prediction-error filter defined through the following recursion for all $t \geq 0$.

$$z_{t|t-1} = -\sum_{k=1}^{p} a_k z[t-k] + \sum_{k=0}^{h} b_k u^g[t-l-k] \quad + \sum_{k=1}^{r} c_k \tilde{z}[t-k], \tag{44}$$

$$\tilde{z}[t] = z[t] - z_{t|t-1}. \tag{45}$$

We assume that the filter is initialized with $\tilde{z}[-k] = \lambda[-k], k \in \{-1, -2, ..., -r\}$. Note that this filter produces $\tilde{z}[t] \equiv \lambda[t]$ if $z[t] \equiv y[t]$. Based on this observation, we propose that the actuator perform the following two tests of sensor veracity:

1. **Test 1:** Check if

$$\lim_{T \to \infty} \frac{1}{T} \sum_{k=0}^{T-1} (\tilde{z}[k] - e[k-l])^2 = \sigma_w^2. \tag{46}$$

2. **Test 2:** Check if

$$\lim_{T \to \infty} \frac{1}{T} \sum_{k=0}^{T-1} \tilde{z}^2[k] = \sigma_w^2 + \sigma_e^2. \tag{47}$$

The following theorem establishes the fundamental security guarantee of Dynamic Watermarking for ARMAX systems.

Theorem 4. *[6] Define* $v[t] := \sum_{k=0}^{p} a_k z[t-k] - \sum_{k=0}^{h} b_k u^g[t-l-k] - \sum_{k=0}^{r} c_k \lambda[t-k]$, *so that for an honest sensor reporting* $z[t] = y[t]$ *for all* t, *the sequence* $v[t]$ *is identically zero, i.e.,* $v \equiv 0$. *If the sensor passes tests (46) and (47), then,*

$$\lim_{T \to \infty} \frac{1}{T} \sum_{k=0}^{T-1} v^2[k] = 0.$$

Proof. See [6]. □

6.2   The Nonlinear Intelligent Transportation System

The experimental setup, which is shown in Fig. 6, is a prototype of an automated transportation system, housed in the Cyber-Physical Systems laboratory at Texas A&M University. The system consists of a collection of vehicles whose high-level control objective is to track a given trajectory. It contains a collision avoidance module that is designed to avoid collisions with other vehicles *provided* it receives accurate sensor measurements of its and other vehicles' positions. Generally, automated or semi-automated transportation systems rely on various sensors to determine the state of the system which includes the position of every vehicle and its velocity, etc. An adversary can compromise the safety of such a system by subverting some of the sensors in the system and reporting false measurements on their behalf. We first demonstrate such an attack which results in collisions.

A set of ten cameras monitor the area in which the vehicles are operated, and capture an image of the field once every 100 ms. These images are relayed to the vision sensors which compute the coordinates (x_i, y_i) and orientation θ_i of vehicle i at each sampling instant t from these images. A low-level controller determines the control input to be applied to each vehicle in order to track the desired trajectory based on the information it receives from the vision sensors.

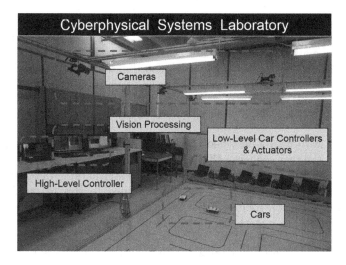

Fig. 6. Experimental facility for dynamic watermarking

It computes these control inputs using Model Predictive Control, and relays this information to the collision avoidance module of the system.

The plant model for vehicle i is given by its kinematic equations:

$$x_i[t+1] = x_i[t] + h\cos(\theta_i[t])v_i[t] + h\cos(\theta_i[t])w_{ix}[t], \tag{48}$$

$$y_i[t+1] = y_i[t] + h\sin(\theta_i[t])v_i[t] + h\sin(\theta_i[t])w_{iy}[t], \tag{49}$$

$$\theta_i[t+1] = \theta_i[t] + h\omega_i[t] + hw_{i\theta}[t], \tag{50}$$

where h is the sampling time period (100 ms in this case), $v_i[t]$ is the speed of the vehicle at sampling epoch t and is one of the control inputs of the vehicles, while $\omega_i[t]$ is the angular speed of the vehicle at sampling epoch t and is the second control input of the vehicles. Also, $w_{ix}[t]$, $w_{iy}[t]$, and $w_{i\theta}[t]$ are random variables whose variances we denote by σ_x^2, σ_y^2, and σ_θ^2 respectively, and they model the ambient noise entering the system as a consequence of small, random drifts in the actual values of the applied control inputs from their set points. For the purposes of our demonstration, it suffices to use just two vehicles, so that $i \in \{1, 2\}$. We make both of them follow an elliptical trajectory, one behind the other.

Using this control input and knowledge of the plant model, the collision avoidance module predicts the position of each vehicle during the next sampling epoch. If a collision is detected based on this prediction, it instructs the actuator to halt the cars, thereby avoiding collision. If not, it relays the control input computed by the controller to the actuator, which then applies that particular input. In a prior work [32], it was shown that *in the absence of attacks on the sensors*, this system indeed guarantees collision freedom.

Next, we construct a specific attack which targets the vision sensor, spoofs the collision avoidance module, and ultimately causes a collision. Specifically, we introduce maliciousness in the vision sensor which computes the x−coordinate of the vehicles' position from the image that it receives from the cameras. Let t_A denote the time at which the attack begins. Then, $z_{2x}[t_A] = x_2[t_A] + \tau$, where τ is the bias that the sensor adds to the x−coordinate of the vehicle. For $t > t_A$, the malicious sensor reports measurements $\{z_{2x}\}$ given by

$$z_{2x}[t+1] = z_{2x}[t] + h\cos(\theta_2[t])u_2^g(\mathbf{z}_1^t, \mathbf{z}_2^t) + \cos(\theta_2[t])n[t], \tag{51}$$

where $n[t] \sim \mathcal{N}(0, \sigma_x^2)$. The video clip in [33] demonstrates this attack which culminates in the two vehicles colliding with each other.

As reported in [31], the theory of Dynamic Watermarking developed for linear systems in the prior sections can be extended to this class of nonlinear systems. Consider a controller which computes the control policy-specified input and superimposes the watermark on it. The system evolves as

$$x_i[t+1] = x_i[t] + h\cos(\theta_i[t])u_i^g(\mathbf{z}_1^t, \mathbf{z}_2^t) + h\cos(\theta_i[t])e_{iv}[t] + h\cos(\theta_i[t])w_{ix}[t], \tag{52}$$

$$y_i[t+1] = y_i[t] + h\sin(\theta_i[t])u_i^g(\mathbf{z}_1^t, \mathbf{z}_2^t) + h\sin(\theta_i[t])e_{iv}[t] + h\sin(\theta_i[t])w_{iy}[t], \tag{53}$$

$$\theta_i[t+1] = \theta_i[t] + h\omega_i[t] + he_{i\theta}[t] + hw_{i\theta}[t], \tag{54}$$

where $\mathbf{z}_i[t] = [z_{ix}[t], z_{ix}[t], z_{ix}[t]] = [z_{ix}[t], y_i[t], \theta_i[t]]^T$, and $z_{ix}[t]$ is vehicle-i's x−coordinate reported by the vision sensor at time t, which is different from its true value $x_i[t]$. $z_{iy}[k]$ and $z_{i\theta}[k]$ are the values reported for $y_i[k]$ and $\theta_i[k]$ respectively, which are equal to their true values at all times. The specific strategy that the sensor uses to fabricate the measurements is the same as (51), except that now, $n[t] \sim \mathcal{N}(0, \sigma_x^2 + \sigma_e^2)$.

The controller performs the following tests to check for sensor maliciousness. The tests are specified only for $\{z_{ix}\}$, but equivalent tests are also performed for $\{z_{iy}\}$ and $\{z_{i\theta}\}$.

1. **Test 1:** The controller checks if

$$\lim_{t\to\infty} \frac{1}{t}\sum_{k=0}^{t-1}(z_{ix}[k+1] - z_{ix}[k] - h\cos(z_{i\theta}[k])u_i^g(\mathbf{z}_1^t, \mathbf{z}_2^t)$$

$$-h\cos(z_{i\theta}[k])e_{iv}[k])^2 = \tilde{\sigma}_x^2. \tag{55}$$

2. **Test 2:** The controller checks if

$$\lim_{t\to\infty} \frac{1}{t}\sum_{k=0}^{t-1}(z_{ix}[k+1] - z_{ix}[k] - h\cos(z_{i\theta}[k])u_i^g(\mathbf{z}_1^t, \mathbf{z}_2^t))^2 = \sigma_c^2, \tag{56}$$

where $\tilde{\sigma}_x^2$ and σ_c^2 are defined as the values that would be obtained in the limit as $t \to \infty$ for the LHSs of (55) and (56) respectively had $\{z_{ix}\}$ been equal to $\{x_i\}$. We assume these limits to exist for the chosen trajectories. They were computed experimentally in our demonstration, and are indicated in Figs. 7 and 8.

The following theorem establishes the fundamental security guarantee for the nonlinear vehicular cyber-physical system.

Theorem 5. *[31] Define*

$$v_x[t + 1] := z_{2x}[t + 1] - z_{2x}[t] - h\cos(\theta_2[t])u_2^g(\mathbf{z}_1^t, \mathbf{z}_2^t)$$
$$-h\cos(\theta_2[t])e_{2v}[t] - h\cos(\theta_2[t])w_{2x}[t], \qquad (57)$$

so that for an honest sensor, $v_x \equiv 0$. If the reported sequence of measurements satisfy (55) and (56), then,

$$\lim_{t\to\infty} \frac{1}{t} \sum_{k=0}^{t-1} v_x^2[k + 1] = 0 \qquad (58)$$

Proof. See [31]. □

In the demonstration, the two tests (55) and (56) of sensor veracity, employed by the controller, are converted to finite-time statistical tests by checking if at each time, the test variances are within predetermined thresholds of their asymptotic value. This is indicated in Figs. 7 and 8.

Figure 7 plots the LHS of the error signal (55) as a function of time, and Fig. 8 plots that of (56) as a function of time. As can be seen, the false measurements pass test 2 but fail test 1, indicating an attack. As expected from the theory, when the attack is initiated, the reported sequence of measurements fails at least one of the two tests. The restoration of collision freedom for the automatic transportation system is shown in the video clip in [33].

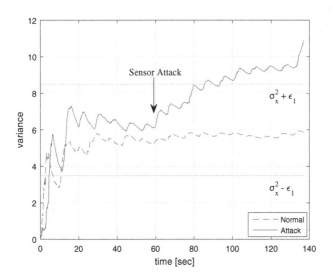

Fig. 7. Test statistic of error Test 1 as a function of time

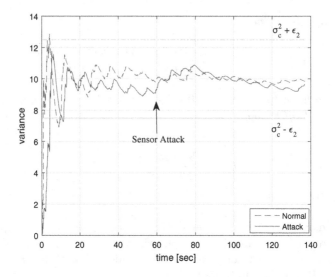

Fig. 8. Test statistic of error Test 2 as a function of time

7   Conclusion

This paper addresses the problem of securing the physical layer of a cyber-physical system from malicious sensors. The approach of dynamic watermarking was developed for partially observed stochastic MIMO linear dynamical system, a model which encompasses some of the previous models for which dynamic watermarking was established to guarantee security. These guarantees are contingent on the controller conducting two particular tests of sensor veracity, and it was shown via explicit construction of two attack strategies that both of these tests are required in that neither can be dropped if the security guarantees are to hold. A brief survey of additional results on Dynamic Watermarking for securing (i) ARMAX systems with colored noise, a model frequently encountered in process control, and (ii) A prototypical automated transportation system (from [31]) have been presented. The theoretical security guarantees, complementary laboratory demonstration, and the ability to implement it on existing control systems with minimal reconfiguration, suggest that Dynamic Watermarking could potentially be a promising candidate for securing critical infrastructure, industrial control systems, and other large-scale cyber-physical systems.

Acknowledgments. The laboratory demonstration of Dynamic Watermarking, summarized in Sect. 6.2, is from [31].

References

1. Langner, R.: Stuxnet: dissecting a cyberwarfare weapon. IEEE Secur. Priv. **9**(3), 49–51 (2011)
2. Mo, Y., Sinopoli, B.: Secure control against replay attacks. In: 47th Annual Allerton Conference on Communication, Control, and Computing, September 2009
3. Mo, Y., Chabukswar, R., Sinopoli, B.: Detecting integrity attacks on SCADA systems. IEEE Trans. Control Syst. Technol. **22**(4), 1396–1407 (2014)
4. Cardenas, A., Amin, S., Sinopoli, B., Giani, A., Perrig, A., Sastry, S.: Challenges for securing cyber physical systems. In: Workshop on Future Directions in Cyber-Physical Systems Security (2009)
5. Abrams, M.: Malicious Control System Cyber Security Attack Case Study-Maroochy Water Services, Australia (2008)
6. Satchidanandan, B., Kumar, P.R.: Dynamic watermarking: active defense of networked cyber-physical systems. Proc. IEEE **105**(2), 219–240 (2017)
7. Ponniah, J., Hu, Y.-C., Kumar, P.R.: A clean slate approach to secure wireless networking. Found. Trends Netw. **9**(1), 1–105 (2014). doi:10.1561/1300000037 http://dx.doi.org/10.1561/1300000037
8. Hou, I.-H., Borkar, V., Kumar, P.R.: A theory of QoS for wireless. In: IEEE INFO-COM. IEEE (2009)
9. Satchidanandan, B., Kumar, P.R.: On minimal tests of sensor veracity for dynamic watermarking-based defense of cyber-physical systems. In: 9th International Conference on Communication Systems and Networks (COMSNETS) (2017, to appear)
10. Cardenas, A.A., Amin, S., Sastry, S.: Secure control: towards survivable cyber-physical systems. In: The 28th International Conference on Distributed Computing Systems Workshops. IEEE (2008)
11. Cardenas, A.A., Amin, S., Sastry, S.: Research challenges for the security of control systems (2008)
12. Amin, S., Cárdenas, A.A., Sastry, S.S.: Safe and secure networked control systems under denial-of-service attacks. In: Majumdar, R., Tabuada, P. (eds.) HSCC 2009. LNCS, vol. 5469, pp. 31–45. Springer, Heidelberg (2009). doi:10.1007/978-3-642-00602-9_3
13. Abur, A., Exposito, A.G.: Power System State Estimation: Theory and Implementation. CRC Press, Boca Raton (2004)
14. Sou, K.C., Sandberg, H., Johansson, K.H.: Data attack isolation in power networks using secure voltage magnitude measurements. IEEE Trans. Smart Grid **5**(1), 14–28 (2014)
15. Sandberg, H., Teixeira, A., Johansson, K.H.: On security indices for state estimators in power networks. In: First Workshop on Secure Control Systems (SCS), Stockholm (2010)
16. Hendrickx, J.M., Johansson, K.H., Jungers, R.M., Sandberg, H., Sou, K.C.: Efficient computations of a security index for false data attacks in power networks. IEEE Trans. Autom. Control **59**(12), 3194–3208 (2014)
17. Guo, Z., Johansson, K.H., Shi, L.: A study of packet-reordering integrity attack on remote state estimation. In: 2016 35th Chinese Control Conference (CCC), pp. 7250–7255, July 2016
18. Guo, Z., Shi, D., Johansson, K.H., Shi, L.: Optimal linear cyber-attack on remote state estimation
19. Teixeira, A., Shames, I., Sandberg, H., Johansson, K.H.: A secure control framework for resource-limited adversaries. Automatica **51**, 135–148 (2015)

20. Pasqualetti, F., Dörfler, F., Bullo, F.: Attack detection and identification in cyber-physical systems. IEEE Trans. Autom. Control **58**(11), 2715–2729 (2013)
21. Fawzi, H., Tabuada, P., Diggavi, S.: Secure state-estimation for dynamical systems under active adversaries. In: 49th Annual Allerton Conference on Communication, Control, and Computing (Allerton). IEEE (2011)
22. Fawzi, H., Tabuada, P., Diggavi, S.: Secure estimation and control for cyber-physical systems under adversarial attacks. IEEE Trans. Autom. Control **59**(6), 1454–1467 (2014)
23. Teixeira, A., Shames, I., Sandberg, H., Johansson, K.H.: Revealing stealthy attacks in control systems. In: 2012 50th Annual Allerton Conference on Communication, Control, and Computing (Allerton), pp. 1806–1813, October 2012
24. Gisdakis, S., Giannetsos, T., Papadimitratos, P.: SHIELD: a data verification framework for participatory sensing systems. In: Proceedings of the 8th ACM Conference on Security and Privacy in Wireless and Mobile Networks, WiSec 2015. ACM, New York (2015). http://doi.acm.org/10.1145/2766498.2766503
25. Weerakkody, S., Mo, Y., Sinopoli, B.: Detecting integrity attacks on control systems using robust physical watermarking. In: 53rd IEEE Conference on Decision and Control, pp. 3757–3764, December 2014
26. Mo, Y., Weerakkody, S., Sinopoli, B.: Physical authentication of control systems: designing watermarked control inputs to detect counterfeit sensor outputs. IEEE Control Syst. **35**(1), 93–109 (2015)
27. Satchidanandan, B., Kumar, P.R.: Secure control of networked cyber-physical systems. In: 2016 IEEE 55th Conference on Decision and Control (CDC), pp. 283–289, December 2016
28. Kumar, P.R., Varaiya, P.: Stochastic Systems: Estimation, Identification and Adaptive Control. SIAM Classics in Applied Mathematics. SIAM, Philadelphia (2015)
29. Lai, T.L., Wei, C.Z.: Least squares estimates in stochastic regression models with applications to identification and control of dynamic systems. In: The Annals of Statistics, pp. 154–166 (1982)
30. Kailath, T.: The innovations approach to detection and estimation theory. Proc. IEEE **58**(5), 680–695 (1970)
31. Ko, W.-H., Satchidanandan, B., Kumar, P.R.: Theory and application of dynamic watermarking for cybersecurity of advanced transportation systems. In: International Workshop on Cyber-Physical Systems Security (to appear)
32. Robinson, C.L., Schutz, H.-J., Baliga, G., Kumar, P.: Architecture and algorithm for a laboratory vehicle collision avoidance system. In: IEEE 22nd International Symposium on Intelligent Control, vol. 2007, pp. 23–28. IEEE (2007)
33. Secure control of an intelligent transportation system. https://youtu.be/qMSakEtkk_0

Exploring Functional Slicing in the Design of Distributed SDN Controllers

Yiyang Chang[1], Ashkan Rezaei[2], Balajee Vamanan[2(✉)], Jahangir Hasan[3], Sanjay Rao[1], and T.N. Vijaykumar[1]

[1] Purdue University, West Lafayette, USA
[2] University of Illinois at Chicago, Chicago, USA
bvamanan@uic.edu
[3] Google Inc., Menlo Park, USA

Abstract. The conventional approach to scaling Software-Defined Networking (SDN) controllers today is to partition switches based on network topology, with each partition being controlled by a single physical controller, running all SDN applications. However, topological partitioning is limited by the fact that (i) performance of latency-sensitive (e.g., monitoring) SDN applications associated with a given partition may be impacted by co-located compute-intensive (e.g., route computation) applications; (ii) simultaneously achieving low convergence time and response times might be challenging; and (iii) communication between instances of an application across partitions may increase latencies. To tackle these issues, in this paper, we explore *functional slicing*, a complementary approach to scaling, where multiple SDN applications belonging to the same topological partition may be placed in physically distinct servers. We present *Hydra*, a framework for distributed SDN controllers based on functional slicing. Hydra chooses partitions based on convergence time as the primary metric, but places application instances across partitions in a manner that keeps response times low while considering communication between applications of a partition, and instances of an application across partitions. Evaluations using the Floodlight controller show the importance and effectiveness of Hydra in simultaneously keeping convergence times on failures small, while sustaining higher throughput per partition and ensuring responsiveness to latency sensitive applications.

1 Introduction

Software-Defined Networking (SDN) is becoming prevalent in datacenter and enterprise networks [11,12]. The central idea behind SDN is to consolidate control plane functionality (e.g., routing, access control) at a *logically* centralized controller which monitors and manipulates network state [8,19]. An SDN controller for a small network with hundreds of switches could be hosted on a single physical server. However, as networks grow in size and functionality, the controller's compute and memory requirements exceed one single server's capacity. Therefore, large datacenter and enterprise networks distribute the controller functionality over multiple servers or VMs [7,9,16,21].

© Springer International Publishing AG 2017
N. Sastry and S. Chakraborty (Eds.): COMSNETS 2017, LNCS 10340, pp. 177–199, 2017.
DOI: 10.1007/978-3-319-67235-9_12

Real SDN deployments typically consist of several tens of SDN applications for diverse network tasks such as routing, load-balancing, security, and Quality of Service (see Fig. 1). Because these applications handle different events (e.g., link failure vs. path lookup) and perform diverse functions, they impose varying demands on the underlying machine resources. We broadly classify them into three groups:

(1) *Real-time* applications that periodically refresh network state (e.g., link manager, heart-beat handler) expect a response within a timeout interval; failing to respond before deadline would trigger expensive false alarms (e.g., a spurious link failure).
(2) *Latency-sensitive* applications that are invoked during flow setup (e.g., path lookup, bandwidth reservation or QoS) are in the critical path of applications and directly impact flow completion times. Therefore, it is crucial to reduce their latency. However, they don't have a hard deadline constraint.
(3) *Computationally intensive* applications such as shortest-path computation are triggered less often due to infrequent events such as link failures. But when triggered, these applications exert substantial pressure (load spikes) on compute and memory. Convergence time, which is the time required for *global* state convergence (e.g., time required for find alternate paths in all partitions after a link failure in one partition), is an important metric for these applications.

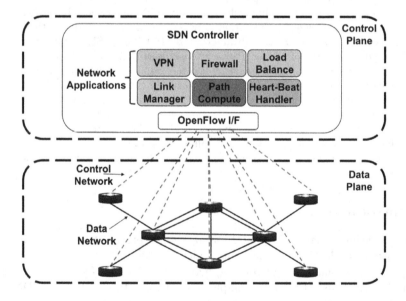

Fig. 1. An example SDN network

Designing a distributed control plane that scales well with network size and application heterogeneity is an important problem. The conventional approach to scaling SDN deployments [7,9,16,21] is *topological slicing* where the network topology is partitioned across multiple controller instances. Each controller instance, which runs on a single server machine, co-locates all applications and handles all events from a network partition containing a subset of switches.

Topological slicing suffers from a few shortcomings:
(1) Because topological slicing co-locates all applications, finding the best partition size that satisfies all applications (i.e., missed deadlines for real-time applications, latency for latency-sensitive applications, and convergence time for computationally intensive applications) is hard. For instance, co-locating computationally intensive applications with other applications may require smaller partition sizes (i.e., higher number of partitions) in order to satisfy resource constraints on the server machine. However, increasing the number of partitions would likely worsen convergence time for route recomputation on failures. Also, latency-sensitive applications such as bandwidth reservation and QoS may require communication across multiple instances of the application running across partitions at flow setup time, potentially leading to an increase in packet-in response times as the number of partitions increase. Finally, there could be other administrative constraints on partition sizing (e.g., a unit within an organization may want to have a separate controller instance). In summary, while there is substantial diversity among applications, topological slicing is agnostic of the different applications' requirements, and, therefore, does not scale well. (2) Topological sizing hurts real-time and latency-sensitive applications. Because computationally intensive applications are susceptible to load spikes, co-locating computationally intensive applications with real-time and latency-sensitive applications adversely affects their latencies (real-time applications are most affected by co-location) as we show in Fig. 7.

We propose *functional slicing*, an approach that complements topological slicing by splitting different control-plane functions across multiple servers. Functional slicing adds a new dimension to the partitioning problem and provides more freedom for placement of applications on different servers. With functional slicing, a switch may forward different events to different controllers (e.g., one could install a forwarding rule at the switch for each event or have the original server forward the events to other servers). With functional slicing, we can optimize the number of partitions to minimize *only* convergence time, without violating administrative constraints and without affecting real-time or latency-sensitive applications.

While functional slicing offers *one more degree of freedom* for partitioning the control plane, it complicates placement. For instance, placing control-plane functions that are in the critical path in different machines would lead to longer flow completion times (i.e., the overhead of crossing machine boundaries would increase response times for packet-in messages during path setup). Therefore, our placement algorithm must be aware of the dependencies between the different control-plane functions.

We present *Hydra*, a framework for partitioning and placement of SDN control-plane functions in different servers. *Hydra* leverages *functional slicing* to increase flexibility in partitioning and placement. Moreover, Hydra's partitioning is *communication-aware* – Hydra considers the communication graph to avoid placing control-plane functions that are in the critical path in different machines. We first formulate the placement of application instances across partitions as an optimization problem with the objective of minimizing the latency of latency-sensitive applications that are in the critical path, subject to resource constraints (i.e., number of servers, CPU and memory per server). We then reduce our formulation to a multi-constraint graph partitioning problem and solve it using well-known heuristics [15]. To shield real-time applications from other applications, Hydra uses thread prioritization. Hydra assigns the highest priority to threads of real-time applications and next highest priority to latency-sensitive applications, while separating computationally intensive applications from the other two categories. Most applications fall in only one of these three categories (e.g., shortest-path calculation is computationally intensive but is neither latency sensitive nor real time). However, if an application belongs to more than one category, we could consider the application in its most critical category and still use Hydra for partitioning and placement.

Hydra is relevant for both reactive controllers (where rules are installed after examining the first packet of each flow), and proactive controllers (where rules are pre-installed in switches) [5]. Our optimization formulation is agnostic to the choice of the model. Our formulation considers the packet-in rates, which may be high for reactive SDNs and low for pro-active SDNs, and the rates, among other factors, influence the best partition chosen by *Hydra*. Our evaluation shows a range of packet-in rates to capture a continuum of this choice.

In summary, we make the following contributions:

- We propose *functional slicing*, which adds a new dimension to partitioning and provides more flexibility.
- We introduce a *communication-aware* placement algorithm that leverages functional slicing and avoids its potential shortcomings.
- We evaluate *Hydra* using Floodlight [2] controller and show the effectiveness of *Hydra's* key techniques – functional slicing, communication-aware placement, and prioritization.

The rest of the paper is organized as follows. Section 2 presents an overview of Hydra's approach, and Sect. 3 delves into the details of Hydra. Section 4 describes our experimental methodology and Sect. 5 presents our results. Section 6 discusses related work. Finally, Sect. 7 concludes the paper. This paper is an extended version of [4]. This extended version includes a section on modeling convergence time (Sect. 3.2) and presents more results on sensitivity.

2   Background and Hydra's Rationale

We begin by discussing alternative ways to scale SDN controllers, and present Hydra's approach and rationale:

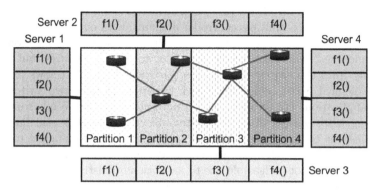

(a) Topological slicing

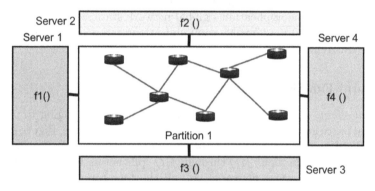

(b) Pure functional slicing

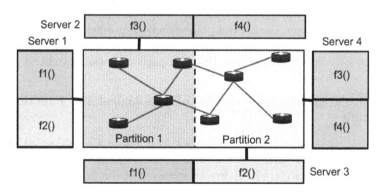

(c) Hybrid slicing with Hydra

Fig. 2. Approaches to partitioning controller functionality.

2.1 Topological Partitioning

Current distributed controllers [7,9,16,21], de facto assume topological partitioning of the network into multiple controller domains, with one controller instance
per domain. Each controller instance runs all the control-plane applications (e.g.,
topology modules, heart-beat handler that monitors switch failures) but handles
events only from the switches in its own partition. Figure 2a shows an example of topological partitioning where each partition contains two switches and
the four applications (*f1* through *f4*) run on each controller. While topological
partitioning helps with scaling, the sustainable throughput is still limited by
the fact that the compute and memory capabilities must be sufficient to handle
all applications in that partition. Increasing the number of partitions to reduce
partition sizes may not be feasible due to network administrator constraints and
since this may potentially increase route convergence time when recomputing
paths on a switch or link failure. Finally, state changes in any partition of an
application may need to be propagated to other partitions in order to maintain consistency of the application's global network state, and flow set up (e.g.,
for a QoS application) may involve communications across application instances
located in different partitions.

2.2 (Pure) Functional Slicing

Functional slicing partitions the control-plane functions belonging to the same
topological partition and places the functions in different servers. Figure 2b shows
an example of functional slicing for the same network as in Fig. 2a. The example shows the four functions *f1()* through *f4()* split across four controllers each
of which covers the entire network (i.e., all the four topological partitions in
Fig. 2a). While this tackles some of the issues with topological partitioning, the
sustainable throughput may now be bottlenecked by the most demanding application. Further, *pure* functional slicing may worsen the latency to handle critical
packet-in events because the control-plane functions needed to handle each such
event may be spread across multiple machines (i.e., kernel overheads and networks delays would lie in the critical path of packet-in event-handlers).

2.3 Hydra's Approach: A Hybrid of Topological and Functional Slicing

With Hydra, we explore a hybrid scheme that employs a combination of topological and functional slicing to reduce both convergence times and packet-in
processing latencies. Figure 2c shows an example of our hybrid slicing for the
same network as in Fig. 2a. The example shows two topological partitions. Each
controller and two functional partitions of each of the topological partitions, so
that only two servers for each function have to converge as opposed to the four
servers in topological partition in Fig. 2a. At the same time, an event involving
all four functions needs communication only between two servers as opposed to
four servers in functional slicing in Fig. 2b.

While Hydra separates computationally-intensive applications (i.e., path re-computation) from the other two categories, Hydra shields real-time applications (e.g., heart-beats) from latency-sensitive applications (e.g., path lookup) using *thread prioritization*. Hydra assigns the highest priority to real-time applications and second highest priority to latency-sensitive applications.

3   Hydra

In this section, we discuss Hydra's *communication-aware* placement algorithm. Recall that Hydra leverages *functional slicing* to calculate the number of partitions that minimizes convergence time, without negatively impacting real-time and latency-sensitive applications or violating administrative constraints.

3.1   Finding the Right Partition Size

In the first step, we compute the number of partitions by considering *only* the most critical computationally intensive application that directly impacts convergence time on failures. Often, the topology (route computation) application is the most critical application. While the exact number of partitions that minimizes convergence time is implementation dependent, in general, as we increase the number of partitions (starting from 1), the convergence time would decrease as the computation gets parallelized across partitions. But, after some point, the communication overheads between parallel computing instances would start to overwhelm the benefits from parallelization. Thus, it is reasonable to expect a U-curve with the best partition size somewhere in the middle. But, Hydra's placement algorithm does not depend on the relationship between convergence time and the number of partitions.

3.2   A Simple Convergence-Time Model

We present a simple model for studying the relationship between convergence time and the number of partitions. For our model, we consider the topology module which re-calculates the routes between all pairs of vertices in the topology graph upon failure. We consider border switches to be those switches that must be traversed when the source and destination lie in different partitions. Intuitively, internal-switch failures have lower cost than border-switch failures. However, the exact convergence cost would depend on the topology and partitioning strategy. Fortunately, most datacenter and enterprise networks have hierarchical topologies (e.g., fat-tree, B-cube) and lead to symmetric partitions with *some* fixed number border switches which greatly simplifies our model. For example, most datacenters have *fat-tree* topologies, with each (or a group) of POD(s) forming a partition. Similarly, most enterprise networks have a *hub-and-spoke* structure, with some switches providing connectivity across many sub-networks (e.g., different parts of the organization), which could have further hierarchy. Therefore, we assume symmetric partitions with a fixed number of border switches per partition in our model.

We start with a network with N switches and P symmetric partitions. Let the total number of border switches be B. Thus, each partition contains $n = \frac{N-B}{P}$ internal switches. The partitions are symmetric and each partition contains k border switches. In general, k could be greater than $\frac{B}{P}$ if some border switches belong to more than one partition. Naturally, each border switch is associated with $\frac{kP}{B}$ partitions. For example, in a network with 20 border switches, 5 partitions, and 5 border switches per partition, one of the 5 border switches in each partition also belongs to one other partition. The total number of switches in each partition is $n + k = \frac{N-B}{P} + k$.

For scalability, large networks are hierarchically organized as interconnections of many small networks; switches maintain fine-grained routes within its domain but aggregate routes to outside world. When aggregating an entire partition, a border switch could advertise a summary metric such as the average cost to switches in that partition, or the minimum, or maximum. Thus, our model maintains routes to all the internal switches (i.e., fine-grained routes) but aggregates routes to the external world (i.e., other partitions). For example, in Fig. 3, switches in partition P1 maintain routes to each of the internal switches within P1 and one for each of the other partitions P2 and P3.

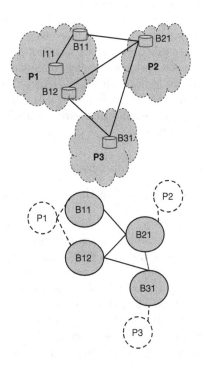

Fig. 3. Example network and its border-switch network

In such a network, route calculation involves three steps:

(1) Internal switches compute internal routes by calculating All-Pair Shortest Paths (APSP) – Dijkstra's algorithm, within each partition. This step has a cost of $(n + k)^2 \log(n + k)$. (Dijkstra's algorithm has a complexity of $O(V^2 log V)$ for V nodes.)

(2) Border switches advertise costs of connecting to their respective partitions (e.g., min-cost path to any of the internal switches within the partition) to other border-switches, which then run APSP in the border-switch network. The border-switch network has (P+B) nodes – see Fig. 3. This step has a cost of at most $(P + B)^2 \log(P + B)$. Note that in certain settings, the graph of border routers need not be connected (e.g., our evaluation section discusses such a scenario with fat-tree topologies). In such scenarios, the cost of this step can be discounted.

(3) Internal-switches update their external routes from their border-switches. There are n internal switches, and each internal switch needs to update paths to all partitions, P. For each internal switch and each partition, we pick the lowest cost path from potentially k border switches (and their cost to other partitions). Thus, the cost of this step is nPk.

When a border switch fails, all steps 1–3 are needed in the worst case [6]. However, when an internal switch fails, we could simplify steps 2 and 3. Specifically, in step 2, we *only* need to compute Single Source Shortest-path from the failed partition, which reduces the cost of step 2 from $(P + B)^2 \log(P + B)$ to $(P + B) \log(P + B)$. Similarly, step 3 only needs to compute the routes to the failed partition i.e., cost reduces from nPk to nk. Thus, we have:

$$conv\_cost_{border} = (n + k)^2 \log (n + k)$$
$$+ (P + B)^2 \log(P + B) \qquad (1)$$
$$+ nPk$$

$$conv\_cost_{internal} = (n + k)^2 \log (n + k)$$
$$+ (P + B) \log(P + B) \qquad (2)$$
$$+ nk$$

The expected convergence time can be calculated from Eqs. 2 and 1, using the probabilities of internal-switch and border-switch failures. If all switches are equally likely to fail, then the probability of border-switch and internal-switch failure are $\frac{B}{N}$ and $1 - \frac{B}{N}$, respectively.

Thus, the total convergence cost (t_{conv}) is $\frac{B}{N} * conv\_cost_{border} + (1 - \frac{B}{N}) * conv\_cost_{internal}$. Hydra computes the convergence time associated with different partitioning strategies and picks one that is desirable from the perspective of minimizing convergence time. The partitioning strategies are constrained by (i) a specification of the acceptable set of border routers specified by the network administrator; and (ii) the requirement of symmetric partitions. Thus, Hydra's formulation allows us to honor administrative constraints, unlike conventional topological slicing.

3.3   Communication-Aware Placement: Formulation

Hydra takes as input the different (topological) partitions of applications and their demands (CPU and memory), resource constraints (i.e., CPU, memory, and number of servers), and the communication graph to calculate the best placement of the applications' partitions that minimizes latency. We assume that computationally-intensive applications (e.g., path computation) are isolated by placing those applications in separate machines (or VMs); simple prioritization might be sufficient in some cases as well. We cast placement of the applications' partitions as an integer linear programming (ILP) optimization problem. Because our problem is NP hard, we identify a efficient heuristic that can solve it in reasonable time.

Let P be the number of topological partitions, N the number of SDN applications deployed in the network, and S the number of physical servers dedicated for the SDN control-plane. We want to bin-pack $P \times N$ application slices within S server machines such that the average packet-in processing latency is minimized.

We represent the communication between the different application slices using a *communication graph* whose vertices are application slices. Thus, there are $P \times N$ vertices in this graph. The edges in the graph denote communication between slices. Communication can occur between two different applications in the same partition (e.g., packets permitted by a firewall module may then be forwarded to a load-balancer), as well as between two slices of the same application in different partitions (e.g., a bandwidth reservation application between a source and destination in two different partitions will require communication between the application slices in the two partitions).

Let d_{ij} denote the communication cost between two slices. Because we are interested in latency, the communication cost denotes the additional latency overhead if the slices are placed in different machines. Let A_i denote a vertex in the communication graph where $i \in [1, P \times N]$. Then, depending on placement, we have the vector $F[i] = k$ which denotes that application slice A_i is placed in machine k.

Objective Function. Next, we model latency of latency-sensitive events. Because these events typically traverse multiple application slices, event-handling latency would depend on the total communication cost across these applications slices (i.e., path delay). Let $E = \{e_1, e_2, ..., e_r\}$ be the events of interest, with their associated paths, $\{p_1, p_2, .., p_r\}$, in the communication graph. Naturally, each path is a sequence of edges in the graph.

Then, the cost of an event is given by:

$$\forall p_m \in P, \; t_{lat}(p_m) = \sum_{<i,j> \in p_m, F[i] \neq F[j]} d_{ij} \tag{3}$$

In this formulation, two slices would incur latency overhead of d_{ij} when placed in different servers but no overhead when co-located in the same physical machine.

We can assign a weight (e.g., relative priority, probability) to each event and calculate the weighted latency as follows.

$$t_{lat} = \sum_{p_m \in \{p_1, p_2, \dots p_r\}} \gamma(p_m) t_{lat}(p_m) \tag{4}$$

The weights could be relative priorities of the events based on semantic knowledge or could just be event probabilities. Our objective is to minimize Eq. (4) subject to capacity (i.e., CPU and memory), latency, and correctness constraints.

Capacity Constraints. Let the compute and memory capacity of each server be R_{cpu} and R_{mem}, respectively. Let A_i's compute and memory requirements be C_i and M_i, respectively. Then, we have the following constraints based on CPU and memory capacities.

$$\max_k \left(\sum_{\forall i: F[i]=k} C_i \right) \leq R_{cpu}$$

$$\max_k \left(\sum_{\forall i: F[i]=k} M_i \right) \leq R_{mem} \tag{5}$$

Real-Time Constraints. We can bound the latency for real-time applications using an additional constraint of the form:

$$t_{lat}(p_m) <= deadline_m \tag{6}$$

where p_m is a path of a real-time event m in the graph.

3.4 Communication-Aware Placement: Simplification

The final form of the objective function t_{lat} is the linear combination $t_{lat} = \sum_{F[i] \neq F[j]} \alpha_{ij} d_{ij}$, for some coefficients α_{ij}. If we ignore the constraints (i.e., Eqs. (6) and (5)), we see that t_{lat} only depends on the weight of the edge-cut between the partitions and our aim is to find such a mapping F. If we ignore only Eq. (6), the problem reduces to the well-known *multi-constraint graph partitioning* [15] problem. If each vertex A_i is assigned a vector of weights $\langle C_i, M_i \rangle$ denoting the compute and memory requirement of each slice, then the problem is *equivalent* to finding a *S-way* partitioning such that the partitioning satisfies a constraint associated with each weight, while attempting to minimize the weight of edge-cut. Because multi-constraint graph partitioning is a known NP-hard problem [15], we employ heuristic methods from [14] which deliver high quality results in reasonable time. While our heuristic solution ignores Eq. (6), we did not observe appreciable degradation in our experiments.

3.5 Discussion

We discuss dynamic load adaptation and fault tolerance.

Load Adaptation. Some previous papers ([7,17]) argue for the controller's partitioning and placement to change according to instantaneous load from switches (e.g., packet-in rate). However, such dynamic re-partitioning and placement requires applications to re-partition and migrate their state which drastically affects controller performance and offsets the cost advantage of dynamic re-partitioning. This cost of reorganizing state applies to controllers that store state locally as well as to those that use a distributed datastore. While controllers that store state locally must aggregate/split/migrate their state whenever partitioning/placement changes [17], controllers that use a distributed datastore must reshard their datastore whenever the partitioning changes [7]. Because the cost of provisioning for the peak load is a small fraction (e.g., dedicating 100 servers for a 100,000-server datacenter is only 0.1%) of total cost of ownership (TCO) of large datacenters, we provision enough servers to accommodate the peak load and do not change our partitioning based on packet-in rate (load). Nevertheless, if desired, *Hydra's* placement algorithm is fast enough to respond to load variations.

Fault Tolerance. For fault tolerance reasons, it may be desirable to replicate SDN controllers in each partition, either using a simple master-slave design for each partition, or a more strongly consistent approach based on the Paxos algorithm [18]. While fault tolerance mechanisms are orthogonal to our work, it is easy to generalize *Hydra* to handle the placement of replicas. Specifically, a simple approach is to replicate the configuration produced in the previous section as many times as needed for adequate fault tolerance. If it is also desirable to consolidate the number of physical controller machines, our model could be extended by including additional variables for each replica, and using the same placement algorithms described in the previous section. To ensure that replicas of a given application/partition slice are not placed on the same physical host, additional constraints may be added to require replicas be placed in different hosts. Finally, there might be additional requirements that parts of the network supplied by different power sources need controller isolation for fault tolerance. This constraint can be added to our formulation by requiring that applications corresponding to these partitions not be co-located with each other.

4   Experimental Methodology

In this section, we present the details of our implementation and our evaluation methodology.

SDN Applications: We use the Floodlight SDN controller [2], which is a widely used OpenFlow controller. We evaluate four control-plane functions:

1. *Shortest path computation* (DJ): Shortest path computation based on Dijkstra's algorithm, which runs whenever a new link (switch) is discovered or an existing link (switch) fails.
2. *Firewall* (FW): Filters packet-in messages based on a set of rules.
3. *Route Lookup* (RL): Returns the complete path based on source/destination pair in a packet-in header.
4. *Heart-beat handler* (HB): Generates and forwards heart-beat messages between switches and controllers;

DJ is a *computationally intensive* intensive application; FW and RL are *latency-sensitive* applications and are invoked during path setup; HB is *real-time* application – if a heart-beat is not processed within a deadline (i.e., heart-beat interval), a spurious link/switch failure would result which would trigger DJ. While a production SDN deployment would include tens of applications, it is hard for researchers to study a large number of applications at production scales.

Load Generation: *Hydra's* evaluation requires large topologies with a few thousand switches. Because network emulators such as *Mininet* model both control and data plane, they do not scale beyond a few tens of switches [7]. Therefore, we use *CBench* [1]. CBench generates packet-in events that stress the control-plane without modeling a full-fledged data-plane. While the current implementation of *CBench* generates random packet-in messages (to potentially non-existent destinations), we modified CBench to generate packets that are meaningful to our topology. We use a reactive model of SDN in our experiments. However, our results are generalizable to both pro-active or reactive models.

Topology: Datacenters typically employ hierarchical topologies which provide high bisection bandwidth and good fault tolerance [3,13,22]. Our datacenter topology is a fat-tree with 2560 switches. The topology is organized into 512 core switches, and 32 pods, with each pod containing 32 Top of Rack (ToR) switches.

5   Results

In this section, we compare *Hydra* to *Topological slicing* for the three types of applications. Recall that we care about different metrics depending on the application type – lower missed heart-beats (deadlines) for real-time applications (HB), lower latency (higher throughput) for latency-sensitive applications (FW,RL), and lower convergence time for computationally-intensive applications (DJ).

We begin by showing how convergence time varies with the number of partitions which enables us to choose the right partition size. Then we show how our *communication-aware placement* co-locates different application slices. Because our placement depends on CPU and memory utilization, we show CPU and memory utilizations which are sensitive to a variety of parameters such as packet-in rates, topology sizes, and other parameters. After placement, we compare missed heart-beats for HB and throughput (at near-saturåtion high loads, throughput is a *proxy* for latency as queuing becomes the dominant latency component) for FW and RL.

5.1 Convergence Time

We study convergence time for our fat-tree topology with 2560 switches. Because fat-tree is hierarchical, it is straight-forward to create partitions by grouping neighboring pods. For example, we can create two partitions by grouping 16 pods in one partition and the other 16 in the other partition (each pod contains 32 ToR switches). Recall that convergence time is the time to recalculate shortest paths after a link failure. So, to measure convergence time, we take down a *random* link in our fat-tree which could be a border link (i.e., core link) or a partition-local link (i.e., ToR or aggregate links). We then measure the time required for *all* partitions to recompute their paths which includes time for inter-partition communication. While all neighboring partitions need to recompute on a border-link failure, a local link failure might also require partitions to advertise new costs to other partitions similar to BGP. For each partition size, we simulate 100 random link failures.

We show the average convergence time for DJ vs. number of partitions (partition size) in Fig. 4. We vary the number of partitions (ToR switches per partition) as 1(1024), 2(512), 4(256), 8(128), 16(64), and 32(32) along X-axis and show convergence time along Y-axis. We see that convergence time decreases *rapidly* as we increase the number of partitions from 1 to 8 due to amortization of compute from parallelization. However, after 8, convergence time starts to climb as

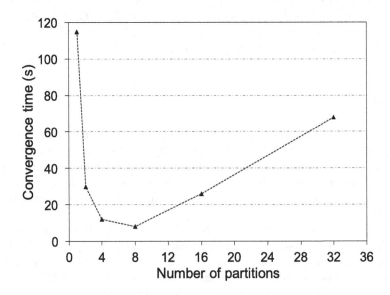

Fig. 4. Convergence time

communication overhead overwhelms gains from parallelization. Because topological slicing co-locates other applications with DJ, higher number of partitions are needed to accommodate the aggregate CPU and memory requirements. In contrast, Hydra's *functional slicing* enables us to choose the best partition size (e.g., 8 in this case), *independent* of other applications.

5.2   Communication-Aware Placement

We start by showing the CPU and memory demands of applications. For these measurements, we ran Floodlight controller on our machine with 4 cores of CPU and 64 GB of memory. The demand of each application depends on the amount of application state and controller's load. Application state impacts both CPU and memory usage – applications maintain state in memory and look up state for each packet-in message. RL must keep local topology information which depends on the partition size. The number of firewall rules impacts FW's state overhead. In our experiments, we use 50, 000 firewall rules which is typical for large networks. DJ maintains both local and global topology information. DJ's CPU usage depends on link failure rate and partition size. We simulate a random link failure every 10 seconds which is reasonable for large networks. From Fig. 4, we expect that DJ's CPU usage to be *highly* sensitive to partition size. HB's CPU and memory usage are minimal – its CPU usage slowly grows with heart-beat frequency but negligible overall.

The CPU demands of applications also depend on load (i.e., rate at which the controller receives packet-in messages from switches). We modified *CBench* to precisely control packet rate. Our base controller saturates around 50,000 packets per second. Therefore, we make measurements from 10,000 to 50,000 packets per second. Even without any applications, SDN controllers run some common functions (e.g., south-bound *OpenFlow* protocol handlers) which cannot be turned off. Therefore, we initially measure the idle CPU and memory usage without any applications (no incoming packets to the controller) which represents the overhead of starting a new controller instance. The overhead is about 15% CPU usage and 512 MB of memory. We enable applications one-by-one and measure CPU and memory usage for each application (excluding idle overhead) at 100 ms intervals for 30 s. We discard initial and final samples to capture *steady-state* usage.

Figure 5 shows the CPU requirements of different applications as as we vary the load. DJ and HB do not depend on load – DJ's CPU usage depends on partition size and link failure rate (1 every 10 s), and HB's usage depends on heart-beat frequency (we ran HB at 10/second and 100/second but they are both insignificant). We show DJ for varying partition sizes – for example, DJ(4P) is for 4 partitions each with one fourth the number of switches as DJ(1P). We observe that DJ's CPU usage reduces with increasing number of partitions due to reduced number of switches. As discussed in the previous section, with topological slicing, the state overheads of other applications (e.g., RL, FW) determine the partition size which negatively impacts convergence time. For instance, we can see that the combined CPU usage of *Idle, RL, FW, HB, and DJ(4P)* is close to 100%

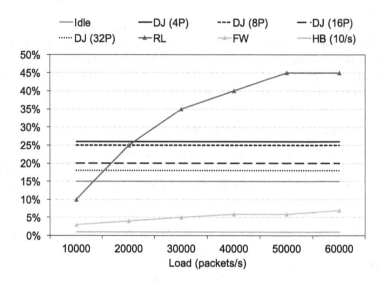

Fig. 5. Average CPU requirements

$(15 + 45 + 7 + 3 + 25)$ for higher loads. In fact, only when there are more than 8 partitions, the combined CPU usage falls well below 100% (servers usually operate at less than 90% loads to provide reasonable response times). Therefore, topological slicing is forced to choose a partition size of 16 or more which leads to high convergence times (see Fig. 4). *Hydra*, on the other hand, separates DJ from other applications, enabling DJ to use the *best* partition size.

Memory usage is largely independent of load. Table 1 shows the average memory overheads of DJ, FW, and RL for the one partition case containing all switches. From the table, it is clear that memory does not impact our placement in our controller as all of applications comfortably fit within our memory capacity. However, we expect production controllers to have large state overheads that will not fit within one server's memory. We do not show HB's memory overhead as it is negligible.

Table 1. Memory requirements

DJ	RL	FW
6.25 GB	3.75 GB	1.25 GB

Recall from Sect. 4 that our communication graph has only one edge between RL and FW, as RL and FW are the only applications that lie in the critical path of flow's path setup; DJ and HB do not have edges between them or to either RL or FW. From Fig. 5 and Table 1, it is straight forward to see the difference between Topological slicing's and Hydra's placement decisions. Topological partitioning requires 16 controller instances (16 partitions) requiring 16 cores. Each instance would host all the applications. In contrast, *Hydra* creates 8 network partitions (*minima* in Fig. 4). For each partition, it assigns two controller instances which run on separate CPU cores. While one controller instance hosts DJ for that partition, another instance hosts all the *other* applications – RL, FW, and HB. While we could manually calculate optimal placements in this simple controller, deployment-scale controllers would likely consist of tens of applications with complex communication patterns, and, therefore, would require a rigorous approach such as Hydra. Unfortunately, it is harder for researchers to experiment with production-scale controllers without access to production-scale networks and workloads.

5.3 Latency-Sensitive Applications

In this experiment, we compare the performance of latency-sensitive applications in *one network partition*. Recall that Hydra creates 8 network partition ($1/8^{th}$ switches) as opposed to topological slicing which creates 16 partitions ($1/16^{th}$ switches). In Fig. 6, we compare the scalability of latency-sensitive applications in Hydra vs. topological slicing. We show load (injected packets per second) along X-axis and the achieved throughput after route lookup (RL) and firewall processing (FW) along Y-axis. As we can see, Hydra scales well beyond 60,000 packets per second whereas topological slicing saturates at about 40,000. As a result, latency-sensitive events incur high queuing inside the controller in the case of topological slicing. It is also interesting to note that even though Hydra handles events from a larger number of switches, the latency-sensitive applications

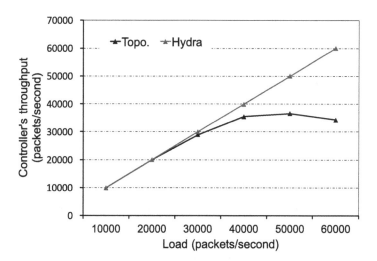

Fig. 6. Scalability of latency-sensitive applications in Hydra

(RL and FW) are isolated from the load spikes caused by computationally-intensive DJ application, thanks to *functional slicing*.

5.4   Real-Time Applications

Separating computationally-intensive DJ application also helps our real-time heart-beats (HB) application. Figure 7 shows the CDF of heart-beat latency between Hydra and topological slicing. Our default heart-beat frequency is 10 heart-beats per second. We see a marked difference between the two – while *Hydra's* 95th and 99th %-iles are about 10 ms, topological slicing's 95th %-ile is about 30 ms. With a deadline of 100 ms (i.e., periodicity of heart-beats), topological slicing would suffer about 3% missed deadlines, whereas Hydra would not miss *any*. While 3% may look like a small number, but penalty for missed deadlines is very high (i.e., missed deadlines trigger expensive path recomputation which would further exacerbate the problem).

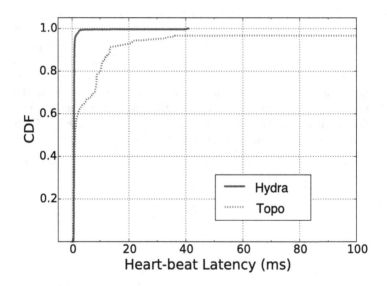

Fig. 7. Performance of real-time apps. in Hydra

5.5   Isolating the Impact of Prioritizing

In this section, we isolate the gains from prioritizing real-time applications over latency-sensitive applications. In Fig. 8, we compare the CDF of heart-beat latency between Hydra with and without prioritization. In this experiment, we use a heart-beat frequency of 10 heart-beat messages per second. Further, we pump packet-in messages such that RL operates close to its saturation in terms of packets per second that can be processed by RL. We show the heart-beat processing latency in *milliseconds* along X-axis and cumulative percent of

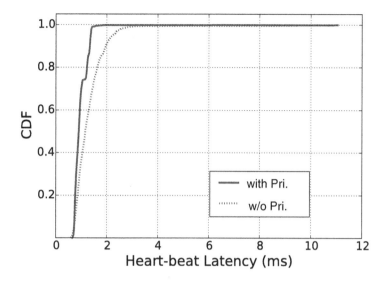

Fig. 8. Isolation of prioritization's gains

requests along Y-axis. We observe that the responses are received in a timely fashion when HB is prioritized over RL (i.e., Hydra). However, when heart-beats are not prioritized (i.e., topological slicing), the performance modestly degrades. As we increase the heart-beat frequency, which is desired for quicker failure detection, prioritizing becomes even more critical as we show next.

5.6 Sensitivity to Heart-Beat Frequency

In this experiment, we increase the heart-beat frequency to 100 per second to facilitate quicker failure detection (While 10 heart-beats per second implies a failure detection time of 100 ms, 100 heart-beats per second implies a failure detection time of 10 ms). Similar to the previous experiment, we pump packet-in messages such that RL operates close to its saturation in terms of packets per second that can be processed by RL. Similar to Figs. 8 and 9 shows heart-beat processing latency in *milliseconds* along X-axis and cumulative percent of requests along Y-axis. We see that *almost* all HB messages meet the deadline when prioritized but *no* messages meet the deadline when not prioritized. In fact, some HB messages take as long as 1800 ms to get a response. Figure 10 which shows the same data as Fig. 9 but truncates the X-axis to 100 ms to show highlight the impact of prioritization. These results clearly show that it is better not to co-locate HB and RL (i.e., functional slicing helps) unless a less aggressive failure detection is acceptable.

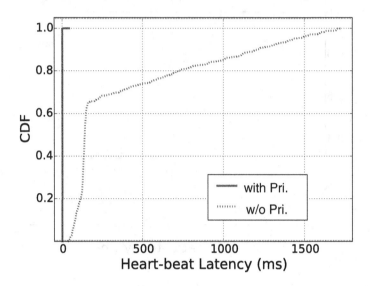

Fig. 9. Sensitivity to heart-beat rate

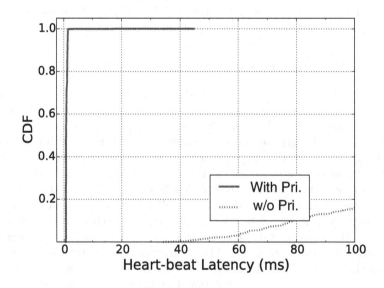

Fig. 10. Sensitivity to heart-beat rate (X-axis truncated to 100 ms)

6   Related Work

SDN has received a lot of attention from the research community over the last several years. While there is a plethora of work that cover many aspects of SDN, a systematic analysis of controller partitioning and placement is not well-studied. Onix [16] focuses on providing APIs for control-plane and state distribution. Beehive [23] enables applications to express their state-dependence and uses the inferred state-dependence to co-locate functions *within* each application. In contrast, Hydra considers event-processing pipeline across applications and considers others constraints (e.g., CPU load, memory) to partition applications as well as the state (i.e., topology).

Hyperflow [21] improves controller performance by pro-actively synchronizing state but does not deal with partitioning. Kandoo [9] offloads switch-local events to switches but does not address a large subset of events that are not local to the switch. ElastiCon [7] topologically partitions the controller based on CPU load. In contrast, Hydra employs a hybrid of topological and functional partitioning. A few other papers address the placement of the controller on the network to reduce network delays and to topologically-slice the network for better performance [10,20]. But none of them employ functional slicing and they do not target specific response times and convergence costs. While some papers [7,16] argue for a logically-separate, globally-consistent, distributed datastore for storing state to ease communication among different controllers, others [17] prefer that the state be distributed among controller instances like many distributed or parallel applications today. Nevertheless, our optimization formulation is agnostic to the choice of state management. In our evaluation, we use Floodlight [2] which assumes the latter alternative where there is no separate datastore but other communication costs (e.g., datastore) can be easily incorporated into our model.

7   Conclusion

In this paper, we have presented *Hydra*, a framework for distributing SDN control functions across servers. *Hydra* combines well-known topological slicing with our novel *functional slicing* and distributes applications based on their communication pattern. We have demonstrated the importance of functional slicing and *communication-aware* placement in the scalability of SDN with extensive evaluations.

Our results, while promising, are only a start. First, while we evaluated using applications that are available publicly controllers, we expect *Hydra's* benefits to be even higher with large-scale deployments. Getting access to production SDN deployments can enable larger-scale evaluations, which is an interesting direction for future work. Second, we are building a more comprehensive system based on functional slicing, that can handle other issues such as incrementally modifying application placement as loads drastically change and incorporating consistency guarantees into the model.

References

1. Controller benchmark. http://www.openflowhub.org/display/floodlightcontroller/Cbench
2. Floodlight. http://www.projectfloodlight.org
3. Al-Fares, M., Loukissas, A., Vahdat, A.: A scalable, commodity data center network architecture. In: Proceedings of the ACM SIGCOMM 2008, pp. 63–74 (2008)
4. Chang, Y., Rezaei, A., Vamanan, B., Hasan, J., Rao, S., Vijaykumar, T.: Hydra: leveraging functional slicing for efficient distributed SDN controllers. In: Proceedings of the International Conference on Communication Systems and Networks (COMSNETS), pp. 1–8, January 2017
5. Curtis, A.R., Mogul, J.C., Tourrilhes, J., Yalagandula, P., Sharma, P., Banerjee, S.: Devoflow: Scaling flow management for high-performance networks. In: Proceedings of the ACM SIGCOMM, pp. 254–265 (2011)
6. Demetrescu, C., Eppstein, D., Galil, Z., Italiano, G.F.: Dynamic graph algorithms. In: Algorithms and Theory of Computation Handbook, p. 9 (2010)
7. Dixit, A.A., Hao, F., Mukherjee, S., Lakshman, T., Kompella, R.: ElastiCon: an elastic distributed SDN controller. In: Proceedings of the ANCS, pp. 17–28 (2014)
8. Greenberg, A., Hjalmtysson, G., Maltz, D.A., Myers, A., Rexford, J., Xie, G., Yan, H., Zhan, J., Zhang, H.: A clean slate 4D approach to network control and management. SIGCOMM Comput. Commun. Rev. 35(5), 41–54 (2005)
9. Hassas Yeganeh, S., Ganjali, Y.: Kandoo: a framework for efficient and scalable offloading of control applications. In: Proceedings of the HotSDN, pp. 19–24 (2012)
10. Heller, B., Sherwood, R., McKeown, N.: The controller placement problem. In: Proceedings of HotSDN, pp. 7–12 (2012)
11. Hong, C.Y., Kandula, S., Mahajan, R., Zhang, M., Gill, V., Nanduri, M., Wattenhofer, R.: Achieving high utilization with software-driven WAN. In: Proceedings of the ACM SIGCOMM, pp. 15–26 (2013)
12. Jain, S., Kumar, A., Mandal, S., Ong, J., Poutievski, L., Singh, A., Venkata, S., Wanderer, J., Zhou, J., Zhu, M., Zolla, J., Hölzle, U., Stuart, S., Vahdat, A.: B4: experience with a globally-deployed software defined WAN. In: Proceedings of the ACM SIGCOMM, pp. 3–14. ACM (2013)
13. Kabbani, A., Vamanan, B., Hasan, J., Duchene, F.: FlowBender: flow-level adaptive routing for improved latency and throughput in datacenter networks. In: Proceedings of CoNEXT, pp. 149–160 (2014)
14. Karypis, G., Kumar, V.: A fast and high quality multilevel scheme for partitioning irregular graphs. SIAM J. Sci. Comput. 20(1), 359–392 (1998)
15. Karypis, G., Kumar, V.: Multilevel algorithms for multi-constraint graph partitioning. In: Proceedings of the ACM/IEEE Conference on Supercomputing, SC 1998, 7–13 November 1998, Orlando, FL, USA, p. 28 (1998)
16. Koponen, T., Casado, M., Gude, N., Stribling, J., Poutievski, L., Zhu, M., Ramanathan, R., Iwata, Y., Inoue, H., Hama, T., Shenker, S.: Onix: a distributed control platform for large-scale production networks. In: Proceedings of OSDI, pp. 1–6 (2010)
17. Krishnamurthy, A., Chandrabose, S.P., Gember-Jacobson, A.: Pratyaastha: an efficient elastic distributed SDN control plane. In: Proceedings of the HotSDN, NY, USA, pp. 133–138. ACM, New York (2014)
18. Lamport, L.: Paxos made simple. ACM Sigact News 32(4), 18–25 (2001)
19. McKeown, N., Anderson, T., Balakrishnan, H., Parulkar, G., Peterson, L., Rexford, J., Shenker, S., Turner, J.: OpenFlow: enabling innovation in campus networks. SIGCOMM Comput. Commun. Rev. 38(2), 69–74 (2008)

20. Tam, A.W., Xi, K., Chao, H.: Use of devolved controllers in data center networks. In: INFOCOM WKSHPS, pp. 596–601, April 2011
21. Tootoonchian, A., Ganjali, Y.: HyperFlow: a distributed control plane for Open-Flow. In: Proceedings of INM/WREN, p. 3 (2010)
22. Vamanan, B., Hasan, J., Vijaykumar, T.: Deadline-aware datacenter TCP (D2TCP). Proceedings of the ACM SIGCOMM 2012, pp. 115–126 (2012)
23. Yeganeh, S.H., Ganjali, Y.: Beehive: towards a simple abstraction for scalable software-defined networking. In: Proceedings of HotNets-XIII, pp. 13:1–13:7 (2014)

Near-Optimal Placement of Virtualized EPC Functions with Latency Bounds

David Dietrich[1]([✉]), Chrysa Papagianni[2], Panagiotis Papadimitriou[3], and John S. Baras[2]

[1] Institute of Communications Technology, Leibniz Universität Hannover, Hanover, Germany
david.dietrich@ikt.uni-hannover.de
[2] Institute for Systems Research, University of Maryland, College Park, USA
{chrisap,baras}@isr.umd.edu
[3] Department of Applied Informatics, University of Macedonia, Thessaloniki, Greece
papadimitriou@uom.edu.gr

Abstract. The proliferation of mobiles devices, application sprawl, and the ever-increasing data volume generates significant stress on cellular networks and particularly on the cellular core, also known as the Evolved Packet Core (EPC), *i.e.,* the cellular network component residing between the radio access network and the Internet. This is further exacerbated by the deployment of hardware appliances for the implementation of a wide range of network functions (*e.g.,* gateways, mobility management, firewalls, network address translation), hindering any opportunity for elastic provisioning, and eventually leading to high operational costs and a significant degree of load imbalance across the EPC.

Network Function Virtualization (NFV) has been seen a promising solution in order to enable elasticity in the cellular core. Applying NFV to the EPC raises the need for network function (NF) placement, which in turn entails significant challenges, due to the stringent delay budgets among cellular core components and the coexistence of communicating data and control plane elements. To address these challenges, we present a linear programming (LP) formulation for the computation of NF placements that strikes a balance between optimality and time complexity. Our evaluation results show that the LP achieves significantly better load balancing, request acceptance rate, and resource utilization compared to a greedy algorithm that performs NF placement inline with carriers' common practice today.

1 Introduction

Cellular networks have been facing a significant growth both in terms of coverage and capacity in order to cope with increasing traffic volumes. The latter stems from the proliferation of mobile devices and the increasing application diversity. This trend is expected to continue in the future with the rise of Machine-to-Machine (M2M) communications [33] and Internet-of-Things (IoT). Control plane traffic is also expected to grow at more than 100% annually [7].

© Springer International Publishing AG 2017
N. Sastry and S. Chakraborty (Eds.): COMSNETS 2017, LNCS 10340, pp. 200–222, 2017.
DOI: 10.1007/978-3-319-67235-9_13

The ever-growing data volume raises the need for more elasticity in terms of network function (NF) deployment. In particular, the cellular core, *i.e*, the cellular network components residing between the radio access network and the Internet - also known as the Evolved Packet Core (EPC), provides data (*e.g*, Serving and Packet Data Network Gateways) and control plane functions (*e.g*, mobility management and signaling [11]). In the EPC, operators also tend to deploy middleboxes for packet inspection and network address translation (NAT) [36]. In fact, the middlebox diversity tends to increase along with the number of offered services and the pressing need for faster service deployment.

Network Function Virtualization (NFV) has been seen as a promising solution to cope with the increasing stress on the cellular core. NFV promotes the consolidation of NFs on platforms built of commodity servers components, deployed in virtualized network infrastructures (*i.e*, datacenters [DCs]) [1–5]. As such, NFV provides a great opportunity for the reduction of investment and operational costs, as it obviates the need to acquire, deploy, and operate specialized equipment on clients' premises, either by introducing new functionality in the network or by scaling existing network services. Besides cost reduction, NFV allows for elastic provisioning, which can lead to the rapid instantiation of new services and enhanced response to evolving demands via virtualized NF instance scale-out [15,23]. In the EPC, NFV can mitigate the problem of load imbalance across the DCs, as operators tend to utilize middleboxes in DCs close to base stations [28].

Leveraging on NFV towards an elastic cellular core poses significant challenges in terms of NF placement. First, NF placement should be optimized jointly for load balancing and latency, since there are stringent delay budgets among communicating data and control plane elements, such as the eNodeB (eNB), the Serving Gateway (S-GW), the Packet Data Network Gateway (P-GW), and the Mobility Management Entity (MME). Second, NF placement should be scalable with a large number of User Equipment (UE) and DCs. This will allow for rapid NF placement decisions in reaction to sudden changes in the traffic load (*e.g.,* flash crowds). In this respect, KLEIN [28] decomposes the NF placement problem into region selection, DC selection and server selection within the assigned DC to reduce the problem complexity.

Since there is full visibility across all DCs in the cellular core, we seek to provide a single-stage scalable solver for the EPC NF placement problem. To this end, we initially present a mixed-integer linear programming (MILP) formulation for the computation of near-optimal NF assignments onto the cellular core at a single stage. To reduce the time complexity of the MILP, we employ relaxation and rounding techniques, transforming the initial MILP into a linear program (LP) that trades a small degree of optimality for fast retrievable NF placements. Our evaluation results show that the proposed LP yields significant gains in terms of load balancing, request acceptance rate, and resource utilization compared to a greedy algorithm at which EPC elements are assigned to DCs in proximity to the eNB (*i.e.,* which is a common practice today). In our evaluation environment, we carefully inspected and took into consideration both data plane and signalling traffic to account for all CPU and bandwidth required for NF placement.

This paper extends our previous work in [20], by providing additional evaluation results, a more elaborate problem description, further details on the EPC signaling model, as well as a more extensive related work discussion. The remainder of the paper is organized as follows. Section 2 describes the NF placement problem, while the corresponding request and network model are presented in Sect. 3. In Sect. 4, we introduce our MILP formulation, its relaxed variant (LP), and a heuristic algorithm for the NF placement. Section 5 presents our evaluation results and discusses the efficiency of the proposed NF placement methods. In Sect. 6 we provide an overview of related work, and finally in Sect. 7, we highlight our conclusions and discuss directions for future work.

2   Problem Description

In this section, we provide background on cellular networks and elaborate on the problem of NF placement on the EPC.

2.1   Cellular Core Background

Overview. An LTE cellular network comprises the Evolved Universal Terrestrial Radio Access Network (E-UTRAN) and the cellular core, known as the Evolved Packet Core (EPC). The E-UTRAN mainly contains the base stations, termed as eNodeBs (eNBs), which provide radio access to the UEs. The EPC consists of a range of data and control plane elements, responsible for routing, session establishment, mobility management, and billing (among others). In the user plane, S-GW and P-GW are used for data forwarding. The S-GW acts as a mobility anchor, whereas the P-GW routes cellular traffic to the Internet. The S-GW interacts with the MME which, in turn, is responsible for UE authentication and authorization, session establishment and mobility management. The eNBs are connected to MME and SGW by means of S1-MME and S1-U interfaces, respectively. The S-GW supports the S11 interface with the MME and S5/S8 interface with P-GW. The eNBs are also interconnected with each other via the X2 interface, mainly used for inter-eNB handover. The QoS level for each transmission path (termed as EPS bearer) between the UE and the P-GW is decided by the P-GW. When a UE is attached to the network, a default bearer is established supporting best-effort QoS. Additional bearers can be set up with different QoS levels. The EPS bearer is made up of the radio data bearer (*i.e.*, between UE and eNB), the S1 data bearer (*i.e.*, between eNB and S-GW) and the S5 data bearer (*i.e.*, between the SG-W and the P-GW). The GPRS tunneling protocol (GTP) is used for setting up the user plane data-paths between the eNB, S-GW and P-G. During handovers, the MME re-establishes the data-path between the S-GW and the new eNB.

LTE-EPC Signaling. Signaling procedures in LTE allow the control plane to manage the data flow between the UE and the P-GW, as well as UE mobility.

Each procedure implies processing and exchange of signaling messages between the control plane entities. However, significant signaling load is considered to be generated by the *Service Request* and *X2 handover* [24,27]. In terms of signaling load on the S-GW, *Attach* and *S1 handover* procedures are the most expensive [6,30]. In our study, we are considering only the costly *Service Request* procedure related to data plane management and consequently also *Service Release*, both of which are explained hereafter.

At the highest layer of the Control Plane protocol stack (Non-Access Stratum - NAS) two signaling protocols are used between the UE and the MME; the EPS Mobility Management (EMM) protocol and the EPS Connection Management (ECM) protocol. The EMM is responsible for handling UE mobility, supporting functions for attaching/detaching the UE from the network and performing location updates in between (tracking area update). The ECM is used to handle signaling connections between the UE and the EPC.

Once a UE is registered/attached to the network (*EMM-REGISTERED*), it can be either in *ECM-CONNECTED* or *ECM-IDLE* state. In the *ECM-IDLE* state, the UE has no radio (Radio Resource Control–RRC) connection to the eNB or S1 connections to the EPC. If, at this time, new traffic is generated from the UE, or from the network to the UE, the UE moves to the *ECM-CONNECTED* state, where radio and S1 signaling connections are established. Following the service request, the radio and S1 bearers are established at the user-plane allowing the UE to receive or send traffic. Service requests can be triggered by a UE or by the network (UE-originated or Network-originated). Service Release is triggered by the eNB due to detected UE inactivity or UE-generated signaling connection release.

As shown in Fig. 1, when the UE has new traffic to send, or learns about the network's intent to send new traffic, it establishes an RRC connection and sends a *Service Request* to the eNB. The *Service Request* is forwarded to the MME from the eNB, through an *Initial UE Message*, leading to S1 connection establishment. We skip UE authentication initiated by the MME and NAS security setup between the UE and MME, as they are optional when UE context exists in the network. Upon receiving the *Service Request*, the MME sends an *Initial Context Setup Request* to the eNB that leads to setting up the data radio bearer with the UE and the SI bearer, leading to end-to-end user-plane traffic paths for the UL. Following the *Initial Context Setup Response*, exchanging the *Modify Bearer* messages, between the MME and SGW, leads to the DL S1 bearer setup. If the UE's cell or tracking area has been changed at the time of the request, the UL/DL S5 bearers are modified.

2.2 Problem Description

Following the recent trends on EPC virtualization, we consider the deployment of its main elements as virtualized NFs (vNFs) in DCs. This creates opportunities for elasticity in resource provisioning and better load balancing, avoiding traffic and processing overload at DCs close to base stations [28]. In this respect, we

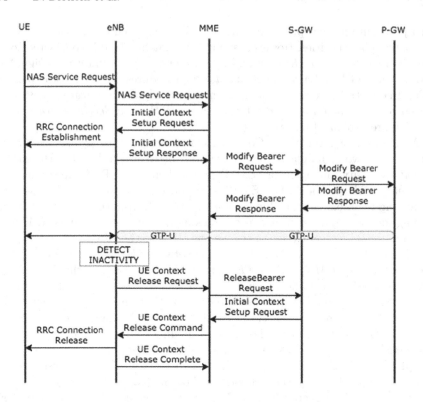

Fig. 1. Service Request/Release workflows.

consider sequences of EPC vNFs expressed as service chains. For instance, Fig. 2 illustrates a service chain consisting of datapath elements and a MME.

EPC virtualization essentially requires the placement of vNFs on servers and orchestration for service chaining, *i.e.*, routing cellular data traffic through a set of vNFs, as prescribed in the service chain. Service chaining in DCs has been addressed by recent work [8,22,29], so in this work we mainly focus on the NF placement problem.

In this respect, we consider a mobile operator's network, consisting of NFV Infrastructure (NFVI) and the RAN. The NFVI is composed of NFVI Points of Presence (PoPs), where EPC elements can be deployed as vNFs. These could extend to the operator's WAN infrastructure, including local or regional PoPs for small or larger-scale NFVI deployments. The NFVI PoP is essentially a DC, therefore we consider a 2-level hierarchical network topology, although any common DC topology could be used for each site depending on the processing and bandwidth demands [21]. On each NFVI PoP, one or more NFs can be dynamically instantiated on demand for a requested service chain.

The problem at hand is to move the EPC's individual components (*i.e.*, MME, S/P-GW, middleboxes) that are traditionally deployed on specialized hardware to the operator's NFVI in order to support efficiently the operator's

RAN, adhering to delay budgets between the individual control and data plane components. Therefore, the objective is to efficiently map the corresponding vNF forwarding graph(s), creating on demand an elastic EPC environment, optimized jointly for load balancing and latency.

In order to provide compatibility with 3GPP standard, specific constraints are taken into consideration for NF placement, *e.g.*, a single S-GW is attached to a UE at any point in time. We also assume that the traffic of a single eNB is routed to a single S-GW [28] and the UE is anchored to a single P-GW, leading to the service chain(s) per eNB depicted in Fig. 2. In this context, an exemplary NF placement is further illustrated in Fig. 3 (*e.g.*, P-GWs belonging to two different chains are assigned to the two distinct servers of an NFVI PoP). Such placements provide the number and location of NFVI PoPs that will provision the vNFs as well as the servers where these vNFs will be deployed, and the physical paths that data (*i.e.*, GTP) and control traffic will traverse.

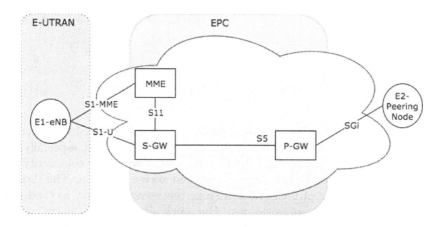

Fig. 2. EPC service chain.

Along these lines, NF placement on the EPC entails the following challenges:

Coordinated Placement of Data and Control Plane Elements. NF placement has been recently tackled for the migration of middleboxes from enterprise networks to virtualized DCs [9,16,19,25,26]. However, proposed methods optimize the placement only of data plane functions for specific objectives, such as minimization of embedding footprint or load balancing. In contrast, EPC requires a coupling between data plane and control plane functions (*e.g.*, S-GW and MME). This has led to the specification of communication delay budgets between EPC elements [32]. These delay constraints should be taken into account in the NF placement, raising the need for NF assignments optimized jointly for load balancing and latency. In this respect, our NF placement methods (Sect. 4) fulfil the latency and resource requirements of the EPC elements.

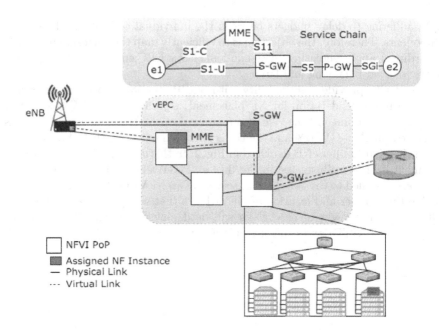

Fig. 3. Example of NF placement on the EPC.

Time Complexity. The NF placement problem can be formulated as an integer linear program which yields high complexity and solver runtime, especially for a large number of UEs and DCs. KLEIN [28] copes with this complexity by decomposing the problem into region, DC, and server selection. This brings some benefits in terms of orchestration (*e.g.*, the server selection method can be invoked for intra-DC optimizations). Our work aims at global optimization of the NF placement, given the network-wide view on the cellular core. In this respect, we derive a LP formulation to reduce the time complexity.

3   Request and Network Model

In the following, we introduce models for the service chains and the cellular core network.

Request Model. We use a directed graph $G_F = (V_F, E_F)$ to express a service chain request. The set of vertices V_F include all virtualized EPC elements, such as S-GW, P-GW, MME, as well as any NFs (*e.g.*, NAT, firewall) that the traffic has to traverse. Each vertex in the graph is associated with a computing demand g^i, which we estimate based on the inbound traffic rate and the resource profile of the EPC element (*i.e.*, CPU cycles/packet). The edges are denoted by $(i, j) \in E_F$ while their bandwidth demands are expressed by g^{ij}. Each request is associated with a maximum delay $d_{(i \to j),max}$ over the virtual links eNB$\to$MME, MME$\to$S-GW, and S-GW$\to$P-GW.

Network Model. We specify the cellular core network topology as an undirected graph $G_S = (V_S, E_S)$, where V_S represents the set of all nodes (*i.e.,* routers, servers, gateways, end-points). We further use $V_{servers} \subset V_S$ to explicitly express the servers in a DC. The delay incurred to a flow when assigned to a graph edge $(u,v) \in E_S$ is denoted by d_{uv}. Furthermore, nodes and links are associated with their residual capacity, denoted by r_u and r_{uv}, respectively. Their maximum capacity is given by $r_{u,max}$ and $r_{uv,max}$. A list of all notations is given in Table 1.

Table 1. Notations in the network model and the MILP/LP.

Symbol	Description
g^i	Computing demand of NF i in GHz
g^{ij}	Bandwidth demand of edge (i,j) in $Mbps$
$d_{(i \to j),max}$	Maximum delay of the virtual link (i,j) in ms
d_{uv}	Delay of the link (u,v) in ms
r_u	Residual capacity of server u in GHz
$r_{u,max}$	Maximum capacity of server u in GHz
r_{uv}	Residual capacity of link (u,v) in $Mbps$
$r_{uv,max}$	Maximum capacity of link (u,v) in $Mbps$
x_u^i	Assignment of NF i to DC or server u
f_{uv}^{ij}	Amount of bandwidth assigned to link (u,v) for NF graph edge (i,j) in $Mbps$
ϵ	Helper variable in the MILP/LP objective function
γ_u^i	Feasibility indicator of the mapping of NF i to server u
λ_{links}	Link load balancing factor
$\lambda_{servers}$	Server load balancing factor
Φ	Link-to-node balancing factor in the MILP/LP objective function

4   NF Placement Methods

In this section, we present our NF placement methods: (i) a MILP formulation for retrieving optimal mapping solutions, (ii) a scalable LP model that is used in conjunction with a rounding algorithm for retrieving near-optimal solutions in polynomial time, and (iii) a greedy algorithm as baseline.

4.1   MILP Formulation

In our MILP formulation, we use the binary variable x_u^i to express the assignment of NF i to the EPC node u. The real variable f_{uv}^{ij} expresses the amount of bandwidth assigned to link (u, v) for NF graph edge (i, j). The MILP is formulated as follows:

Minimize

$$
\sum_{i \in V_F} \sum_{u \in V_S} \left(1 - \frac{r_u}{r_{u,max}}\right) g^i x_u^i \gamma_u^i + \Phi \sum_{(i,j) \in E_F} \sum_{\substack{(u,v) \in E_S \\ (u \neq v)}} \left(1 - \frac{r_{uv}}{r_{uv,max}} + \varepsilon\right) f_{uv}^{ij} \quad (1)
$$

subject to:

$$
\sum_{u \in V_S} x_u^i = 1 \quad \forall i \in V_F \tag{2}
$$

$$
\sum_{\substack{v \in V_S \\ (u \neq v)}} (f_{uv}^{ij} - f_{vu}^{ij}) = g^{ij}(x_u^i - x_u^j) \quad i \neq j, \forall (i,j) \in E_F, \forall u \in V_S \tag{3}
$$

$$
\sum_{i \in V_F} g^i x_u^i \leq r_u \quad \forall u \in V_S \tag{4}
$$

$$
\sum_{(i,j) \in E_F} f_{uv}^{ij} \leq r_{uv} \quad \forall (u,v) \in E_S \tag{5}
$$

$$
\sum_{(u,v) \in E_S} \frac{f_{uv}^{eNB,MME}}{g^{eNB,MME}} d_{uv} \leq d_{(eNB \to MME),max} \tag{6}
$$

$$
\sum_{(u,v) \in E_S} \frac{f_{uv}^{MME,SGW}}{g^{MME,SGW}} d_{uv} \leq d_{(MME \to SGW),max} \tag{7}
$$

$$
\sum_{\substack{(i,j) \in \\ \{\{SGW,NF_1\}, \\ \{NF_1,NF_2\}, \cdots \\ \{NF_n,PGW\}\}}} \sum_{(u,v) \in E_S} \frac{f_{uv}^{ij}}{g^{ij}} d_{uv} \leq d_{(SGW \to PGW),max} \tag{8}
$$

$$
x_u^i \in \{0,1\} \quad \forall i \in V_F, \forall u \in V_S \tag{9}
$$

$$
f_{uv}^{ij} \geq 0 \quad \forall (u,v) \in E_S, \forall (i,j) \in E_F \tag{10}
$$

The objective of the MILP is load balancing as expressed by the objective function (1). The first term of this function represents the amount of CPU resources multiplied by the utilization of each assigned server[1]. This term is minimized, if servers with lower utilization are preferred. Similarly, the second term of the objective function expresses the accumulated bandwidth assigned to EPC links multiplied by the corresponding link utilization. By minimizing the right-hand term, the number of assigned links is minimized while less loaded

---

[1] The relative sever utilization is deducted from their residual capacities in the term $1 - \frac{r_u}{r_{u,max}}$. The same applies to the link utilization.

links are preferred. We further use a very small offset ε to avoid unnecessary use of zero-utilized links as they would otherwise result in multiplication by zero in the objective function[2]. In the first term, the input variable γ_u^i is used to avoid infeasible NF/server combinations. γ_u^i is infinite if the mapping $i \leftrightarrow u$ is already known to be infeasible, otherwise it is set to 1. For instance, we adjust the corresponding feasibility indicators $\gamma_{u \in V_S}^{i=SGW}$, $\gamma_{u \in V_S}^{i=MME}$ to mark each the potential servers for the S-GW and MME.

Furthermore, we introduce the link-to-node balancing factor Φ. $\Phi \gg 1$ yields solutions aiming at link load balancing while $\Phi \ll 1$ balances the load among the servers. We adjust Φ to strike a balance between node and link load balancing as follows:

$$\Phi = \frac{\lambda_{links}}{\lambda_{servers}} \cdot \frac{\sum_{i \in V_F} g^i}{\sum_{(i,j) \in E_F} g^{ij}} \tag{11}$$

$$\lambda_{servers} = \frac{max \left\{ 1 - \frac{r_u}{r_{u,max}} \mid u \in V_{servers} \right\}}{\frac{1}{|V_{servers}|} \sum_{u \in V_{servers}} \left(1 - \frac{r_u}{r_{u,max}} \right)} \tag{12}$$

$$\lambda_{links} = \frac{max \left\{ 1 - \frac{r_{uv}}{r_{uv,max}} \mid (u,v) \in E_S \right\}}{\frac{1}{|E_S|} \sum_{(u,v) \in E_S} \left(1 - \frac{r_{uv}}{r_{uv,max}} \right)} \tag{13}$$

Φ essentially depends on the current load balancing factors for the servers $\lambda_{servers}$ (12) and the links λ_{links} (13). The right-hand term of (11) is used for the normalization of CPU and bandwidth units.

Next, we explain the constraints of the MILP. Constraint (2) ensures that each NF $i \in V_F$ is mapped exactly to one server. Constraint (3) enforces flow conservation, i.e., the sum of all inbound and outbound traffic in switches, routers, and servers that do not host NFs should be zero. More precisely, this condition ensures that for a given pair of assigned nodes i, j (i.e., NFs or end-points), there is a path in the network graph where the edge (i, j) has been mapped. The constraints (4) and (5) ensure that the allocated computing and bandwidth resources do not exceed the residual capacities of servers and links, respectively. The constraints (6)–(8) ensure that the delays eNB→MME, MME→S-GW, and S-GW→P-GW do not exceed predefined bounds. The right-hand side of these constraint formulations represents a delay threshold, whereas the left-hand side computes the actual delay between i and j by accumulating the delay over the assigned links. The latter is calculated with the aid of the boolean expression f_{uv}^*/g^*, which is 1 if the link uv is assigned and 0 otherwise. Finally, the conditions (9) and (10) express the domain constraints for the variables x_u^i (binary) and f_{uv}^{ij} (real).

---

[2] We set $\varepsilon = 10^{-10}$ in our simulations.

4.2 LP Relaxation and Rounding Algorithm

In the following, we describe a transformation of the above MILP to an LP model by relaxing the integer domain constraint of x_u^i:

$$x_u^i \in \{0,1\} \rightarrow x_u^i \geq 0 \quad \forall i \in V_F, \forall u \in V_S \tag{14}$$

The LP model can yield solutions with $x_u^i \notin \{0,1\}$ in which the boolean characteristic of x_u^i is not considered, thus constraints (2), (3), and (4) could be omitted. Therefore, we introduce an upper bound to the variables. The final domain constraints that replace (9) and (10) are as follows:

$$0 \leq x_u^i \leq 1 \quad \forall i \in V_F, \forall u \in V_S \tag{15}$$

$$0 \leq f_{uv}^{ij} \leq g^{ij} \quad \forall (u,v) \in E_S, \forall(i,j) \in E_F \tag{16}$$

We use a rounding algorithm to extract feasible solutions from the LP solutions that potentially contain non-boolean x_u^i. More specifically, the algorithm invokes a call to the LP solver and processes the set of feasible LP solutions iteratively. Each iteration includes the rounding of the x_u^i variables of the current solution and either the acceptance or the rejection of the request. If the rounded solution does not violate the capacity and delay constraints then the request is accepted; otherwise it is rejected. Algorithm 1 shows the pseudo code for the LP rounding.

Algorithm 1. NF placement with LP rounding

1: **repeat**
2:    $\{x_u^i, f_{uv}^{ij}\} \leftarrow$ **Solve_LP**(..)
3:    $FeasSol := true$ if solution for LP exists, $false$ otherwise
4:    $X \leftarrow \{x_u^i \mid x_u^i \notin \{0,1\}\}$
5:    **if** $X \neq \emptyset$ **then**
6:       $\{i_{fx}, u_{fx}\} \leftarrow argmax_{\{i \in V_F, u \in V_S\}} X$

7:       **if** $\left(\sum_{i \in \{V_F \mid x_{u_{fx}}^i = 1\}} g^i + g^{i_{fx}} \leq r_{u_{fx}} \right)$ and $\left(\sum_{(i,j) \in E_F} \sum_{(u,v) \in E_S} \frac{f_{uv}^{ij}}{g^{ij}} d_{uv} \leq d_{max} \right)$ **then**

8:          **Add_LP_Constraint**("$x_{u_{fx}}^{i_{fx}} = 1$")
9:       **else**
10:          **Add_LP_Constraint**("$x_{u_{fx}}^{i_{fx}} = 0$")
11:       **end if**
12:    **end if**
13: **until** $(X = \emptyset) \vee (FeasSol = false)$
14: **if** $FeasSol = true$ **then**
15:    **return** $\{x_u^i, f_{uv}^{ij}\}$ {Accept request}
16: **else**
17:    $\forall x_u^i := 0, \forall f_{uv}^{ij} := 0$
18:    **return** $\{x_u^i, f_{uv}^{ij}\}$ {Reject request}
19: **end if**

Our tests[3] show that both MILP and LP lead to server and link load balancing[4] (Figs. 4 and 5). However, the optimality gap between MILP and LP is larger in terms of link load balancing, since our rounding approach results in the acceptance of requests with higher CPU demand and lower bandwidth demand compared to the requests accepted by the MILP. In particular, the LP generates in the long run 95% and 92% of the CPU and bandwidth revenue compared to the MILP. At the same time, the request acceptance rate of the LP is lower (Fig. 6). On the other hand, the LP is known to yield substantially lower time complexity. This is corroborated by our tests, *i.e.,* the solver runtime of the LP is up to two magnitudes lower than the MILP solver runtime (Fig. 7). Consequently, since the LP trades a small degree of optimality for a substantially lower runtime, we use this variant in our evaluations (Sect. 5).

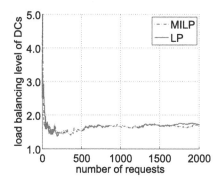

Fig. 4. DC load balancing level (based on server load).

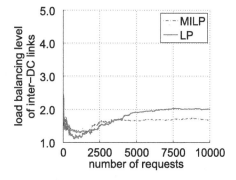

Fig. 5. Inter-DC link load balancing level.

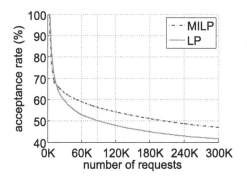

Fig. 6. Request acceptance rate.

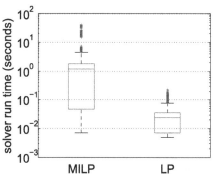

Fig. 7. Solver runtime.

---

[3] The tests were conducted on a 2 GHz AMD Opteron server (restricted to single core).

[4] See Sect. 5.1 for the definition of the load balancing level.

Algorithm 2. NF Placement - Greedy Algorithm (Baseline)

1: $DCs \leftarrow$ DCs, ordered by distance from eNB
2: $NrByDCs \leftarrow DCs$ with $d_{(eNB \to DC)} \leq d_{(eNB \to DC),max}$
3: **if** SGW and MME exist already for the UE group **then**
4:      MapToServer (SGW, currently used server)
5:      MapToServer (MME, currently used server)
6: **else**
7:      $DC :=$ first DC in $NrByDCs$
8:      **while** SGW is **not** mapped to any server **do**
9:          **if** MapToDcServer (SGW, DC) **not** successful **then**
10:             $DC :=$ next DC in $NearByDCs$
11:             **if** $DC = \emptyset$ **then**
12:                 **return** $\forall \{x_u^i, f_{uv}^{ij}\} := 0$ {Reject request}
13:             **end if**
14:         **end if**
15:         Update x_u^{SGW}
16:     **end while**
17:     **while** MME is **not** mapped to any server **do**
18:         **if** MapToDcServer (MME, DC) **not** successful **then**
19:             $DC :=$ next DC in $NearByDCs$
20:             **if** $DC = \emptyset$ **then**
21:                 **return** $\forall \{x_u^i, f_{uv}^{ij}\} := 0$ {Reject request}
22:             **end if**
23:         **end if**
24:         Update x_u^{MME}
25:     **end while**
26: **end if**
27: Compute least-delay paths:
28: -from eNB to $Server(MME)$ and $Server(SGW)$
29: -and from $Server(MME)$ to $Server(SGW)$
30: **if** $d_{(eNB \to MME)} \leq d_{(eNB \to MME),max}$ and $d_{(MME \to SGW)} \leq d_{(MME \to SGW),max}$ **then**
31:     Update f_{uv}^{ij}
32: **else**
33:     **return** $\forall \{x_u^i, f_{uv}^{ij}\} := 0$ {Reject request}
34: **end if**
35: Reorder DCs such that $DC(1) = DC$ of SGW
36: $DC :=$ first DC in DCs
37: **for** $NFi = \{NF_1, NF_2, \cdots, NF_n, PGW\}$ **do**
38:     $prevDC := DC$
39:     **while** MapToDcServer (NFi, DC) **not** successful **do**
40:         $DC :=$ next DC in DCs
41:     **end while**
42:     **if** $DC = \emptyset$ **then**
43:         **return** $\forall \{x_u^i, f_{uv}^{ij}\} := 0$ {Reject request}
44:     **else**
45:         Update x_u^i
46:     **end if**
47: **end for**
48: Compute least-delay path from SGW to PGW
49: **if** $d_{(SGW \to PGW)} \leq d_{(SGW \to PGW),max}$ **then**
50:     Update f_{uv}^{ij}
51:     **return** $\{x_u^i, f_{uv}^{ij}\}$ {Accept request}
52: **else**
53:     **return** $\forall \{x_u^i, f_{uv}^{ij}\} := 0$ {Reject request}
54: **end if**

4.3   Greedy Algorithm

In addition, we have developed a greedy algorithm, which is shown in Algorithm 2. This algorithm assigns the NFs to the DC located most proximately to the eNB. In the case of lack of resources in proximate DCs, the algorithm seeks placements on other DCs, subject to delay budgets and capacity constraints. For the mapping of NFs to the servers of each DC, the algorithm calls the routine *MapToDcServer*, which strives to co-locate the NFs in order to save link capacity and reduce delays among the assigned NFs. More specifically, the algorithm uses a list of servers of the DC, ordered by decreasing residual CPU capacity, and maps all the NFs to the first server. If the capacity of the first server is not sufficient, the remaining NFs will be mapped to the next servers in the list. Similar to the LP, the greedy algorithm allocates a single S-GW and MME per UE.

Greedy algorithms are generally known to be time-efficient but sub-optimal. Based on our analysis, there is a substantial optimality gap between the MILP solutions and the solutions of the greedy algorithm. More precisely, the MILP yields approximately 100% better load balancing compared to the greedy variant. We use the greedy algorithm as a baseline in our evaluation in Sect. 5.

5   Evaluation

In this section, we assess the efficiency of our NF placement methods on virtualized EPC. To this end, we compare the efficiency between:

- The **LP** that aims at achieving load-balancing across the EPC,
- The **greedy** algorithm that maps NFs to the DC which is most proximate to the associated eNB, similar to what we consider a common practice today.

In the following, we discuss the evaluation environment (Sect. 5.1), the evaluation metrics (Sect. 5.2), and the evaluation results (Sect. 5.3).

5.1   Evaluation Environment

We have implemented an evaluation environment in C/C++, including a service chain generator and a cellular core network topology generator. We use CPLEX for our MILP/LP models. In the following we provide further details about our evaluation setup.

Cellular Core Network. We have generated a PoP-level cellular core network topology, spanning 10 homogeneous NFVI PoPs. Each PoP is essentially a micro-DC with a two-level fat-tree network topology. Table 2 shows additional cellular core network parameters.

Radio Access Network. We rely on a multi-cell scenario for the RAN, similar to the one presented in [18] that was based on real statistics from a region in Paris. However, in our case, we consider varying user density ($\rho = U[385, 2308]UEs/km^2$), so that the number of active UEs per eNB ranges from 500 to 3000 (Table 3). Considering uniform circular cells with an overlapping factor γ of 1.2, the required cell radius is $r = \gamma\sqrt{A_t/C\pi}$.

Table 2. Cellular core network parameters

NFVI PoPs	10
Servers per DC	20 in 2 racks
Server capacity	$16 \cdot 2\,\text{GHz}$
ToR-to-Server link capacity	4 Gbps
Inter-rack link capacity	16 Gbps
Inter-DC link capacity	100 Gbps

Table 3. User modeling parameters

Area size (A_t)	$4500\,\text{km}^2$
Total number of eNBs in the area (C)	5000
Active UEs per eNB	$500 \ldots 3000$

Table 4. Session parameters

Application type (and NFs)	Arrival rate (1/hour)	Duration (seconds)	Nominal rate (Kbps)	Pr(0)
Voice (FW, NAT, Echo cancellation)	0.67	180	12.65	0.5
Streaming (FW, NAT, Transcoder)	5	180	256	1
Background traffic (FW, NAT)	40	10	550	0.8

Traffic Classes. Based on 3GPP, traffic is classified into three types, *i.e.*, voice, media streaming, and background traffic, with their busy-hour parameters shown in Table 4 [17]. $Pr\{O\}$ is the probability that a session of a specific application type is originated by a UE.

Service Chains. We generate vNF-forwarding graphs per traffic class based on service chain templates. In particular, each service chain contains the main EPC elements (*i.e.*, S/P-GW, MME) and a set of security and application-specific NFs depending on the traffic class (see Table 4). We derive the CPU demands for each NF from resource profiles, similar to [19]. Based on the session parameters of Table 4, we generate service chain requests that express a periodic update of active sessions (UEs). Upon its generation, each service chain request is embedded replacing the existing chain that handles the traffic of the same class.

Delay Budgets. The delay budgets among the communicating EPC elements (*i.e.,* eNB-MME, MME-SGW, SGW-PGW) are set to 50 ms, inline with [32].

MME Signaling Load and Traffic. We quantify the processing load and the uplink/downlink traffic generated by LTE/EPC data management procedures, using the aforementioned traffic profile based on the analysis provided in [17,18] and 3GPP LTE/EPC signaling messages (Fig. 1) and their sizes provided in [31]. In this respect, applications are modeled as ON-OFF state machines, while we assume that each UE is registered in the LTE/EPC network (EMM-registered) and alternates between Connected (*ECM-Connected*) and Idle (*ECM-Idle*) states, as described in Fig. 1. In other words, only *Service Request/Release* procedures are taken into account. The RRC inactivity timer defines the inactivity period required for the UE to switch to IDLE state. This timer is adjusted to 10 s, which is a widely used setting in cellular networks.

Based on the model provided in [17,18], the processing load at the MME for a *Service Request - Release* is given by:

$$L_{MME} = \beta \rho A_c C [M_{MME}^{UE-SR} P_{UE} + M_{MME}^{NET-SR}(1 - P_{UE}) + M_{MME}^{SRel}]$$

where A_c, C, ρ denote the cell area, number of eNBs, and the UE density, respectively. The number of messages M per case for the Service Request (SR) and Service Release ($SRel$), depending on where the session is originated (UE or NET), are given in Fig. 1. The same methodology is used for all SR involved control plane elements. In a similar manner, we estimate the UL/DL bandwidth demands, given the sizes of the various packets exchanged during the *Service Request*. For example, in the case of UL between eNB and MME, the bandwidth demand is given by:

$$T_{eNB-MME}^{UL} = \beta \rho A_c [P_{ICSR} + P_{CRQ} + P_{CRTE}]$$

where P_{ICSR}, P_{CRQ}, P_{CRTE} denote the packet size for the *Initial Context Setup Response*, the *UE Context Release Request*, and the *UE Context Release Complete*, respectively [31]. The same methodology is used for all control links.

5.2 Evaluation Metrics

We use the following metrics for the evaluation of NF placement efficiency:

- **Load Balancing Level (LBL)** is defined as the maximum over the average load. We report the LBL for DCs (based on server load) and for inter-DC links. Lower values of LBL represent better load balancing, while $LBL = 1$ designates optimal load balancing.
- **Request Acceptance Rate** is the number of successfully embedded service chain requests over the total number of requests.
- **Revenue per Request** is the amount of CPU and bandwidth units specified in the request.
- **Resource Utilization** is the amount of CPU and bandwidth units allocated for the embedded requests.

5.3   Evaluation Results

Initially, we discuss the load balancing in the cellular core, which is the main objective of our LP. Figure 8 shows the load balancing level among the DCs, based on server load. The LP achieves a significant improvement in the DC load balancing level (Fig. 8) compared to the baseline which corresponds to the common practice today. We note that LP's load balancing efficiency is achieved while complying with 3GPP. These constraints most of the times inhibit the partitioning of service chains across DCs. This is corroborated in Table 5, which shows the number of DCs used for the assignment of each service chain, on average. Relaxing the 3GPP-associated constraints is expected to yield even better load distribution across the DCs, as inter-DC service chaining partitioning will not be restricted.

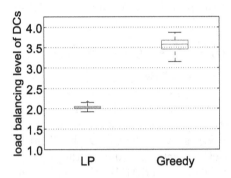

Fig. 8. DC load balancing level (based on server load).

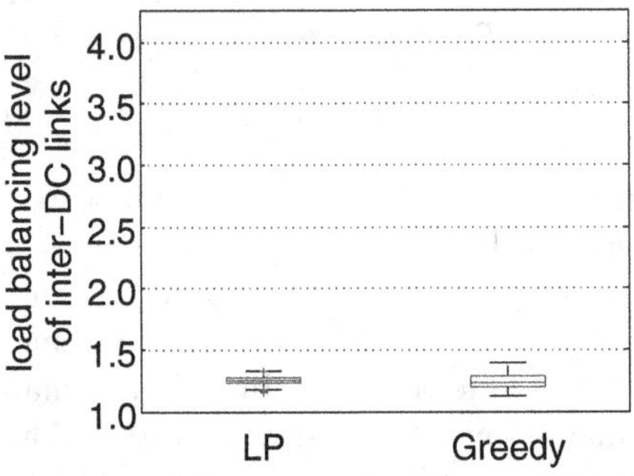

Fig. 9. Inter-DC link load balancing level.

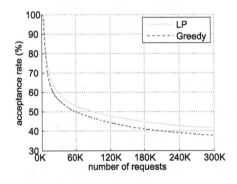

Fig. 10. Request acceptance rate.

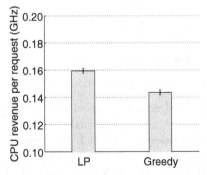

Fig. 11. Revenue from CPU per request.

Table 6 provides additional insights into the NF placement by the LP and the greedy algorithm. We observe that both NF placement methods minimize the

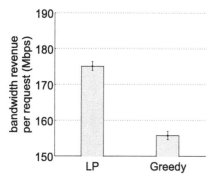

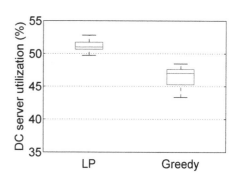

Fig. 12. Revenue from bandwidth per request.

Fig. 13. Server utilization.

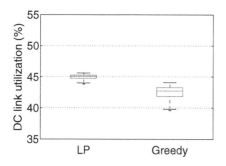

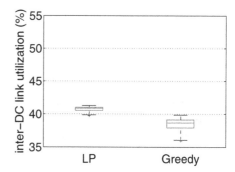

Fig. 14. Intra-DC link utilization.

Fig. 15. Inter-DC link utilization.

number of servers assigned to each service chain (subject to capacity constraints), thus minimizing inter-rack traffic within DCs. In certain cases, both methods accomplish the co-location of all NFs in the same server, which reduces the provisioning cost for cellular network operators.

We further investigate load balancing across the links connecting the DCs. As shown in Fig. 9 both the LP and the greedy algorithm yield an equally high level of inter-DC link load balancing.

Figure 10 illustrates the request acceptance rate of the LP and the greedy algorithm. The optimized NF placement of the LP leads to notable gains in terms of acceptance rate. More precisely, at steady state the LP variant accepts 11% more requests which are further associated with higher resource demands,

Table 5. Number of DCs per service chain

Method	1 DC	2 DCs
LP	74.56%	25.95%
Greedy	77.48%	22.52%

Table 6. Number of servers per service chain

Method	1 server	2 servers	3 servers
LP	18.63%	81.27%	0.10%
Greedy	23.76%	76.18%	0.06%

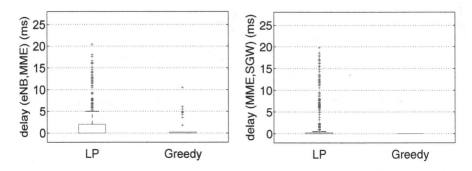

Fig. 16. Delay between eNB and MME.   **Fig. 17.** Delay between S-GW and MME.

i.e., 12% more CPU and 13% more bandwidth demand per request relatively to the revenue generated by the baseline (Figs. 11 and 12). A high request acceptance rate is crucial for a carrier, since he can increase his revenue by fulfilling QoS requirements of a larger number of UEs. The ability to accommodate and process larger volumes of data traffic can also lead to higher revenues for carriers that lease network slices to Mobile Virtual Network Operators (MVNO).

Since a fraction of requests are rejected even with the LP (Fig. 10), we investigate the potential reasons that lead to these rejections. Our logs indicate that delay budgets and 3GPP's requirement of a single instance of S-GW and MME per UE rarely lead to rejections; instead, they merely restrict the solution space. In fact, the main reason for the request rejections is the inability to meet CPU or bandwidth requirements within highly utilized DCs.

Figures 13, 14 and 15 depict the utilization level of the servers, the intra-DC links, and the inter-DC links, respectively. The higher utilization levels achieved by the LP stem from the higher request acceptance rate (Fig. 10). Essentially, our optimized NF placement allows a carrier to utilize his resources more effectively accommodating larger volumes of traffic. Furthermore, in the case of cellular network slicing and leasing, the carrier will be able to monetize much more efficiently his infrastructure.

Finally, we investigate the delays incurred between communicating data and control plane EPC elements. In this respect, Figs. 16 and 17 illustrate the delay between the eNB and the MME, and the delay between the MME and S-GW, respectively. It can observed that delays are below the 50 ms threshold (mandated by 3GPP) for both NF placement methods. As expected, the greedy algorithm yields very low delays, since it strives to assigns all EPC vNFs close to the eNB. On the other hand, the LP exploits the delay budgets to achieve a more flexible placement in order to achieve DC load balancing. The mean delays incurred with the LP are significantly lower than the 50 ms delay budget.

6 Related Work

In this section, we provide an overview of related work on NF placement for virtualized EPC. NF placement has been tackled for the migration of LTE mobile core gateways (S-GW and/or P-GW) to DCs [10,35,37]. In the same direction, additional approaches to the problem [14,34] take into consideration data-plane delay constraints. However, the proposed methods optimize the placement only of data-plane functions for design or operational objectives (*e.g.,* minimizing the EPC resource provisioning cost or GW relocations, load balancing).

Recently, the placement of virtualized EPC control plane functions (*e.g.,* MME, HSS) along S/P-GWs has been also considered towards the instantiation of a 3GPP-compliant elastic cellular core [12,28]. Furthermore, latency bounds for control as well as data plane traffic have also been considered to match real-world deployments [12,28].

KLEIN [28] proposes an orchestration framework for a software-defined mobile core network. The corresponding NF placement problem is formulated as an ILP, with the goal to minimize the total resources (capacity per DC) allocated to the virtualized mobile core, subject to capacity constraints of the physical resources and delay budgets for each traffic class supported. KLEIN argues that the attempt to model latency constraints between the control and data plane functions yields quadratic constraints. As such, potential solutions include the co-location of control and data plane functions or a two step procedure, *i.e.,* control function placement followed by data function placement problem, with an additional constraint on the delay budgets between the MME and S-GW components. To deal with complexity and scalability issues, KLEIN decomposes the global optimization into a three-level hierarchy; (i) UE aggregates are assigned to specific regions (Region Selection Problem) solving the aforementioned ILP problem, assuming the regional collocation of control and data plane functions (ii) then these aggregates are further assigned to DCs (DC Selection Problem) running a two step placement procedure to break the quadratic dependency issue, and (ii) finally KLEIN solves the Server Selection Problem using an appropriate greedy heuristic.

In [12], authors also decompose the EPC network graph into a data-plane chain and several control-plane ones. The service chain endpoints are (i) the RAN traffic aggregation point (for a cluster of eNodeBs) and (ii) Internet Exchange Point(s). Their goal is to jointly embed them into the underlying virtualized infrastructure. The problem is formulated as an ILP and solved optimally for small problem instances. Authors have extended their work in [13], taking into account delay budgets. Specifically, they propose a MILP formulation for the joint embedding of individual 3GPP-compliant core network service chains, considering end-to-end data- and control-plane latency bounds.

In our proposed solution (i) we investigate the embedding of service chains, containing both data and control-plane EPC elements as well as service-specific

NFs, tailored to specific traffic classes and service delivery (*e.g.*, with the addition of service-specific NFs) and (ii) we consider delay budgets among individual EPC components, based on LTE design and deployment strategies provided by vendors. Our main aim is global optimization, therefore we derive the NF placement in a single step, given the fact that virtual EPC providers (potentially telecom operators) will have a network-wide view on the cellular core.

7   Conclusions and Future Work

In this paper, we tackled the challenging problem of NF placement onto the cellular core. In this respect, we introduced a MILP and its relaxed variant for NF placement optimization, subject to capacity constraints, delay budgets between EPC components, and 3GPP-related restrictions. We further presented a greedy algorithm that strives to map NFs proximately to eNBs, inline with carriers' common practice.

We set up a realistic evaluation environment after a careful inspection of a wide range of cellular core network settings as well as signaling load and UE session models. According to our evaluation results, the proposed LP mitigates the load imbalance problem in today's cellular networks, spreading the load more evenly across the EPC's DCs, while maintaining compliance with the 3GPP standard. This leads to notable gains in terms of request acceptance and resource utilization, enabling the carrier to better monetize his infrastructure. Compared to the MILP, the LP exhibits substantially lower time complexity and solver runtime. As such, the LP can enable reprovisioning at lower timescales and thus better responses to traffic load variations. A small penalty is paid by the LP in terms of inter-DC link load balancing, whereas the DC load balancing level is similar for both variants.

In future work, we plan to couple our NF placement methods with service chaining and NF state transfer for EPC-wide orchestration. We will further investigate techniques for scaling in/out existing NF instances (*e.g.*, based on our previous work in [15]) to provide better responses to evolving service demands.

Acknowledgments. This work was partially supported by the EU FP7 T-NOVA Project (619520).

References

1. ETSI Network Function Virtualization. http://www.etsi.org/technologies-clusters/technologies/nfv
2. OPNFV. https://www.opnfv.org/
3. T-NOVA Project. http://www.t-nova.eu/
4. SONATA Project. http://www.sonata-nfv.eu/
5. UNIFY Project. http://www.fp7-unify.eu/
6. 3GPP TS 24.301: 3GPP Non-Access-Stratum (NAS) protocol for Evolved Packet System (EPS). http://www.3gpp.org/DynaReport/24301.htm

7. Business Case for Juniper Networks Virtualized Mobile Control Gateway, White Paper, Juniper (2013)
8. Abujoda, A., Kouchaksaraei, H.R., Papadimitriou, P.: SDN-based source routing for scalable service chaining in datacenters. In: Mamatas, L., Matta, I., Papadimitriou, P., Koucheryavy, Y. (eds.) WWIC 2016. LNCS, vol. 9674, pp. 66–77. Springer, Cham (2016). doi:10.1007/978-3-319-33936-8_6
9. Abujoda, A., Papadimitriou, P.: MIDAS: middlebox discovery and selection for on-path flow processing. In: IEEE COMSNETS, Bangalore, India, January 2015
10. Bagaa, M., Taleb, T., Ksentini, A.: Service-aware network function placement for efficient traffic handling in carrier cloud. In: IEEE WCNC, Istanbul, Turkey, April 2014
11. Banerjee, A., et al.: Scaling the LTE control-plane for future mobile access. In: ACM CONEXT, Heidelberg, Germany, December 2015
12. Baumgartner, A., Reddy, V.S., Bauschert, T.: Mobile core network virtualization: a model for combined virtual core network function placement and topology optimization. In: IEEE NetSoft 2015, London, UK, April 2015
13. Baumgartner, A., Reddy, V.S., Bauschert, T.: Combined virtual mobile core network function placement and topology optimization with latency bounds. In: EWSDN 2015, Bilbao, Spain, September 2015
14. Basta, A., et al.: Applying NFV and SDN to LTE mobile core gateways, the functions placement problem. In: 4th Workshop on All Things Cellular, ACM SIGCOMM 2014, Chicago, US, August 2014
15. Cao, Z., Abujoda, A., Papadimitriou, P.: Distributed data deluge (D3): efficient state management for virtualized network functions. In: IEEE INFOCOM SWFAN, San Francisco, USA, April 2016
16. Cohen, R., Lewin-Eytan, L., Naor, J., Raz, D.: Near optimal placement of virtual network functions. In: IEEE INFOCOM, Hong Kong, China, April 2015
17. Diego, W., Hamchaoui, I., Lagrange, X.: The cost of QoS in LTE/EPC mobile networks evaluation of processing load. In: IEEE VTC, Boston, MA, USA (2015)
18. Diego, W., Hamchaoui, I., Lagrange, X.: Cost factor analysis of QoS in LTE/EPC mobile networks. In: IEEE CCNC, Las Vegas, USA, January 2016
19. Dietrich, D., Abujoda, A., Papadimitriou, P.: Network service embedding across multiple providers with nestor. In: IFIP Networking, Toulouse, France, May 2015
20. Dietrich, D., Papagianni, C., Papadimitriou, P., Baras, J.: Network function placement on virtualized cellular cores. In: IEEE COMSNETS, Bangalore, India, January 2017
21. Bari, M.F.: Data center network virtualization: a survey. IEEE Commun. Surv. Tutorials 15(2), 909–928 (2013)
22. Fayazbakhsh, S., et al.: Enforcing network-wide policies in the presence of dynamic middlebox actions using flowtags. In: USENIX NSDI 2014, Seattle, USA, April 2014
23. Gember-Jacobson, A., et al.: OpenNF: enabling innovation in network function control. In: ACM SIGCOMM 2014, Chicago, USA, August 2014
24. Hirschman, B., et al.: High-performance evolved packet core signaling and bearer processing on general-purpose processors. IEEE Netw. 29(3), 6–14 (2015)
25. Lukovszki, T., Schmid, S.: Online admission control and embedding of service chains. In: Scheideler, C. (ed.) Structural Information and Communication Complexity. LNCS, vol. 9439, pp. 104–118. Springer, Cham (2015). doi:10.1007/978-3-319-25258-2_8
26. Mehraghdam, S., Keller, M., Karl, H.: Specifying and placing chains of virtual network functions. In: IEEE CloudNet, Luxembourg, October 2014

27. Prados-Garzon, J., et al.: Latency evaluation of a virtualized MME. In: IEEE Wireless Days, Toulouse, France, March 2016
28. Qazi, Z., et al.: KLEIN: a minimally disruptive design for an elastic cellular core. In: ACM SOSR 2016, Santa Clara, USA, March 2016
29. Qazi, Z., et al.: SIMPLE-fying middlebox policy enforcement using SDN. In: ACM SIGCOMM 2013, Hong Kong, China, August 2013
30. Rajan, A.S., et al.: Understanding the bottlenecks in virtualizing cellular core network functions. In: IEEE LANMAN, Beijing, China, April 2015
31. Sama, M.R., Ben Hadj Said, S., Guillouard, K., Suciu, L.: Enabling network programmability in LTE/EPC architecture using OpenFlow. In: WiOpt 2014, Hammamet, Tunisia, May 2014
32. Savic, Z.: LTE Design and Deployment Strategies - CISCO. http://tinyurl.com/lj2erpg
33. Shafiq, M.Z., Ji, L., Liu, A.X., Pang, J., Wang, J.: A first look at cellular machine-to-machine traffic: large scale measurement and characterization. In: ACM SIGMETRICS, London, UK, June 2012
34. Taleb, T., Bagaa, M., Ksentini, A.: User mobility-aware virtual network function placement for virtual 5G network infrastructure. In: IEEE ICC 2025, London, UK, June 2015
35. Taleb, T., Ksentini, A.: Gateway relocation avoidance-aware network function placement in carrier cloud. In: ACM MSWiM, Barcelona, Spain, November 2013
36. Wang, Z., et al.: An untold story of middleboxes in cellular networks. In: ACM SIGCOMM 2011, Toronto, Canada, August 2011
37. Yousaf, F., et al.: SoftEPC: dynamic instantiation of mobile core network entities for efficient resource utilization. In: IEEE ICC, Budapest, Hungary, June 2013

A Buffer Aware Resource Allocation Framework for Video Streaming over LTE

Satish Kumar$^{(\boxtimes)}$, Dheeraj Puri Goswami, Arnab Sarkar, and Arijit Sur

Department of Computer Science and Engineering,
Indian Institute of Technology Guwahati, Guwahati, India
`satish.kr@iitg.ernet.in`

Abstract. Latency sensitive high bandwidth multimedia data is expected to capture more than 70% of the available bandwidths in *LTE* and future wireless networks. This is expected to pose enormous challenges on the radio resource and management mechanisms in these networks. One of the most important factors that diminish the quality of viewing experience of delivered videos is frequent client side rebuffering events. This paper proposes a buffer-aware downlink scheduling framework (called *BA-TLS*) for streaming video applications. The problem of scheduling a set of video streams over *LTE* has first been formulated as an *Integer Linear Programming (ILP)* problem. It has been shown that a conventional *Dynamic Programming (DP)* solution for the *ILP* imposes prohibitive online overheads. Then, by utilizing analytical properties of the problem, a genetic algorithm based stochastic solution has been implemented. Further, a fast and efficient deterministic heuristic known as *Proportionally Balanced Robustness-level Allocator (PBRA)* has been implemented over the proposed framework. Experimental results show that while the optimal *DP* based solution performs significantly better at reducing rebuffering events with respect to the stochastic as well as the deterministic solutions, both of them incur much lower temporal overheads compared to *DP*. Further, it may be observed that although the stochastic and deterministic solutions are comparable in performance, the deterministic heuristic solution *PBRA* is about *300* to *600* times faster on average compared to its stochastic counterpart.

Keywords: Video streaming · LTE · Radio resource allocation · Buffer awareness · Genetic algorithm · Low overhead scheduling

1 Introduction

Multimedia applications over cellular networks have been growing at an exponential rate due to the ever increasing demand for video content and proliferation of heterogeneous mobile devices with increased processing capabilities. Therefore, video streaming over wireless is expected to be one of the main revenue generators for the current and future mobile broadband networks. However, satisfactory transmission of such *Quality of Service (QoS)* sensitive high data rate

© Springer International Publishing AG 2017
N. Sastry and S. Chakraborty (Eds.): COMSNETS 2017, LNCS 10340, pp. 223–242, 2017.
DOI: 10.1007/978-3-319-67235-9_14

video streams over limited wireless bandwidths poses an enormous challenge for the service provider.

The Long Term Evolution (LTE) [1] technology recently devised by the *Third Generation Partnership Project (3GPP)* is expected to cater to the high bandwidth and low latency demands of multimedia applications. However, it is still conceivable that these improvements will not be enough to meet the expected *QoS* demands of real time applications. Consequently, service providers are continually looking for effective techniques which permit them to provide improved capacity and *QoS* for their video users with their limited resources. It is evident from recent studies [2,3] that state-of-the art strategies for multiplexing multiple video streams over wireless are often susceptible to performance issues when competing for a bottleneck link. Literature also suggests that solution to these critical issues largely lies in the development of effective radio resource allocation strategies. However, an on-line scheduling policy which attempts to optimally utilize available resources in the face of uncertainties such as fading, data-rate demands variates etc. will pose a prohibitive computational budget (NP hard) at eNodeB.

In this paper, we propose a downlink resource allocation framework called *Buffer-aware Three Level Scheduler (BA-TLS)* which endeavors to deliver smooth viewing experience to each active end user even during transient network overloads. Founded on the basic architecture of *Three Level Scheduler (TLS)* [4], *BA-TLS* inherits all its salient facets including low *resource block*[1] *(RB)* allocation overheads, minimum guaranteed delay bounds for the flows, high spectral efficiency etc. However, TLS does not consider client side buffer status in its RB allocation strategy. Due to this buffer status ignorance, basic *TLS* is susceptible to frequent buffering events which may induce stutters in the transmitted videos which ultimately pulls down the *quality of viewing experience.* One of the principal objectives of *BA-TLS* is to mitigate this problem by minimizing re-buffering events caused by client side buffer outages. It may be noted that seamless playout experience in the face of temporally varying wireless bandwidths, may only be ensured by continuously maintaining playout buffer size above a specific threshold [5]. The robustness of a flow against buffer outages is directly proportional to the length of the video playout duration that can be transmitted in the ensuing super-frame (higher this length, higher will be the number of video frames contained in the buffer's repository). However at any given time, the exact video playout length required to quantitatively achieve a specific degree of robustness depends on the instantaneous channel quality being experienced. This is because, flows encountering poor channel qualities typically tend to suffer higher packet loss rates which in turn effects increased packet retransmissions. Thus, in such a situation, buffer outages may only possibly be avoided by maintaining a relatively larger number of video frames in the playout buffer. This problem has been posed as an *Integer Linear Programming (ILP)* based formulation such that aggregate robustness against buffer outages for a given set of flows over a limited wireless bandwidth, is maximized. The optimal

---

[1] Basic unit of resource that may be assigned to an UE in LTE.

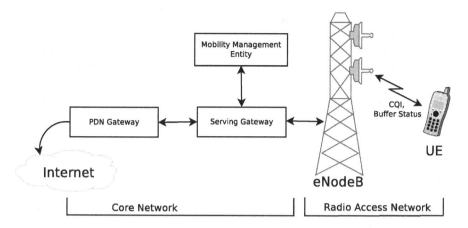

Fig. 1. LTE system overview

Dynamic Programming (DP) solution for the *ILP* has been shown to incur substantially high computational overheads which makes it impractical for it to be employed as an on-line resource allocation policy in dynamically evolving networks. In order to control on-line complexity, we have first proposed an efficient genetic algorithm [6] based stochastic solution strategy. Next, we have designed a deterministic heuristic strategy known as *Proportionally Balanced Robustness-level Allocator (PBRA)*, which is able to achieve robustness levels which are comparable to the stochastic solution, while incurring drastically lower computational overheads. Experimental results show that *PBRA* is about *300* to *600* times faster on average compared to the genetic algorithm approach. An initial version of this work has been published in [7].

The rest of the paper is organized as follows. A brief overview of LTE systems in general along with a discussion of the *TLS* framework is provided in the next section. Section 3 summarizes related works. Section 4 provides a detailed description of the proposed framework. Experiments and results along with a discussion on the same have been presented in Sect. 5. Finally, we present the conclusions in Sect. 6.

2 Background

2.1 LTE Architecture

LTE (Long Term Evolution) [8] is an architectural standard for cellular communication technology, which is designed to support the ever growing demands of bandwidth intensive multimedia applications and to provide high *Quality of Service (QoS)* for users in mobile networks. As shown in Fig. 1, the architecture has been designed as compared to previous architectures such as *GPRS*, *UMTS*, *HSDPA* etc., and consists of two main elements, namely the *Core Network (CN)* and the *Radio Access Network (RAN)*. *Core Network* (which includes the serving gateway, the *Mobility management entity* and the *Packet Data Network (PDN)* gateway) provides functionalities like IP connectivity, authentication, authorization, accounting and routing of traffic to and from several base stations. *RAN* is mainly composed of eNodeB, where wireless resource allocation across multiple flows, is performed.

Founded on the *Orthogonal Frequency Division Multiplexing (OFDM)* mechanism in the downlink, *LTE* systems provide an elaborate resource allocation infrastructure by allowing the total radio resource bandwidth (BW) to be simultaneously frequency multiplexed into multiple sub-channels (of 180 KHz each), each of which may further be time multiplexed at very fine granularities of a *Transmission Time Interval (TTI)* (1 *TTI* = 1 ms). A *TTI* is made up of two time slots of duration 0.5 ms. A time/frequency radio resource spanning over 180 kHz wide in frequency domain and over one time slot in the time domain is called a *Resource Block (RB)*. A resource block is the smallest unit of resources that can be assigned to an user equipment.

In this work, a single cell with interface scenario has been generated using *LTE-Sim* [9], an open source simulator for LTE networks. In this scenario, the total available transmission power (equal to 43 dBm) at eNodeB is uniformly spread over all the available sub-channels. Each User Equipment (UEs) calculates the *Signal-to-Interference plus Noise Ratio (SINR)* of the received reference signals for all the downlink sub-channels. The calculated values of SINR are mapped to a corresponding set of *Channel Quality Indicator (CQI)*. Each user equipment periodically feeds back their calculated Channel Quality Index (CQI), client side buffer status, and decodable quality levels with their required data rates to the eNodeB at the MAC layer.

The Packet scheduler available at eNodeB is responsible for allocating RBs to the active flows in each TTI. For each scheduled flow, an Adaptive Modulation and Coding (AMC) module selects a proper Modulation and Coding Scheme (MCS) based on CQI feedback. The Transport Block Size, or in other words, the amount of data that a flow can transmit at the MAC layer during a TTI using a sub-channel, is obtained from the selected MCS, taking into account the physical configuration proposed in [10]. Before presenting the detailed description of the proposed framework, we present an overview of the *TLS* Framework.

2.2   An Overview of Three Level Scheduler (TLS) Framework

Three Level Scheduler (TLS) [4] is a flexible resource allocation framework aimed at enabling mobile operators to effectively achieve good *Quality of Service (QoS)* and high cell spectral efficiency while incurring low overall scheduling overheads. As depicted in Fig. 2, the *TLS* framework has been designed as a three layered architecture (the super-frame layer, the frame layer and the TTI layer). These layers interact together in order to dynamically allocate RBs to the active flows, taking into account the instantaneous channel status, system load and maximum tolerable delays of flows.

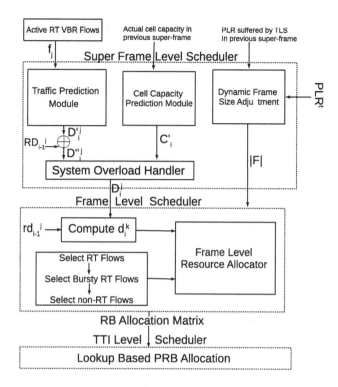

Fig. 2. Three Level Scheduler (TLS)

At the outermost layer, *TLS* divides time into a sequence of fixed sized intervals called super-frames. At each super-frame boundary, the *Traffic Prediction Module* calculates the amount of data that the flows should transmit in the following super-frame in order to satisfy their delay constraints. The *System Overload Handler* is also embedded at this layer and imposes an upper cap on the transmission data rates (during system overload) for each flow such that the total data rate demand may be reduced to atmost the total available cell capacity (computed in the *Cell Capacity Prediction Module*).

A super-frame is further divided into a specific number of frames whose duration may be dynamically adjusted at each super-frame boundary based on required scheduling accuracy and RB selection overheads under a given overall *CQI*. The *Frame Level Resource Allocator (FLRA)* at each frame boundary allocates the required number of RBs to a selected set of flows so that their data rate demands may be satisfied after execution within the next frame. *FLRA* selects the available traffic flows (RT flows having the highest priority, followed by bursty RT flows and non-RT flows) in three distinct rounds.

Finally, at the third and innermost level, the RBs are physically allocated to the flows for transmission at each TTI through an $O(1)$ lookup operation on the *RB Allocation Matrix* obtained from the *FLRA* module. During such RB allocation at any given TTI, an appropriate *Modulation and Coding Scheme (MCS)* is selected for each flow based on the instantaneous CQI feedback received for that flow-RB pair at that TTI.

3 Related Work

Effective radio resource management is an important tool by which the service provider tunes the amount of bandwidth resources received by its subscribers. As discussed in [2,3], significant performance gains may possibly be achieved by efficiently multiplexing the total available wireless bandwidth in both frequency and time among the different user equipments.

Riiser et al. [11] have tested the performance of various HTTP based video streaming services in a 3G mobile network scenario. They found a significant difference in performance and optimization objectives between the scheduling techniques of these services. For example, the Adobe HTTP Dynamic Streaming service was found to be quite responsive to bandwidth fluctuation and thus achieved a good bandwidth utilization. However, it experienced frequent video stuttering due to short buffering at the client. Microsoft IIS Smooth Streaming achieved better video quality with respect to Apple HTTP Live Streaming, but at the same time encounters a higher degree of re-buffering. A cross-layer *QoE* aware optimization framework called Re-buffering Aware Gradient Algorithm (RAGA) for LTE networks has been presented in [12]. *RAGA* attempts to restrict rebuffering probability of flows through periodic feedbacks of the playout buffer status for a set of adaptive streaming clients. Chen et al. [13] have proposed a *Playout Buffer Aware* scheduling scheme (*PBA*) in the endeavour to improve playout continuity of the video streaming services over *LTE*. They classify the users based on their urgencies and proposed a resource allocation scheme to keep buffer occupancy at acceptable levels. Authors in [5] evaluated video streaming using profiled bandwidth traces obtained in a vehicular scenario and inferred that re-buffering events may be minimized by maintaining playout buffer sizes above a certain threshold.

4 The BA-TLS Framework

According to a set of recent statistics by Conviva [14], viewer interruption from re-buffering affects ~20.6% of video streams while ~19.5% of users are impacted by slow video startups. In an endeavor to alleviate this problem, we have proposed an efficient radio resource allocation framework called *Buffer Aware Three Level Scheduler (BA-TLS)*. The *BA-TLS* framework provides a certain degree of robustness against re-buffering events and slow startups by attempting to quickly ramp-up and maintain playout buffer sizes of each flow above a threshold value. Such a protective shield against buffer outages enables the service provider to effectively deliver smooth viewing experience to all UEs under varying wireless channel conditions.

Typically, flows encountering poor channel qualities tend to suffer higher packet loss rates which in turn effects increased packet retransmissions. In such a situation, a flow naturally undergoes through a higher risk of buffer outages. One of the possible ways in which a flow may avoid buffer outages (improve robustness) during such transient durations of low CQIs, is to maintain comparatively larger playout buffer sizes. With this insight, we have designed buffer threshold (BS^{th}) for each flow to be a dynamic quantity which is proportional to the instantaneous value of the CQI feedback for the flow. Buffer threshold for the ith flow (BS_i^{th}) is calculated as:

$$BS_i^{th} = 2 \times (CQI_{max} - CQI_i + 1) \tag{1}$$

where, CQI_{max} (=15) is the maximum possible CQI feedback in LTE and CQI_i is the current CQI feedback received by the ith flow. As Eq. 1 shows, the value of BS_i^{th} for the ith flow increases as its channel quality degrades. In this work, lower and upper bounds on BS_i^{th} has been set to be 2 s (putting $CQI_i = CQI_{max} = 15$) and 30 s (putting $CQI_i = 1$), respectively.

As discussed above, a targeted degree of robustness against varying channel conditions may only be guaranteed by maintaining the playout buffer size of each flow above the threshold value BS_i^{th}. Therefore, BA-TLS calculates the amount of data to be transmitted for each flow in the ensuing super-frame such that the playout buffer achieves its threshold size BS_i^{th}. However, achieving threshold buffer sizes may not always be possible for all flows due to limited instantaneous wireless bandwidth. In such a situation, the framework attempts to provide a fraction of the targeted threshold robustness to each flow such that the total data transmission demand of all flows remains less than the expected cell capacity. The value of the fractional robustness to be chosen for a given flow depends on its relative urgency towards buffer replenishment. For the flow f_i, this urgency is proportional to the difference ($BS_i^{th} - BS_i^{cur}$) between its targeted threshold buffer size (BS_i^{th}) and its current buffer size (BS_i^{cur}). However, it may be noted that, choosing an optimal fractional robustness value for each flow such that the overall system level urgency is maximally reduced while simultaneously avoiding resource capacity overloads, is a very hard problem. Therefore, in order to control its complexity, the problem has been discretized as follows. The interval ($BS_i^{th} - BS_i^{cur}$) for each flow f_i has been partitioned into a constant number K of robustness levels (In this work, we have considered 10 levels, i.e. $K = 10$). The degree of urgency of a flow has been quantitatively represented in the form of an exponential reward function. The system obtains a reward R_{ij} if it is able to successfully transmit the ith flow at the jth robustness level. R_{ij} is given by:

$$R_{ij} = exp\left(\frac{(BS_i^{th} - BS_i^{cur})}{1 + \sqrt{1/N \sum_i (BS_i^{th} - BS_i^{cur})}}\right) \times j \tag{2}$$

where, N is the total number of active flows. It may be noted from the above equation that reward R_{ij} is a linearly increases function of the selected robustness level j. In the *BA-TLS* framework, the *System Overload Handler* of *TLS* is replaced by the *Robustness Level Selection module* which judiciously selects an appropriate robustness level for each flow.

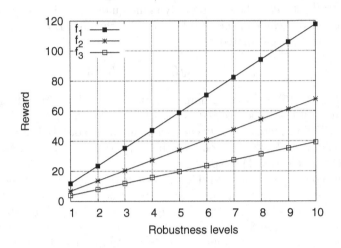

Fig. 3. Reward values for the flows f_1, f_2 and f_3 at all the available robustness levels

We now present a simplistic example in order to unfold the concealed properties of the reward function. Assume a system consisting of three flows f_1, f_2 and f_3 with 10 robustness levels for each flow. Let the current playout buffer size (BS_i^{cur}) for all the flows be same and equal to 5 s. Also, let the CQI feedbacks received by f_1, f_2 and f_3 be 9, 10 and 11, respectively. Hence, their corresponding buffer threshold values (refer Eq. 1) become 14 s, 12 s and 10 s. The differences between their threshold and current playout buffer size $(BS_i^{th} - BS_i^{cur})$ are 9, 7 and 5, respectively. Figure 3 depicts plots for the reward value obtained by f_i, f_2 and f_3 as the robustness levels j varies from 1 to 10. It may be observed from the figure that for any given robustness value, higher the value of the difference $BS^{th} - BS_i^{cur}$, higher is the obtained reward. Thus, the designed reward function implicitly auto-tunes the system towards quick buffer ramp-up and thereby endeavours to mitigate possibilities of buffer outages.

4.1   Problem Formulation

Assume that the length of a super-frame interval is t TTIs and the number of RBs available in a TTI is p. Then, the total number of RBs available in a super-frame duration becomes $B = t \times p$. These RBs are required to be distributed among the N active flows $(Q = \{f_1, f_2, .., f_N\})$ at a given super-frame boundary. Let K be the total number of available robustness levels. Also, let b_{ij} be the total number of RBs required to transmit the ith flow at the jth *robustness level*. x_{ij} is a binary variable which is equal to 1 if flow f_i is selected for transmission at robustness level j. We then formulate the resource allocation problem as:

$$\text{maximize} \sum_{i=1}^{N} \sum_{j=1}^{K} R_{ij} \times x_{ij} \tag{3a}$$

subject to

$$\sum_{i=1}^{N} \sum_{j=1}^{K} b_{ij} \times x_{ij} \leq B, \tag{3b}$$

$$\sum_{j=1}^{K} x_{ij} \leq 1, \ x_{ij} \in \{0,1\}, \forall i \tag{3c}$$

The first constraint in Eq. 3b guarantees that the total number of RBs allocated to all flows do not surpass the total available number of RBs (B) at eNodeB. The second constraint as given in Eq. 3c forces each flow to select atmost one robustness level.

4.2 Proposed Resource Allocation Schemes

The above formulation (refer Eq. 3) may be classified as a Multiple Choice Knapsack Problem (MCKP) [15], where each video flow is analogous to a class and the distinct robustness levels of each video flow are the items within each class. Multiple Choice Knapsack Problem can be optimally solved through a dynamic programming (DP) procedure. We first propose a standard dynamic programming procedure (described in Algorithm 1) to solve this MCKP.

The Dynamic Programming Robustness-level Allocator. This strategy which we refer to as the *Dynamic Programming Robustness-level Allocator* (BA-TLS-Optimal), selects a robustness level for each flow in such a manner that the aggregate reward over all flows is maximized. A step by step analysis of the working principle of the algorithm is as follows: Steps 1 to 12 select robustness levels for all flows. Let $R(i,\beta)$ be the optimal aggregate reward value for flows 1 through i given β, the total number of available RBs. The initialization of the optimal aggregate reward matrix ($R(i,\beta)$) is done in steps 2 to 6. The matrix $R(i,\beta)$ is built iteratively for all the flows, and for each flow the problem is solved for all the available RBs in a super-frame interval (B). The optimal aggregate reward value $R(i,\beta)$ depends on the robustness level selected for the ith flow. Hence, for each robustness level (1 to K), the allocator checks the optimal aggregate reward value obtained by the first $i-1$ flows given ($\beta - b_{ij}$) resource blocks, where b_{ij} is the total additional number of RBs required to transmit the ith flow at the jth robustness level. To obtain optimal aggregate reward value $R(i,\beta)$, the allocator selects the robustness level for the ith flow that gives the highest reward.

Algorithm 1: The Dynamic Programming based Robustness-level Allocator (BA-TLS-Optimal)

Input: N : Number of active video flows,

B : Total number of resource block in a super-frame interval,

K: Total number of robustness levels available for each video flow,

b_{ij} : RBs demand for the ith video flow at the jth robustness level,

R_{ij} : Reward value for the ith video flow at the jth robustness level

Output: Selected robustness level for each video flow

1 **begin**
2   **for** β *from 1 to B* **do**
3         $R(1, \beta) = 0$;
4   **for** i *from 2 to N* **do**
5   **for** β *from 1 to B* **do**
6             $R(i, \beta) = -\infty$
7   **for** i *from 1 to N* **do**
8   **for** β *from 1 to B* **do**
9             $R(i, \beta) = U(i - 1, \beta)$;
10   **for** j *from 1 to K* **do**
11                 $R(i, \beta) = \max \left(R(i, \beta), R(i - 1, \beta - b_{ij}) + r_{ij} \right)$
12   Output the solution that gives $R(N, B)$;
13 **end**

The computational complexity of the dynamic programming solution is $\mathcal{O}(N \times L \times B)$ where, N is the number of active users, L is an upper bound on the number of robustness levels corresponding to a flow and B is the total number of resource blocks in a super-frame. This overhead proves to be quite expensive as the number of RBs to be scheduled (B) is typically high even for moderately sized super-frames. For example, in a system with 20 MHz bandwidth (i.e. 100 RBs per TTI), the value of R is 100000 for a super-frame duration of just one second. Our experimental results show that given an LTE bandwidth of 20 MHz in a system with 100 active users and 1 GHz processing capacity, conventional DP takes ~1.89 ms (~4 times the size of resource block) on average to generate a solution for a super-frame interval of size of 1 s. The above overhead estimates indicate that to be practically useful, we require lower overhead heuristics for the online buffer aware RB allocation problem. Therefore, a *Genetic Algorithm* based fast and efficient resource allocation heuristic called *BA-TLS-Genetic* has been proposed over the *BA-TLS* framework. For the example system mentioned above, our *GA* strategy is able to produce good and acceptable solutions in ~0.03 ms which is ~60 times faster than conventional DP (which takes ~1.89 ms). A detailed description of the proposed strategy is presented in the next subsection.

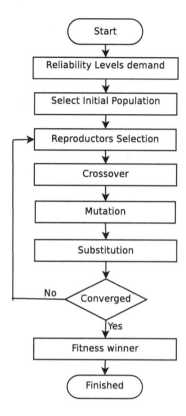

Fig. 4. Optimization strategy based on genetic algorithm

4.3   Genetic Algorithm Strategy for Robustness Level Selection

Genetic algorithm [6] is an optimization search procedure which samples the solution space of the problem iteratively and tries to locate a globally optimal solution after examining a limited number of candidates in the solution space. Effectiveness and efficiency of genetic algorithm comes from its potential to analyze the search space and maintain the traits of the best candidates already found while searching through the state space.

As depicted in Fig. 4, our proposed genetic algorithm *BA-TLS-Genetic* selects a solution providing candidate robustness levels for each flow in five steps, namely, (1) Initialization, (2) Reproductors Selection, (3) Crossover, (4) Mutation Operator and (5) Substitution. The steps 2–5 are repeated until the solutions converge. Once, the solutions are converged, the algorithm determines a final solution which has the highest fitness value. Now, we discuss each step of our genetic algorithm strategy in detail.

Initialization: In this step, initial candidate solutions are generated. Here, a solution represents a distinct set of selected robustness levels for the flows.

Initialization may be done through a *random* strategy or using the *first fit* scheme. However, with the *random* strategy, the candidate solutions are selected without investigating their feasibility. On the other hand, *best-fit* scheme only selects feasible candidate solutions. A solution is feasible if the total number of RBs required to transmit all flows do not surpass the total available RBs (B) at eNodeB. It may be noted that the *first fit* process is myopically greedy in choosing feasible candidate solutions and may induce poor overall performance of the genetic algorithm. On the other hand, random generation may provide good candidate solutions, but the chances for their infeasibility are also high. To ensure a good variety of selected robustness levels in the initial solutions, we have selected 30% of the candidate robustness levels in the initial configuration by the *first-fit* method while robustness levels for the rest of the candidates have been generated randomly.

Reproductors Selection: This step identifies the better solutions within a given generation using a metric called *Fitness Value (FV)*. These identified solutions act as reproductors for the creation of a new population. Feasible candidate solutions with relatively higher fitness values are closer to the optimal solution. The fitness value (FV_z) for the zth candidate solution is defined as the sum of the rewards of all flows at their selected robustness levels i.e.

$$FV_z = \sum_{i=1}^{N} \sum_{j=1}^{L_i} R_{ij} \times x_{ij}^z \tag{4}$$

It may be noted that FV is same as the expression for the objective function of the *ILP* in Eq. 3.

Crossover: One of the principal motivations towards the use of a genetic algorithm approach is to transfer the best traits in the parent solutions to the subsequent candidate generations. This is achieved through the mechanism of crossover where new child solutions are generated by combining parts of the configurations from two different parent solutions. For example, in the scenario shown in Fig. 5, two offspring solutions O_a and O_b have been generated through a crossover operation on the parent solutions S_a and S_b. Here, both O_a and O_b are obtained by combining half of the robustness levels from S_a and remaining from S_b. The Primary goal of the crossover operation is to generate a good variety for a new population. This is typically referred to as *"Survival of the fittest"*. However, good offspring candidates can only be generated by intelligently choosing parents having the best traits. This is achieved by assigning a selection probability to each parent solution based on its goodness/fitness. This work calculates selection probability SP_z of the zth candidate using its *fitness value* as:

$$SP_z = \frac{FV_z}{\sum\limits_{z=1}^{P} FV_z} \tag{5}$$

where, P denotes the size of the population.

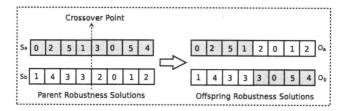

Fig. 5. Single-point crossover procedure

It may be observed from the above equation that higher the fitness value of a candidate solution, higher will be its selection probability. Then, roulette wheel [6] selection scheme has been used to choose the parents based on their selection probability and traits of the parents are combined to generate new candidates. As shown in Fig. 5, the algorithm calculates a single crossover point [16] on both parents' and then, a new candidate solution is generated using robustness levels from the beginning of the chromosome to the crossover point from one parent, the rest being copied from the second parent. After that, a second child solution is generated from the remaining robustness levels of both the parent solutions.

Mutation Operator: It may be noted that just selecting the best solutions based on their fitness values is not enough for obtaining the global maximum reward because the approach may get stuck at a local maxima. The main purpose of the mutation operator is to maintain diversity by purturbing the solutions within a population and avoid premature convergence. The mutation operator randomly selects a flow (also called mutation flow) from the candidate solutions and assigns all possible robustness levels to it. Then, the algorithm calculates the fitness values corresponding to all newly assigned robustness levels to the mutation flow. The robustness level which corresponds to highest fitness value is assigned to the mutation flow.

Substitution: The improved solutions which are obtained by the crossover and mutation steps are included in the population, and the solutions which are infeasible are removed. Then, the algorithm repeats steps 2–5 until the solutions are converged.

GA thus produces good solutions at appreciably lower computational cost with respect to *DP*. However, insight obtained through a deeper look into the structure of the problem revealed that it is possible to design a poised proportionally balanced step by step heuristic solution approach which is capable of providing comparable performance with that of *GA* while incurring drastically lower computational overheads. This approach, which we call the *Proportionally Balanced Robustness-level Allocator (PBRA)* is discussed next.

4.4   Proportionally Balanced Robustness-level Allocator

The underlying philosophy of the *Proportionally Balanced Robustness-level Allocator (BA-TLS-PBRA)* is to select the robustness levels of a subset of the flows in each super-frame boundary, such that the robustness of the system is optimized. However, in order to obtain good and acceptable solutions, the heuristic strategy must be aware of the constraint on the available number of RBs. Hence, the algorithm must not only consider the individual reward gains during robustness level selections, but also the number of incremental RBs incurred during such a selection process. Therefore, we have transformed the original objective function, i.e. *Reward (R)* into *Reward per RB (RpR)*. *RpR* is calculated as:

$$RpR_{il} = \frac{R_{il}}{RB_{il}} \tag{6}$$

where, R_{il} is the reward value obtained by the system when it transmits the ith flow at the lth robustness level and RB_{il} is the total number of RBs required to transmit the ith flow at the lth robustness level. *RpR* proves to be a better performance metric than *Reward* as the former takes into account the spectral efficiencies of different flows and is able to provide higher overall Reward per super-frame interval.

At any given time during the *robustness level* allocation process of the *BA-TLS-PBRA* heuristic, the flows are maintained in a priority queue organized as a *max heap*. The priority of a flow within the *max-heap* is decided on the basis of a *key* which is defined for each flow as follows:

$$key_i = \mathbf{max}\{d[RpR_{lK}^i], \ d[RpR_{l(l+1)}^i]\} \tag{7}$$

Here, $d[RpR_{lK}^i]$ denotes the difference in *Reward per RB* values between its current (l) and highest (K) *robustness levels* and $d[RpR_{l(l+1)}^i]$ represents the *Reward per RB* difference of its current and immediately higher *robustness levels*.

It was observed that key_i is able to provide an appropriate balance between the immediate gain obtained through a *robustness level* shift from l to $l+1$ and the overall obtainable gain for the flow $d[RpR_{lK}^i]$. A situation (shown for robustness level upgradation here) where the consideration of such overall gains may be useful is as follows: Let us consider the relative prioritization of two flows f_i and f_j, currently allocated *robustness levels* x and y respectively (say), at an arbitrary intermediate stage of the *robustness level* allocation process using *BA-TLS-PBRA*. Assume $d[RpR_{x(x+1)}^i]$ is lower than $d[RpR_{y(y+1)}^j]$. However, $d[RpR_{xK}^i] >> d[RpR_{yK}^i]$. In such a situation, if overall gain values are not considered as part of the *key*, f_j will be selected for the *robustness level* upgradation by one level over f_i even if its overall gain $(d[RpR_{xK}^i])$ is much greater than $\mathbf{max}\{d[RpR_{yK}^i], \ d[RpR_{y(y+1)}^i]\}$. A more severe case is that, if $f_i's$ immediate gain $d[RpR_{x(x+1)}^i]$ is relatively very low, f_i may be indefinitely starved in spite of potentially handsome overall gains. Defining the *key* as $\mathbf{max}\{d[RpR_{lK}^i], \ d[RpR_{l(l+1)}^i]\}$ appropriately handles the situation.

The algorithm proceeds by repeatedly extracting the flow at the root of the *max heap*, incrementing its *robustness level* by 1, updating its *key* value and reheapifying it, until either the system capacity is completely exhausted, or all flows have been assigned their maximum possible *robustness levels*. The asymptotic worst-case time complexity of this heuristic is $\mathcal{O}(N) + \mathcal{O}(\sum_i L_i log N)$

Algorithm 2: The Proportionally Balanced Robustness-level (BA-TLS-PBRA)

Input: N : Number of active video flows,

B : Total number of resource block in a super-frame interval,

K: Total number of robustness levels available for each video flow,

b_{ij} : RBs demand for the ith video flow at the jth robustness level,

R_{ij} : Reward value for the ith video flow at the jth robustness level

Output: Selected robustness level for each flow

1   Assume the current and highest *robustness levels* of flow f_i are l and K, respectively;

2   Initialize $l = 0$ for all flows;

3   Remaining Excess Capacity $REC = B$;

4   Compute the $d[RpR_{l(l+1)}]$ and $[RpR_{lK}]$ values for each active flow f_i;

5   Compute key_i: $\mathbf{max}\{d[RpR^i_{lK}], d[RpR^i_{l(l+1)}]\}$ for each flow f_i ;

6   Create a *max-heap* of the flows with the *key* values obtained;

7   **begin**

8   Extract the flow f_i from the root of the *max-heap*;

9   Let $RB^i_{l(l+1)}$ be the RBs required to increment the robustness level of the flows f_i by one;

10   Increment the *current robustness level* l of f_i by one if the incremental RBs $(RB^i_{l(l+1)})$ is at most equal to REC;

11   Update $REC = REC - RB^i_{l(l+1)}$;

12   If $(REC \leq \epsilon)$ Exit;

13   If $(l < K)$, update key_i, reheapify f_i, go to step 9;

14 **end**

---

where, N is the total number of active flows. The complexity $\mathcal{O}(N)$ is for the formation of the heap data structure for the N active flows. The $\mathcal{O}(\sum_i L_i log N)$ overhead is for the reheapify operation and updating the remaining excess /deficient capacity at each *robustness level* modification. A step wise description of the *Proportionally Balanced Robustness-level Allocator (BA-TLS-PBRA)* is presented in Algorithm 2.

5   Experiments and Results

The performance of the *BA-TLS* framework has been experimentally evaluated using LTE-Sim [9], an open source simulator for LTE networks. All simulations run for 120 s. A summary of the main simulation parameters are presented in Table 1. A series of experiments have been conducted in order to measure the performance achieved by the proposed strategy. The obtained performance results have also been compared against the *TLS* [4] framework. The specific performance metrics which have been considered for evaluation are: (i) Average buffering (%), (ii) Instantaneous playout buffer status and (iii) Average execution time.

Table 1. Simulation parameters

Simulation time	120 s
Bandwidth	20 MHz
Number of RBs	100
Frame structure	FDD
Cell radius	1.0 km
Number of cells	19
Carrier frequency	2 GHz
Number of video flows	10 to 100
Video traffic generator	Trace based
RLC ARQ	Maximum 5 retransmissions

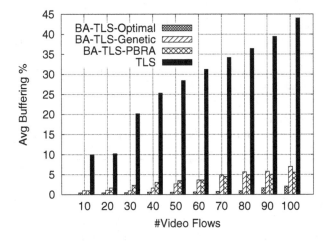

Fig. 6. Avg buffering % vs. #Video flows

Figure 6 depicts plots for the average buffering suffered by the different resource allocation strategies against varying number of video flows (or system load) during the entire simulation length. It may be noted that average buffering (%) for all the strategies increases as the number of flows/system load increase. This is expected because the average number of RBs that may be allocated for a video flow reduces as the total number of video flows increases under a fixed resource block budget within a super-frame interval. Although, trends for all the methodologies in Fig. 6 are similar, *BA-TLS-Optimal* is seen to encounter less buffering events compared to both the heuristic strategies, namely, *BA-TLS-Genetic* and *BA-TLS-PBRA*, while the basic *TLS* algorithm performs poorly in all cases. The reason for the poor performance of basic *TLS* originates from its ignorance of client side buffer status during the resource allocation process. On the other hand, the endeavour to maintain stable playout

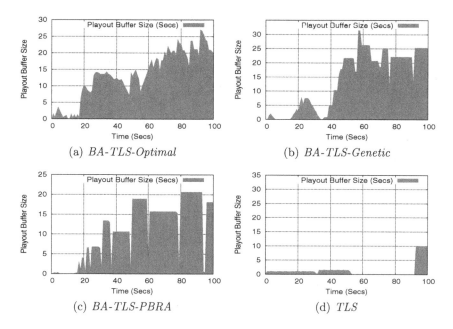

Fig. 7. Instantaneous playout buffer size achieved by *BA-TLS-Optimal*, *BA-TLS-Optimal* and *TLS* strategies

buffer sizes for each flow considerably reduces rebuffering events in the proposed buffer aware schemes. In Fig. 6, *BA-TLS-Genetic* and *BA-TLS-PBRA* are seen to suffer slightly higher average buffering with respect to *BA-TLS-Optimal*, due to their inherent heuristic nature.

Figures 7(a) to (d) shows instantaneous buffer sizes achieved by *BA-TLS-Optimal*, *BA-TLS-Genetic*, *BA-TLS-PBRA* and TLS strategies respectively, for a single flow (namely, Star Wars) over the entire simulation duration. The scenario considers a cell with 100 active flows. It may be observed from the figures that the buffer-aware strategies, namely *BA-TLS-Optimal*, *BA-TLS-Genetic* and *BA-TLS-PBRA* are able to maintain approximately stable buffer sizes for the flow during the entire simulation duration. Stable playout buffer sizes in *BA-TLS* is achieved by two principle mechanisms: (i) Providing a certain degree of robustness to each flow against varying channel conditions and (ii) Auto tunning the priority of the flow during resource allocation based on its instantaneous playout buffer size and received CQI feedback (i.e. assigning relatively higher reward values to flows having comparatively lower playout buffer sizes and/or CQIs).

Table 2 shows the average number of clock cycles taken by *BA-TLS-Optimal*, *BA-TLS-Genetic* and *BA-TLS-PBRA* as the number of video flows vary from 10 to 100. It may be observed from the table that the average number of clock cycles required for *BA-TLS-Optimal* is comparatively much higher than the *BA-TLS-Genetic* and *BA-TLS-PBRA* strategies. This happens because *BA-TLS-Optimal* calculates partial solutions for all possible bounds on number of flows

Table 2. Comparative results for number of clock cycles

# Flows	BA-TLS-Optimal	BA-TLS-Genetic	BA-TLS-PBRA
10	186749	4533	15
20	365207	7395	20
30	551498	11022	24
40	727642	12915	30
50	903856	15923	25
60	1101784	18268	31
70	1257624	21616	35
80	1451931	23825	59
90	1681833	27541	45
100	1885498	30051	58

($\forall i \in [0, N]$), robustness levels ($\forall l \in [0, L_i]$) and RBs ($\forall \beta \in [0, B]$). On the other hand, the stochastic strategy *BA-TLS-Genetic* is observed to generate good and acceptable solutions much quicker as compared to the optimal strategy. This is expected because the *BA-TLS-Genetic* tries to locate a globally optimal solution after examining a limited number of candidates in the solution space. Therefore, the *BA-TLS-Genetic* strategy may be seen to achieve good speedups ($\sim$50 to 60 times) with respect to the *BA-TLS-Optimal* strategy. On the other hand, it may be observed that *BA-TLS-PBRA* perform far better than *BA-TLS-Optimal* and *BA-TLS-Genetic* in terms of computational overhead. This is because the computational complexity of *BA-TLS-PBRA* only depends on the available number of flows and the number of available robustness level. Therefore, *BA-TLS-PBRA* is able to achieve drastic speed-ups with respect to the other two strategies. Comparative results for achieved speed-ups are shown in Table 3.

Table 3. Comparative results for speed-ups achieved by the proposed heuristics

# Flows	Optimal vs. Genetic	Optimal vs. PBRA	Genetic vs. PBRA
10	41	12450	302
20	49	18260	370
30	50	22979	459
40	56	24255	431
50	57	36154	637
60	60	35541	589
70	58	35932	618
80	61	24609	404
90	61	37374	612
100	63	32509	518

6 Conclusion

In this work, a new Buffer Aware Three Level Scheduling framework (called *BA-TLS*) has been proposed. *BA-TLS* is based on *TLS* and hence, inherits all its salient facets. The framework is aimed at enabling the service provider to deliver smooth viewing experience to the end users even during transient overloads through a buffer aware adaptive scheduling strategy that attempts to minimize client-side re-buffering events. The resource allocation model has been formulated as an *Integer Linear Programming (ILP)* problem for which conventional dynamic programming solution is shown to impose substantial overheads. Thus, two fast and efficient solution strategies, namely *BA-TLS-Genetic* and *BA-TLS-PBRA* have been designed with the endeavor to achieve efficient but low-overhead resource adaptability. Experimental results show that the genetic algorithm *BA-TLS-Genetic* produces good solutions and at the same time is about *40* to *60* times faster than the optimal strategy *BA-TLS-Optimal*. The deterministic heuristic strategy *BA-TLS-PBRA* in-turn is comparable in performance while being about *300* to *600* times faster on average compared to *BA-TLS-Genetic*.

References

1. Cox, C.: An Introduction to LTE: LTE, LTE-advanced, SAE and 4G Mobile Communications. Wiley, London (2012)
2. Capozzi, F., Piro, G., Grieco, L.A., Boggia, G., Camarda, P.: Downlink packet scheduling in LTE cellular networks: key design issues and a survey. IEEE Commun. Surv. Tutorials **15**(2), 678–700 (2013)
3. Chen, J., Mahindra, R., Khojastepour, M.A., Rangarajan, S., Chiang, M.: A scheduling framework for adaptive video delivery over cellular networks. In: Proceedings of the 19th Annual International Conference on Mobile Computing & Networking, pp. 389–400. ACM (2013)
4. Kumar, S., Sarkar, A., Sriram, S., Sur, A.: A three level LTE downlink scheduling framework for RT VBR traffic. Comput. Netw. **91**, 654–674 (2015)
5. Müller, C., Lederer, S., Timmerer, C.: An evaluation of dynamic adaptive streaming over HTTP in vehicular environments. In: Proceedings of the 4th Workshop on Mobile Video, pp. 37–42. ACM (2012)
6. Golberg, D.E.: Genetic Algorithms in Search, Optimization, and Machine Learning, vol. 1989, p. 102. Addison Wesley, Boston (1989)
7. Kumar, S., Goswami, D., Sarkar, A., Sur, A.: Buffer aware three level scheduler for video streaming over LTE. In: 2017 9th International Conference on COMmunication Systems and NETworkS (COMSNETS). IEEE (2017)
8. Nossenson, R.: Long-term evolution network architecture. In: IEEE International Conference on Microwaves, Communications, Antennas and Electronics Systems, COMCAS 2009, pp. 1–4. IEEE (2009)
9. Piro, G., Grieco, L., Boggia, G., Capozzi, F., Camarda, P.: Simulating LTE cellular systems: an open-source framework. IEEE Trans. Veh. Technol. **60**(2), 498–513 (2011)
10. 3GPP: Tech. Specif. Group Radio Access Network; Conveying MCS and TB Size via PDCCH. 3GPP TSG-RAN WG1 R1–081483

11. Riiser, H., Bergsaker, H.S., Vigmostad, P., Halvorsen, P., Griwodz, C.: A comparison of quality scheduling in commercial adaptive HTTP streaming solutions on a 3G network. In: Proceedings of the 4th Workshop on Mobile Video, pp. 25–30. ACM (2012)

12. Ramamurthi, V., Oyman, O.: Video-QoE aware radio resource allocation for HTTP adaptive streaming. In: 2014 IEEE International Conference on Communications (ICC), pp. 1076–1081. IEEE (2014)

13. Chen, Y., Liu, G., Chen, X.: Playout buffer aware scheduling scheme for video streaming over LTE networks. In: 2014 IEEE/CIC International Conference on Communications in China (ICCC), pp. 840–845. IEEE (2014)

14. Conviva: Think Streaming Will Replace Cable TV. http://www.conviva.com/think-streaming-will-replace-cable-tv-this-data-on-streaming-quality-proves-otherwise/

15. Sinha, P., Zoltners, A.A.: The multiple-choice knapsack problem. Oper. Res. **27**(3), 503–515 (1979)

16. Kaya, Y., Uyar, M., et al.: A novel crossover operator for genetic algorithms: ring crossover. arXiv preprint arXiv:1105.0355 (2011)

Convolutional Regression Framework for Human Health Prediction Under Social Influences

Srinka Basu[1(✉)], Saikat Roy[2], and Ujjwal Maulik[2]

[1] Department of Engineering and Technological Studies,
University of Kalyani, Kalyani, India
srinka.basu@gmail.com
[2] Department of Computer Science and Engineering,
Jadavpur University, Kolkata, India
saikat_roy@hotmail.com, umaulik@cse.jdvu.ac.in

Abstract. Understanding the propagation of human health behavior, such as smoking and obesity, and identification of the factors that control such phenomenon is an important area of research in recent years mainly because, in industrialized countries a substantial proportion of the mortality and quality of life is due to particular behavior patterns, and that these behavior patterns are modifiable. Predicting the individuals who are going to be overweight or obese in future, as overweight and obesity propagate over dynamic human interaction network, is an important problem in this area. The problem has received limited attention from the network analysis and machine learning perspective till date, though. In this work, we propose a scalable supervised prediction model based on convolutional regression framework that is particularly suitable for short time series data. We propose various schemes to model social influence for health behavior change. Further we study the contribution of the primary factors of overweight and obesity, like unhealthy diets, recent weight gains and inactivity in the prediction task. A thorough experiment shows the superiority of the proposed method over the state-of-the-art.

1 Introduction

In recent days, dynamic social networks have been leveraged in various fields to analyze time-varying events involving social connectivity including computational epidemiology to study the propagation of diseases and other public health issues [1,2]. The area of public health, in particular, has been one of increased scrutiny with the advances in information technology playing an increased role in health care and medicine. Obesity has been identified, alongside cancer, to be one of the biggest epidemics of the 21st century [3,4]. World Health Organization (WHO) defines obesity and overweight as the medical conditions due to abnormal or excessive fat accumulation that may impair health. Body mass index (BMI) is a weight-for-height index commonly used to classify overweight as persons having BMI over 25 and obesity as persons having BMI over 30 in adults [5]. The major

N. Sastry and S. Chakraborty (Eds.): COMSNETS 2017, LNCS 10340, pp. 243–261, 2017.
DOI: 10.1007/978-3-319-67235-9_15

health concern associated with people being overweight or obese is that it increases the risks of developing other more chronic ailments [6,7]. No longer exclusive to urban areas in high income countries, obesity has reached a pandemic stage with populations from middle income countries showing increased cases of obesity [7]. Classified as a disease by the American Medical Association in 2013, obesity has been identified even amongst an increasing populations of children [8]. With over 10% of the world's population being obese or overweight, the spread of obesity is a major cause for concern in the modern world [9].

In this context, as overweight and obesity propagate over human interaction network, predicting the individuals who are going to be overweight or obese in future, is an important problem. However, the problem has received limited attention from the network analysis and machine learning perspective till date. A few recent works applied regression based techniques to such prediction problems [10]. To the best of authors knowledge, in this context the performance of alternative scalable supervised learning models such as Convolutional Neural Networks (CNN) have been explored to a limited extent.

In this work, we particularly focus on the problem of prediction of overweight status amongst the individuals connected through dynamically changing temporal interaction network. We propose a scalable convolutional regression framework for the prediction task. Further, referring to [11], the proposed model considers the major contributing factors to the propagation of weight gain, in the current or past neighborhoods of nodes in the network. We propose various schemes for encoding self-influence and social influence factors - both present and historical in propagation of overweight. The proposed CNN based model followed by multiple hidden layers of non-linear transformations, results in a rich and compact feature representation of self and social influences of the population at previous time periods. Finally, the regression layer predicts the weight gain state of the population in the future. We extend on previous work in this area using convolutional regression frameworks by exploring combinations of influence schemes used previously, as well as varying the depth and width of architectures of the predictive model [12]. A thorough experiment on the synthetic as well as real networks demonstrates the superiority of the proposed method over the existing baseline approaches.

The paper is organized as follows. Section 2 formally defines the problem. The proposed method is illustrated in Sect. 3 and the implementation details are described in Sect. 4. Sections 5, 6 and 7 describes the data sets used in the experiment, the experimental setup and the results and observations, respectively. Section 8 involves a brief discussion of related works. Section 9 concludes with a general summary of the paper and possible future work.

2   Problem Definition

In real life, social networks evolve over time – that is, the actors may form new ties or even lose old ties with the passage of time. Additionally, the actors (or node) exhibit change in behavior (or feature) over time. Let, $G_t = (V_t, E_t)$ be the undirected graph representing social ties E_t amongst the set of n actors, V_t at time instance t. Let, $F_t = \{F_t^1, F_t^2, ..., F_t^n\}$ represent the feature sets of all actors V_t at time t. Here F_t^i is the set of features of node i, where $F_t^i = \{f_t^1, f_t^2, ..., f_t^k\}$ and $f_t^i \in \mathbb{R}$ is a particular feature of node i at time t.

The general problem of behavior prediction can be defined as, *given a temporal network* $G_{1..T}$ *observed during time instances* $t = \{1, ..., T\}$ *and the set of node features* $F_{1..T}$ *observed during* $t = \{1, ..., T, \}$ *predict one or multiple features of nodes at time* $T + 1$, *represented by* F_{T+1}.

In the current scope of work, we particularly focus on the prediction of the propagation of weight gain over a social contact network defined as, *given* $< G_{1,...,t}, F_{1,...,t} >$ *and a node* i *in the network, predict whether* i *will have an increase in his weight at time* $T + 1$.

The varying degrees of influence by the neighbors of a node in deciding its future behavior, the temporal change in contact network and the sparsity of connections make the weight gain prediction on a temporal network a particularly challenging problem.

3   The Proposed Method

We propose a convolutional regression framework to model the behavior prediction problem. The basic steps of the method are described using the flowchart in Fig. 1a. The flowchart begins with a basic preprocessing step where non-repeating nodes are removed, height and weight are converted to BMI etc. This is followed by feature extraction for nodes and their neighbor connectivity data at multiple time instances from Health and Bluetooth Proximity Reports. These features are used to generate neighborhood influence models. Multiple influence schemes have been explored in this work for modeling weight gain. The neighborhood influence features obtained are aggregated with user features to form the dataset for a convolutional regression framework which is used to predict the propagation of weight gain.

3.1   Modeling Influence

In a social network, the behavior of a node can be influenced by multiple factors. Along with the influence of their own behavior at past instances of time, there is a tendency for nodes to exhibit behavior similar to what is demonstrated by their neighbors, which is the well-known principle of homophily [13]. Thus, we consider the *self-influence*, and *influence by neighbors or social influence* separately in our model. Both self influence and social influence are derived from the current interaction record and current feature values along with the past instances of interaction and feature values. Given $< G_{1,...,t}, F_{1,...,t} >$, without loss of generality we assume that $F_{t+1} = f(G_{t-1}, F_{t-1}, G_t, F_t)$. That is, F_{t+1} is determined by the current state of the system and the immediate past state of the system only, where a state comprises of both interaction record and feature values, and F_{t+1} is independent of all its previous historical states.

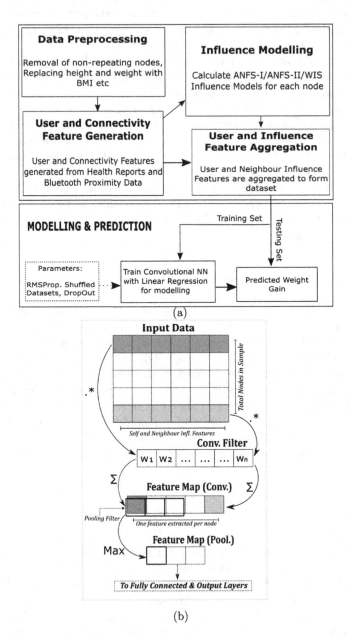

Fig. 1. (a) Flowchart of weight gain prediction via convolutional regression network. (b) Illustration of the convolution and pooling layers of the convolutional regression model

Further, the proposed model considers four major factors that contribute to the propagation of weight gain (obesity), namely, unhealthy diets, recent weight gains, obesity and inactivity, in the current or past neighborhoods of nodes in the network. The various schemes used for determining the social influence are discussed below.

Weighted Interaction Scheme (WIS). Considering the binary connections is not a sufficiently good indicator of the degree neighbors' influence. For example, let node j and k both influences node i to gain weight at time t. While j only exhibits the factor recent weight gain, k exhibits both the factors obesity and inactivity and unhealthy diet. In such scenario, degree of influence of node k is assumed to be more than that of node j. In other words, two neighbors of node i, node j and node k, will have differing influence on node i if they have different number of weight gain causative factors associated.

To address the issue, we propose to use weighted connections where weights are derived based on the number of weight gain causative factors a neighbor of a node exhibits. This enables us to retain the connectivity information of a node, while incorporating the varying degree of influence of each neighbor.

Formally, a connection weight $W_i^t(j)$ associated with edge $i-j$ at time stamp t is derived as -

$$W_i^t(j) = \sum_{p \in \Pi} \mathbf{I}_p^t(j) \tag{1}$$

where, the set of causative factors for weight gain, $\Pi = \{overweight,\ recent\ weight\ gain,\ bad\ diet,\ inactivity\}$ and the indicator function, $I_p^t(j) = 1$ if node j demonstrate a trait $p \in \Pi$ at time t and 0 otherwise. For a node pair (i, j) where no connection exists between i and j, $W_i^t(j) = 0$. The input features X_i^t for node i, under this scheme are generated by concatenating $F_i^{t-1}, W_i^{t-1}, F_i^t, W_i^t$.

Average Neighbor Feature Scheme - I (ANFS-I). Another simplistic way of representing social influence of neighbors is to use weighted average of the feature values of neighbors of a node at a given point in time. The intuition behind this scheme is that for any node i, if neighbor j has more weight gain causation factors than the average weight gain causation factors in the neighborhood of i, then j is more likely to have higher influence on i. This scheme allows us to emphasize the features of a highly influential neighbor.

Formally, this scheme determines social influence on node i by assigning weights N_i^t to the corresponding feature set, such that,

$$N_i^t = \sum_{j \in \mathbb{N}(i)} \frac{W_i^t(j)}{\bar{W}_i^t} \times F_j^t \tag{2}$$

where, F_j^t is the feature vector for node j at time t, $W_i^t(j)$ is given by Eq. 1, $\mathbb{N}(i)$ is the neighborhood of node i for whom $W_i^t(j) > 0$, $\bar{W}_i^t$ is the average connection weight of the neighbors of node i given by $\frac{1}{|\mathbb{N}(i)|} \sum_{k \in \mathbb{N}(i)} W_i^t(k)$.

Average Neighbor Feature Scheme - II (ANFS-II). An alternative to ANFS-I is based on the intuition that for any node i, if the neighborhood of neighbor j has more weight gain causation factors than the mean of the neighborhood of other neighbors of i, then j is more likely to have higher influence on i. In this scheme, the feature weight is computed using a normalized degree count of node j to weigh the influence it has on node i.

Formally, this scheme determines social influence on node i by assigning weights N_i^t to the corresponding feature set, such that,

$$N_i^t = \sum_{j \in \mathbb{N}(i)} \frac{D_j^t}{\bar{D}_i^t} \times F_j^t \qquad (3)$$

where, F_j^t is the feature vector for node j at time t, D_j^t is given by $\sum_{k \in \mathbb{N}(j)} W_j^t(k)$, $W_i^t(j)$ is given by Eq. 1, $\mathbb{N}(i)$ is the neighborhood of node i for whom $W_i^t(j) > 0$, $\bar{D}_i^t$ is given by $\frac{1}{|\mathbb{N}(i)|} \sum_{k \in \mathbb{N}(i)} D_k^t$.

ANFS-I can be considered to model direct influence of the neighbors on a node, while, ANFS-II can be considered as a measure of transitive neighbor influence on a node. The input features X_i^t for node i, under the schemes ANFS-I and ANFS-II are generated by concatenating $F_i^{t-1}, N_i^{t-1}, F_i^t, N_i^t$.

3.2   Feature Extraction Using CNN

Convolutional Neural Networks. Convolutional Neural Network (CNN) is an adaptation of multi-layered neural deep architecture that reduces the number of free parameters [14]. This is achieved by weight sharing principle that makes use of the local receptive fields whose parameters are forced to be identical for all its possible locations. Schematically, the CNN architecture is a succession of alternating convolution layers (to capture salient information) and sub-sampling layers (to reduce dimension), both with trainable weights.

Although CNN models were historically used in the areas of image and video processing, recent deeper CNN architectures have enjoyed success in multiple research areas [15–17]. To the best of authors knowledge, the applicability of CNN in modeling human behavior dynamics over social networks still remains unexplored, in spite of the problem nature being inherently correlated with the CNN functionality. In other words, while, human behavior prediction over a social network involves learning a global function which emerges from the locally correlated behavior of a node and its neighbors, CNN exploits the local correlation within a small data neighborhood where the data neighborhood serves as the receptive fields to read feature values from input space. Thus making CNN a potential model for learning and predicting human behavior. Besides, the shared weight architecture of CNN helps us model the contribution of self and neighborhood influence successfully.

Table 1. Mean and Max AUROC with various influence schemes on the CNN model

Propagation factors for weight gain	ANFS								WIS	
	ANFS–I		ANFS–II		ANFS–SUM		ANFS–PROD			
	Max	Mean	Max	Mean	Max	Mean	Max	Mean	Max	Mean
(a) Obesity/Overweight	0.6722	0.6406	0.6722	0.6170	0.6751	0.6482	0.6722	0.6169	0.7065	0.6616
(b) Unhealthy diet	0.6729	0.6149	0.6777	0.6207	0.6731	0.6253	0.6777	0.6207	0.6802	0.6441
(c) Inactivity	0.6944	0.6498	0.6873	0.6507	0.6742	0.6508	0.6873	0.6507	0.6987	0.6479
(d) Recent wt. gain	0.6742	0.6422	0.6641	0.6171	0.6758	0.6377	0.6641	0.6171	0.6789	0.6347
a + d	0.6878	0.6415	**0.7156**	**0.6731**	0.6775	0.6349	0.7031	0.6634	0.6896	0.6519
a + c + d	**0.7014**	**0.6543**	0.6761	0.6399	0.6989	0.6563	0.6957	0.6549	**0.7162**	**0.6662**
a + b + c + d	0.6853	0.6491	0.6840	0.6425	0.6853	0.6526	0.6887	0.6292	0.6988	0.6653
None	Max = 0.6867				Mean = 0.6441				0.6952	0.6490

Table 2. Variation in AUROC with change in model architecture – consisting of Convolutional (Conv), Pooling (Pool) and Fully Connected (FC) layers

Model architecture	Influence scheme					
	ANFS-I		ANFS-II		WIS	
	Max	Mean	Max	Mean	Max	Mean
Original architecture	**0.7014**	**0.6543**	**0.7156**	**0.6731**	**0.7162**	0.6662
Add 1 conv. layer (8 filters of 3 × 1)	0.6415	0.6023	0.6233	0.5936	0.6529	0.5836
Add 1 conv. & pool layer (8 filters of 3 × 1 & 2 × 1 pool filters of 2 × 1 stride)	0.6624	0.5721	0.6630	0.6075	0.6852	0.6569
Add 1 FC layer (10 units)	0.6571	0.6256	0.6700	0.6277	0.6769	0.6162
Add 1 FC layer (25 units)	0.6416	0.6026	0.6740	0.5992	0.6736	0.6047
Remove last FC layer	0.6890	0.6133	0.6932	0.6331	0.7090	**0.6713**

Shared Weights for Social Network Data Representations. The key requirement for modeling data with a convolutional neural network is to adopt the concept of shared weights for that particular data representation. Hence, the use of shared features for the problem must be justified. This requires the filter shape, which searches for common features, to be customized in an intuitive manner. We also discuss the appropriateness of our data representation schemes in the context of weight sharing. For the current problem, the usability of shared weights is interpreted in two areas: (1) user features denoting self-influence, (2) neighbor influence representations.

Nodes demonstrating similar behavioral outcome, irrespective of the neighborhood, are expected to share common features of self-influence as those nodes can be said to work in similar ways under self-influence. For example, frequent exercise habits of nodes i and j are expected to result in weight loss for both the nodes.

Under WIS scheme, for two identical nodes, degree of social influence by a common neighbor is expected to be similar. For example, if node i and j both have a connection to node k, who is obese, it can be thought of that k will influence both i and j similarly. Again, for ANFS scheme, the weighing schemes already captures the influence of the different neighbors. The resultant feature vector, can be said to contribute towards social influence for different nodes.

In the ANFS representation, an example similar to that for self-influence can be thought of - that is, in the presence of a feature vector which provides a compact representation of neighbor influence, nodes i and j will be influenced similarly by each component of that feature. Hence, shared weights can be applied in this case as well.

Using filters of size $n \times 1$, where n is the length of feature vector representing a node, each filter f can be said to learn the mapping,

$$g \colon X_t \longrightarrow \mathbb{R}^m \tag{4}$$

where, m is the number of nodes in the social network and each component of the co-domain is the output of a neuron.

Thus, if $(x_1, x_2, ..., x_m) \in \mathbb{R}^m$, then $x_i = \phi(M_i^t W_f)$, where M_i^t is a row vector of the features of node i at time t, W_f is a column vector of the weights of filter f and $\phi(.)$ is the activation unit of the neuron. In the present work rectified linear activation units (ReLU) are used [18]. This entire procedure is computationally performed as a convolution, thus speeding up calculations when generating the feature maps. The extracted feature maps are higher level representations of the raw behavioral input and hence, aid in extracting salient features for the prediction problem.

Max Pooling of Feature Maps. Max Pooling is used for pooling the outputs of multiple neurons across feature maps [19]. The pooling operation helps reduce the problem complexity and overlapping pooling filters were used for better performance of the model.

Depth of the Network. In theory, the CNN could be deepened significantly with further convolutional, pooling and fully connected layers in the model. However, in this study, the depth of the network, and thus the free parameters, are constrained by the short time series data. A layer of convolution, pooling followed by two fully connected layers guarantee decent results, while minimizing generalization issues.

3.3 RMSProp for Faster Convergence

RMSProp is a technique for using an adaptive learning rate for each neuron in the network. RMSProp maintains a moving average of the squared gradient for each weight and divides the global learning rate by this value at each weight update step. RMSProp prevents too large or small error gradients from drastically increasing or decreasing the value of the weight updates. It helps maintain consistency in weight updates, helps in faster convergence and has been used while learning the proposed model.

3.4   Multivariate Multiple Regression

The output layer used in this model is a multivariate multiple linear regression layer. The neural network is trained to model all nodes available at a given snapshot of the network. Hence, the regression layer contains response variables corresponding to the states of weight gain of all the nodes in the entire network at a point of time. This can be represented as,

$$Y_t^{(n \times 1)} = A^{(n \times 1)} + B^{(n \times m)} \psi_t^{(m \times 1)} + \epsilon^{(n \times 1)} \tag{5}$$

where, Y_t is a column vector of response variables of size n where n is the number of nodes in the social network, A is a column vector of size n representing the biases, ψ_t is a column vector of size m representing the output of the m hidden units of the previous layer, B is $n \times m$ matrix of regression coefficients and ϵ is a column vector of size n of errors. The loss function used in the Regression layer is the $l2$ loss function.

3.5   Preventing Over-Fitting with Dropout

Over-fitting is a particularly important problem in neural networks which are trained with a small amount of data. Constrained by the short time series data, alternative methods of reducing the over-fitting like dropout technique [20] has been used that improves generalization by reducing co-adaptions between neurons.

3.6   Combination of Influence Schemes

We try combinations of ANFS-I, ANFS-II and WIS influence models using at both the model and feature level in an attempt to improve prediction performance.

Model Level. We combine the ANFS and WIS influence schemes at the model level by using the mean as well as max of the regression outputs for their three corresponding models, to average out errors in the ensembled model.

Feature Level. While it is not possible to combine ANFS and WIS models at the feature level, it is possible to combine the two ANFS models. This is done by combining the weights derived using the ANFS-I with those derived using ANFS-II before calculating the weighted features. We explore simple additive and multiplicative combinations of the two influence models.

4   Implementation Details

The Convolutional Neural Network architecture used has been carefully designed for the short time series data. The general idea of the architecture is keeping the layers of the network narrow (that is, least number of hidden units possible), and the total network as deep as possible without suffering any severe degradation in performance due to over-fitting. This minimizes the trainable weights for the entire network.

With $|V_t|$ number of nodes (assuming for all t) and $|X_i^t|$ number of features per node, the model consists of an input layer of size $|V_t| \times |X_i^t|$, a convolutional layer of 8 filters with size of $1 \times |X_i^t|$ and a pooling layer with pool shape of 4×1 and pool stride of 2×1 (which enables overlapping pooling), 2 fully connected layers of 50 and 25 fully connected units respectively and a Linear Regression layer with $|V_t|$ response variables.

A high dropout rate of 80% is used in the proposed model to regularize the effects of low amount of data and to achieve increased generalization.

The training was done with approximately 60% of the available data (say t time instances) in each data split variation (monthly, fortnightly and weekly), where instances from 0 to $0.6t$ were included. Stochastic gradient descent was used to train each model for 100 iterations. The testing was performed on the remaining data samples which contained instances from $0.6t$ to t.

5   Data Description

For the prediction of weight gain status, we used a real life data set, the Social Evolution (SE) dataset [21]. The data consists of proximity information of approximately 80 undergraduate MIT students sharing a dormitory captured by digitally tracking their location, proximities, phone calls and messages through a pre-installed mobile phone application. An interaction network is formed out of the proximity data where a node represents a participant and an edge $i - j$ indicate that node i and j were in proximity of less than 10 m. Further, we use the health assessments data of the participants including the features like, weight, height, diet, exercise frequency and more.

The social network is generated by sampling the frequency of physical proximity, given by bluetooth proximity data of mobile phones, among the nodes, wherein a new link is introduced between 2 nodes on the occurrence of a pre-defined number of proximity counts between them. A snapshot of the network is generated at monthly, bimonthly and weekly intervals to obtain temporally evolving social networks in each case.

In order to construct discrete temporal networks, we first divided the survey period into shorter time quantum (weekly, fortnightly, monthly) and aggregated the interactions falling in a particular time quantum. Further we pruned the nodes those do not appear in every time quantum. We also pruned edges for which number of interactions within a time quantum is below certain threshold. The temporal reference frame with which the interaction data changes are not same as that of health feature. While the health surveys were performed at 1 or 2 month(s) intervals – bluetooth proximity data were collected near continuously during the course of the survey. To make the two time frames comparable, we disaggregate the health feature sets using linear interpolation. For example,

Considering a monthly time quantum, say health surveys have been performed for months 1 and 4, while connectivity data is available for every month. In this case, the features in the two months are interpolated linearly to provide features for months 2 and 3. This allows us the freedom to sample interaction data at relatively frequent intervals such as monthly, fortnightly and weekly basis and integrate it with the corresponding feature data.

It would be further interesting to study the prediction behavior on a family of generalized networks, instead of focusing on a particular instance of a real life graph. For that, we simulated a set of synthetic networks using Temporal Exponential Random Graph Model (TERGM) [22] that adopted the properties of the SE interaction network. Subsequently, the features of the nodes of the simulated temporal networks are mapped to that of the nodes of the original SE network. To achieve this, we use the PATH algorithm which is a fairly effective algorithm for graph matching [23].

6 Experimental Setup

We first carry out a parameter sensitivity study of our model that would also help to decide upon the best parameters to be used for the evaluation. Subsequently, the performance of our proposed method is compared with the performance of the existing baseline methods, using the metric area under the receiver-operator-characteristic curve (AUROC). An ROC curve is obtained by plotting the false positive rate against the true positive rate while varying the discriminating threshold for classification. The area under the ROC curve (AUROC) offers a simple yet insightful metric for quantifying the performance of classifiers and can be used to compare the optimality of classification models [24].

During the experiment multiple tests are run on the data sets with learning rate ranging between 0.001 to 0.005, step size of 0.0002. Further, we experiment with various temporal window sizes, that is number of historical variables seen.

For the comparative study we use the Personalized autoregression [10] and the socialized autoregression models [10]. While Personalized autoregression provides a simple and basic benchmark for behavior prediction tasks based on the feature set only, Socialized Autoregression uses social influence measures.

7 Results and Analysis

7.1 Parameter Sensitivity

The various parameters of the Convolutional Regression (Conv-Reg) model as well as the temporal window size have been varied to trace their influence in the model outputs. They are as follows:

Table 3. Variation of AUROC of different methods based on the frequency of splits for the different methods

Split frequency	WIS		ANFS-I		ANFS-II	
	Max	Mean	Max	Mean	Max	Mean
Monthly	0.6221	0.5966	0.6288	0.6022	0.6534	0.6111
Fortnightly	0.7162	0.6662	0.7014	0.6543	0.7156	0.6761
Weekly	0.7311	0.7019	0.6464	0.6437	0.6919	0.6316

Monthly, Fortnightly and Weekly Splits. Longitudinal splits of the network are varied on a monthly, fortnightly and weekly basis. The AUROC scores obtained are shown in Table 3. It is observed that on increasing the number of splits from weekly to fortnightly, the WIS scheme shows decreasing performance while the performances of the ANFS schemes (both I & II) improves. However, on further decreasing the number of splits to a monthly level, the performances of all the schemes decreases. This is possibly, because the true periodicity of the data is 14 days.

Dropout Rate. Figure 2 shows effect of the Dropout rate on the AUROC obtained from different influence schemes. The plot shows a clear increase in performance with the increase in Dropout rate. This observation is consistent with the premise that a high Dropout rate can reduce over-fitting in the model brought on by less data by preventing the neurons from co-adapting.

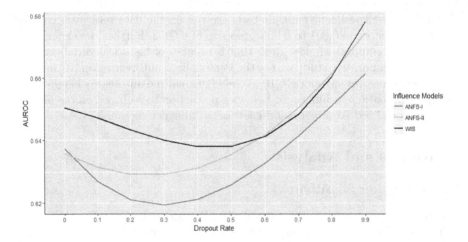

Fig. 2. Smoothed plot of the change of mean AUROC for different influence models vs. change in dropout rate

Temporal Window. The temporal window size (t) or the number of historical variables seen is varied from 0 to 2 and the performance of various influence schemes are evaluated. The result is plotted in Fig. 3. As shown in the figure, the best result is obtained when temporal window size is 1. This clearly supports our first-order Markovian assumption of the model, that given the present behavioral state, the future behavioral state is independent of the past behavioral states. While exploring further higher order behavioral states is an interesting idea, it remains a difficult task due to very real problem of not having a large enough dataset, in terms of survey sampling frequency, to draw from.

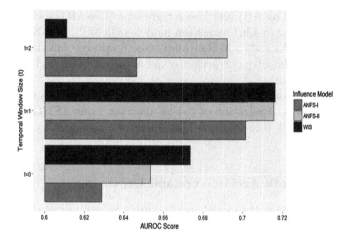

Fig. 3. Variation in AUROC with change in temporal window size for different influence techniques

Causative Factors for Weight Gain. We analyzed the effects of the individual weight gain factors on the prediction accuracy. When considered individually, the factors inactivity, Obesity/Overweight and recent weight gain is observed to have higher predictive power than unhealthy diet. We also analyzed combined effect of the three causative factors. As shown in the results, these three factors and their combination have higher predictive power than the predictive power of all the four factors. We can infer from the results that the unhealthy diet of an individual or her neighbor has less impact on the propagation of weight gain when compared to the other factors namely, inactivity, Obesity/Overweight and recent weight gain.

Proximity Reading Counts for Forming a Connection. We varied the threshold weight used to prune edges while forming the interaction network from 10 to 100 counts. However, the predictive performance is observed to be invariant to this change.

7.2   Comparative Performance Analysis

Having studied the effects of the parameters on the predictive results, we select the following parameters that gives the best predictive performance: fortnightly temporal splits - with the samples for 10 fortnights being used for training and the remaining 7 fortnights being used for testing purposes, high dropout rate of 0.8, temporal window of size 1, combination of all four causative factors, bluetooth proximity count of 10 to form a connection very liberally in the social network graph.

The results of the comparative study are summarized in Table 4. We compare the performance of the proposed method with the personalized autoregression model with logistic (Log-AR) and linear regression (Lin-AR), socialized logistic (S-Log-AR) and linear (S-Lin) regression models with WIS, ANFS-I and ANFS-II influence models. As shown in the results, the proposed convolutional regression framework significantly out-performs the auto-regressive and the socialized auto-regressive models.

We further carry out the comparative performance analysis on the synthetic data set which is a generalization of the SE data set using TERGM model. We observe an increase of 16%–20% predictive accuracy achieved by the proposed method.

7.3   Neural Network Architecture and Depth

The number of weights in the model architecture was kept minimal to both guarantee generalization and minimize overfitting. While the architecture used for most experiments is described in Sect. 4, additional experiments are also carried

Table 4. AUROC scores of the influence model-learning technique pairs on the SE data set

Infl. model	ML technique	AUROC
None	Lin-AR	0.6965
	Log-AR	0.6812
WIS	S-Lin-AR	0.6239
	S-Log-AR	0.6022
	Conv-Reg	**0.7162**
ANFS-I	S-Lin-AR	0.6799
	S-Log-AR	0.6491
	Conv-Reg	**0.7156**
ANFS-II	S-Lin-AR	0.6852
	S-Log-AR	0.6543
	Conv-Reg	**0.7014**

out to justify an admittedly shallow 5 layer neural network model. Specifically, we test models with increased number of convolution, pooling and fully connected layers.

With a relatively low amount of training data, it is observed, as evidenced by Table 2, that gains in descriptiveness provided by a deeper architecture are superseded by the effects of overfitting on the training data. Although convolution layers have relatively lesser free parameters or number of weights to add to the model, it is seen that increase in the number of layers whether convolution or fully connected or otherwise result in a degradation of the AUROC score. The reduction in AUROC scores on deepening the architecture is replicated with experiments on all influence models. It can be inferred from the results that increasing the depth further than that of the original model results in overfitting.

We also validate the claim of a smaller architecture underfitting the data by trying a model with the fully connected layer removed. It is seen that a lower AUROC score than the original model validates our claims against a model with lesser depth as well.

7.4 Combination of Influence Schemes

The prediction of weight gain with different schemes are combined at two levels – feature level (for only ANFS) and model level. Table 1 shows the feature level combinations for the additive (ANFS-SUM) and the multiplicative scheme (ANFS-PROD) for the ANFS influence model. While ANFS-PROD in general performs better than the ANFS-SUM, neither is able to surpass the performance of the individual ANFS influence schemes.

Similarly, in case of the model level combination, we use a max (Preds-Max) and mean (Preds-Mean) scheme for averaging. Since a combination of weight gain factors has been seen to give the highest AUROC, we combine the scores of these models, as summarized in Table 5. However, despite Preds-Max usually performing marginally better than Preds-Mean, they are unable to outperform individual influence scheme models.

Table 5. Model level combination of influence schemes

Weight gain factors	Preds-Max		Preds-Mean	
	Max	Mean	Mean	Max
Obesity + Recent weight gain	0.6922	0.6659	0.6924	0.6720
Obesity + Inactivity + Recent weight gain	0.6940	0.6573	0.6922	0.6641
Obesity + Recent weight gain + Inactivity + Unhealthy diet	0.6955	0.6590	0.6873	0.6633

8   Related Work

Although the propagation of information, opinion, or disease over social network has a long history of research, only a fairly recent work [25] highlights that obesity could spread through human interactions over a period of time. [25] demonstrates the propagation of obesity over a temporal social network data collected over a period of 25 years, sparked further interest in the social network research community.

Human interaction data available usually refers to data obtained by querying the population (eg. friendship nominations). However this can be noisy and prone to directed edges in a relationship graph due to unreciprocated nominations. In [21], the authors introduced the idea of pervasive capturing of human interactions by analyzing the pattern of daily proximity data recorded through sensors, instead of manually collected survey data. Social contact, it was deemed, could be inferred through continued close proximity through individuals. It was further demonstrated in [26] that proximity measured through mobile phones is a strong indicator for inferring friendship ties among a population. Unlike the previous works which looked at obesity propagation over more than two decades at a low sampling frequency, the dataset in [26] was collected over a rather short period of 10 months at a higher sampling frequency and the study focused on weight gain propagation, particularly that of being overweight. In [11], a regression framework considering various causative factors for weight gain were explored to model the propagation of weight gain. It was concluded that weight gain, similar to obesity, is influenced by neighbors in an interaction network.

In literature, problems related to inferring health conditions from social networks were modeled with Socialized and Personalized Logistic Regression Models which formed decent benchmarks for prediction of behavior propagation over temporal social relationship networks [10,27]. However, unlike the simple regression based models, the present work uses neural networks with a larger number of layers of non-linear transformations to model the data.

In a recent related work [28], Restricted Boltzmann Machines (SRBM) have been used for modeling the propagation of exercise habits across a temporal social network. However, [28] developed a significantly more complex neural network connected to all historical variables of all users which is not highly scalable and like all other deep networks require very large amount of training data.

9   Conclusion and Future Work

Understanding the propagation of obesity and overweight, and identification of the underlying controlling factors is an important research area of recent days. Particularly, the prediction of the individuals who are going to be overweight or obese in future, as overweight and obesity propagate over dynamic human interaction network, would help the healthcare providers take preventive and precautionary measures to contain the propagation and improve the quality of life by modifying behavior patterns.

In this work, we address the problem from the social network analysis perspective. We developed a scalable supervised prediction model based on convolutional regression framework that is particularly suitable for prediction of short time series data. While existing models such as the SRBM and Regression based models mentioned previously are fully connected architectures and assign weights to all historical variables, we use the concept of shared weights to significantly restrict the free parameters of our model. We propose various schemes to model social influence for health behavior change. These schemes are successfully used to create feature embeddings for our convolutional network and extract similar features from the feature representation of the users in our dataset. An exhaustive comparative study on the Social Evolution data set shows the superiority of the proposed method over comparable techniques.

Further we study the contribution of the primary factors of overweight and obesity, like unhealthy diets, recent weight gains and inactivity in the prediction task. The results reveal an important observation - in contrary to the common belief, unhealthy diet of an individual or her neighbor has less impact on the propagation of weight gain when compared to the other factors namely, inactivity, obesity/overweight and recent weight gain.

Finally, we generalized the Social Evolution data set using Separable Temporal Exponential Random graph model and run the experiments to verify the performance of the proposed methods. The results show an improvement of over 16% in the predictive accuracy achieved by the developed method.

As future extension, it would be interesting to study the seasonality of interaction pattern and its effect on the propagation of obesity and overweight. As basic CNN and auto-regressive models are unable to capture the seasonal variations, a modification of the CNN and its integration with auto-regressive models that support seasonality, like Holt-Winter model could open up a future research avenue.

References

1. Christensen, C., Albert, I., Grenfell, B., Albert, R.: Disease dynamics in a dynamic social networks. Phys. A **389**(13), 2663–2674 (2010)
2. Read, J.M., Eames, K.T., Edmunds, W.J.: Dynamic social networks and the implications for the spread of infectious disease. J. Royal Soc. Interface **4**(26), 1001–1007 (2008)
3. Caballero, B.: The global epidemic of obesity: an overview. Epidemiol. Rev. **29**(1), 1–5 (2007)
4. Zagorsky, J.L.: Health and wealth: the late-20th century obesity epidemic in the US. Econ. Hum. Biol. **3**(2), 296–313 (2005)
5. Dietz, W.H., Bellizzi, M.C.: Introduction: the use of body mass index to assess obesity in children. Am. J. Clin. Nutr. **70**(1), 123s–125s (1999)
6. Poulain, M., Doucet, M., Major, G.C., Drapeau, V., Sériès, F., Boulet, L.P., Tremblay, A., Maltais, F.: The effect of obesity on chronic respiratory diseases: pathophysiology and therapeutic strategies. Can. Med. Assoc. J. **174**(9), 1293–1299 (2006)

7. Derek Yach, D.S., Brownell, K.D.: Epidemiologic and economic consequences of the global epidemics of obesity and diabetes. Nature Med. **12**, 62–66 (2006)
8. Chang, V.W., Christakis, N.A.: Medical modelling of obesity: a transition from action to experience in a 20th century American medical textbook. Sociol. Health Illn. **24**(2), 151–177 (2002)
9. Eknoyan, G.: A history of obesity, or how what was good became ugly and then bad. Adv. Chronic Kidney Dis. **13**(4), 421–427 (2006)
10. Shen, Y., Jin, R., Dou, D., Chowdhury, N., Sun, J., Piniewski, B., Kil, D.: Socialized Gaussian process model for human behavior prediction in a health social network. In: 2012 IEEE 12th International Conference on Data Mining, pp. 1110–1115, December 2012
11. Madan, A., Moturu, S.T., Lazer, D., Pentland, A.S.: Social sensing: obesity, unhealthy eating and exercise in face-to-face networks. In: Wireless Health, pp. 104–110 (2010)
12. Basu, S., Roy, S., Maulik, U.: Convolutional regression framework for health behavior prediction. In: 9th International Conference on Communication Systems and Networks (COMSNETS) (2017)
13. McPherson, M., Lovin, L.S., Cook, J.M.: Birds of a feather: homophily in social networks. Ann. Rev. Sociol. **27**(1), 415–444 (2001)
14. LeCun, Y., Bottou, L., Bengio, Y., Haffner, P.: Gradient-based learning applied to document recognition. Proc. IEEE **86**(11), 2278–2324 (1998)
15. Krizhevsky, A., Sutskever, I., Hinton, G.E.: Imagenet classification with deep convolutional neural networks. In: Advances in Neural Information Processing Systems, pp. 1097–1105 (2012)
16. Abdel Hamid, O., Mohamed, A.R., Jiang, H., Deng, L., Penn, G., Yu, D.: Convolutional neural networks for speech recognition. IEEE/ACM Trans. Audio Speech Lang. Process. **22**(10), 1533–1545 (2014)
17. Kim, Y.: Convolutional neural networks for sentence classification, CoRR, abs/1408.5882 (2014)
18. Nair, V., Hinton, G.E.: Rectified linear units improve restricted Boltzmann machines. In: Proceedings of the 27th International Conference on Machine Learning, pp. 807–814 (2010)
19. Scherer, D., Müller, A., Behnke, S.: Evaluation of pooling operations in convolutional architectures for object recognition. In: Diamantaras, K., Duch, W., Iliadis, L.S. (eds.) ICANN 2010. LNCS, vol. 6354, pp. 92–101. Springer, Heidelberg (2010). doi:10.1007/978-3-642-15825-4_10
20. Srivastava, N., Hinton, G., Krizhevsky, A., Sutskever, I., Salakhutdinov, R.: Dropout: a simple way to prevent neural networks from overfitting. J. Mach. Learn. Res. **15**, 1929–1958 (2014)
21. Madan, A., Cebrian, M., Moturu, S., Farrahi, K., Pentland, S.: Sensing the "health state" of a community. IEEE Pervasive Comput. **11**(4), 36–45 (2012)
22. Hanneke, S., Fu, W., Xing, E.P.: Discrete temporal models of social networks. Electron. J. Stat. **4**, 585–605 (2010)
23. Zaslavskiy, M., Bach, F., Vert, J.P.: A path following algorithm for the graph matching problem. IEEE Trans. Pattern Anal. Mach. Intell. **31**(12), 2227–2242 (2009)
24. Bradley, A.P.: The use of the area under the ROC curve in the evaluation of machine learning algorithms. Pattern Recogn. **30**(7), 1145–1159 (1997)
25. Christakis, N.A., Fowler, J.H.: The spread of obesity in a large social network over 32 years. N. Engl. J. Med. **357**(4), 370–379 (2007)

26. Eagle, N., Pentland, A.S., Lazer, D.: Inferring friendship network structure by using mobile phone data. In: Proceedings of the National Academy of Sciences, vol. 106, no. 36, pp. 15274–15278 (2009)
27. Shen, Y., Phan, N., Xiao, X., Jin, R., Sun, J., Piniewski, B., Kil, D., Dou, D.: Dynamic socialized Gaussian process models for human behavior prediction in a health social network. In: Knowledge and Information Systems, pp. 1–25 (2015)
28. Phan, N., Dou, D., Piniewski, B., Kil, D.: Social restricted Boltzmann machine: human behavior prediction in health social networks. In: Proceedings of the 2015 IEEE/ACM International Conference on Advances in Social Networks Analysis and Mining, pp. 424–431 (2015)

Designing 2-Hop Interference Aware Energy Efficient Routing (HIER) Protocol for Wireless Body Area Networks

Moumita Roy[1], Chandreyee Chowdhury[1(✉)], and Nauman Aslam[2]

[1] Department of Computer Science and Engineering,
Jadavpur University, Kolkata, India
chandreyee.chowdhury@gmail.com
[2] Department of Computer and Information Sciences,
Northumbria University, Newcastle upon Tyne, UK

Abstract. With the evolution of wireless communication and advent of low power, miniaturized, intelligent computing devices, sensor network technology initiates the era of Wireless Body Area Network (WBAN) for medical applications. This new trend of healthcare empowers continuous supervision of vital physiological parameters under free living conditions. However, the potency of WBAN applications are subject to reliable data delivery. Inherent challenges of WBAN such as scarce energy resource, varying link quality, propensity of tissue damage necessitate optimal routing strategy to combat with hostilities. In addition, coexistence of multiple WBANs within proximity results in severe degradation of throughput as well. In this paper, a cost-based energy efficient routing protocol has been designed which ensures satisfactory performance without fostering thermal effect and adapts itself in adverse situations like intra BAN as well as inter BAN interference. The performance of the proposed algorithm is analyzed through comprehensive simulations. The protocol is analyzed for different mobility models signifying relative body movement due to posture change. The simulation results demonstrate that our proposed protocol out performs other protocols with respect to energy efficiency while maintaining a stable packet delivery ratio under interference.

Keywords: WBAN · Routing · Intra BAN interference · Inter BAN interference

1 Introduction

Application of sensor network technology in human health monitoring has revolutionized the conventional concept of health care. The new era of proactive health monitoring involves collection of light-weight, small-size, ultra-low powered, intelligent micro or nano technology bio sensors to be placed in, on or around human body to monitor vital physiological parameters [1]. Consequently,

© Springer International Publishing AG 2017
N. Sastry and S. Chakraborty (Eds.): COMSNETS 2017, LNCS 10340, pp. 262–283, 2017.
DOI: 10.1007/978-3-319-67235-9_16

Wireless Body Area Network (WBAN) is formed to transmit the acquired data to a remote server via network coordinator for real time diagnosis by medical personnel as depicted in Fig. 1. These devices are generally powered by batteries with bounded lifetime [2]. Hence, to acquire everlasting welfare of WBAN applications network lifetime should be enhanced which necessitates the use of ultra low power transceiver as well as power efficient MAC protocol for intra BAN communication. On top of that, designing energy efficient protocol [3] for network layer communication alleviate preservation of this scarce resource to a greater extent. Mostly, sensor nodes in WBAN follow star topology [1] where the network co-ordinator resides at the center. Intra-BAN communication can be done using Bluetooth (IEEE 802.15.1), ZigBee (IEEE 802.15.4) or IEEE 802.15.6 standard (mainly for implantable nodes). However, to bring down the power expenditure due to direct (single hop) communication between source and sink, multi-hop communication is often preferred. The latest version of the IEEE standard proposed for WBANs in February 2012 recommends at most two hops for IEEE WBAN standards compliant communication [2]. However, more than two hops could be exploited by the proprietary systems with the cost for handling inter-operability issue. The bio-sensor nodes are in direct contact with human body; thus the absorption of electromagnetic radiation by human body causes imprudent temperature rise of human tissue [4] leading to several health hazards [1,5] such as reduced blood flow, tissue damage, enzymatic disorder etc. The amount of radiation absorbed in human body is measured in terms of Specific Absorption Rate (SAR) [6]. Designing network protocol for WBAN must ensure reliable data delivery with least thermal impact. Repeated participation in network activities could cause rate capacity effect [3] leading to prompt energy depletion. Furthermore, posture change may result in relative node movement in WBAN which imposes difficulties in choosing the optimal transmission power subject to varying link quality. In addition, link degradation due to channel fading increases packet error rate and overall network performance is affected as well; the case is worse when multiple WBAN coexist within a small region.

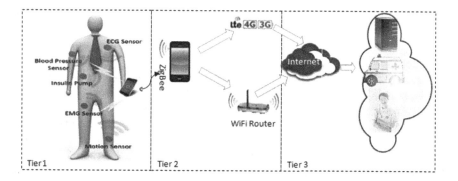

Fig. 1. 3-tier network architecture of WBAN

The existing routing protocols contemplate predominantly one or more of these issues, however, optimal solution is still indispensable. Thermal aware protocols such as [3,4] mostly go for multi-hop communication to prevent temperature upswing of individual nodes, however, that may not result in energy efficient routing. Besides, additional overhead like delay could be imposed as well. Interference aware protocols [7,8] emphasize on hindering throughput degradation due to co-existing communicating nodes, inherent challenges are yet to be incorporated into the solutions. Accordingly, a 2-Hop Interference aware Energy efficient Routing protocol (HIER) has been proposed in this work. This work is the extended version of the work presented in [9]. In this work, our contributions are as follow: The protocol exhibits adaptive routing strategy in situations like intra BAN interference and inter BAN interference; it omits acknowledgment policy as regarded in [9] to bring down energy expenditure and control packets overhead; a detailed study has been carried out in performance evaluation subject to different mobility models.

The paper is organized as follows: State of the art works on BAN routing protocols are presented in the next section. Section 3 gives detailed description of our proposed routing protocol. Experimental setup and simulation results are discussed in Sect. 4. Finally, Sect. 5 concludes.

2   Related Work

The trends in existing researches on WBAN routing protocols are organized according to time-line in Table 1. Existing routing protocols are grouped into six categories focusing on their objective in solving routing problems. In earlier days researches were focused towards addressing a specific issue of BAN routing such as temperature control [3,4], clustering [10,11]. However, the trend does not go far due to some inherent limitations associated with it. Thermal aware routing [3,4] often fails to resolve other major issues such as energy efficiency, reliability. In addition, cluster based routing protocols [10,11] group the nodes in WBAN into clusters and each cluster is supervised by a cluster head. Data communication between sensor nodes of a cluster and sink is governed by the respective cluster head. However, periodic cluster formation and cluster head selection cause significant overhead for a network of 15 to 20 nodes i.e. the average network size in case of WBAN [1].

Herewith, researches move towards addressing multiple issues which are often cross layer [14,15] or furnish modules for different QoS parameters [16,21]. Cross layer protocols combine the routing layer challenges with medium access issues. Time is divided into slots and nodes reserve slots prior to actual data transfer as in [14,15]. Protocols in this category enhance collision free data transfer, hence throughput increases. To foster energy use up, nodes turn off their transceiver when not required. However, these protocols are not well suited subject to substantial body movement. In QoS based routing protocols data traffic is divided into several categories as in [16,21] based on QoS requirements and separate modules are devised to meet with desired criteria. Although these protocols

Table 1. Timeline of existing routing protocols

Year	Temperature based protocols	Cluster based protocols	Cross layer protocols	Cost effective protocols	QoS based protocols	Interference aware protocols
2004		[12]				
2005	[4]	[13]				
2006	[3]		[14]			
2007	[5]	[10]	[15]		[16]	[17]
2008	[18,19]		[20]		[21]	
2009	[22]		[23]	[24,25]	[26]	[27]
2010				[28]		[29]
2011				[30]	[31]	[7]
2012				[32,33]		
2013		[11]		[34,35]	[36]	
2014					[37]	[8,38,39]
2015				[41–43]		
2016			[40]	[44]		
2017				[9]		

enhance throughput as well as reliability with low end-to-end delay, the system overhead increases to a large extent for designing several modules for QoS metric. In addition, another trend in designing routing solutions for WBAN is to address interference issue [8,38]. Hitherto strategies are devised to oversee intra BAN interference issue as in [17,29]. However, WBAN yields constant medical supervision under free living condition leading to potential interference with coexisting WBANs as well. Accordingly, researches [7,8] move towards perceiving solutions to combat with inter BAN interference complications. To cope up with interference issue a system is designed prior to adopting routing protocol to operate in that framework [8,17]. But this trend is yet to be explored more and a compact policy is still required to overcome intra BAN as well as inter BAN interference along with inherent challenges of WBAN routing.

Consequently, the trend moves towards cost based routing [24,25] where the major issues of BAN routing such as temperature control, link quality, energy efficiency, mobility are considered in cost calculation and a trade off is made. Data is routed through the least cost route. However, cost evaluation process is either centralized or distributed. In case of centralized cost computation as in [34,41,42], sink acquires relevant information of other sensors such as remaining energy, distance from sink etc. and formulates costs for each node and these costs are exploited during data forwarding. Unlike centralized approach, in distributed cost assessment [32,33] each node evaluates cost for its neighbors relies on multiple criteria such as remaining energy, link quality, temperature etc. and opts for suitable least cost relay node for data forwarding. However, the centralized cost evaluations are subject to the energy expenditure due to periodical exchange of node information with sink. Nodes in WBAN often choose forwarder opportunistically in case of intermittent network connections [28,30] and data is routed in store, carry, forward modes. Cost based protocols in WBAN mostly select least cost relay for data forwarding; however few approaches [28] take into account cumulative path cost to the sink node leading to less intermediate storage delay but intensify the overhead of caching cumulative path cost. Herewith, a cost based 2 hop energy efficient routing protocol has been designed in [9] where distinct sources of energy consumption in WBAN and its effect in human body and communication system as well as the network are analyzed and incorporated in routing decision. Authors demonstrated that more energy consumption by the body sensors may improve performance of a particular link but it affects both the human body and the network in many ways (shown in Fig. 2). The protocol in [9] selects forwarder considering issues such as remaining energy, link reliability, node reliability. Besides, increase in Specific Absorption Rate (SAR) of the forwarder resulting from relaying data is also contemplated in relay selection. As shown in Fig. 2, most of the routing protocols incorporate one or more of the existing issues like increase in SAR or link reliability etc. In [9], the authors have dealt with some combination of issues. In this work the protocol in [9] is extended to handle the effect of intra BAN and inter BAN interference in routing.

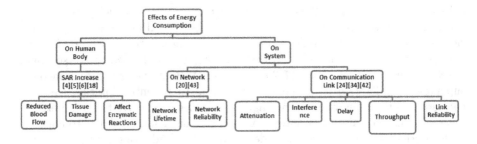

Fig. 2. Effect of energy consumption of body sensors both on human body and on system as in [9]

3   Proposed Work

Existing researches exhibit the major issues of WBAN and how these exert influence on routing. Our protocol has been devised to address the issues as presented in previous sections. A brief description of the proposed algorithm is as follows.

Any node i in the network that wants to communicate its data to the sink broadcasts $SETUP\_REQ$ in one hop neighborhood with substantially low transmission power. The node may receive $SETUP\_RES$ from either sink or those neighbors which has direct connectivity with the sink. Here the communication is restricted within 2 hops i.e. either from source to sink (1 hop) or from source to relay plus relay to sink (2 hops). On receiving reply from sink, the node communicates its data directly to the sink. Besides, if the rate of energy depletion at node i is less, then node i may act as potential relay for others. Since the node is capable of communicating with the sink at low transmission power, the energy consumption as well as SAR reduces even if working as relay. The nodes that do not receive $SETUP\_RES$ from sink s, may check whether they have received any $SETUP\_RES$ from neighbors and evaluate fitness $F^j(t)$ of each neighbor j to act as relay in terms of energy ratio $ER^j(t)$, link reliability $R_{(i,j)}(t)$ and SAR ratio $SARRatio^j(t)$ defined in Eqs. 3, 4 and 6 respectively. If there remains any node that does not receive $SETUP\_RES$ from either sink or relays, it attempts to communicate with enhanced transmission power. Whenever communicating with sink as well as neighbors node i observes for sudden degradation of Signal to Noise Ratio (SNR) which may result due to intra ban as well as inter ban interference and behaves accordingly.

System model: The network consists of N sensor nodes, and each node can act as source as well as relay. In this work we have considered single sink node which performs as network coordinator although the proposed approach may be applied to multiple sink scenario as well. Every node in the network carries out transmissions with uniform transmission power P_{tx}. The bio-sensor nodes communicate with each other through electro-magnetic radio frequency waves. The radiation absorbed in human body is quantified in terms of SAR. SAR is quantified subject to the distance 'R' from the sensor node position; if the reference point is located in the near field region of the source node, SAR is quantified as follows [6]

$$SAR = \frac{\sigma}{\rho} \frac{\mu\omega}{\sqrt{\sigma^2 + \epsilon^2\omega^2}} \left(\frac{Idl sin\theta}{4\pi} e^{-\alpha R} \left(\frac{1}{R^2} + \frac{|\gamma|}{R}\right)\right)^2 \quad (1)$$

Here σ, ϵ, μ represent conductivity (S/m), permittivity (F/m) and permeability (H/m) of the medium respectively. γ is the complex propagation constant and complex intrinsic impedance $\eta = \frac{\gamma}{\alpha+j\omega\epsilon}$ at frequency ω. dl is the dipole length and current I is uniform and varies sinusoidally with time. Likewise, if the reference point is located at far field region of the source node, SAR is computed as follows [6]

$$SAR = \frac{\sigma}{\rho}(|\eta||\gamma|\frac{Idl sin\theta}{4\pi R}e^{-\alpha R})^2 \quad (2)$$

In addition, at any point of time t each node i measures its own energy ratio $(ER^i(t))$ as follows [9]

$$ER^i(t) = \frac{E^i_{rem}(t)}{E^i_{ini}} \quad (3)$$

This ratio is a prerequisite for relay selection process. It is evident that a node with more remaining energy is more eligible to act as relay.

Following is the details of the proposed algorithm (Algorithm 1).

In a network of N nodes, a node i initiates the algorithm when it has data for sink in other words, the protocol operates on demand. The algorithm works in two phases. During setup phase node i exchanges SETUP packets with neighbors to identify its connectivity with sink as well as other nodes and this is followed by data transfer phase. A node acquires neighbor information in setup phase. Setup phase is initiated when node i broadcasts $SETUP\_REQ^i$ in one hop neighborhood. The transmission is conducted with substantially low transmission power. The aim is to discern whether sink is reachable even at this low power level. This has both way benefits: if sink is reachable then subsequent communications could be made directly to the sink with such low transmission power which may not lead to excessive temperature rise of human tissue; besides the node may participate in data relaying for others as well without much energy depletion. Node i confirms direct connectivity to the sink s when it receives $SETUP\_RES^s$ from sink. At this point, node i may broadcast itself as potential relay if its energy depletion rate $\left(\frac{E_{rem}(t-\Delta t)-E_{rem}(t)}{\Delta t}\right)_i$ is within pre-specified limit $E_{threshold}$. However, node i may receive $SETUP\_RES^j$ from neighbor j as well if neighbor j has direct connectivity with sink. Neighbor j includes its energy ratio ER^j quantified following Eq. 3 along with $SETUP\_RES^j$ for i. However, if node i does not receive $SETUP\_RES^s$ from sink, it looks for $\forall j \in k\ SETUP\_RES^j$ received from k neighbors. Node i also observes the Received Signal Strength Indicator (RSSI) and evaluates reliability $\forall j \in k\ R_{(i,j)}(t)$ of the link between node i and each neighbor j as follows [9]

$$R_{(i,j)}(t) = \frac{RSSI_{avg}^{(i,j)}(t)}{RSSI_{max}^{(i,j)}} \tag{4}$$

The link reliability evaluation reflects potential existence of the link over time subject to its maximum quality instead of just considering a single scenario. Node i caches the information received during setup phase for certain time in routing table RT_i so that a number of data packets may be sent without setup overhead. After the time period is over, node i again initiates setup phase if it has more data for the sink. However, each node in WBAN is provided with limited storage capacity. Thus if buffer exceeds, the node i discards information of the neighbor j with comparatively low energy ratio $ER^j(t)$. Accordingly, node i enters into the data transfer phase which includes forwarder selection process in case sink does not reside in one hop neighborhood. In such case node i computes fitness $\forall j \in k\ F^j(t)$ of k neighbors to identify suitable forwarder. In addition to energy ratio ER^j and link reliability $R_{(i,j)}(t)$, increase in SAR in neighbor j to act as relay is also assessed by node i as a parameter for fitness calculation. Authors have analyzed in [9] how SAR is related to the transmission power (P_{tx}) given other parameters of Eq. 1 remain constant. Node i predicts increase in SAR at neighbor j to relay q bits data with transmission power P_{tx} as [9]

$$SAR^j = m \times q \times P_{tx} \tag{5}$$

Here m is constant relies on the network conditions. With this, node i evaluates $SARRatio^j(t)$ as follows [9]

$$SARRatio^j(t) = \frac{SAR^j(t)}{SAR_{Lim}} \tag{6}$$

Here SAR_{Lim} is retained much less as compared to its regulatory limit 1.6 W/Kg [1] assuming the node j is engaged in other activities as well apart from data relaying. $SARRatio^j(t)$ is updated after relaying each data packet accordingly. Hereafter, node i finally computes fitness $\forall j \in k$ $F^j(t)$ as follows [9]

$$F^j(t) = w_1 ER^j(t) + w_2 R_{(i,j)}(t) + w_3(1 - SARRatio^j(t)) \qquad (7)$$

A neighbor with maximum fitness value is selected as potential forwarder to relay data to sink. Fitness of a neighbor is assessed contemplating energy ratio ER^j, link reliability $R_{(i,j)}$ and $SARRatio^j$ and each metric is weighted accordingly such that $w_1 + w_2 + w_3 = 1$. Value for these weights are chosen empirically such that the prime objective of this protocol is reflected in decision process.

Unlike energy ratio ER^j and link reliability $R_{(i,j)}$, $SARRatio^j$ has negative impact on fitness calculation. This metric regulates the distribution of forwarding traffic among potential relays such that the most suitable relay does not get overburdened with forwarding traffic. During communication with sink or neighbors, node i observes the rate of change in signal to noise ratio (SNR) such that sudden degradation in rate of change in signal to noise ratio could be measured. Signal to noise ratio degrades suddenly due to interference resulting from intra ban or inter ban communication. If such event occurs during communication with the sink, node i waits for some time which is less than the time out interval of upper layer and then retries. However, node i opts for another relay in case of communication with any neighboring node. The step-by-step description of the proposed protocol is stated in Algorithm 1 and frequently used terms are listed along with their meaning in Table 2.

Following data structure are needed by the algorithm.

– Boolean variable con_s which is true when there is direct connection with sink;
– Neighbor Information Table $RT_i\{SNR^j, avgRSSI^j, F^j\}$ where each entry consists of
  1. SNR^j to hold signal to noise ratio while receiving from node j at time t
  2. $avgRSSI^j$ to store average RSSI over the link between node i and neighbor j
  3. F^j to hold the fitness value of neighbor j

Complexity analysis: Algorithm 1 pursues numerous data delivery at sink s with the cost of setup packet overhead. However, single setup phase may lead to collective data transmissions hence bringing down the control message complexity to its deprecated form when evaluated with respect to the amount of data. Nevertheless, a distinct setup phase may result in one of the following scenario subject to the transmission range of a node i ready with data for the sink s and having no routing information at RT_i.

Best case: When only sink s lies in the transmission range of node i single $SETUP\_REQ^i$ from node i and single $SETUP\_RES^s$ from s are adequate to initiate data transmission. Hence, in this scenario the control message required is 2, that is complexity is constant.

input : :
1 control information of neighbors
output: :
2 reliable data delivery to sink
3 **repeat**
4   **if** *((ready(data)^i OR receive(data)^j) AND !con$_s$)* **then**
5   *broadcast(SETUP_REQ^i)* ;
6   **if** *receive(SETUP_RES^s)* **then**
7   **if** $\frac{SNR(t-\Delta t)^s - SNR(t)^s}{\Delta t}{}_i < SNR_{threshold}$ **then**
8   *update(RT_i);*
9   *set con$_s$ = true;*
10   *send(data)^i to s ;*
11   **if** *($\frac{E_{rem}(t-\Delta t) - E_{rem}(t)}{\Delta t}$)$_i$ < E$_{threshold}$* **then**
12   *broadcast($ID^i, ER^i(t)$);*
13   **if** *receive(data)^j* **then**
14 | *forward(data)^j*
15   **end**
16   **end**
17   **else**
18 | *wait($t_{backoff}$)*
19   **end**
20   **else**
21   **if** $\frac{SNR(t-\Delta t)^j - SNR(t)^j}{\Delta t}{}_i < SNR_{threshold}$ **then**
22   *update(RT_i) ;*
23   *calculate($F^j(t)$) using Eqn7*
24   **else**
25 | *drop(SETUP_RES^j)*
26   **end**
27   *set(r = j if $F^j(t) = F^j(t)_{max}$);*
28   *forward(data)^i to r;*
29   **end**
30   **end**
31   **if**
     receive(broadcast)^j AND !con$_s$ AND $\frac{SNR(t-\Delta t)^j - SNR(t)^j}{\Delta t}{}_i < SNR_{threshold}$
     then
32   **while** *exceed(buffer)* **do**
33 | *discard(record) for $ER^j(t)_{min}$*
34   **end**
35   *update(RT_i)*
36   **else**
37 | *discard(broadcast)^j*
38   **end**
39 **until** *every t time unit;*

Algorithm 1: FindRouteToSink()

Table 2. Frequently used terms and their descriptions

Terms	Description
i, j	Any node in the network
s	Sink
$ER^j(t)$	Energy ratio of node j at time t
$E_{rem}(t)$	Remaining energy of a node at time t
E_{ini}	Initial energy of a node
$R_{(i,j)}(t)$	Reliability of the link between node i and node j at time t
$SARRatio^j(t)$	SAR ratio of the node j at time t
con_s	Connectivity to sink s
$F^j(t)$	Fitness of the node j at time t
P_{tx}	Transmission power
w_1, w_2, w_3	weights assigned to different metric
$SNR^j(t)_i$	Signal to noise ratio at node i while communicating with node j at time t
RT_i	Routing table of node i

Average and worst case: Besides, two further situations are likely to happen-
(i) sink s along with other relays $j \in N$ are covered within the transmission
range of i and (ii) only relay nodes are connected to node i.

In both cases, the message complexities are subject to the number of potential
relays which may vary in the range $1 \leq j \leq (N-1)$ for a network of N nodes.
Hence, on an average node i may receive $SETUP\_RES$ from $N/2$ neighbors
with single $SETUP\_REQ^i$ and $(N-1)$ in worst case leading to control message
complexity as $O(N)$ in either case.

Although the control message complexity is $O(N)$, after each setup phase, a
number of data packets can be transmitted without needing the setup phase if
the network topology remains stable.

4   Simulation Results

The proposed work is evaluated through immense simulations using Castalia-3.2
[45] simulator based on OMNeT++ platform which provides support to implement distributed algorithms and/or protocols with advanced wireless channel
and radio models illustrating a realistic node behavior particularly in accessing
the physical layer. Highly parametric design of Castalia-3.2 enables researchers
to study discrete platform characteristics relating to specific applications such
as IEEE 802.15.4 functionality could be exploited to prototype intra BAN communications. Different simulation parameters used while simulating HIER are

listed in Table 3 along with their default values. Any changes to it are stated precisely.

Table 3. Simulation parameters and their default values

Parameter	Default value
No. of nodes	12
No. of sink	1 (Node 0)
Time	500 s
Sending data rate	14 packets per sec (all nodes except sink)
Mobility model	Line mobility
Transmission power	−15 dBm
Sink location	Waist

12 nodes are deployed at different positions on human body as shown in Fig. 3(a) and sink is placed at waist. Simulation area of 20 m × 20 m has been exploited to provide support for relative node movements due to posture change. Experiments are carried out using ZigBee MAC protocol and Line mobility model [45]. All transmissions are made with −15 dBm transmission power. Radio parameters are regulated with values from CC2420 datasheet [45].

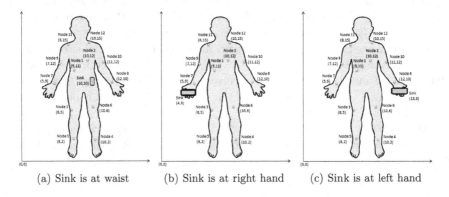

(a) Sink is at waist   (b) Sink is at right hand   (c) Sink is at left hand

Fig. 3. Node deployment strategies following different sink placements

To evaluate performance of the proposed protocol the following metrics are introduced as follows.

The ratio of total data delivered at sink ($Data^s_{rec}$) to the total data sent by each sensor i ($\Sigma_{i \in N} Data^i_{sent}$) is defined as packet delivery ratio.

$$DelRatio = \frac{Data^s_{rec}}{\Sigma_{i \in N} Data^i_{sent}} \qquad (8)$$

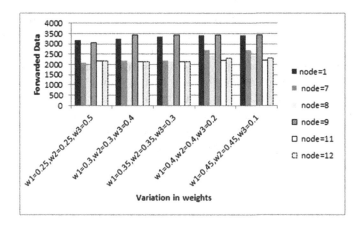

Fig. 4. Selection of weights w_1, w_2, w_3

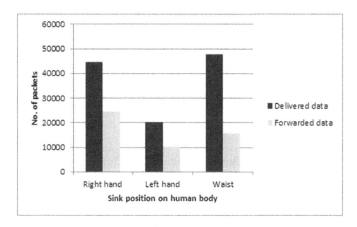

Fig. 5. Variation of forwarding traffic with corresponding delivered data at different sink positions

Likewise, forwarding ratio is measured in terms of ratio between total forwarding traffic of each sensor i ($\Sigma_{i \in N} Data^i_{fwd}$) to delivered data at sink s.

$$FwdRatio = \frac{\Sigma_{i \in N} Data^i_{fwd}}{Data^s_{rec}} \quad (9)$$

In the first experiment, we have observed weights(w_1, w_2, w_3) assigned to each metric for fitness calculation (that is $ER^j(t), R_{(i,j)}(t), SARRatio^j(t)$) (Eq. 7). The nodes are deployed such that few nodes are incompetent to get direct connection to sink. In such case the nodes follow the proposed routing strategy and select suitable relay to forward their data. At this point, our first focus is to assign appropriate weights such that the entire forwarding traffic is distributed among potential relays and not to overburden a single node with forwarding traffic. As we can observe from Fig. 4, due to incorporation of the metric $SARRatio^j(t)$ in fitness calculation, our goal to distribute forwarding traffic among relays is met. Herewith, we have gradually varied w_3 starting from 0.5 and accordingly adjusted two other weights w_1 and w_2 and what we found here is with w_3 as 0.2 and w_1 and w_2 as 0.4 each the forwarding traffic is not only distributed but also forwarding ratio intensifies. The scenario is even similar with w_3 as 0.1 and w_1 and w_2 as 0.45 each. Hence, we have taken w_1 and w_2 as 0.4 each and w_3 as 0.2 for our reference to carry out subsequent experiments.

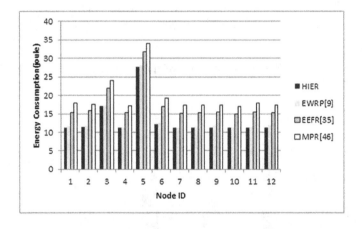

Fig. 6. Energy consumed at each node

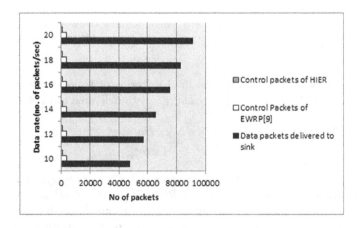

Fig. 7. Delivered data packets with corresponding control packets overhead

In the next experiment, we have varied the location of sink to perceive its effect on data routing. Here as presented in Fig. 3(a), (b) and (c) we have considered three major positions to place sink over human body i.e. waist, right hand and left hand. Results as obtained from Fig. 5 when sink is located at waist, most of the nodes are in a position to get direct connectivity with sink. Hence, the forwarding traffic is less with respect to the entire data delivered to sink. Accordingly, when sink is positioned on right hand, forwarding traffic grows more as few more nodes become incompetent to deliver data directly to the sink. However, according to our deployment strategy, when sink is located at left hand most of the nodes loose connectivity to sink which affects the delivery ratio as well. Hence, if sink is placed at waist it not only gets better connectivity but also becomes least affected due to posture change.

In the next experiment, we have analyzed the energy consumption of each node and compared it to the state of the art protocols. We have implemented the strategies described in [35, 46] for similar simulation set up. It is observed in Fig. 6 that due to incorporation of energy efficient routing strategy, the proposed protocol requires less energy consumption as compared to the state of the art protocols. Even this protocol exhibits slightly less energy consumption than our previous work [9] as acknowledgement policy is omitted here.

In the following experiment, we have evaluated our work in terms of overhead. Variations of delivered data packets at sink with increasing data rate are plotted with corresponding control packets. It is found in Fig. 7 that data delivery increases with rising data rate but as caching mechanism is employed in this work, more data packets could be routed with a single setup phase (i.e. control message exchange). Hence the control packets overhead remains unchanged irrespective of growing data rate and it is found to be nominal with respect to delivered data. The associated overhead is even less as compared to our previous work [9] in similar experimental setup since the acknowledgement overhead is avoided.

Next two experiments are conducted to study the behavior of the proposed protocol with time and increasing data rate respectively. The state of the art protocols are also compared with the proposed protocol HIER for similar simulation setup. As it can be seen from Fig. 8(a) HIER is able to sustain reasonable packet delivery ratio with time and outperforms existing works as well. As obtained from Fig. 8(b) channel got saturated gradually with increasing data rate, hence packet delivery ratio descends accordingly for every protocol. However, HIER exhibits better performance as compared to the existing works since this approach requires minimum control packet overhead.

In the next experiment performance of HIER is analyzed subject to increasing network size. The experiment was initiated with 5 nodes forming the network and more nodes were introduced subsequently following the deployment strategy of Fig. 3(a) to observe the behavior of packet delivery ratio in comparison to corresponding forwarding ratio. Since each node can act as relay as well, the number of forwarder increases accordingly with growing number of nodes. A

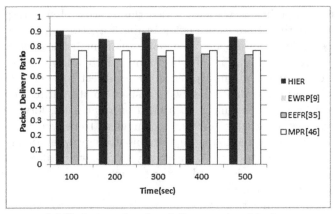

(a) Variation of packet delivery ratio with time

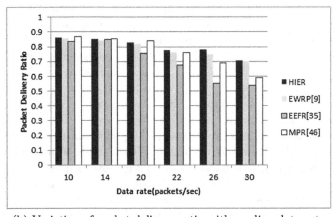

(b) Variation of packet delivery ratio with sending data rate

Fig. 8. Variation of packet delivery ratio with different simulation parameters

stable performance in terms of packet delivery ratio is observed with increasing network size as seen from Fig. 9 subject to increase in forwarding traffic.

Next experiment measures the delivered data in comparison to corresponding forwarding traffic with varying transmission power. This experiment shows how the proposed protocol manages data delivery with low transmission power regulating the forwarding traffic. Performance is recorded for different data rates. The results are depicted in Fig. 10. With high transmission power, nodes are capable to communicate directly to the sink and hence no forwarding traffic is required. However, with low transmission power few nodes are incompetent to transmit data directly to the sink causing more forwarding traffic in order to retain the delivery rate.

In the next experiment the performance of the proposed protocol HIER is studied subject to inter-BAN interference. When a WBAN encounters another

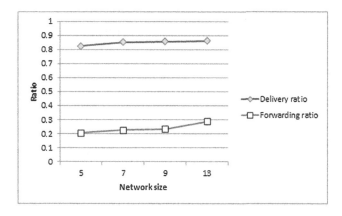

Fig. 9. Variation of packet delivery ratio with corresponding forwarding ratio with varying network size

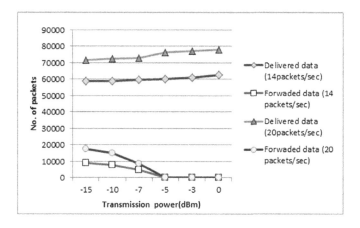

Fig. 10. Variation of delivered data with corresponding forwarding data with varying transmission power

WBAN within its communication range, inter BAN interference occurs leading to sudden degradation in SNR resulting in detrimental performance. This experiment is carried out subject to two scenarios to reflect the effect of inter BAN interference. Firstly the performance is measured when sink suffers from inter BAN interference and subsequently the behavior is noticed when a sensor node placed on right hand got affected. In the experimental setup such coexistence is introduced after 200 s and as seen from Fig. 11 performance got affected more when sink is interfered whereas packet delivery ratio could be retained well in later case by refraining the affected sensor to act as forwarder.

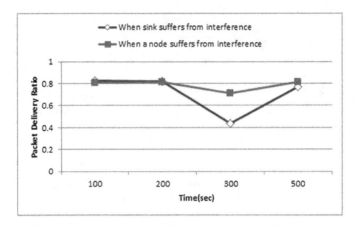

Fig. 11. Timely variation of packet delivery ratio in case of inter BAN interference

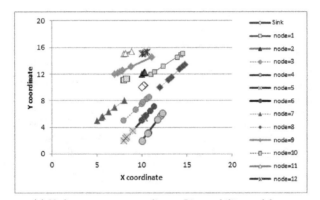

(a) Node movements according to Line mobility model

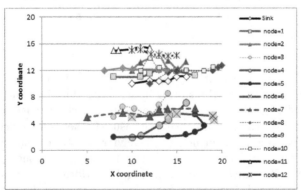

(b) Node movements according to Smooth Random mobility model

Fig. 12. Node movement with varying mobility models

A detailed analysis has been made in the next two experiments regarding relative node movements employing different mobility models. Node locations in time domain are plotted accordingly. As observed from Fig. 12(a) with line mobility model [45] movement pattern is linear and follows diagonal path starting from initial location to the corner point of the working area i.e. (20, 20) in this scenario. According to the node deployment strategy as illustrated above in Fig. 3(a) sink node placed at waist along with two other nodes (that is, node 1 and node 2) placed at chest exhibit imperceptive movements with respect to others. Besides, two more nodes (that is, node 11 and node 12) located at shoulders move unrushed as compared to the nodes deployed in hands or legs. Similar scenario has been exploited in case of smooth random mobility model [47]. Accordingly, as seen from Fig. 12(b) node movement pattern is smooth and less likely to take sharp turn. Nodes placed on hands and legs are subject to frequent posture changes than the nodes on waist or chest. This is reflected in Fig. 12(b) as well. However, the intrinsic random nature of this model influences the connectivity between nodes to a greater extent as compared to line mobility model.

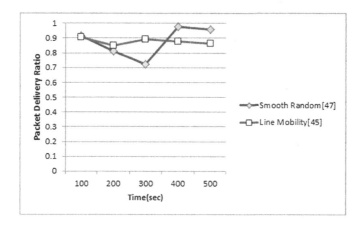

Fig. 13. Timely variation of packet delivery ratio with varying mobility model

In the subsequent experiment performance of the proposed protocol HIER is studied subject to the aforementioned mobility models. As obtained from Fig. 13, with linear movement pattern, HIER imparts steady throughput in terms of packet delivery ratio since all nodes move with comparable speed in the same direction according to the trace in Fig. 12(a). However, in case of smooth random mobility model, the different movement patterns of hands, legs with respect to waist or chest can be reflected resulting in topology change due to posture change when the transmission power of the nodes are low. Thus the packet delivery ratio obtained for Smooth Random Mobility Model is more realistic.

5 Conclusion

This paper presents a cost based energy efficient 2 hop routing protocol HIER for WBAN which addresses the inherent challenges of WBAN architecture and empowers a trade off between contradictory issues in routing decision with minimal overhead. The proposed algorithm exhibits adaptive nature in circumstances when inter BAN interference takes place. Performance of HIER is evaluated with respect to various simulation parameters for different environments such as varying sink position, varying network size etc. It is observed that, HIER outperforms the state of the art protocols for similar simulation setup in terms of energy consumed. In addition, smooth random mobility model has been implemented to trace the relative node movements in WBAN and comparative analysis has been accomplished with respect to line mobility model to elaborately investigate the effect of movement patterns on performance of routing protocols.

References

1. Cavallari, R., Martelli, F., Rosini, R., Buratti, C., Verdone, R.: A survey on wireless body area networks: technologies and design challenges. IEEE Commun. Surv. Tutorials **16**(3), 1635–1657 (2014)
2. Movassaghi, S., Abolhasan, M., Lipman, J., Smith, D., Jamalipour, A.: Wireless body area networks: a survey. IEEE Commun. Surv. Tutorials **16**(3), 1658–1686 (2014)
3. Bag, A., Bassiouni, M.A.: Energy efficient thermal aware routing algorithms for embedded biomedical sensor networks. In: IEEE International Conference on Mobile Adhoc and Sensor Systems (MASS), pp. 604–609. IEEE (2006)
4. Tang, Q., Tummala, N., Gupta, S.K.S., Schwiebert, L.: TARA: Thermal-Aware Routing Algorithm for implanted sensor networks. In: Prasanna, V.K., Iyengar, S.S., Spirakis, P.G., Welsh, M. (eds.) DCOSS 2005. LNCS, vol. 3560, pp. 206–217. Springer, Heidelberg (2005). doi:10.1007/11502593_17
5. Bag, A., Bassiouni, M.A.: Hotspot preventing routing algorithm for delay-sensitive biomedical sensor networks. In: IEEE International Conference on Portable Information Devices, PORTABLE 2007, pp. 1–5. IEEE (2007)
6. Gupta, S.K., Lalwani, S., Prakash, Y., Elsharawy, E., Schwiebert, L.: Towards a propagation model for wireless biomedical applications. In: IEEE International Conference on Communications, ICC 2003, vol. 3, pp. 1993–1997. IEEE (2003)
7. Wu, G., Ren, J., Xia, F., Yao, L., Xu, Z., Shang, P.: A game theoretic approach for interuser interference reduction in body sensor networks. Int. J. Distrib. Sensor Netw. **7**(1), 12–30 (2011)
8. Sarra, E., Moungla, H., Benayoune, S., Mehaoua, A.: Coexistence improvement of Wearable Body Area Network (WBAN) in medical environment. In: IEEE International Conference on Communications (ICC), pp. 5694–5699. IEEE (2014)
9. Roy, M., Chowdhury, C., Aslam, N.: Designing an energy efficient WBAN routing protocol. In: COMSNETS. IEEE (2017)
10. Watteyne, T., Augé-Blum, I., Dohler, M., Barthel, D.: Anybody: a self-organization protocol for body area networks. In: Proceedings of the ICST 2nd International Conference on Body Area Networks, pp. 1–7. ICST (Institute for Computer Sciences, Social-Informatics and Telecommunications Engineering) (2007)

11. Murthy, J.K., Rao, V.S.: Improved routing protocol for health care communications. Open J. Appl. Biosensor **2**, 51–56 (2013)
12. Culpepper, B.J., Dung, L., Moh, M.: Design and analysis of Hybrid Indirect Transmissions (HIT) for data gathering in wireless micro sensor networks. ACM SIGMOBILE Mob. Comput. Commun. Rev. **8**(1), 61–83 (2004)
13. Moh, M., Culpepper, B.J., Dung, L., Moh, T.S., Hamada, T., Su, C.F.: On data gathering protocols for in-body biomedical sensor networks. In: Global Telecommunications Conference, GLOBECOM 2005, vol. 5. IEEE (2005)
14. Braem, B., Latre, B., Moerman, I., Blondia, C., Demeester, P.: The wireless autonomous spanning tree protocol for multihop wireless body area networks. In: Third Annual International Conference on Mobile and Ubiquitous Systems: Networking and Services, pp. 1–8. IEEE (2006)
15. Ruzzelli, A.G., Jurdak, R., O'Hare, G.M., Van Der Stok, P.: Energy-efficient multi-hop medical sensor networking. In: Proceedings of the 1st ACM SIGMOBILE International Workshop on Systems and Networking Support for Healthcare and Assisted Living Environments, pp. 37–42. ACM (2007)
16. Liang, X., Balasingham, I.: A QoS-aware routing service framework for biomedical sensor networks. In: 4th International Symposium on Wireless Communication Systems, ISWCS 2007, pp. 342–345. IEEE (2007)
17. Latré, B., De Poorter, E., Moerman, I., Demeester, P.: MOFBAN: a lightweight modular framework for body area networks. In: Kuo, T.-W., Sha, E., Guo, M., Yang, L.T., Shao, Z. (eds.) EUC 2007. LNCS, vol. 4808, pp. 610–622. Springer, Heidelberg (2007). doi:10.1007/978-3-540-77092-3_53
18. Takahashi, D., Xiao, Y., Hu, F., Chen, J., Sun, Y.: Temperature-aware routing for telemedicine applications in embedded biomedical sensor networks. EURASIP J. Wirel. Commun. Networking **2008**, 1–11 (2008)
19. Bag, A., Bassiouni, M.A.: Routing algorithm for network of homogeneous and id-less biomedical sensor nodes (rain). In: Sensors Applications Symposium, SAS 2008, pp. 68–73. IEEE (2008)
20. Braem, B., Latré, B., Blondia, C., Moerman, I., Demeester, P.: Improving reliability in multi-hop body sensor networks. In: Second International Conference on Sensor Technologies and Applications, SENSORCOMM 2008, pp. 342–347. IEEE (2008)
21. Liang, X., Balasingham, I., Byun, S.S.: A reinforcement learning based routing protocol with QoS support for biomedical sensor networks. In: First International Symposium on Applied Sciences on Biomedical and Communication Technologies, ISABEL 2008, pp. 1–5. IEEE (2008)
22. Ahourai, F., Tabandeh, M., Jahed, M., Moradi, S.: A thermal-aware shortest hop routing algorithm for in vivo biomedical sensor networks. In: Sixth International Conference on Information Technology: New Generations, ITNG 2009, pp. 1612–1613. IEEE (2009)
23. Bag, A., Bassiouni, M.A.: Biocomm-a cross-layer Medium Access Control (MAC) and routing protocol co-design for biomedical sensor networks. Int. J. Parallel Emergent Distrib. Syst. **24**(1), 85–103 (2009)
24. Quwaider, M., Biswas, S.: Probabilistic routing in on-body sensor networks with postural disconnections. In: Proceedings of the 7th ACM International Symposium on Mobility Management and Wireless Access, pp. 149–158. ACM (2009)
25. Quwaider, M., Biswas, S.: On-body packet routing algorithms for body sensor networks. In: First International Conference on Networks and Communications, NETCOM 2009, pp. 171–177. IEEE (2009)

26. Djenouri, D., Balasingham, I.: New QoS and geographical routing in wireless bio-medical sensor networks. In: Sixth International Conference on Broadband Communications, Networks, and Systems, BROADNETS 2009, pp. 1–8. IEEE (2009)
27. de Francisco, R., Huang, L., Dolmans, G.: Coexistence of WBAN and WLAN in medical environments. In: IEEE 70th Vehicular Technology Conference Fall (VTC 2009), pp. 1–5. IEEE (2009)
28. Quwaider, M., Biswas, S.: DTN routing in body sensor networks with dynamic postural partitioning. Ad Hoc Netw. **8**(8), 824–841 (2010)
29. Chen, B., Varkey, J.P., Pompili, D., Li, J.K., Marsic, I.: Patient vital signs monitoring using wireless body area networks. In: Proceedings of the 2010 IEEE 36th Annual Northeast Bioengineering Conference, pp. 1–2. IEEE (2010)
30. Maskooki, A., Soh, C.B., Gunawan, E., Low, K.S.: Opportunistic routing for body area network. In: Consumer Communications and Networking Conference (CCNC), pp. 237–241. IEEE (2011)
31. Razzaque, M.A., Hong, C.S., Lee, S.: Data-centric multiobjective QoS-aware routing protocol for body sensor networks. Sensors **11**(1), 917–937 (2011)
32. Liang, X., Li, X., Shen, Q., Lu, R., Lin, X., Shen, X., Zhuang, W.: Exploiting prediction to enable secure and reliable routing in wireless body area networks. In: Proceedings of INFOCOM 2012, pp. 388–396. IEEE (2012)
33. Movassaghi, S., Abolhasan, M., Lipman, J.: Energy Efficient Thermal and Power Aware (ETPA) routing in body area networks. In: 23rd International Symposium on Personal Indoor and Mobile Radio Communications (PIMRC), pp. 1108–1113. IEEE (2012)
34. Nadeem, Q., Javaid, N., Mohammad, S., Khan, M., Sarfraz, S., Gull, M.: Simple: stable increased-throughput multi-hop protocol for link efficiency in wireless body area networks. In: Eighth International Conference on Broadband and Wireless Computing, Communication and Applications (BWCCA), pp. 221–226. IEEE (2013)
35. Chen, Y.M., Peng, Y.: Energy efficient fuzzy routing protocol in wireless body area networks. Int. J. Eng. **4**(1), 59–63 (2013)
36. Murthy, J.K., Thimmappa, P., Sambasiva Rao, V.: Investigations on the routing protocols for wireless body area networks. In: Aswatha Kumar, M., Selvarani, R., Suresh Kumar, T.V. (eds.) Proceedings of International Conference on Advances in Computing. AISC, vol. 174, pp. 483–490. Springer, New Delhi (2013). doi:10.1007/978-81-322-0740-5_59
37. Monowar, M.M., Hassan, M.M., Bajaber, F., Hamid, M.A., Alamri, A.: Thermal-aware multiconstrained intrabody QoS routing for wireless body area networks. Int. J. Distrib. Sensor Networks **10**(3), 1–14 (2014)
38. Movassaghi, S., Abolhasan, M., Smith, D., Jamalipour, A.: AIM: Adaptive Inter-network Interference mitigation amongst co-existing wireless body area networks. In: Global Communications Conference (GLOBECOM), pp. 2460–2465. IEEE (2014)
39. Almashaqbeh, G., Hayajneh, T., Vasilakos, A.V.: A cloud-based interference-aware remote health monitoring system for non-hospitalized patients. In: 2014 IEEE Global Communications Conference (GLOBECOM), pp. 2436–2441. IEEE (2014)
40. Elhadj, H.B., Elias, J., Chaari, L., Kamoun, L.: A priority based cross layer routing protocol for healthcare applications. Ad Hoc Netw. **42**, 1–18 (2016)
41. Ahmed, S., Javaid, N., Yousaf, S., Ahmad, A., Sandhu, M.M., Imran, M., Khan, Z.A., Alrajeh, N.: Co-LAEEBA: cooperative link aware and energy efficient protocol for wireless body area networks. Comput. Hum. Behav. **51**, 1205–1215 (2015)

42. Javaid, N., Ahmad, A., Nadeem, Q., Imran, M., Haider, N.: iM-SIMPLE: improved stable increased-throughput multi-hop link efficient routing protocol for wireless body area networks. Comput. Hum. Behav. **51**, 1003–1011 (2015)
43. Sahndhu, M.M., Javaid, N., Imran, M., Guizani, M., Khan, Z.A., Qasim, U.: BEC: a novel routing protocol for balanced energy consumption in wireless body area networks. In: Wireless Communications and Mobile Computing Conference (IWCMC), pp. 653–658. IEEE (2015)
44. Ayatollahitafti, V., Ngadi, M.A., bin Mohamad Sharif, J., Abdullahi, M.: An efficient next hop selection algorithm for multi-hop body area networks. PloS One **11**(1), 1–14 (2016)
45. https://castalia.forge.nicta.com.au/index.php/en/
46. Lu, Y.M., Wong, V.W.S.: An energy-efficient multipath routing protocol for wireless sensor networks. Int. J. Commun. Syst. **20**(7), 747–766 (2007)
47. Bettstetter, C.: Smooth is better than sharp: a random mobility model for simulation of wireless networks. In: Proceedings of the 4th ACM International Workshop on Modeling, Analysis and Simulation of Wireless and Mobile Systems, pp. 19–27. ACM (2001)

Techno-Economics Behind Provisioning 4G LTE Mobile Services over Sub 1 GHz Frequency Bands

A Case Study for Indian Telecom Circles

Ashutosh Jha[✉] and Debashis Saha

Management Information Systems Group, Indian Institute of Management Calcutta,
Kolkata 700104, India
{ashutoshj14,ds}@iimcal.ac.in

Abstract. The fourth generation (4G) mobile cellular networks are being deployed rapidly across both the developed and the developing world. The choice of Long-Term Evolution (LTE) for 4G deployment is driven primarily by its technical superiority in catering to the rising consumer demand for high-speed mobile broadband services. The total cost of ownership (TCO) for deploying 4G LTE services, however, involve massive investments in spectrum acquisition and radio network infrastructure provisioning. Since spectrum bands in different frequencies have different wave propagation characteristics, their individual valuations also differ, leading to varying implications on an operator's TCO and profitability. To clearly establish these financial and technical implications, this paper performs a comparative evaluation of 4G LTE deployment over sub 1 GHz, 1–2 GHz, and 2–3 GHz cohorts of frequency bands. With the help of a suitable techno-economic model, we forecast the number of 4G LTE subscribers, determine the achievable coverage and capacity, and analyze their comparative profitability through a discounted cash flow approach over a 20-year horizon across 22 telecom circles in India. Our results indicate that sub 1 GHz bands result in lower TCO and higher profitability for operators across all the 22 telecom circles when compared to other two cohorts. Interestingly, we also note that, among the four types of telecom circles, Category C circles, which are crucial to ensure the mandated last-mile coverage for rural Indian villages, come next to only Metro circles in terms of profitability, thereby increasing their attractiveness further in future spectrum auctions in India.

Keywords: Cellular mobile · 4G · LTE · Spectrum · Techno-economic assessment · Total cost of ownership (TCO) · Discounted cash flow (DCF)

1 Introduction

The newly emerging patterns of socioeconomic interactions in an information economy today rely on the presence of a high-speed broadband[1] connectivity. The transformative

---

[1] Recommendation I.113 of the ITU Standardization Sector defines broadband as a "transmission capacity that is faster than primary rate Integrated Services Digital Network (ISDN) at 1.5 or 2.0 Megabits per second (Mbits)".

© Springer International Publishing AG 2017
N. Sastry and S. Chakraborty (Eds.): COMSNETS 2017, LNCS 10340, pp. 284–306, 2017.
DOI: 10.1007/978-3-319-67235-9_17

benefits of ensuring broadband connectivity are very similar to those provided by major infrastructure services, such as road, rail, and electricity [1]. Considering the positive impacts of broadband connectivity on the national economy, various governments have taken several steps towards facilitating ubiquitous access to broadband in their countries [2–4]. The governments in the developing world, especially, have conceived and implemented several initiatives to enable accessibility to broadband infrastructure for their citizens [1, 5]. India, for instance, started the National Optical Fiber Network (NOFN) initiative in 2011 with a view to connecting its 250,000 *gram panchayats* (democratic village councils) via the broadband network. In the recently launched 'Digital India' initiative of the Government of India (GoI), provisioning broadband connectivity across the country is one of the most important priorities [5]. Similar such initiatives can be mentioned for many other developing countries [2]. However, there are several challenges faced by telecom operators towards meeting the policy objectives of the government [6]. The costs incurred by the operators in acquiring the spectrum and provisioning the radio network infrastructure are massive. The decision to acquire spectrum in a particular frequency band is also crucial, considering the fact that the bands vary in their wave propagation characteristics and therefore are priced differently by the government [6–8]. There are also challenges of ensuring the last-mile coverage and the promised data rate, apart from estimating the data volume demands of customers over the varied demography. The variation in purchasing power and literacy levels in the rural and urban parts of the country also lead to apprehensions about the adoption behavior of the customers. Each of these challenges translates into differing policy and business objectives, for the governments and the telecom operators, respectively. In this context, the fourth generation (4G) of mobile services can address some of the challenges related to the provisioning of the high-speed broadband services in a country such as India. There is a rapid deployment of 4G services in both the developed and developing world. This is due to the technical superiority of 4G over the previous generations, to meet the ever-increasing consumer demand.

In most of the countries, the 4G mobile services make use of the Long-Term Evolution (LTE) network architecture for provisioning voice and data services. Recent studies have highlighted the potential of 4G LTE as an efficient vehicle to deliver high-speed broadband connectivity [2–4, 8]. 4G LTE has been proven to be technologically superior to its predecessor technologies, such as HSDPA [8]. 4G LTE has also been shown to be cost-effective for provisioning broadband connectivity in the rural areas of Spain and India and can, therefore, serve as the technology of choice for the operators willing to provision high-speed broadband services [2–4]. The deployment of 4G LTE networks includes provisioning compatible Base-Transceiver-Stations (BTSs), upgrading core network components, and installing backhaul fiber links. However, prior to the decision to deploy 4G LTE services, the operators need to evaluate the likely return vis-à-vis the total expenditure and assess the profitability scenarios. This process of due diligence is known as techno-economic assessment in the literature [2–4]. The decisions to invest in the radio network infrastructure and further procurement of spectrum blocks for increasing the bandwidth rely on the scope of profitability as evaluated by the techno-economic assessment. Profitability, in turn, eventually, depends upon the revenue generated from the potential customers who adopt the 4G LTE mobile services offered by the telecom operator.

Therefore, forecasting the likely adoption of 4G LTE services forms the basic step of a techno-economic evaluation [2–4]. Given the paucity of literature on the circle-wise broadband adoption forecasts for India, and considering that we can approximate the 4G LTE subscription through broadband adoption forecasts, we make use of the Bass model of innovation diffusion to forecast the 4G LTE adoption in India [9]. The forecasts are done for all the 22 telecom circles in India over a twenty-year horizon with 2016 as the base year. Depending upon the forecasts of 4G LTE adoption the technical parameters of the radio transceiver equipment are configured, in order to ensure the given network coverage, maintain service quality, and support promised data rate. Here, the role of the frequency band over which the service is to be provisioned becomes important. This is due to the fact that the achievable cellular coverage depends on the frequency band under consideration since there are variations in the wave propagation characteristics at different frequencies [7, 8]. Accordingly, the spectrum blocks offered in each frequency band are priced differently by the government, leading to varying investments incurred by the operators [8]. This requires separate techno-economic evaluations for each frequency band under consideration, with varying technical specifications suited to the 4G LTE services.

We extend our previous work[2] in this study, to include the techno-economic implications of provisioning 4G LTE services over the three frequency cohorts, namely, sub 1 GHz (700 and 800 MHz), 1–2 GHz (1800 MHz), and 2–3 GHz (2100 MHz) [10]. The choice of the frequency band(s) in each cohort, viz. 700 MHz, 800 MHz, 1800 MHz and 2100 MHz, reflect the prevailing global 4G LTE deployment scenario [6, 7]. For the case of India, the bands in 700 MHz and 800 MHz were recently introduced in the prior spectrum auctions[3] [7]. Notably, 700 MHz which was put up for auction for the first time did not see any takers citing high valuation prices [7]. However, given the wider coverage capabilities of the lower frequency band such as 700 MHz, an exact implication of this advantage on the financial liability is warranted [6]. Therefore, our study attempts to evaluate the relative profitability of sub 1 GHz cohort, compared to 1–2 GHz cohort and above 2 GHz cohort, and its implications for the 700 MHz band in future spectrum auctions. We also evaluate in this study both the technical aspects related to coverage and capacity as well as the financial aspects, such as total cost of ownership (TCO) and Net Present Value (NPV) of the investments incurred for provisioning 4G LTE services over the three frequency cohorts. The analysis covers all the 22 telecom circles in India, taking into account the subscriber adoption and geographical characteristics of each circle. Through this analysis, we intend to comparatively assess the technical and financial implications of provisioning 4G LTE services over the three frequency cohorts.

In the Indian context, 700 MHz band may serve to be an important addition to the kitty of both a new entrant and an incumbent operator. However, the spectrum acquisition strategy of an operator needs to appropriately select spectrum blocks from all the available bands, keeping in mind its existing spectrum holdings, with a view to reducing the TCO while maximizing the profitability. Since the operators use bands in sub 1 GHz cohort to

---

[2] This paper is an extension of work originally reported in *Proceedings of the 9th International Conference on Communication Systems and Networks (COMSNETS)*.

[3] The 700 MHz band was introduced for bidding for the first time, in the 2016 spectrum auctions in India. The 800 MHz band has been auctioned twice in the spectrum auctions of 2013 and 2015.

increase the breadth of coverage, while simultaneously using bands in 1–2 GHz and 2–3 GHz cohorts for dense deployments, this combination is extremely crucial. These decisions are also subject to constraints with specific governmental mandates pushing for the last-mile coverage, and limits imposed on the circle-wise as well as aggregate spectrum holding for a particular operator [3, 11]. In this study, we demonstrate through the profitability analysis of both a new entrant and an incumbent operator, how both the decisions, namely (i) the choice of the telecom circles to bid for, and (ii) particular frequency band to go for, are crucial for them. We also attempt to highlight in the process, the circles that are financially more lucrative, and the spectrums that are relatively cost-efficient.

The paper consists of five sections. Section 2 covers the prior literature related to the techno-economic assessment and empirical models of diffusion of innovations. Section 3 presents an overview of theoretical underpinnings of our techno-economic model. Section 4 highlights the main results and the detailed explanations along with the input parameters used for calculating the model parameters. Finally, Sect. 5 concludes the work.

2 Literature Review

The use of broadband positively benefits the GDP both directly and indirectly [1]. There are numerous positive externalities associated with the use of broadband, manifesting through the creation of consumer surplus and improvement in firm efficiencies [1]. The economic impacts and business implications of broadband connectivity have been the subject of various studies in the extant literature [1–4, 12–15]. The problems addressed in these studies range from assessing the macroeconomic impact [1] to addressing the capacity-cost aspects of provisioning broadband [12].

Across the world, 4G LTE is rapidly becoming the most favored choice for provisioning of mobile broadband services [2, 4, 11]. 4G LTE services have already been deployed across 151 countries comprising of over a billion subscriptions [13]. Various reports have predicted that by 2020, 4G LTE services will constitute one-third of the overall mobile connections across the world [13]. These developments have mostly come about due to the rapid deployment of 4G LTE networks in the developing world. India, for example, is soon poised to become the second largest mobile broadband market in the world according to the GSMA [13]. The potential of 4G LTE services for a country such as India, therefore, are huge.

The deployment of 4G LTE network takes place over several frequency bands belonging to either of the three major frequency cohorts, namely, sub 1 GHz (700–900 MHz), 1–2 GHz (1800–1900 MHz), and above 2 GHz (2100–2600 MHz). Of these, 4G LTE deployments in the majority of countries where services are already in place, make use of 700 MHz, 800 MHz, 1800 MHz and 2100 MHz bands. Other bands such as 900 MHz, 1900 MHz, 2300 MHz and 2500 MHz, have not yet seen the rollout of the service in many countries. However, for all the above-mentioned frequency bands, the future roll-out plans are already in place. The details on frequency bands currently being used for 4G LTE deployment across countries have been summarized in Table 1 below.

Table 1. Frequency bands used for 4G LTE deployment globally

Frequency (MHz)	Countries with LTE networks planned or deployed
700	*Africa* – Kenya, South Africa, Tanzania
	Americas – Bermuda, British Virgin Islands, Curacao, Jamaica, Trinidad and Tobago, Cayman Islands, Argentina, Brazil, Colombia, Costa Rica, Ecuador, Honduras, Mexico, Nicaragua, Paraguay, Peru, United States
	Asia – Bangladesh, China, India, Kazakhstan, Malaysia, Mongolia, Nepal, South Korea, Thailand
	Europe – Austria, Finland, France, Iceland, Russia, Slovenia
	Australia
800	*Africa* – Ghana, Kenya, Nigeria, Senegal, Seychelles, Somalia, South Africa
	Americas – Trinidad and Tobago, Argentina, Brazil, Paraguay, Canada, United States
	Asia – Azerbaijan, Kyrgyzstan, South Korea, Taiwan, Cambodia, China, India, Thailand
	Europe – Austria, Cyprus, Denmark, Greece, Iceland, Ireland, Malta, Moldova, Montenegro, Romania, Serbia, Ukraine
1800	*Africa* – Senegal, South Africa, Tanzania
	Americas – Brazil, Costa Rica
	Asia – Bangladesh, Cambodia, China, Hong Kong, India, Malaysia, Mongolia, Myanmar, Nepal, Pakistan, South Korea, Taiwan, Thailand, Vietnam
	Europe – Crimea, Czech Republic, Hungary, Italy, Malta, Moldova, Montenegro, Russia, Sweden, Ukraine
	Australia
2100	*Americas* – Costa Rica
	Asia – Bangladesh, China, Hong Kong, India, Indonesia, Philippines, South Korea, Sri Lanka, Taiwan, Thailand,
	Europe – Albania, Austria, Croatia, Iceland, Italy, Kosovo, Moldova, Montenegro, Netherland, Norway, Poland, Switzerland, Ukraine, United Kingdom

2.1 Previous Works on Techno-Economic Assessment

Techno-economic models are used to evaluate the parameters of the financial feasibility of technology-intensive investments. The aspects addressed by the techno-economic models comprises of financial recoverability, break-even period, and profits and losses associated with a capital-intensive project such as the deployment of 4G LTE networks. The dimensions of the model take into account, the estimated future market potential, the number of competitors, technical parameters, overall cost considerations, and the expected revenue. Techno-economic evaluations have been used previously to evaluate the technical and financial feasibility of LTE deployment in the rural areas of Spain [2] and India [3, 4]. The studies have concluded that 4G LTE could be profitable for the operators if the right combination of data offerings is provided [2–4]. The studies have also highlighted the need for demand-inducing initiatives on the part of the government [2]. The studies, however, have not performed comparative evaluations between various frequency bands for the circle-wise deployment scenarios. Techno-economic evaluations for the case of a single fictitious operator for the countries of Germany and Sweden have also been undertaken with a view to analyzing the impacts of the spectrum on the capital expenditure [11]. This particular study analyzed the dynamics of network design, customer demand, and investments, through evaluating the impacts on capital expenditure for differential access to 800 MHz and 2.6 GHz spectrums [11]. The study, however, does not undertake any empirical model based demand forecasting and excludes the future adoption scenarios. The effects of provisioning 4G LTE services, having different mobile broadband capacity configurations, over the capital and operational expenditures has been highlighted in the report by Nokia [12]. Through a range of possible configurations, the variations in expenditures are traced, for both 4G LTE and HSPA technologies [12]. The evaluation of TCO and profitability parameters as well as the regional variations in demand have not been addressed by the report, though. Another report by LS Telecom [14] has evaluated the financial feasibility of providing Public Protection and Disaster Relief (PPDR) services for the case of Greater London area, by comparing the network performance of 700 MHz with 2 GHz. This independent report prepared for Solaris Mobile, however, only considers the specific case of provisioning PPDR services by Solaris Mobile without incorporating future variations in user demand [14].

We in this work have considered the case of 4G LTE deployment across the 22 telecom circles in India, and have attempted to incorporate the above-mentioned limitations. The analysis, however, is generic enough to accommodate similar situations in several other countries as well.

2.2   Related Works on Mobile Diffusion Models

To understand the likely response of the customers towards a newly launched product or service in a given market, researchers often forecast the adoption with the help of an empirical model of innovation diffusion [2–4, 11]. For example, Gompertz model was used to estimate the 4G LTE subscriber adoption in the rural areas of Spain [2]. The forecasts, however, did not take specific geographical regions into account, since they were performed at an aggregate level of the combined rural area. The Gompertz model has been found to perform poorly when compared to the Bass model [15] for the case when a limited data set is available [15, 16]. The Bass model has been extensively used to forecast new product sales in marketing and it can adequately describe the diffusion process even when a very limited data set is available [7]. We in this study use the Bass model to forecast the adoption of 4G LTE services in all the 22 telecom circles of India. We had earlier used the Bass model for forecasting the broadband diffusion in the rural parts of India by only considering the aggregate rural population [4]. The previous study, however, did not perform any model parameter estimation over the historical data set of broadband subscription in India. This is also pertinent considering that no prior study has performed a circle-wise forecast of broadband adoption in India, to the best of our knowledge. The analysis performed in this study attempts to address this gap in the literature.

3   Techno-Economic Evaluation Model

The techno-economic model used in this study is a major extension to that in [3, 4]. Assuming a single operator market, the model comparatively evaluates the TCO and profitability parameters for provisioning 4G LTE services over 700 MHz, 800 MHz, 1800 MHz, and 2100 MHz. We have considered separate scenarios for both an incumbent operator, and a new entrant in the market, for our calculations. Figure 1 highlights the various steps involved in the techno-economic model.

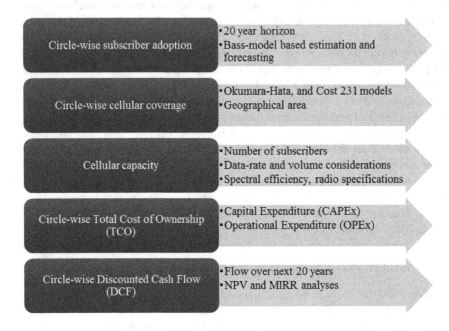

Fig. 1.   Techno-economic evaluation procedure

The first step consists of forecasting the likely adoption of 4G LTE services across the 22 telecom circles in India. This is done with the help of Bass model parameter estimation and subsequent forecasting [9, 15, 16]. We have considered 2016 as the base year and also taken into account the rise in India's population between the 20-year forecast duration, i.e., 2016–2036 [17]. We then use the standard values of 4G LTE radio parameters to calculate the total allowable loss value for a given BTS specification. The total allowable loss value thus determined, are used as inputs to the chosen radio propagation models (Okumura-Hata and Cost 231) for determining the achievable cellular coverage over a particular frequency band. The values of cellular coverage are used to estimate the total number of BTSs (henceforth called sites) required, given the geographical area of the circle. While the number obtained is an indication of the total number of sites required to provide the full coverage, it might not be sufficient for ensuring the levels of subscriber demand for data rate and volume. This is due to the variations in subscriber demand for data volume and data rate in different regions, and given that each site can deliver only a finite amount of data volume in a period. To evaluate the number of sites that can meet the specified levels of capacity as well as coverage, we estimate the levels of annual data demands in each telecom circle. Suitable assumptions regarding the monthly data requirements of customers in different circles are made by taking into account the past trends of data consumption. The aggregate annual data demand is calculated therefrom.

Given the annual data demand, the spectral efficiency of the frequency band, modulation scheme, standard LTE radio equipment, and the busy-hour traffic constraints, we determine the cellular data capacity of a single site. The actual number of sites required to provide the promised service can then be calculated. Calibrations are performed so that there are no mismatches between the number of sites needed for coverage and capacity.

The aggregate annual investment in the radio network infrastructure is then evaluated depending on the number of sites required in each circle [3, 4]. The number of sites over future years are kept constant for the case of an incumbent operator. This is considering the fact that the incumbent operators upgrade their site incrementally, depending on the growing customer demands and future increases in the subscription. For the case of a new entrant, however, the number of sites have been made to continuously increase over the period of study till the maximum value of adoption is reached. For both the new entrant and the incumbent operator, the circle-wise aggregate annual investment in the network infrastructure, over the four chosen frequency bands (viz. 700 MHz, 800 MHz, 1800 MHz, and 2100 MHz), are then calculated. The circle-wise spectrum acquisition costs for a fixed size of spectrum block in each band is then added to the investments in network infrastructure, to calculate the aggregate capital expenditure (CAPEX) incurred by an operator. The CAPEX represents the fixed upfront cost an operator incurs in procuring the spectrum, assets, equipment, and the physical infrastructure. The variable cost components are included in the Operational expenditure (OPEX) portion and comprise of site maintenance, rental, electricity, and spectrum usage charges (SUC). The TCO for an operator is the sum of CAPEX and OPEX incurred during a given period.

Reasonable assumptions related to the average revenue per user (ARPU) are made in order to evaluate the circle-wise revenue given the estimated subscriber population. The circle-wise net present value (NPV) and modified internal rate of return (MIRR) are then evaluated for the estimated revenue and the TCO [3, 4] using the discounted cash flow (DCF) approach. The calculations are repeated for all the four chosen frequency bands. The MIRR and NPV values are used as measures to indicate financial recoverability of operator investments in 4G LTE deployments.

3.1 Forecasting 4G LTE Subscribers Using Bass Model

The Bass model categorizes all the potential adopters into *innovators* and *imitators* [9]. Innovators do not get influenced by other adopters and the decision to adopt is purely based on the information collected from the formal communication channels. In contrast, imitators are easily influenced by other members in the social system and their decision to adopt an innovation is based on the information gathered from informal sources, such as direct observations of the service usage and personal interactions with other users [9]. Essentially, the Bass model posits that *"the probability that an initial purchase will be made at time t, given that no purchase has yet been made, is a linear function of the number of previous buyers*" [9]. Hence, the probability density function for adoption at time t is expressed as [9]:

$$\frac{dF(t)}{dt} = f(t) = (p + qF(t))(1 - F(t)) \tag{1}$$

where, f(*t*) is the likelihood of purchase at time *t*, F(*t*) is the fraction of the ultimate potential of the market that has adopted by time *t*, *p* is the coefficient of innovation, and *q* is the coefficient of imitation. The solution to Eq. (1) is given as [15]:

$$F(t) = m \left[\frac{1 - e^{-(p+q)t}}{1 + \frac{q}{p} e^{-(p+q)t}} \right] \tag{2}$$

where m is the ultimate market potential. The ultimate market potential is the maximum sales expected of the innovation during its lifetime. The Bass model assumes a finite market size, due to which the adoption curve reaches a saturation once the peak sales have occurred and start to decline afterward.

To estimate the Bass model parameters we apply ordinary least squares (OLS) regression [9, 15] on the historical data set of broadband subscription in India. The discrete version of the Bass model [9, 15] is used for the regression analysis. The discrete version of the Bass model is expressed as:

$$N(t_i) = b_1 + b_2 N(t_{i-1}) + b_3 (N(t_{i-1}))^2 \tag{3}$$

where N(*t_i*) is the cumulative number of adoptions till time period *i*, and b_1, b_2, and b_3 are the coefficients of the discrete Bass model [9, 15]. Knowing the parameters b_1, b_2, and b_3, we can calculate *m*, *p* and *q* using the relations mentioned below:

$$m = \frac{-b_1 - \sqrt{b_1^2 - 4b_2 b_3}}{2b_3}; p = \frac{b_1}{m}; q = -mb_3 \tag{4}$$

The estimated coefficients are subsequently used in forecasting the future adoption of 4G LTE services in the 22 telecom circles of India.

3.2 LTE RF Link Budgeting Model

The link budget calculations are needed for the calculation of cellular coverage parameters. A link budget takes into consideration all the losses and gains involved in equipment (say BTS), end-terminals (i.e., mobile devices), and communication medium (i.e., free space). The results obtained indicates the maximum allowable propagation loss (MAPL). The formulae used in the link budget calculations are expressed below:

$$EIRP_{Tx} = P_{Tx} + G_{Tx} - L_b \tag{5}$$

$$EIRP_{Tx} = NB_{noise} + Th_{noise} + SINR \qquad (6)$$

$$MAPL = EIRP_{Tx} + R_{SENS} - IM - L_{cable} + G_{Rx} - M + G_{soft} \qquad (7)$$

where $EIRP_{Tx}$ is the Equivalent Isotropically Radiated Power of the Transmitter, P_{Tx} is the maximum transmitter power, GT_x is the transmitter antenna gain, L_b is the body loss, R_{SENS} is the receiver sensitivity, NB_{noise} is the noise value for Node-B, Th_{noise} is the thermal noise, SINR is the signal to noise interference ratio, MAPL is the maximum allowable propagation loss, IM is the interference margin, L_{cable} is the cable loss, G_{Rx} is the receiver antenna gain, M is the fast-fade margin, and G_{soft} is the soft handover gain.

3.3 Radio Propagation Model for Coverage Calculation

We use the MAPL values, calculated earlier, as inputs to the radio propagation model to calculate the cell radius and the coverage area for each site [3, 4]. Standard values of 4G LTE transceiver specifications are used towards the same [18]. As per convention, we have used two different propagation models for determining cell range and coverage area values: Okumura-Hata model is used for 700 MHz and 800 MHz bands, whereas the Cost-231 model is used for 1800 MHz and 2100 MHz bands.

Okumura-Hata (700 MHz and 800 MHz) and Cost-231 Model (1800 MHz and 2100 MHz)

$$d(km) = 10^{((MAPL-A-B)/C)} \qquad (8)$$

$$A = 69.55 + 26.16\log_{10}(f_c) - 13.82\log_{10}(h_b) - a(h_m) \qquad (9)$$

$$B = 44.9 - 6.55\log_{10}(h_b) \qquad (10)$$

$$Coverage\ Area = 1.9485 \times d^2 \qquad (11)$$

$$MAPL = 46.3 + 33.9\log_{10}(f_c) - 13.82\log_{10}(h_b) - a(h_b, f_c) + \\ [44.9 - 6.55\log_{10}(h_b)]\log_{10}d + C \qquad (12)$$

$$a(h_b, f_c) = (1.1\log_{10}(f_c) - 0.7)h_b - (1.56\log_{10}(f_c) - 0.8) \qquad (13)$$

where $C = \{0$ dB for medium cities and sub-urban areas; 3 dB for metropolitan areas$\}$; d is the cell radius (km), f_c is the carrier frequency (MHz), h_m is the effective antenna height of the mobile station (m) and h_b is the base station antenna height (m).

3.4 Cell-Dimensioning for a Given Data Rate

Given the size of the spectrum block and the 4G LTE radio equipment configuration, the monthly data capacity of a single site is determined [3, 4, 18]. The data capacity per site is used to evaluate the maximum number of subscribers that could be served by each site. For the specific data rate and the user demand of data volume, the total number of sites required in each circle are calculated. The cell radius calculations are calibrated in order to achieve congruence between the number of sites needed, to meet both the coverage and the capacity requirements of a circle. The number of users sharing the same data capacity at the same time is captured by the overbooking factor or the contention ratio [18]. This value is usually taken to be 20 [18]. Busy hour is the hour during a 24 h time frame that sees the greatest number of calls. In our conservative approach, we have taken 50% of the assumed busy hour traffic, but it can be easily changed in the formula. We have assumed antenna configuration to be 3-sectors per site.

$$N_{sub} = \frac{C_{cap} \times L_{BH}}{N_{sector} \times \{R_{sub}/O_{factor}\}} \tag{14}$$

where N_{sub} is the maximum number of subscribers, C_{cap} is the cell capacity, L_{BH} is the busy hour average loading, R_{sub} is the required user data rate, O_{factor} is the overbooking factor, and N_{sector} is the number of sectors per site.

3.5 TCO Calculation

The investments in the network infrastructure (sites, backhaul, transport network and core network) and the annual license charges[4] for the spectrum, together yield the net CAPEX for an operator. The base price valuations fixed by the GoI for the bands 700 MHz, 800 MHz, 1800 MHz, and 2100 MHz in each circle are used as the spectrum costs [6]. The annual SUC (paid at 3% of the Adjusted Gross Revenue per circle [7]) have been treated as the OPEX in our calculations. The rate of inflation is adjusted to reflect the net increase in the OPEX value in every year. Suitable assumptions related to the aggregate values of CAPEX and OPEX per site are made based on standard industry reports [11].

$$CAPEX = \left(BS_i \times NC_j\right) + SP_{license} \tag{15}$$

$$OPEX = \left(BS_i \times SC_i\right) + SUC_i \tag{16}$$

where BS_i is the number of base stations in the ith year, NC_i is the aggregate network cost per unit base station, $SP_{license}$ is the annual spectrum license installment, SC_i is the combined site related expenses, and SUC_i is the annual spectrum usage charges.

3.6 DCF Valuation

DCF is used to evaluate the potential returns on a capital-intensive project. The evaluation depends on the positive and negative cash flows generated over the entire project life-cycle. DCF approach takes into account the weighted-average cost of capital (WACC) and the savings rate, in order to estimate the profitability parameters of NPV and MIRR. In our

---

[4] According to the mandates of the last spectrum auction in India, 10% of the total license charges had to be paid upfront at the time of acquiring the spectrum, while the rest were supposed to be paid in 18 equal annual installments in future.

case, WACC is the discount rate for the telecommunications sector in India and the savings rate is the reinvestment rate decided by the Reserve Bank of India. The DCF approach yields the NPV and the MIRR figures over the total period of evaluation. NPV signifies the present value of the net cash flows generated over the entire project duration. Positive NPVs signal a profitable investment scenario, and vice versa. MIRR is the profitability metric assessing the rate of return on a project, which can then be compared with projects of similar investment size. MIRR calculation follows a practical approach by taking into account the reinvestment of positive cash flows at the rate of reinvestment and discounting of the negative cash flows with the WACC. MIRR and NPV values together, help in simplifying the investment related decisions, since a larger project with smaller MIRR value may still have a higher NPV, and vice-versa. The profitability related calculations make use of the formulae mentioned below:

$$Revenue = Number\ of\ subscriber \times Market\ Share \times ARPU \qquad (17)$$

$$NPV = \sum \left\{ \frac{CF_i}{(1+r)^i} \right\} \qquad (18)$$

where CF_i is the cash flow for the ith year ($i = 1$ to 20) and r is the discount rate or the weighted-average cost of capital (WACC).

4   Results and Discussion

The subsequent sections highlight the main results of our techno-economic analysis. The assumptions of the analyses have also been represented in tabular formats in the individual sections. We have made use of the STATA software package for the statistical calculations involved in the Bass model forecasting.

4.1   Forecasting 4G-LTE Adoption Using Bass Model

We use the quarterly broadband subscription data of last 11 years (2005-2016) for our regression analysis [19]. The data set consists of 44 data points of prior broadband adoption in India [19]. We use the discrete Bass model equation for our regression analysis. The coefficients of the model, as expressed by Eqs. (1)–(4), are estimated through the ordinary least-squares (OLS) approach [16]. The results of the regression analysis are highlighted in Table 2. We can infer the robustness of the model from the high adjusted R^2 and acceptable Root Mean Square Error (RMSE) values [16]. After calculating the Bass model parameters with the help of regression coefficients, we forecast the 4G LTE adoption scenario till the year 2036 in all the 22 telecom circles. Figure 2 illustrates the results of the forecasts for the 12 largest telecom circles (i.e., all circles from Metro, and larger circles from Categories A, B, and C) by subscriber volume. Together, these circles constitute over 45% of the total subscription.

We have assumed the aggregate value of predicted cellular subscriptions by the year 2036, as the ultimate market potential for each telecom circle [20]. The aggregate mobile subscriptions as of June 2016 is taken as the base value [19], which is then modulated by the rise in India's population between the period 2016–2036 [17]. The premise that every mobile subscriber can be a potential adopter of 4G LTE services in future, forms the basis of this assumption. A minimum subscription of 2% of the ultimate market potential is also assumed for the initial year (i.e., 2016) [20] .

Table 2. Regression results for Bass model parameter estimation

Adj. R^2	RMSE	p	q	m
0.9794	5.9781	0.009	0.45	986.3

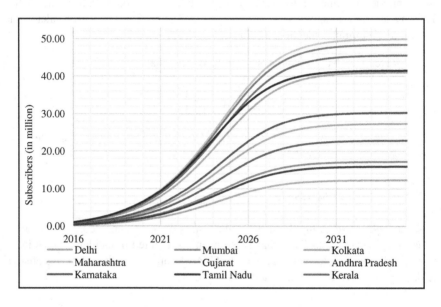

Fig. 2. 4G LTE adoption forecast using Bass model (sample of 12 circles)

We observe from Fig. 2 that the adoption trend rises with a positive slope till the year 2027. This signifies the sustained influence of strong imitative behavior among the potential adopters of 4G LTE services in India. The number of adoptions is also the maximum between this duration. The adoption trend begins to plummet after the year 2028, and by the year 2033 saturation sets in. This signals the end of late adoptions as well as the diffusion life-cycle of 4G LTE mobile services. The dynamics of 4G LTE diffusion in India, implies the need for vigorous investments and rapid provisioning of radio infrastructure during the initial years, so as to meet the growing customer demand for data-intensive services.

4.2 Link Budget and Coverage Calculations

We calculate the MAPL by taking the standard values of BTS specifications as inputs to the link budget model [3, 4]. Table 3 highlights the input values used in the link budget calculations. MAPL is later used as input to the radio propagation models, in order to evaluate the achievable cell-range under different frequency bands [13]. We can observe from Table 3, that the resultant MAPL value for our case is 144.45 dB (for both uplink and downlink). Further details related to the standard specifications for LTE link budget calculations have been explained in [18].

Table 3. Assumptions for link budget calculation

P_{Tx}	46	R_{SENS}	−106.45
G_{Tx}	18	IM	3
Lb	2	L_{cable}	20
$EIRP_{Tx}$	62	G_{Rx}	0
NB_{noise}	7	M	0
Th_{noise}	−104.45	G_{soft}	0
SINR	−9	MAPL	145.45

We use the BTS antenna height and the mobile station antenna height to evaluate the achievable cell-radius values for 700 MHz, 800 MHz, 1800 MHz, and 2100 MHz frequency bands. The input assumptions for BTS antenna height and mobile station antenna height are mentioned in Table 4 [3, 4]. The results of the cell radius calculations have been summarized in Table 5.

Table 4. Input parameters for radio propagation model

Carrier frequency (MHz)	BS height (h_b)	MS height (h_m)
700, 800, 1800, and 2100	30 m	1.5 m

Table 5. Cell-range calculation results

Frequency (MHz)	Urban (km)	Sub-urban (km)	Rural (km)
700	1.25	2.51	4.31
800	1.11	2.12	3.81
1800	0.707	1.16	2.49
2100	0.625	0.99	2.24

We can observe that the cell radius for 700 and 800 MHz bands are approximately 1.5 times that of 1800 MHz and 2 times that of 2100 MHz. These findings related to the achievable cell-radius under different frequency bands validate the argument about lower frequency bands (sub 1 GHz) being better in terms of cellular coverage than the higher frequency bands (1–2 GHz). The coverage results under each frequency band matches roughly with the results mentioned in [15], which in a way validates our proposed techno-economic model. The urban, suburban and the rural cell radius values are taken as inputs for calculating the achievable cellular coverage in Metro, Category A and B, and C circles, respectively. The number of sites required in each circle to ensure coverage has been highlighted in Fig. 3.

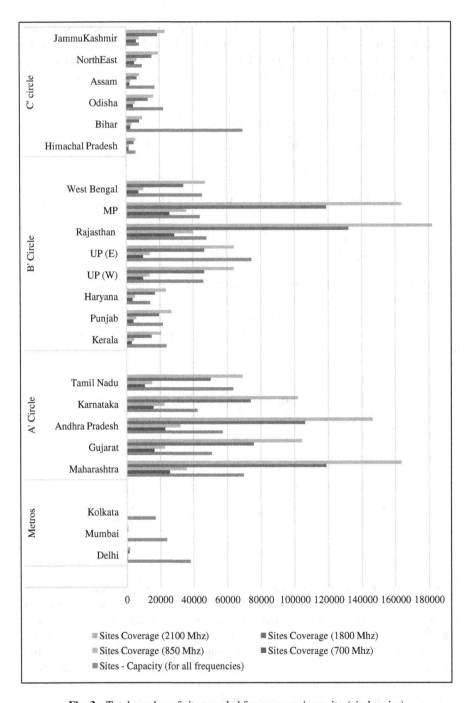

Fig. 3. Total number of sites needed for coverage/capacity (circle-wise)

4.3 Capacity-Tuned Cell-Dimensioning

Specific assumptions related to the size of available spectrum block, downlink data rate, LTE spectral efficiency, average loading, and busy hour constraints, are made, in order to calculate the potential capacity of each site. The assumptions are standard in the literature [3, 4] and have been summarized in Table 6. Considering that the data-rate and busy hour constraints remain the same, irrespective of the frequency deployed, we have used similar assumptions for all the four chosen frequency bands [18].

Table 6. Calculations for data volume capacity per site

Spectrum bandwidth (MHz)	2 × 5 MHz FDD LTE
Average downlink rate	20 Mbps
LTE downlink spectral capacity	2.7 bps/Hz
Average loading	50%
Busy hour % daily traffic	20%
Data volume capacity per site per month	5932.61 GB

The data volume demand has been modeled to increase exponentially from 12 GB/year/customer to 90 GB/year/customer, over the period of study [12, 18]. As evident from Table 6, under the given assumptions each site can handle an annual data volume demand of up to 7.12 TB/MHz. We then calculate the total number of sites required for meeting the capacity in each circle. The results have been highlighted in Fig. 3, which also provides the details on the number of sites required for coverage in each circle. However, if the operators wish to use conservative values, they may increment the data demand linearly, and recalculate the subsequent values accordingly.

4.4 TCO and Profitability Analysis

The input assumptions related to the cost aspects of site upgrade, spectrum license, OPEX per site and the discount rates, have been summarized in Table 7. These assumptions are used as inputs to the CAPEX, OPEX, and TCO calculations under each frequency band [3, 4]. WACC and savings rate for all the profitability related calculations are assumed at 15% and 8%, respectively [21]. The ARPU values are assumed at Rs. 300 for Metro circles, Rs. 250 for Category A and B circles, and Rs. 200 for Category C circles [20].

Table 7. Input for TCO calculation

LTE upgrade cost per site (million INR)	3
Fixed spectrum license charges	10% of the base price
Number of annual installments	18 equal installments
Average OPEX per site (in million INR)	Metro – 6, Category A – 3, Category B – 1, Category C – 0.6
Rate of Inflation (%)	3.78%
Spectrum Usage Charges as % of AGR	3%
WACC	15%
Savings rate	8%

Since CAPEX comprises of the major portion of the overall investment incurred by the operators, we highlight the CAPEX for an incumbent under each frequency band in Fig. 4. The projections of OPEX for an incumbent, over the study durations, has also been highlighted in Fig. 5. We can observe that both the CAPEX and OPEX incurred in the cases of 4G LTE deployment over higher frequency bands (1800 and 2100 MHz) are much higher when compared to the lower frequency bands (700 and 800 MHz). We also determine the TCO scenarios for both an incumbent operator and a new entrant. The TCO values for a new entrant is much lower as compared to an incumbent, given their low OPEX values due to the absence of legacy sites. For an incumbent, however, all the legacy sites existing in each circle need to be included in the TCO calculations [19]. The circle wise TCO calculations for an incumbent under each frequency band, have been highlighted in Figs. 6, 7, 8 and 9. We can observe from Figs. 6, 7, 8 and 9 that 700 and 800 MHz have much smaller TCO values as compared to the higher frequency bands (one-fourth of that for 1800 MHz and one-sixth of that for 2100 MHz, approximately).

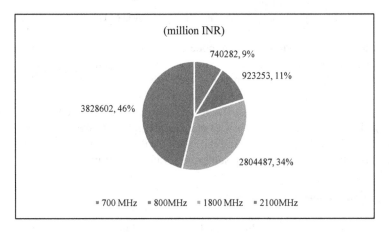

Fig. 4. CAPEX for an incumbent

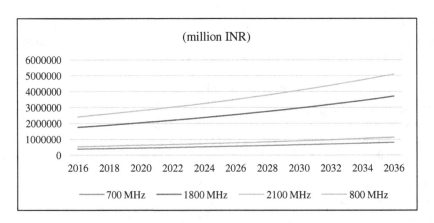

Fig. 5. OPEX projections for an incumbent operator

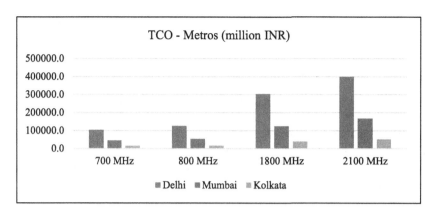

Fig. 6. TCO in metro circles

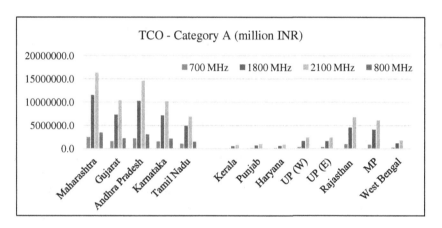

Fig. 7. TCO in cat. A circles

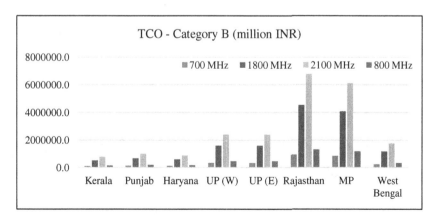

Fig. 8. TCO in cat. B circles

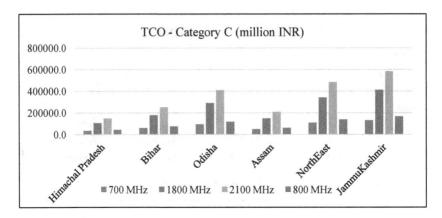

Fig. 9. TCO in cat. C circles

The highest TCO in the metro category is incurred in the Delhi circle, whereas Mumbai and Kolkata have TCOs similar to the circles in Category C, namely Himachal Pradesh, Assam, and Bihar. Circles in Category A have higher TCO compared to that in Category B. This is due to the fact that more number of sites are required for ensuring coverage and capacity in Category A circles, given their large geographical areas and higher subscriber volumes.

Figures 10 and 11 highlights the profitability aspects (MIRR) under different frequency bands, for a new entrant and an incumbent operator, respectively. We can infer from Fig. 10 that in terms of profitability, the circles in Category C come next to the Metro circles, followed by circles in Category B and Category A. We must note that Category C circles are already important from the perspective of the governmental mandate to ensure the last-mile coverage, since they include villages with sparse population. The reflected potential for profitability adds to the importance of Category C circles for the incumbents. Circles in Categories A and B remain highly important in terms of subscriber volume. However, with the assumed ARPU values the chances of

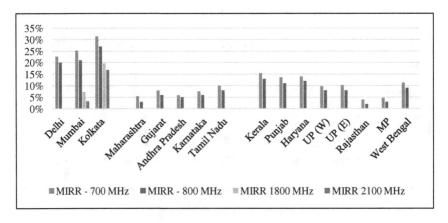

Fig. 10. Circle-wise profitability (MIRR %) over 20 year period for a new-entrant

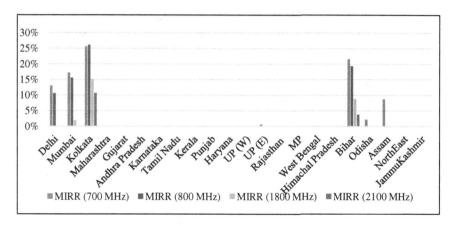

Fig. 11. Circle-wise profitability (MIRR %) over 20 year period for an incumbent

profitability are low in Category A as compared to Category B. Smaller circles in Category B hold out better promises in terms of profitability, as compared to the larger ones. For the new entrants, however, both 700 MHz and 800 MHz bands display potential for profitability across various circles, as evident from Fig. 10. However, very few circles show positive returns for 1800 MHz and 2100 MHz for the new entrant scenario.

4.5 Implications Related to Spectrum Acquisition by Incumbents

The profitability calculations done for the chosen frequency bands have implications for the spectrum acquisition strategies of an incumbent operator, especially for the recently made available spectrum in the 700 MHz frequency band by the GoI. The NPV for 4G LTE deployment over 700 MHz band for an incumbent has been summarized in Fig. 12. We posit that the acquisition of spectrum in a combination of circles belonging to Metro,

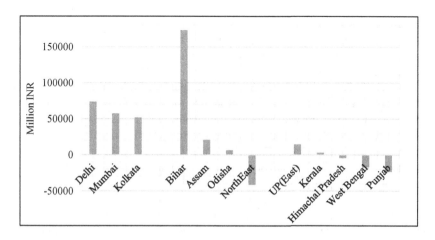

Fig. 12. NPV values over 20 years for incumbent operators in 700 MHz

Category C and Category B, is likely to prove profitable for an incumbent. Several possible subsets of circles from these categories may result in positive NPV scenarios, subject to certain minimum acquisitions in the Metro and Category C circles. The larger circles from Category A and B continue to remain important, though, given their potential for higher subscriber volume. Acquisition of spectrum in 700 MHz band is, therefore, highly recommended for incumbents for both the short and long terms advantages.

5 Conclusion

This work evaluates the technical and financial feasibility of provisioning 4G LTE services across the 22 telecom circles in India. This is done with the help of a techno-economic model that takes into consideration the future data volume demand of customers, achievable coverage and capacity over four frequency bands, and the costs involved in both the radio network infrastructure and spectrum acquisition. The frequency bands chosen for the evaluations include 700 MHz, 800 MHz, 1800 MHz, and 2100 MHz. These bands have been chosen from the three cohorts of frequency bands over which 4G LTE services are provisioned across the globe as well as in India. These cohorts include 700–900 MHz, 1800–1900 MHz, and 2100–2500 MHz. The choice is also driven by the fact that some of the bands in the lower frequency (viz. 700 MHz) are being considered for future spectrum auctions in countries such as India. The results of our evaluations have implications for both new entrants and the incumbent operators.

As expected, since the bands in the lower frequency (700 MHz and 800 MHz) have much higher cellular coverage compared to the bands in the higher frequency (1800 MHz and 2100 MHz), the CAPEX and the OPEX incurred over lower frequencies are much less than those over higher frequencies. For both new entrants and the incumbents, total TCO is much less for 700 and 800 MHz, as compared to 1800 MHz and 2100 MHz. The TCO for an incumbent over 700 and 800 MHz is approximately $1/4^{th}$ and $1/6^{th}$ as that of 1800 and 2100 MHz, respectively, while, for a new entrant, the TCO is approximately $1/7^{th}$ and $1/10^{th}$ that of 1800 MHz and 2100 MHz, respectively. Therefore, the potential of financial recoverability for provisioning 4G LTE services is higher over lower bands of frequency for both incumbent and the new entrant.

4G LTE deployment over lower frequency bands leads to lower TCO for all scenarios. Therefore, the potential for profitability is higher for operators already possessing sufficient spectrum holdings if they provision 4G LTE over lower frequency bands, especially 700 and 800 MHz. Specifically, telecom circles from Metro, Category C and Category B are found to be more profitable for 4G LTE provisioning over lower frequency bands. Operators who want to simultaneously increase the spectrum holdings and the customer subscription may acquire spectrum blocks from a combination of circles belonging to the Metro, Category C and Category B. In terms of subscriber volume the larger circles in Category B and C continue to remain important for every operator without compromising much on profitability.

In the light of these findings, the provisioning of 4G LTE services in India can be cost effective for operators considering deployment over lower frequency bands such as 700 MHz and 800 MHz. We also find that in all possible cases, a right combination of circles from Metro, Category C and Category B exhibits profitable returns for operators in the long term. The importance of bands in the lower frequencies is, therefore, likely to witness a rise in the future spectrum auctions in India.

Acknowledgments. This paper is an extended version of our earlier work presented in the 9th International Conference on Communication Systems and Networks (COMSNETS), Bangalore, India, held during January 4–8, 2017. We sincerely thank the reviewers and the participants of COMSNETS 2017 for their insightful comments and suggestions toward improving the paper.

References

1. Qiang, C.Z.-W., Rossotto, C.M., Kimura, K.: Economic impacts of broadband. In: Information and Communications for Development: Extending Reach Increasing Impact, pp. 35–50. The World Bank, Washington, D.C. (2009)
2. Ovando, C., Pérez, J., Moral, A.: LTE techno-economic assessment: the case of rural areas in Spain. Telecomm. Policy. **39**, 269–283 (2015)
3. Jha, A., Saha, D.: Techno-economic assessment of the potential for LTE based 4G mobile services in rural India. In: 2015 IEEE International Conference on Advanced Networks and Telecommuncations Systems (ANTS), pp. 28–33. IEEE, Kolkata (2015)
4. Jha, A., Saha, D.: Offering fourth generation (4G) mobile services in India: a techno-economic assessment from the operators' perspective. IIM Calcutta WPS No. 764 (2015). https://www.iimcal.ac.in/sites/all/files/pdfs/wps_764.pdf
5. Digital India: http://www.digitalindia.gov.in/content/vision-and-vision-areas
6. TRAI: On valuation and reserve price of spectrum in 700 MHz, 800 MHz, 900 MHz, 1800 MHz, 2100 MHz, 2300 MHz and 2500 MHz bands (2016). http://www.trai.gov.in. Accessed 10 Sept 2016
7. TRAI: Recommendations on valuation and reserve price of spectrum in 700 MHz, 800 MHz, 900 MHz, 1800 MHz, 2100 MHz, 2300 MHz and 2500 MHz bands (2016). Accessed 10 Sept 2016
8. Rao, A.M., Weber, A., Gollamudi, S., Soni, R.: LTE and HSPA+: revolutionary and evolutionary solutions for global mobile broadband. Bell Labs Tech. J. **13**(4), 7–34 (2009)
9. Bass, F.M.: A new product growth for model consumer durables. Man. Sci. **5**, 216–278 (1969)
10. Jha, A., Saha, D.: Why is 700 MHz band a good proposition for provisioning pan-India 4G LTE services? In: 9th International Conference on Communication Systems & Networks, pp. 1–8. IEEE, Bangalore (2017)
11. Mölleryd, B., Markendahl, J., Mäkitalo, Ö.: Impact assessment and business implications of options for allocation of spectrum in the 800 and 900 MHz band. In: 18th Biennial Conference of the International Telecommunications Society, pp. 1–23 (2010)
12. Nokia: Mobile broadband with HSPA and LTE – capacity and cost aspects (2014). http://resources.alcatel-lucent.com/asset/200183. Accessed 07 Aug 2016
13. GSMA: 4G connections hit one billion as mobile broadband momentum extends to the developing world (2016). http://www.gsma.com/newsroom/press-release/4g-connections-hit-one-billion-as-mobile-broadband-momentum-extends-to-the-developing-world/
14. Telecom, L.: Comparison of the performance of 700 MHz versus 2 GHz networks for PPDR services (2013)
15. Naseri, B.M., Elliott, G.: The diffusion of online shopping in Australia: comparing the bass, logistic and Gompertz growth models. J. Mark. Anal. **1**, 49–60 (2013)

16. Srinivasan, V., Mason, C.H.: Nonlinear least squares estimation of new product diffusion models. Mark. Sci. **5**, 169–178 (1986)
17. Division, U.N.P.: The World Bank - Annual Population Growth Data (2016)
18. Holma, H., Toskala, A.: LTE for UMTS: OFDMA and SC-FDMA based radio access (2009)
19. TRAI: The Indian telecom services performance indicators (2015). http://www.trai.gov.in. Accessed 10 Sept 2016
20. Indiastat: Indiastat database. http://www.indiastat.com/default.aspx
21. Ernst and Young: India's cost of capital: a survey (2014). Accessed 21 Nov 2016

Modeling Request Patterns in VoD Services with Recommendation Systems

Samarth Gupta and Sharayu Moharir$^{(\boxtimes)}$

Department of Electrical Engineering,
Indian Institute of Technology Bombay, Mumbai 400076, India
samarthg@andrew.cmu.edu, sharayum@ee.iitb.ac.in

Abstract. Video on Demand (VoD) services like Netflix and YouTube account for ever increasing fractions of Internet traffic. It is estimated that this fraction will cross 80% in the next three years. Most popular VoD services have recommendation engines which recommend videos to users based on their viewing history, thus introducing time-correlation in user requests. Understanding and modeling this time-correlation in user requests is critical for network traffic engineering. The primary goal of this work is to use empirically observed properties of user requests to model the effect of recommendation engines on request patterns in VoD services. We propose a Markovian request model to capture the time-correlation in user requests and show that our model is consistent with the observations of existing empirical studies.

Most large-scale VoD services deliver content to users via a distributed network of servers as serving users requests via geographically co-located servers reduces latency and network bandwidth consumption. The content replication policy, i.e., determining which contents to cache on the servers is a key resource allocation problem for VoD services. Recent studies show that low start-up delay is a key Quality of Service (QoS) requirement of users of VoD services. This motivates the need to pre-fetch (fetch before contents are requested) and cache content likely to be requested in the near future. Since pre-fetching leads to an increase in the network bandwidth usage, we use our Markovian model to explore the trade-offs and feasibility of implementing recommendation based pre-fetching.

1 Introduction

Internet usage patterns are shifting towards content distribution and sharing with Video-on-demand (VoD) services like Netflix [21] and YouTube [27] accounting for over 50% of all Internet traffic. This fraction is expected to cross 80% by 2019 [7]. Most popular VoD services provide recommendations to users which heavily influence their viewing patterns. More specifically, recommendations lead to correlation in the videos requested by a user across time. The primary goal of this work is to model the viewing patterns of users of VoD services with recommendation engines. An accurate model of usage patterns is a crucial ingredient

© Springer International Publishing AG 2017
N. Sastry and S. Chakraborty (Eds.): COMSNETS 2017, LNCS 10340, pp. 307–334, 2017.
DOI: 10.1007/978-3-319-67235-9_18

in the design of resource allocation algorithms which effectively manage Internet traffic and ensure high Quality of Service (QoS) to the users.

Meeting the QoS demands of users is critical for a VoD service to retain and expand its customer base. A recent study by Akamai [14] found that users start leaving if a video takes more than two seconds to start streaming. Moreover, for each additional second of start-up delay, the rate of abandonments increases by approximately 5.8%. The probability of a user returning to the VoD service within one day after watching a failed video is 8% versus 11% after watching a normal one. Evidently, frequent start-up delays can lead to a loss of customers, thus reducing the revenue of the VoD service.

Most large-scale VoD services serve their users via Content Delivery Networks (CDNs) which have multiple servers/caches with storage and service capabilities spread across the world. Efficient use of the available storage resources, e.g., serving user requests via geographically co-located servers can enhance the QoS for the user. More specifically, a frequent cause of start-up delay is that videos requested by users are not available on geographically co-located servers, and have to be fetched from other servers *after* they are requested. The delay in start-up is caused by the large geographical/network distance between the users and servers which cache the requested content.

The goal of reducing start-up delay motivates caching policies that are aggressive in adapting the content stored on the local servers in order to minimize the probability of delayed start-up. One possible solution is to pre-fetch (fetch before videos are requested) and cache videos that are likely to be requested in the near future [9,13,15,17,22]. Since pre-fetching leads to an increase in the bandwidth consumption of the CDN, there is a trade-off between bandwidth usage of the network and the quality of service provided to the users. We explore this trade-off in this work.

1.1 Contributions

The contributions of this work can be summarized as follows.

Modeling the request process: In a preliminary version of this work [11], we propose a Markovian model which captures the time-correlation in user requests in VoD services due to the presence of recommendation systems. We show that our model is consistent with empirically observed properties of request patterns in such VoD services [5,6,16,29]. A limitation of this model is that it imposes the constraint that the recommendations are symmetric (i.e., Video A recommends Video B implies Video B recommends Video A). In this work, we generalize our model to allow for non-symmetric recommendation relationships.

Performance evaluation of caching policies: We study a caching policy which pre-fetches videos likely to be requested in the future in order to minimize the chance of delayed start-up. More specifically, while a user is watching a video, our policy pre-fetches a pre-determined number of the corresponding recommended videos to the local cache, thus reducing the probability that the next request from this user experiences any start-up delay.

As discussed above, pre-fetching content reduces start-up delay, but, leads to increased bandwidth consumption. Via simulations, we explore this trade-off as a function of the relative costs of bandwidth consumption and delayed start-up. Our results characterize when pre-fetching content can lead to a reduction in the overall cost of service, even with the increased bandwidth usage.

1.2 Organization

The rest of the paper is organized as follows. In Sect. 2, we discuss existing literature on empirical studies of viewing patterns in VoDs with recommendation systems. In Sect. 3, we define our Markovian request model and discuss its properties. We describe our CDN setting in Sect. 4 and discuss the proposed caching scheme in Sect. 5. In Sect. 6, we evaluate the performance of the proposed policy via simulations. We present our conclusions in Sect. 8.

2 Literature Review

2.1 Request Patterns in VoDs with Recommendations

We first summarize the observations of empirical studies which study the effect of recommendation systems on the users' viewing patterns [5,6,16,29]. These studies have been conducted either by crawling the YouTube webpage [29], or via the Youtube API [29], or by collecting browsing data from university networks [16,29]. The studies represent the relationship between videos using a directed graph, where nodes represent videos and each node has a directed edge to all the corresponding recommended videos. They focus on the properties of the graph [5], the effect of the placement/rank of a video in the recommendation list of another video [16,29], and the effect of recommendations on the overall video popularity profile [6].

Small-World Recommendation Graph. The key insight obtained in [5] is that the graph representing the YouTube recommendation network is small-world. We use the following definitions to formally define small-world networks.

(i) *Characteristic Path Length:* The characteristic path length of a network is defined as the mean distance between two nodes, averaged over all pairs of nodes.
(ii) *Clustering Coefficient:* The clustering coefficient of a network is defined as the average fraction of pairs of neighbors of a node that are also neighbors of each other.

Small-world networks are a class of networks that are highly clustered (high clustering coefficient), like regular lattices, yet have small characteristic path lengths, like random graphs [26]. Compared to random graphs with the same average degree, small-world networks are characterized by high clustering coefficients and similar path lengths. In [5], the authors use these two characteristics to conclude that the YouTube recommendation graph is small-world.

Content Popularity Profiles. It has been observed that content popularity for VoD services *without* recommendation systems is heavy-tailed and can often be well-fitted with the Zipf distribution defined as follows: the popularity of the ith most popular video is proportional to $i^{-\beta}$, where β is a positive constant called the Zipf's parameter. Typical values of β for VoD services lie between 0.6 and 2 [1].

Empirical studies have concluded that content popularity for VoD services *with* recommendation systems, e.g., YouTube, can be well-fitted with the Zipf distribution for the popular videos and popularity for the less popular videos decreases faster than the rate predicted by the Zipf distribution [6].

Click Through Rate. The Click Through Rate (CTR) for position r in the recommendation list of Video i is defined as the fraction of times a user requests the video in position r in the recommendation list of Video i right after watching Video i. In [29], the authors found that the mean of the CTR follows the Zipf distribution as a function of r. In addition, Fig. 3 in [16] shows that the CDF of the CTR is concave.

Chain Count. Chain count is defined as the average number of consecutive videos a user requests by clicking on videos in the recommendation list before requesting a video which is not the list of recommended videos for the video currently being watched. For YouTube, the chain count is estimated to be between 1.3 and 2.4 in [16].

Degree Distribution. The degree distribution of the recommendation graph has been found to follow the power law. More specifically, the number of nodes with degree k is approximately proportional to k^{-3} [23].

2.2   Pre-fetching Based Caching Schemes

Caching schemes which use pre-fetching have been shown to be beneficial for TV-on-demand and VoD services [9,13,15,17,22]. To the best of our knowledge, none of the existing works have attempted to model the request arrival process for VoD services with recommendation systems, and instead, use trace data to evaluate the performance of the proposed policies. In addition, another key difference between the existing literature and this work is that we study the trade-off between bandwidth usage and quality of service, while most of the existing works (except [9]) focus only on the improvement in quality of service (cache hit-ratio) by pre-fetching content.

In [13], the authors use trace data from a campus network gateway to analyze the performance of pre-fetching content to serve YouTube requests. A key observation in [13] that it is not necessary to pre-fetch complete videos to avoid start-up delays. Fetching a fraction of the video is often sufficient as the rest of the video can be fetched while the users' watch the initial part of the video.

In [15], the authors compare the performance of pre-fetching+caching and the Least Recent Used (LRU) caching scheme which does not pre-fetch content, for Hulu (a VoD service) on a university network. In [9], trace data from a Swedish TV service provider is used to evaluate the benefits of pre-fetching episodes of shows that a specific user is watching in order to reduce latency. In [22], the authors study the setting where the requests arrive according to a known Markov process. They propose an MDP based pre-fetching scheme and prove its optimality. Although our work also assumes that the underlying request process is Markovian, unlike [22], our caching policy works without the knowledge of the transition probabilities. This is an important distinction, since for VoD services like YouTube with massive content catalogs, content popularity is often time-varying and unknown [20]. In [17], the authors study a pre-fetching and caching scheme for HTTP-based adaptive video streaming. They propose a pre-fetching and caching scheme to maximize the cache hit-ratio assuming the bandwidth between the local cache and the central server is limited.

3 Our Request Model

In this section, we discuss our model for the request process for VoD services with recommendation systems.

3.1 Model Definition

We construct a directed graph $G(V, E)$, where the set V consists of all the videos offered by the VoD service and an edge $e = \{i, j\} \in E$ implies that Video j is one of the recommended videos for Video i. We then assign weights to edges. Each user's request process is a random walk on this weighted graph and therefore, the request arrival process is Markovian and can be completely described by a transition probability matrix.

We use a subset of the properties discussed in Sect. 2.1 to construct this matrix and verify that the remaining properties discussed in Sect. 2.1 are satisfied by our Markovian model.

Motivated by the fact the empirical studies like [5] have found that this graph is small-world, and the degree distribution follows the power law [23] we use the Barabasi-Albert model [2] to generate a random small-world graph. Refer to Fig. 1 for a formal definition of the Barabasi-Albert model.

Since the Barabasi-Albert model generates a undirected graph, we replace each edge by two directed edges to obtain a directed graph on the set of videos. This means that if v_i recommends v_j, our model assumes that v_j also recommends v_i. This is motivated by the fact that YouTube uses the relatedness score [8] for each pair of videos to determine homepage recommendations. The relatedness score of two videos is proportional to the number of times two videos are co-watched in a session. Therefore, by definition, if v_i is closely related to v_j, v_j is closely related to v_i.

1: Initialize: Generate a connected graph of m nodes $(v_1, v_2, ..., v_m)$. Let $v = m + 1$.
2: Introduce a new node n_v which connects to m existing nodes. These m edges from n_v are added in an sequential manner as follows. The probability that each of the m edges from the new node go to an existing node n_i is given by p_i such that

$$p_i = \frac{K_i}{\sum_j K_j},$$

where K_i is the current degree of node n_i.
3: $v = v + 1$. If $v < n$, goto Step 2.

Fig. 1. Barabasi-Albert Model – *an algorithm to generate a random small-world graph with a degree distribution following the power law.*

Users can request videos via multiple sources. We divide them into two categories:

- The first set of requests come via the recommendations made by VoD service when the user is watching a video. We introduce a quantity P_{cont}, defined as the probability that a user requests a recommended video after he/she finishes watching the current video. Formally, after watching a video, each user requests one of the recommended videos with probability P_{cont} independent of all previous requests. By definition, the expected chain count (defined in Sect. 2.1) is given by $1/(1 - P_{cont})$. The value of P_{cont} should be between 0.2 and 0.7 to be consistent with the chain count values observed in [16].
- The second set of requests come from all other sources on the Internet including the VoD homepage, the user's social networking page, etc. To model the second type of requests, we add a dummy node n_0 to the graph G. This dummy node represents all other sources of requests and is connected to all other nodes in the G via two directed edges.

The next step is to assign transition probabilities corresponding to each edge in this directed graph $G(V, E)$. Let $P_{i,j}$ be the probability a node makes the transition from node n_i to node n_j.

- By definition, $P_{i,j} = 0$ if $\{i, j\} \notin E$.
- Recall that P_{cont} is the probability that a user requests one of the recommended videos after watching the current video. If not, we assume that the user goes to node n_0 which represents all other sources of video requests. Therefore, by definition, $P_{i,0} = 1 - P_{cont}, \forall i > 0$.
- Motivated by the fact that for VoD services without recommendations, content popularity follows the Zipf distribution (as discussed in Sect. 2.1), we set the value of $P_{0,j} \propto j^{-\beta}$ for a positive constant β called the Zipf parameter. Typical values of β for VoD services lie between 0.6 and 2 [1].
- To assign transition probabilities to edges between a video and its recommended videos, we use the distance between two videos as a measure

of similarity in the content of the two videos. For each $i, j \in E$, $P_{i,j} \propto P_{cont} \cdot (D(i,j))^{-\kappa}$, where $D(i,j) = |i - j|$ and κ is a positive constant. We use the $P_{i,j}$s to determine the order in which the recommended videos are presented to the user. For Video i, we assume that the recommended videos are ordered in decreasing order $P_{i,j}$s.

Remark 1. Our model is characterized by five parameters, namely, the total number of videos n, the size of the graph used in the first step of the Albert-Barabasi model (Fig. 1) m, the Zipf parameter β, the probability that a user requests one of the recommended videos after watching the current video P_{cont}, and κ.

Remark 2. Another way to assign transition probabilities from a video to its recommended videos is to pick a permutation of the set of recommended videos and assign transition probabilities according to the Zipf law. By construction, this Markov chain will satisfy the property that the mean CTR follows the Zipf distribution and therefore will be consistent with properties observed in Sect. 2.1. Unlike the model we propose, in this construction, the probability of requesting the ith ranked recommendation is the same across all videos.

3.2   Properties

Our model uses the empirically observed properties that the recommendation graph is small-world, its degree distribution follows the power law, content popularity in the absence of recommendations follows the Zipf distribution, and the chain count is between 1.3 and 2.4. In this section, we verify that our Markovian model satisfies the remaining properties discussed in Sect. 2.1.

Content Popularity Profile. The popularity of a video is the fraction of total requests for the video. Since the requests are generated by a finite state irreducible Discrete Time Markov Chain (DTMC), this is equal to the steady state probability of requesting the video. We therefore compute the content popularity profile of our model by calculating the stationary distribution of the Markov Chain. Figure 2 illustrates the content popularity profile for a system consisting of 2000 videos as a function of the Zipf Parameter β. Figure 3 shows how final distribution varies with P_{cont}.

We see that, as desired, the content popularity profile follows the Zipf distribution for the popular videos and decreases faster than as predicted by the Zipf distribution for the unpopular videos. We thus conclude that the content popularity profile for our model is consistent with the observations in [6].

Click Through Rate. As discussed in Sect. 2.1, the median Click Through Rate (CTR) follows the Zipf distribution. To verify this for our model, we compute the probability of requesting the rth ranked recommended video for each video. We plot the median of this quantity across all videos as a function of r in Fig. 4. We see that the median CTR can be approximated by the Zipf distribution. Our model is therefore consistent with the observations in [29]. Varying κ allows us to change the slope of median CTR.

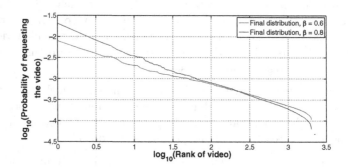

Fig. 2. Content popularity profile for our model with $m = 20$, $P_{cont} = 0.4$, Number of videos $(n) = 2000$ and $\kappa = 0.8$.

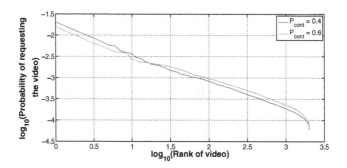

Fig. 3. Content popularity profile for our model with $m = 20$, Zipf parameter $(\beta) = 0.8$, Number of videos $(n) = 2000$ and $\kappa = 0.8$.

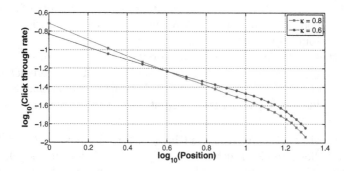

Fig. 4. Median Click through rate (CTR) as a function of position of video in the recommendation list for Number of videos $(n) = 2000$, $m = 20$, Zipf Parameter $\beta = 0.8$, and $P_{cont} = 0.4$.

CDF of Click Through Rate. As mentioned in Sect. 2.1, in [16], the authors compute the Cumulative Distribution Function (CDF) of the Click Through Rate (CTR). To evaluate the CDF, we compute the CTR for the rth ranked video in the recommendation list as follows:

$$\text{CTR}(r) = \sum_{i=1}^{n} \pi(i) \times P_{i,r^{\text{th}} \text{ ranked recommended video}}.$$

We plot the CDF of the CTR as a function of the position r in Fig. 5. Qualitatively, Fig. 5 shows the same trend as observed in Fig. 3 in [16].

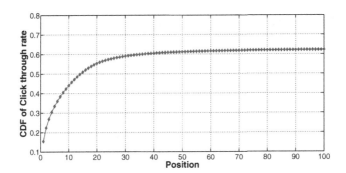

Fig. 5. CDF of CTR vs. position in recommendation list for Number of videos $(n) =$ 2000, $m = 20$, Zipf parameter $\beta = 0.8$, $\kappa = 0.8$, and $P_{cont} = 0.4$.

4   CDN Setting

We consider a Content Delivery Network (CDN) consisting of a central server which stores the entire catalog of contents offered by the VoD service, assisted

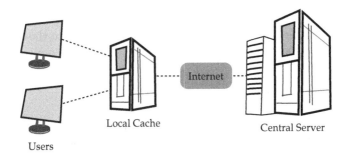

Fig. 6. An illustration of a Content Delivery Network (CDN) with a central server, a local cache and two users.

by a local cache with limited storage capacity (Fig. 6). Content can be fetched from the central server and replicated on the local cache to serve user requests. The motivation behind such a network architecture is to serve most of the user requests via the local cache, thus reducing the load on the network backbone, and therefore reducing the overall bandwidth consumption of the network. In addition, the local cache can serve user requests with a lower start-up delay due to their geographical/network proximity.

4.1 Request Model

We assume that the local cache serves u users concurrently and the arrival requests from each user are generated i.i.d. according to the Markovian process described in Sect. 3. We assume that the service time of each request is an Exponential random variable with mean 1.

4.2 Cost Model

We divide the cost of serving requests into two parts:

(i) Cost of Bandwidth Usage: Each time a video is fetched from the central server and replicated on the local cache, the CDN pays a fetching cost denoted by C_{Fetch}.
(ii) Cost of Delayed Startup: Each time the requested content is not available in the local cache and has to be fetched from the central server *after* the request is made, the CDN pays an additional start-up delay cost denoted by C_{Delay}. This captures the cost of deterioration in the quality of service provided to the users.

Without loss of generality, we normalize $C_{\text{Fetch}} = 1$ and let $C_{\text{Delay}} = \gamma \times C_{\text{Fetch}}$, where γ is the start-up delay penalty.

Let $\text{Cost}(t)$ denote the total cost of serving requests that arrive before time t, $F(t)$ be the number of fetches from the central server to the local cache made before time t and $D(t)$ be the number of delayed start-ups by time t. Then we have that,

$$\text{Cost}(t) = F(t) + \gamma \times D(t).$$

The goal is to design content caching policies to minimize the total cost of serving user requests.

5 Caching Policies

We propose a caching policy which uses the fact that user requests are being generated according to a Markov process to determine which contents to cache. We refer to this policy as the PreFetch policy. The key idea of the PreFetch policy is to pre-fetch the top r recommended videos as soon as a user requests a specific video, thus reducing the chance that the next request from this user will have to face any start-up delay. The policy uses the Least Recently Used (LRU) metric to purge stored content in order to make space to store the fetched content.

We use the following definitions in the formal definition of the PreFetch policy:

Definition 1.

- A video is said to be in use *if it is being used to serve an active request.*
- A video is referred to as a tagged video *if it is one of the top r (where r is a pre-determined integer ≥ 1) recommendations for any one the videos currently in use.*

Refer to Fig. 7 for a formal definition of the PreFetch policy.

1: **Input:** An integer $r \geq 1$.
2: **Initialize:** Set of cached videos, $C = \phi$, set of tagged videos, $T = \phi$, set of videos in use, $U = \phi$, set of cached videos currently not in use or tagged, $V = C \setminus (T \cup U)$.
3: On arrival (request for Video i) **do**,
4: **if** Video $i \notin C$, **then**
5:     **if** $|C| <$ cache size, **then**
6:         fetch Video i; $C = C \cup$ Video i
7:     **else if** $V \neq \phi$, **then**
8:         fetch Video i; replace the Least Recently Used (LRU) video in V with Video i.
9:     **else**
10:         remove a video $\in T$, chosen uniformly at random, and replace it with Video i.
11:     **end if**
12:     Update C, V, T and U.
13: **end if**
14: **if** top r recommendations of Video i not in cache, **then**
15:     pre-fetch missing recommended videos,
16:     **for** each pre-fetched video **do**
17:         **if** $|C| <$ cache size, **then**
18:             add video to the cache, update C,
19:         **else if** $V \neq \phi$, **then**
20:             replace LRU video in V with fetched video,
21:         **else**
22:             remove a video $\in T$, chosen uniformly at random, and replace it with fetched video.
23:         **end if**
24:         Update C, V, T and U.
25:     **end for**
26: **end if**

Fig. 7. PreFetch – *a caching policy which adapts the content stored on cache to ensure that the top r recommended videos for the videos currently being viewed are pre-fetched to the cache in order to reduce the chance of start-up delay for the next request.*

Remark 3. We assume that the storage capacity of the local cache is large enough to store more videos than the number of users it serves simultaneously.

Remark 4. The PreFetch caching policy can be implemented without the knowledge of the relative popularity of various videos. The only information required to implement the PreFetch policy is the list of recommended videos corresponding to each video in the catalog, which is always known to the VoD service.

As discussed in [13], a possible generalization of the PreFetch policy is to pre-fetch only a fraction of the recommended videos instead of pre-fetching entire videos, and fetching the remaining part of the video only after the request is made. If there exists an $\alpha < 1$ such that while the user watches the first α fraction of the video, the remaining $(1 - \alpha)$ fraction of the video can be pre-fetched, the CDN can provide uninterrupted service to the user without any start-up delay by pre-fetching only the first α fraction of the video.

In the next section, we compare the performance of our PreFetch policy with the popular Least Recently Used (LRU) caching policy. The LRU policy has been traditionally used for caching [25] and has been widely studied for decades. Refer to Fig. 8 for a formal definition of the LRU policy.

1: On arrival (request for Video i) **do,**
2: **if** Video i not present in the cache, **then**
3:     fetch Video i; replace the Least Recently Used (LRU) cached video with Video i.
4: **end if**

Fig. 8. Least Recently Used (LRU) – *a caching policy.*

6   Simulation Results

In this section, we compare the performance of the LRU policy and the PreFetch policy. Our goal is to understand if exploiting the time correlation between requests from a user by pre-fetching recommended videos can lead to better performance. In addition, we also study how the performance of the two caching policies depends on the request arrival process and various system parameters like number of users using a local server (u), size of cache, fraction of video pre-fetched (α).

Requests arrive according to the request model discussed in Sect. 3. We assume that the VoD service has a content catalog consisting of 1000 videos. We use the Albert-Barabasi model (Fig. 1) to generate the recommendation graph with $m = 20$. We fix $\kappa = 0.8$ (defined in Sect. 3) for all the results presented in this section. We assume that the service time of each request is an Exponential random variable with mean of one time unit. We assume all videos are of unit size. For each set of system parameters, we simulate the system for 10^5 time units.

6.1   Cost vs. Startup Delay Penalty (γ)

In Fig. 9, we compare the performance of the PreFetch policy and the LRU policy as a function of the Start-up delay penalty (γ). Recall that P_{cont} is the probability that the next video requested by the user is one of the recommended videos. The PreFetch policy pre-fetches the top r (≥ 1) recommendations of a video from the central server to the cache the moment a video is requested, thus ensuring that there is no start-up delay if the user requests one the top r recommended videos. In addition, the total cost of service is the sum of the cost of bandwidth usage and cost due to startup delay. In Fig. 9, for each value of Start-up delay penalty (γ), we use the empirically optimized value of r which leads to the lowest cost of service. The optimal value of the number of recommendations to pre-fetch (r) increases with increase in Start-up delay penalty (γ) as shown in Fig. 10.

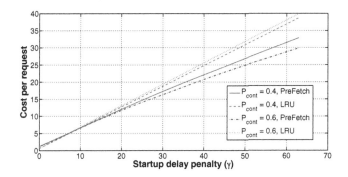

Fig. 9. Cost vs. Start-up delay penalty (γ) for a system with Number of videos = 1000, $m = 20$, Zipf parameter (β) = 0.8, Cache size = 200 and 1 User. As γ increases, PreFetch outperforms the LRU policy.

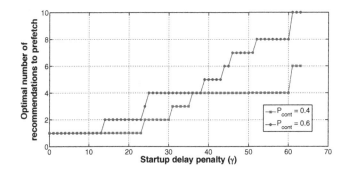

Fig. 10. The optimal number of recommendations to pre-fetch (r) vs. Start-up delay penalty (γ) for a system with Number of videos = 1000, $m = 20$, Zipf parameter (β) = 0.8, Cache size = 200 and 1 User. The optimal number of recommendations to pre-fetch (r) increases with start-up delay penalty γ.

We observe that for low values of Start-up delay penalty (γ), LRU outperforms the PreFetch policy. As the Start-up delay penalty (γ) increases, PreFetch outperforms the LRU policy. This illustrates the tradeoff between bandwidth usage, i.e., number of pre-fetches and quality of service, i.e., reducing startup delay.

6.2   Cost vs. Number of Users (u)

In Figs. 11 and 12, we compare the performance of the two policies where the value of r used by the PreFetch policy is empirically optimized for each value of u and γ. We see that as the number of users increases from 1 to 5, there is a sharp drop in the cost for both LRU and PreFetch policy. Since all the users access videos according to the same Markov process, when there are multiple users accessing the cache, the probability that the popular videos and their top recommendations are always present in the cache increases. This reduces the number of cache misses and the number of pre-fetches for the most popular videos, thus reducing the overall cost of service.

As seen in Fig. 11, when the Startup delay cost γ is low, the LRU caching policy outperforms the (optimized) PreFetch policy for all values of u. For $\gamma = 63$ (Fig. 12), the PreFetch policy outperforms the LRU caching policy. Our simulations shows that for $\gamma \leq 11$, the optimal number of recommendations (r) to cache is 1. The optimal value of r is between 4 and 6 for $\gamma = 63$.

Figure 13 illustrates that cache hit rates are higher for the PreFetch policy as compared to that of the LRU policy for all values of u and γ considered.

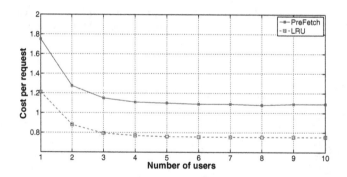

Fig. 11. Cost vs. Number of users for a system with Number of videos = 1000, Startup delay penalty (γ) = 1, Zipf parameter (β) = 0.8, $P_{cont} = 0.4$ and Cache size = 200. LRU outperforms the PreFetch policy.

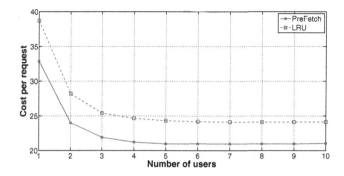

Fig. 12. Cost vs. Number of users for a system with Number of videos = 1000, Startup delay penalty (γ) = 63, Zipf parameter (β) = 0.8, P_{cont} = 0.4 and Cache size = 200. The PreFetch policy outperforms the LRU policy.

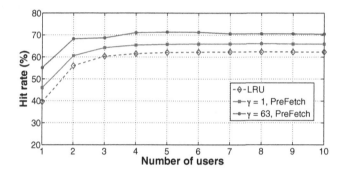

Fig. 13. Hit rate vs. Number of users for a system with Number of videos = 1000, Zipf parameter (β) = 0.8, P_{cont} = 0.4 and Cache size = 200. Cache hit rates are significantly improved by using PreFetch scheme for all values of u and γ.

6.3   Cost vs. P_{cont}

Recall that P_{cont} denotes the probability that the next video is accessed via the recommendation list. We vary the value of P_{cont} between 0.2 and 0.6 (to be consistent with the observations in [16]) and evaluate the performance of LRU and optimal PreFetch policy for $\gamma = 11$ and $\gamma = 63$.

In Fig. 14, we see that LRU outperforms the (optimized) PreFetch policy for low values of P_{cont} and PreFetch outperforms LRU as P_{cont} increases. Since increasing the value of P_{cont} increases the probability that the next video is accessed via the recommendation list, we conclude that if the Startup delay cost is not very high ($\gamma = 11$), for low values of P_{cont}, the excess bandwidth usage due to pre-fetching outweighs the benefits of reducing startup delay.

Figure 15 illustrates that the PreFetch policy outperforms LRU for $\gamma = 63$ for all values of P_{cont} considered. In addition, the relative performance of PreFetch policy improves with respect to LRU policy with increase in P_{cont}.

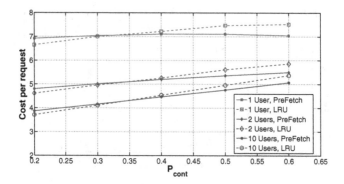

Fig. 14. Cost vs. P_{cont} for a system with Number of videos = 1000, Startup delay penalty (γ) = 11, Zipf parameter (β) = 0.8 and Cache size = 200. For low values of P_{cont}, the excess bandwidth usage due to pre-fetching outweighs the benefits of reducing startup delay, and for higher values of P_{cont}, pre-fetching leads to reduced cost of service.

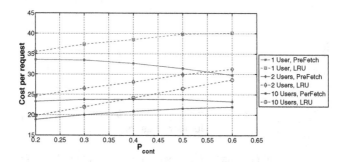

Fig. 15. Cost vs. P_{cont} for a system with Number of videos = 1000, Startup delay cost (γ) = 63, Zipf parameter (β) = 0.8 and Cache size = 200. The PreFetch policy outperforms LRU for all values of P_{cont} considered.

In Fig. 16, we plot the optimal value of r as a function of P_{cont}. We conclude that with increasing P_{cont}, it is beneficial to pre-fetch more videos from the recommendation list.

Figures 17 and 18, corresponding to $\gamma = 11$ and $\gamma = 63$ respectively, illustrate that cache hit rate is higher for the PreFetch policy as compared to the LRU policy.

6.4   Cost vs. Zipf Parameter (β)

As discussed in Fig. 2, increasing the value of the Zipf parameter β makes the overall content popularity more lopsided, i.e., a smaller fraction of the videos account for the same fraction of the total requests. Therefore, the performance for both the LRU policy and the PreFetch policy improves with increasing β (Fig. 19), as the small pool of popular videos are available in the local cache

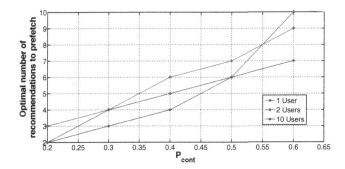

Fig. 16. Optimal number of recommendations to pre-fetch (r) vs. P_{cont} for a system with Number of videos = 1000, Startup delay penalty $(\gamma) = 63$, Zipf parameter $(\beta) = 0.8$ and Cache size = 200. The optimal number of recommendations to pre-fetch increases with P_{cont}.

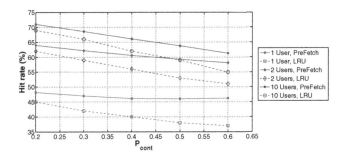

Fig. 17. Hit rate vs. P_{cont} for a system with Number of videos = 1000, Startup delay penalty $(\gamma) = 11$, Zipf parameter $(\beta) = 0.8$ and Cache size = 200. The PreFetch policy has higher hit rate and the difference between the hit rates of the PreFetch policy and the LRU policy increases with increasing P_{cont}.

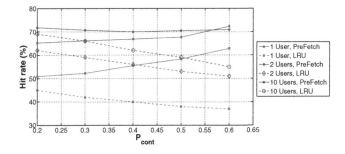

Fig. 18. Hit rate vs. P_{cont} for a system with Number of videos = 1000, Startup delay penalty $(\gamma) = 63$, Zipf parameter $(\beta) = 0.8$ and Cache size = 200. The PreFetch policy has higher hit rate and the difference between the hit rates of the PreFetch policy and the LRU policy increases with increasing P_{cont}.

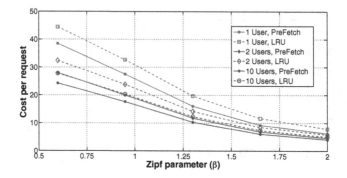

Fig. 19. Cost vs. Zipf parameter (β) for a system with Number of videos = 1000, Start-up delay penalty (γ) = 63, P_{cont} = 0.4 and Cache size = 200. The performance of both the LRU policy and the PreFetch policy improve with increasing β.

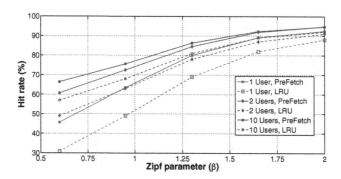

Fig. 20. Hit rate vs. Zipf parameter (β) for a system with Number of videos = 1000, Start-up delay penalty (γ) = 63, P_{cont} = 0.4 and Cache size = 200. The hit rates for both the LRU policy and the PreFetch policy improve with increasing β.

more often for both policies. We focus on β values between 0.6 and 2 since typical values of β lie in that range for most VoD services [4, 10, 12, 18, 19, 24, 28]. For Startup delay penalty $\gamma > 11$, the PreFetch policy outperforms the LRU policy for all β between 0.6 and 2. Optimal r for $\gamma = 63$ falls between 4 and 6 for these values of β. Figure 20 illustrates that cache hit rates increase with increasing β.

6.5   Cost vs. Cache Size

We expect the performance of all policies to improve with the increase in cache size. In Figs. 21 and 22, we see that the PreFetch policy performs considerably better than the LRU policy for all cache sizes considered.

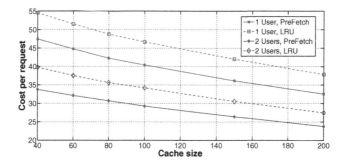

Fig. 21. Cost vs. Cache size for a system with Number of videos = 1000, Startup delay penalty $(\gamma) = 63$, $P_{cont} = 0.4$ and Zipf parameter $(\beta) = 0.8$. The performance of both polices improves with increasing cache size.

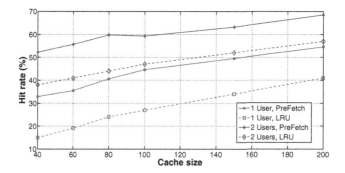

Fig. 22. Hit rate vs. Cache size for a system with Number of videos = 1000, Startup delay cost $(\gamma) = 63$, $P_{cont} = 0.4$ and Zipf parameter $(\beta) = 0.8$. The hit rates for both polices improve with increasing cache size.

6.6   Cost vs. Fraction to Prefetch (α)

In the simulation results discussed so far, we pre-fetch complete videos. We now explore the possibility of pre-fetching only a fraction of the video and fetching the remaining part of the video only after the request is made. If there exists an $\alpha < 1$ such that while the user watches the first α fraction of the video, the remaining $(1 - \alpha)$ fraction of the video can be pre-fetched, the CDN can provide uninterrupted service to the user without any startup delay by pre-fetching only the first α fraction of the video.

Pre-fetching only a fraction of video reduces the bandwidth usage, thus reducing the overall cost of service as shown in Figs. 23 and 24. Since the bandwidth usage per pre-fetch is reduced, this allows the CDN to pre-fetch more recommendations at the same cost (Fig. 25) which leads to improved cache hit rates (Fig. 26).

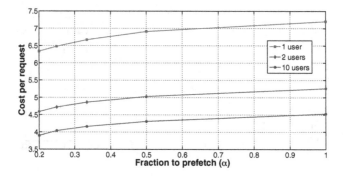

Fig. 23. Cost vs. Fraction to pre-fetch (α) for a system with Number of videos = 1000, Startup delay penalty (γ) = 11, P_{cont} = 0.4, Zipf parameter (β) = 0.8 and Cache size = 200. The cost of service increases with α as larger fractions of videos need to be pre-fetched to avoid start-up delay.

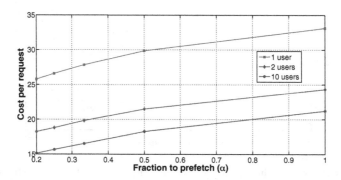

Fig. 24. Cost vs. Fraction to pre-fetch (α) for a system with Number of videos = 1000, Startup delay penalty (γ) = 63, P_{cont} = 0.4, Zipf parameter (β) = 0.8 and Cache size = 200. The cost of service increases with α as larger fractions of videos need to be pre-fetched to avoid start-up delay.

7   Alternative Model

In Sect. 3, we used the Barabasi-Albert model to generate the recommendation graph $G(V, E)$. The Barabasi-Albert model generates an undirected graph. In the model described in Sect. 3, we replace each edge of this graph by two directed edges to get the recommendation relationships. As a result, if v_i recommends v_j, then, v_j also recommends v_i. However, the recommendation links in a VoD service may not always be bidirectional. In this section we explore a directed graph model that can be used to capture this property.

7.1   Model Definition

Motivated by the fact that the degree distribution of the recommendation graph of VoD services follows the power law [23], instead of using the Barabasi-Albert

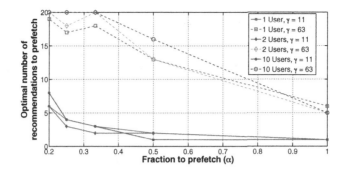

Fig. 25. Optimal number of recommendations to pre-fetch (r) vs. Fraction to pre-fetch (α) for a system with Number of videos = 1000, P_{cont} = 0.4, Zipf parameter (β) = 0.8 and Cache size = 200. The optimal number of recommendations to pre-fetch decrease with α as larger fractions of videos need to be pre-fetched to avoid start-up delay.

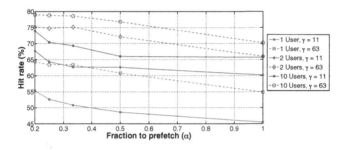

Fig. 26. Hit rate vs. Fraction to pre-fetch (α) for a system with Number of videos = 1000, P_{cont} = 0.4, Zipf parameter (β) = 0.8 and Cache size = 200. Hit-rates decrease with increasing values of α as the number of recommendations to pre-fetch reduce as α increases.

model, we use a variation of the directed random graph model proposed in [3] for which the in-degree distribution follows the power law. The random graph is generated in an iterative manner by adding one node at the time. We start with an initial graph of m nodes. Each new node is connected to the graph via m edges. When a new node is introduced, edges are added to the graph in a sequential manner until there are m edges involving the new node as follows:

– With probability p_{out} a link from new node is created to an existing node v. Node v is chosen randomly in proportion to the in-degree of v.
– With probability p_{in} a link from an existing node v to the new node is created. Node v is chosen randomly in proportion to the out-degree of v.
– Otherwise, a link between 2 existing nodes u and v is created. The originating node (node u) and target node (node v) are chosen randomly in proportion to the in-degree and out-degree of u and v respectively.

A formal description of the algorithm is given in Fig. 27.

1: Initialize: Generate a connected graph of m nodes $(v_1, v_2, ..., v_m)$. Let $v = m + 1$.
2: Introduce a new node n_v in the graph. Until the node gets connected with m existing nodes in the graph, either via inlinks or outlinks, new links are sequentially added as follows: With probability p_{out}, a link from n_v to n_i for $i < v$ is added, the probability p_i of choosing node i is given by

$$p_i = \frac{K_i}{\sum_j K_j},$$

where K_i is the current in-degree of node n_i.
With probability p_{in}, a link from n_i to n_v is added, the probability q_i of choosing node i is given by

$$q_i = \frac{L_i}{\sum_j L_j},$$

where L_i is the current out-degree of node n_i.
With probability $1 - p_{out} - p_{in}$, a link from n_i to n_j is added for $i, j \leq m$, the probability p_i of choosing node n_i, and q_j of choosing node j is given by

$$p_i = \frac{K_i}{\sum_j K_j},$$

$$q_j = \frac{L_j}{\sum_k L_k},$$

3: $v = v + 1$. If $v < n$, goto Step 2.

Fig. 27. A directed random graph model which generates a random small-world directed graph with a degree distribution following the power law.

Once the recommendation graph is generated, we assign transition probabilities to the various edges as discussed in Sect. 3. This completes the definition of our directed graph model.

7.2 Properties

Similar to the model proposed in Sect. 3, the alternative model also uses the empirically observed properties that the content popularity in absence of recommendation follows the Zipf's distribution and that chain count is between 1.3 and 2.4 to assign transition probabilities. Next, we verify if this model which uses a directed random graph model to generate the recommendation graph satisfies the rest of the empirical properties observed in Sect. 2.1.

Degree Distribution. The graph $G(V, E)$ generated as described in Fig. 27 has a power law in-degree distribution, and the average number of out-links from a node is more than mp_{out}. Figure 28 illustrates the in-degree distribution for a graph of 10,000 nodes. The slope of the curve can be changed by changing the values of p_{in} and p_{out}.

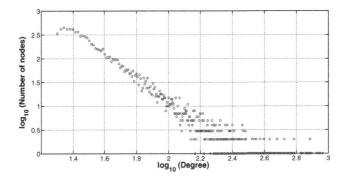

Fig. 28. In-degree distribution for the directed graph model of size 10,000 nodes with $p_{in} = 0.4$ and $p_{out} = 0.4$.

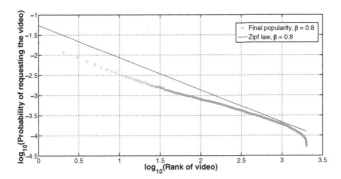

Fig. 29. Content popularity profile for the model with $m = 40$, $p_{out} = 0.4$, $p_{in} = 0.4$, Zipf parameter $(\beta) = 0.8$, number of videos $(n) = 2000$ and $\kappa = 0.8$

Small World Nature. We evaluate the clustering coefficient and average path length for this graph with 2000 nodes, $p_{in} = 0.4$ and $p_{out} = 0.4$. It is observed that this graph has a larger clustering and shorter average path lengths with respect to the Barabasi-Albert graph of the same size. We thus conclude that the construction in 7.1 generates a small world graph.

Content Popularity Profile. We generate the content popularity profile of our model by calculating the stationary distribution of the Markov Chain (as in Sect. 3). Figure 29 shows the content popularity profile in our model. We see that, the content popularity profile follows the Zipf distribution for the popular videos and decreases faster than as predicted by the Zipf distribution for the unpopular videos. Therefore, we conclude that content popularity profile for the alternative model is consistent with the observations in Sect. 2.1.

Click Through Rate. As in Sect. 3, we plot the median Click Through Rate (CTR) for the directed graph model in Fig. 30. We see that the median CTR

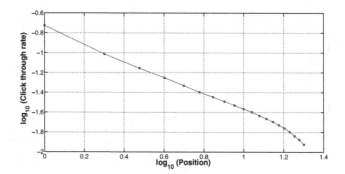

Fig. 30. CDF of CTR vs. position in recommendation list for Number of videos (n) = 2000, $m = 40$, $p_{in} = 0.4$, $p_{out} = 0.4$, Zipf parameter $\beta = 0.8$, $\kappa = 0.8$, and $P_{cont} = 0.4$.

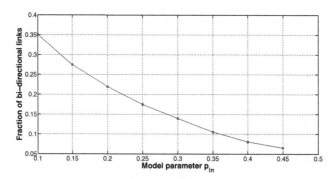

Fig. 31. Fraction of bi-directional links as a function of model parameter p_{in} for a graph of size 2000 nodes and $p_{out} = p_{in}$.

can be approximated by the Zipf distribution. Our model is therefore consistent with the observations in Sect. 2.1.

Fraction of Bi-directional Links. From a small experiment on a sub-graph of the YouTube recommendation graph, we observed that about 30% of the recommendation links are bi-directional. Figure 31 shows the relationship between the model parameter p_{in} and the fraction of bi-directional links in the graph. We conclude that the value of p_{in} can be tuned to obtain the desired fraction of bi-directional links. This flexibility does not exist in the model proposed in Sect. 3 and therefore, is a key point of difference between the model proposed in Sect. 3 and the alternative model discussed in this section. An issue with small values of p_{in} is that it distorts the final popularity from the scale-free nature as shown in Fig. 32.

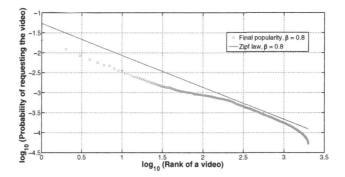

Fig. 32. Content popularity for the model with $m = 40$, $p_{out} = 0.2$, $p_{in} = 0.2$, Zipf parameter $(\beta) = 0.8$, number of videos $(n) = 2000$ and $\kappa = 0.8$. The content popularity gets distorted from the Zipf law for small values of p_{in}.

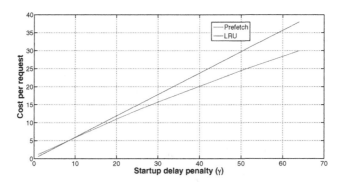

Fig. 33. Cost vs. Start-up delay penalty (γ) for a system with number of videos $= 1000$, $m = 40$, Zipf parameter $(\beta) = 0.8$, cache size $= 200$, $P_{cont} = 0.4$, $p_{in} = 0.4$, $p_{out} = 0.4$ and 1 user. As γ increases, PreFetch outperforms LRU policy.

7.3 Caching Simulations

In this section, we study the performance of the LRU and PreFetch policy when requests arrive according to the model described in Sect. 7.1. We use the same CDN and simulation setting as described in Sects. 4 and 6 respectively.

In Fig. 33, we compare the performance of PreFetch policy and the LRU policy as a function of the Startup delay penalty (γ). In Fig. 33, we use the empirically optimized value of r (number of recommendations to prefetch) which leads to the lowest cost of service. The optimal number of recommendations to pre-fetch (r) increases with increase in Start-up delay penalty (γ) as shown in Fig. 34. Note that these plots exhibit qualitatively similar behavior as in Figs. 9 and 10.

The dependence on other parameters like number of users using a local server (u), size of cache, fraction of videos pre-fetched (α) etc. is qualitatively similar to the results in Sect. 6.

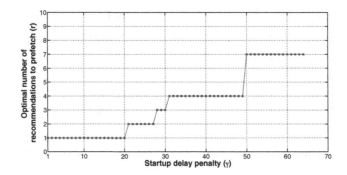

Fig. 34. The optimal number of recommendations to pre-fetch (r) vs. Start-up delay penalty (γ) for a system with number of videos $= 1000$, $m = 40$, Zipf parameter$(\beta) = 0.8$, cache size $= 200$, $P_{cont} = 0.4$, $p_{in} = 0.4$, $p_{out} = 0.4$ and 1 user. The optimal number of recommendations to pre-fetch (r) increases with start-up delay penalty γ.

8   Conclusions

In this work, we propose a Markovian model for request arrivals in VoD services with recommendation engines which captures the time-correlation in user requests and is consistent with empirically observed properties.

Low start-up delay is a key QoS requirement of users of VoD services. In addition, minimizing the bandwidth consumption of the network is key to reduce the cost of service. Given the trade-off between these two goals, we show that the time-correlation in user requests can be used to design caching policies which outperform popular policies like LRU which do not exploit this time-correlation. More specifically, we show that our caching policy *PreFetch* which employs recommendation based pre-fetching outperforms the LRU policy in terms of the joint cost of start-up delay and bandwidth consumption when the relative is cost of start-up delay is high.

References

1. Adamic, L.A., Huberman, B.A.: Zipfs law and the internet. Glottometrics **3**(1), 143–150 (2002)
2. Albert, R., Barabási, A.L.: Statistical mechanics of complex networks. Rev. Mod. Phys. **74**(1), 47 (2002)
3. Bollobás, B., Borgs, C., Chayes, J., Riordan, O.: Directed scale-free graphs. In: Proceedings of the Fourteenth Annual ACM-SIAM Symposium on Discrete Algorithms, pp. 132–139. Society for Industrial and Applied Mathematics (2003)
4. Breslau, L., Cao, P., Fan, L., Phillips, G., Shenker, S.: Web caching and Zipf-like distributions: evidence and implications. In: Proceedings of Eighteenth Annual Joint Conference of the IEEE Computer and Communications Societies, INFOCOM 1999, vol. 1, pp. 126–134. IEEE (1999)
5. Cheng, X., Dale, C., Liu, J.: Understanding the characteristics of internet short video sharing: Youtube as a case study. arXiv preprint arXiv:0707.3670 (2007)

6. Cheng, X., Liu, J.: NetTube: exploring social networks for peer-to-peer short video sharing. In: INFOCOM 2009, pp. 1152–1160. IEEE (2009)
7. Cisco Whitepaper. http://www.cisco.com/c/en/us/solutions/collateral/service-provider/ip-ngn-ip-next-generation-network/white_paper_c11-481360.html
8. Davidson, J., Liebald, B., Liu, J., Nandy, P., Van Vleet, T., Gargi, U., Gupta, S., He, Y., Lambert, M., Livingston, B., et al.: The youtube video recommendation system. In: Proceedings of the Fourth ACM Conference on Recommender Systems, pp. 293–296. ACM (2010)
9. Du, M., Kihl, M., Arvidsson, Å., Lagerstedt, C., Gawler, A.: Analysis of prefetching schemes for TV-on-demand service. In: The Tenth International Conference on Digital Telecommunications, ICDT 2015. International Academy, Research and Industry Association (IARIA) (2015)
10. Fricker, C., Robert, P., Roberts, J., Sbihi, N.: Impact of traffic mix on caching performance in a content-centric network. In: 2012 IEEE Conference on Computer Communications Workshops (INFOCOM WKSHPS), pp. 310–315. IEEE (2012)
11. Gupta, S., Moharir, S.: Request patterns and caching in VoD services with recommendation systems. In: COMSNETS (2017)
12. Iamnitchi, A., Ripeanu, M., Foster, I.: Small-world file-sharing communities. In: Twenty-third Annual Joint Conference of the IEEE Computer and Communications Societies, INFOCOM 2004, vol. 2, pp. 952–963. IEEE (2004)
13. Khemmarat, S., Zhou, R., Krishnappa, D.K., Gao, L., Zink, M.: Watching user generated videos with prefetching. Sig. Process. Image Commun. 27(4), 343–359 (2012)
14. Krishnan, S.S., Sitaraman, R.K.: Video stream quality impacts viewer behavior: inferring causality using quasi-experimental designs. IEEE/ACM Trans. Networking 21(6), 2001–2014 (2013)
15. Krishnappa, D.K., Khemmarat, S., Gao, L., Zink, M.: On the feasibility of prefetching and caching for online TV services: a measurement study on Hulu. In: Spring, N., Riley, G.F. (eds.) PAM 2011. LNCS, vol. 6579, pp. 72–80. Springer, Heidelberg (2011). doi:10.1007/978-3-642-19260-9_8
16. Krishnappa, D.K., Zink, M., Griwodz, C., Halvorsen, P.: Cache-centric video recommendation: an approach to improve the efficiency of youtube caches. ACM Trans. Multimed. Comput. Commun. Appl. (TOMM) 11(4), 48 (2015)
17. Liang, K., Hao, J., Zimmermann, R., Yau, D.K.: Integrated prefetching and caching for adaptive video streaming over HTTP: an online approach. In: Proceedings of the 6th ACM Multimedia Systems Conference, pp. 142–152. ACM (2015)
18. Liu, Y., Li, F., Guo, L., Shen, B., Chen, S.: A server's perspective of internet streaming delivery to mobile devices. In: 2012 Proceedings of INFOCOM, pp. 1332–1340. IEEE (2012)
19. Liu, Y., Li, F., Guo, L., Shen, B., Chen, S., Lan, Y.: Measurement and analysis of an internet streaming service to mobile devices. IEEE Trans. Parallel Distrib. Syst. 24(11), 2240–2250 (2013)
20. Moharir, S., Ghaderi, J., Sanghavi, S., Shakkottai, S.: Serving content with unknown demand: the high-dimensional regime. In: ACM SIGMETRICS (2014)
21. Netflix. www.netflix.com
22. Pleşca, C., Charvillat, V., Ooi, W.T.: Multimedia prefetching with optimal Markovian policies. J. Netw. Comput. Appl. 69, 40–53 (2016)
23. Suman, S., Shubham, S.: Understanding the characteristic of youtube video graph (2016). https://www.dropbox.com/s/vpgxsvm5je9264q/Youtube-Video-Graph.pdf?dl=0

24. Veloso, E., Almeida, V., Meira, W., Bestavros, A., Jin, S.: A hierarchical characterization of a live streaming media workload. In: Proceedings of the 2nd ACM SIGCOMM Workshop on Internet Measurment, pp. 117–130. ACM (2002)
25. Wang, J.: A survey of web caching schemes for the internet. ACM SIGCOMM Comput. Commun. Rev. **29**(5), 36–46 (1999)
26. Watts, D.J., Strogatz, S.H.: Collective dynamics of small-world networks. Nature **393**(6684), 440–442 (1998)
27. YouTube Statistics. http://www.youtube.com/yt/press/statistics.html
28. Yu, H., Zheng, D., Zhao, B.Y., Zheng, W.: Understanding user behavior in large-scale video-on-demand systems. ACM SIGOPS Oper. Syst. Rev. **40**, 333–344 (2006). ACM
29. Zhou, R., Khemmarat, S., Gao, L.: The impact of youtube recommendation system on video views. In: Proceedings of the 10th ACM SIGCOMM Conference on Internet Measurement, pp. 404–410. ACM (2010)

A Hidden Markov Restless Multi-armed Bandit Model for Playout Recommendation Systems

Rahul Meshram[1(✉)], Aditya Gopalan[2], and D. Manjunath[1]

[1] Electrical Engineering Department,
Indian Institute of Technology Bombay, Mumbai 400076, India
rahulmeshram@ee.iitb.ac.in
[2] ECE Department, Indian Institute of Science, Bangalore 560012, India

Abstract. We consider a restless multi-armed bandit (RMAB) in which each arm can be in one of two states, say 0 or 1. Playing an arm generates a unit reward with a probability that depends on the state of the arm. The belief about the state of the arm can be calculated using a Bayesian update after every play. This RMAB has been designed for use in recommendation systems where the user's preferences depend on the history of recommendations. In this paper we analyse the RMAB by first studying single armed bandit. We show that it is Whittle-indexable and obtain a closed form expression for the Whittle index. For a RMAB to be useful in practice, we need to be able to learn the parameters of the arms. We present Thompson sampling scheme, that learns the parameters of the arms and also illustrate its performance numerically.

Keywords: Restless multi-armed bandit · Recommendation systems · POMDP · Automated playlist creation systems · Learning

1 Introduction

Recommendations systems are used in almost all forms of modern media like YouTube and other video streaming services, Spotify and other music streaming services to create playlists. Playlists are also created on personal devices like digital music players. Highly personalised playlists are now being created using a variety of information that is mined from behavior history and social networking sites. A search for patents on playlist creation yields more than handful of items indicating a strong commercial interest in the search for good algorithm. The research literature though is scant.

A possible approach to create a playlist is to treat it as a 'matrix completion' problem, (e.g. [7], and choose a set of items from the completed matrix for which the user has a high preference.) A second approach would be to treat

The work of Rahul Meshram and D. Manjunath was carried out in the Bharti Centre for Communications at IIT Bombay. D. Manjunath is also supported by grants from CEFIPRA and DST. Part of this paper have appeared in COMSNETS-2017 conference, [23].

© Springer International Publishing AG 2017
N. Sastry and S. Chakraborty (Eds.): COMSNETS 2017, LNCS 10340, pp. 335–362, 2017.
DOI: 10.1007/978-3-319-67235-9_19

playlist creation as a recommendation system and generate a sequence of recommendations for the user. This is the view that we take in this paper but with the key of the user's interest in items being influenced by immediate behavioral history. To the best of our knowledge such a system has not been considered in the literature. Specifically, we assume that user will like different items to be repeated at different rates and there will be some randomness in the preferences. The playlist creation system that we describe in this paper generates a dynamic list by taking a binary feedback from the user after an item has been played. Specifically, we allow different items to have different 'return times' in that some items may be played out more frequently than others.

We assume that the items are of two different categories—'normal' or type-A item and 'viral' or type-B item. For a normal item, the user preference goes from high low immediately after playing it and rises slowly after not playing it. The opposite is true for a 'viral' item, i.e., the preference goes to high immediately after play and decreases when it is not played. In this model, the recommendation system observes the user preference for the item only after playing it and not observed for other items. This feedback is accounted in subsequent plays of items. Since the user preferences are not observed for other items, system maintains the belief about the preference of the item. It is updated based on the action and outcome. The goal of system is to maximize a long term reward function. Such system can be modeled a restless multi-armed bandit (RMAB) with hidden states.

Typically, the users may have different preferences towards different items and also have different repetition rates. It may not be known at the beginning. Thus, the learning of associated state transition models and click through probabilities is required.

We next discuss the related literature on RMAB and learning in multi-armed bandits.

1.1 Related Literature

Typical recommendation system models based on multi-armed bandits take the form of contextual bandits, e.g., [15,16]. A key feature in these models is that the user interests are assumed independent of the immediate recommendation history, i.e., the reward model is a static. We introduce the feature of making it dependent on the immediate recommendation history. Other models that address user reaction in recommendations use a finite sequence of past user responses as a basis for deciding the current recommendation, e.g., [13]; these are numerical studies and no provable properties are derived.

The classical stochastic multi-armed bandit problem for recommendation systems (RS) studied in [2,6,14], where RS chooses the items from given set of items at each time step. Play of an item yields a random reward that is drawn from probability distribution associated with item and it is unknown. There goal is to maximize the expected cumulative reward. This model do not have states associated with each item and rewards are drawn independently at each time step. It is studied as online learning problem. The performance is measured via regret, it is defined as difference between reward obtained using optimal strategy and reward obtained from strategy that is used for learning. A variant of stochastic multi-armed bandit considered in [8]. These are solved using efficient algorithms based on upper confidence bound (UCB). Further, it is shown that expected regret scales logarithmically with time steps. Recently, Thompson sampling (TS) based Bayesian algorithm considered for stochastic multi-armed in [1,9,11,12]. In [9], authors have empirically illustrated the performance of Thompson sampling algorithm and observed that it performs better than UCB. TS algorithm is analysed in [1,11] and shown that the regret scales logarithmically with number of time steps.

Another stochastic bandit, a restless multi-armed bandit first studied in seminal work of [29], where each arm has states associated with it and states evolve according to a Markov chain and that evolution is action dependent. Further, author proposed the heuristic index based policy, it is referred to as Whittle index policy. In [19,22], we have considered a general system of a restless multi-armed bandit with unobservable states and action dependent transitions. In [22] we show that such a system is *approximately Whittle-indexable*. The restless bandit that we propose in this paper is a special case of that from [22] for which we can show exact Whittle indexability and also obtain a closed form expression for the Whittle index.

The standard restless multi-armed bandit work assumes that the transition probabilities and rewards are known. In recent work of [17], UCB based learning algorithm studied for a restless multi-armed bandit when transition probabilities and rewards are unknown. Also, Thompson sampling algorithm for a restless single armed bandit proposed and analysed in [20,21]. In this paper, we also propose Thompson sampling based learning algorithm for RMAB and analyse its properties via numerical experiments.

1.2   Contributions

This paper is an extended version of [23]. Here, we extend our earlier work in [23] to long term average reward problem and discuss few variants of models. The detailed contributions from this paper are as follows.

1. We develop a restless multi-armed bandit (RMAB) model for use in recommendation systems and playlist creation. The arms of the bandit correspond to the items that may be recommended. Two types of arms may be defined—type A and type B. Each 'like' for a played arm yields a unit reward. We will seek a policy that maximises the infinite horizon discounted reward and a policy that maximises the long term average reward. The details are in Sect. 2.
2. We derive the value function properties for both type of arms in infinite horizon discounted reward and average reward. Using these properties, we obtain closed form expressions for value functions in Sect. 3.
3. We show that both types of arms are Whittle-indexable and obtain closed form expressions for the Whittle index. It is a function of the state of the

arm. This is obtained for infinite horizon discounted reward case in Sect. 3.1. We also derive the expression for the Whittle index in average reward case, see Sect. 3.2.

4. The Whittle index policy is compared against a myopic policy in numerical experiments. We see that the index based policy indeed outperforms the myopic policy in many cases. This is covered in Sect. 4.
5. In Sect. 5 we discuss dual speed restless bandits for hidden states. For few variations of type A and type B arms, we obtain closed form expression of Whittle index.
6. Finally, in Sect. 6 we provide a Thompson sampling based algorithm for online learning of the parameters of the arms. A numerical comparison of the regret shows that the learning is effective.

We remark that the objective of the paper is not to design a recommendation system but to develop a new framework with provable properties for creating such systems.

2   Preliminaries and Model Description

To anchor the discussion, assume an automated playlist creation system (APCS) with N items in its database. When an item is played, the user provides a binary feedback; a possible mechanism could be by clicking, or not clicking a 'like' button. The user's interest in an item at any time is determined by an intrinsic interest and also on the time since it was last played. These features are captured in the model as follows. Each item in the database corresponds to one arm of the multi-armed bandit. The playout history of an arm is captured via a state variable for the arm and the interest in the item is captured via state-dependent 'like'-probability for the arm. The state of each arm evolves independently of the other arms with transition probabilities that depend on whether it is played or not played.

We now formally describe the model. Time is measured in recommendation steps and is indexed by $t = 1, 2, 3, \cdots$, i.e., a recommendation is made in every step. $X_t(n) \in \{0, 1\}$ is the state of arm n at the beginning of step t. $A_t(n) \in \{0, 1\}$ is the action in step t for arm n with $A_t(n) = 1$ corresponding to playing arm n and $A_t(n) = 0$ corresponding to not playing it. $X_t(n)$ evolves according to transition probabilities that depend on $A_t(n)$. There are two types of arms with arms in $\mathcal{A} = \{1, \ldots, M\}$ being type A arms and those in $\mathcal{B} = \{M + 1, \ldots, N\}$ being the type B arms. $P_{ij}^n(a)$ denotes the transition probability from state i to state j for arm n under action a.

For type A arms, i.e., for $1 \leq n \leq M$, for $P_{00}^n(1) = 1$, $P_{10}^n(1) := 1$, $P_{01}^n(0) := p_n$, $P_{11}^n(0) := 1$ Here, p_n determines the preferred 'repetition rate' of arm n. If p_n is small, then the user prefers a large gap between successive times that the arm is played; if it is large then the preference is for smaller gaps. Type A arms correspond to 'normal' items in that the user prefers sufficient gap between the playing of the item.

For type B arms, i.e., for $M + 1 \leq n \leq N$, the transition probabilities are $P_{01}^n(1) = 1$, $P_{11}^n(1) = 1$, $P_{00}^n(0) = 1$, $P_{10}^n(0) = p_n$. Type B arms correspond to 'viral' items where the preference is to have it played frequently and until it is 'time to forget' it. Thus p_n determines the forgetting rate for a viral item.

When arm n is played and it is in state i, then a unit reward is accrued with probability $\rho_{n,i}$, $0 < \rho_{n,i} < 1$. The reward corresponds to the user liking the playing of the arm and $\rho_{n,i}$ represents the intrinsic preference for the item. No reward is accrued from arms that are not played. The transition probabilities and rewards for the two types of arms are illustrated in Figs. 1 and 2.

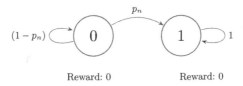

Reward: 0   Reward: 0

State transitions and rewards when $A_t = 0$.

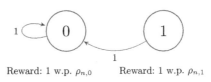

Reward: 1 w.p. $\rho_{n,0}$ Reward: 1 w.p. $\rho_{n,1}$

State transitions and rewards when $A_t = 1$.

Fig. 1. Transition probabilities and reward structure for type-A arms

Observe that in the system, the state of an arm evolves even when it is not played; thus this is a restless multi-armed bandit. For each arm, we maintain a belief for the state of arm at the beginning of time step t, denoted by $\pi_t(n)$, for arm n. At the end of each time step, we can perform a Bayesian update of $\pi_t(n)$ using p_n and $\rho_{n,i}$ along with the observation of the reward if the arm is played. We will define $\pi_t(n) = \Pr\left(X_t(n) = 0 \mid H_t\right)$. Here, H_t denote the history of actions and observed rewards up to the beginning of time t, i.e., $H_t \equiv (A_s(n), R_s(n))_{1 \leq n \leq N, 1 \leq s < t}$, and $R_t(n)$ is the reward obtained in step n from arm n. One arm from the set of N arms is to be played at each time step. Let $\phi = \{\phi(t)\}_{t>0}$ be the strategy where $\phi(t) : H_t \to \{1, \ldots, N\}$ maps the history upto time t to the action of playing one of the N arms at time t. Under the policy ϕ, let the action at time t be denoted by

$$A_t^\phi(n) = \begin{cases} 1 & \text{if } \phi(t) = n, \\ 0 & \text{if } \phi(t) \neq n. \end{cases}$$

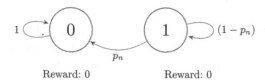

Reward: 0   Reward: 0

State transitions and rewards when $A_t = 0$.

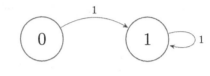

Reward: 1 w.p. $\rho_{n,0}$ Reward: 1 w.p. $\rho_{n,1}$

State transitions and rewards when $A_t = 1$.

Fig. 2. Transition probabilities and reward structure for type-B arms.

The infinite horizon expected discounted reward under policy ϕ is given by

$$V_{\beta,\phi}(\pi) := \mathsf{E}\left(\sum_{t=1}^{\infty} \beta^{t-1}\left(\sum_{n=1}^{N} A_t^{\phi}(n)\,(\pi_t(n)\,\rho_{n,0} + (1-\pi_t(n))\rho_{n,1})\right)\right). \quad (1)$$

Here β is the discount factor, $0 < \beta < 1$, the initial belief is $\pi(n) = \Pr(X_1(n) = 0)$, and $\pi = [\pi(1), \cdots, \pi(N)]^T$. The long term average reward under policy ϕ is given as follows.

$$V_{\phi}(\pi) := \lim_{T \to \infty} \frac{1}{T}\mathsf{E}\left(\sum_{t=1}^{T}\left(\sum_{n=1}^{N} A_t^{\phi}(n)\,(\pi_t(n)\,\rho_{n,0} + (1-\pi_t(n))\rho_{n,1})\right)\right) \quad (2)$$

In this paper, our goal is in a policy ϕ that maximizes $V_{\beta,\phi}(\pi)$ for all $\pi \in [0,1]^N$ assuming that we know p_n, and $\rho_{n,i}$ for all n. Similarly, in case of average reward problem we want to find a policy ϕ that maximizes $V_{\phi}(\pi)$ for all $\pi \in [0,1]^N$.

3   Towards the Whittle Index

As we have mentioned earlier, the problem (1) is a restless multi-armed bandit (RMAB) with partially observable states. In general, RMAB is computationally intractable. It is known to be PSPACE-hard; see [24]. In light of this hardness, heuristic policies are sought. One class of heuristic policies is an index-based policy. Here, at the beginning of each time step, an index is calculated for each arm using the belief of the state of the arm, the transition probabilities and the reward probabilities and the arm(s) with highest index values are played in the step. A popular index-based policy is the Whittle-index policy based on a Lagrangian relaxation of (1). This was first outlined in [29]. In many cases, this policy is known to be asymptotically optimal; see [18], [10, Chap. 6]. To be able to use this heuristic, we first need to show that each arm is indexable. To effectively use it, we need to derive the formulae to calculate the index. Indexability is proved by analysing a single arm. We first analyse a single armed bandit with infinite horizon discounted reward problem. Later, we will examine a single armed bandit with long term average reward problem.

3.1   Discounted Reward Problem

We begin by dropping the reference to n, the sequence number of the arm to simplify the notation. Next, the arm is assumed to be assigned a *subsidy* λ for not playing it. In view of this subsidy, (1) may be rewritten as follows.

$$V_\beta(\pi) := \mathsf{E}\left(\sum_{t=1}^\infty \beta^{t-1}\left(A_t^\phi\left(\pi_t\,\rho_0 + (1-\pi_t)\rho_1\right) + \lambda(1-A_t^\phi)\right)\right). \tag{3}$$

Recall that $\pi_t = \Pr\left(X_t = 0 \mid H_t\right)$. For notational simplicity, we rewrite A_t^ϕ as A_t with policy ϕ. The Bayesian updates for π_t are obtained as follows.

- For a type A arm: If $A_t = 1$, then $\pi_{t+1} = 1$ and if $A_t = 0$, then $\pi_{t+1} = (1-p)\pi_t$.
- For a type B arm: If $A_t = 1$, then $\pi_{t+1} = 0$ and if $A_t = 0$, then $\pi_{t+1} = \pi_t + p(1-\pi_t)$.

If $A_t = 1$, then the expected reward in the step is $\pi_t\rho_0 + (1-\pi_t)\rho_1$. The policy $\phi(t) : H_t \to \{0,1\}$, maps the history up to time t, to an action A_t in t. From [4,5,25], the following is well known.

- π_t captures the information in H_t, and is a sufficient statistic to construct policies that depend on the history.
- Optimal strategies can be restricted to stationary Markov policies.
- The optimum value function for fixed λ and β, denoted $V_\beta(\pi, \lambda)$, is determined by solving the following dynamic program.

$$V_{1,\beta}(\pi, \lambda) := \begin{cases} \pi\rho_0 + (1-\pi)\rho_1 + \beta V_\beta(1, \lambda) & \text{for type A} \\ \pi\rho_0 + (1-\pi)\rho_1 + \beta V_\beta(0, \lambda) & \text{for type B} \end{cases}$$

$$V_{0,\beta}(\pi, \lambda) := \begin{cases} \lambda + \beta V_\beta((1-p)\pi, \lambda) & \text{for type A} \\ \lambda + \beta V_\beta(\pi + p(1-\pi), \lambda) & \text{for type B} \end{cases}$$

$$V_\beta(\pi, \lambda) = \max\{V_{1,\beta}(\pi, \lambda), V_{0,\beta}(\pi, \lambda)\}. \tag{4}$$

$V_{i,\beta}(\pi, \lambda)$ is the optimal value function if $A_1 = i$, $i = 0, 1$.

We next derive properties of the value functions V_β, $V_{0,\beta}$, and $V_{1,\beta}$ in the following Lemma.

Lemma 1.

1. For fixed λ and β, $V_\beta(\pi, \lambda)$, $V_{0,\beta}(\pi, \lambda)$, $V_{1,\beta}(\pi, \lambda)$ are non-increasing convex in π. Furthermore, $V_{1,\beta}(\pi, \lambda)$ is linear in π.
2. For fixed π and β, $V_\beta(\pi, \lambda)$, $V_{1,\beta}(\pi, \lambda)$ and $V_{0,\beta}(\pi, \lambda)$ are non-decreasing convex in λ.
3. For fixed π and β, $V_{1,\beta}(\pi, \lambda)$ and $V_{0,\beta}(\pi, \lambda)$ intersect at least once. This leads us to define (1) $\lambda_{L,\beta}$ such that for all $\lambda < \lambda_{L,\beta}$, the optimal action is to play the arm for all $\pi \in [0,1]$, and (2) $\lambda_{H,\beta} = \lambda_H$ such that for all $\lambda > \lambda_H$ the optimal action is to not play the arm for all $\pi \in [0,1]$. $\lambda_{L,\beta}$ and λ_H are given as follows.

$$\lambda_H = \begin{cases} \rho_1 & \text{for type } A, \\ \rho_1 & \text{for type } B, \end{cases}$$

$$\lambda_{L,\beta} = \begin{cases} \rho_0 + \beta q(\rho_0 - \rho_1) & \text{for type } A, \\ \rho_1 + (1 - \beta)(\rho_0 - \rho_1) & \text{for type } B. \end{cases}$$

The proof of Lemma 1 is analogous to the proofs in [22, Lemmas 2 and 3]. Hence we omit the proof. In the next Lemma, we state the Lipschitz properties of value function with respect to π and λ.

Lemma 2.

1. For fixed λ and β, and $\forall \pi_1, \pi_2 \in [0,1]$, we have

$$\left| V_\beta(\pi_1, \lambda) - V_\beta(\pi_2, \lambda) \right| \leq (\rho_1 - \rho_0)|\pi_1 - \pi_2|$$

2. For fixed $\pi \in [0,1]$, and for $0 < \beta < 1$,

$$\frac{\partial V_\beta(\pi, \lambda)}{\partial \lambda}, \quad \frac{\partial V_{1,\beta}(\pi, \lambda)}{\partial \lambda}, \quad \text{and} \quad \frac{\partial V_{0,\beta}(\pi, \lambda)}{\partial \lambda}$$

are bounded above by $\frac{1}{1-\beta}$.

The proof is given in Appendix A.1.

Remark 1. It is possible that $V_\beta(\pi, \lambda)$ is not differentiable with respect to π or λ. In that case the partial derivative of $V_\beta(\pi, \lambda)$ should be taken to be the right partial derivative. Note that such the right partial derivative exists because $V_\beta(\pi, \lambda)$ is convex in π, λ, and bounded.

Using the Lipschitz property of $V_\beta(\pi, \lambda)$ in π, we derive the next result.

Lemma 3. For fixed λ and β, $V_{1,\beta}(\pi, \lambda) - V_{0,\beta}(\pi, \lambda)$ is decreasing in π.

The proof is detailed in Appendix A.2. We now ready to present our first main result on a threshold policy structure.

Theorem 1 (Single threshold policy). *For the single-armed bandit, $0 < \beta < 1$, and $\lambda_L \leq \lambda \leq \lambda_{H,\beta}$, the optimal policy is of threshold type with a single threshold. That is, there is a unique threshold $\pi_T \in [0,1]$ such that*

$$V_\beta(\pi, \lambda) = \begin{cases} V_{1,\beta}(\pi, \lambda) & \text{if } \pi \leq \pi_T, \\ V_{0,\beta}(\pi, \lambda) & \text{if } \pi \geq \pi_T, \end{cases}$$

where $\pi_T = \{\pi \in [0,1] : V_{1,\beta}(\pi, \lambda) = V_{0,\beta}(\pi, \lambda)\}$.

Proof. Fix β, λ. From Lemmas 1 and 3, we have the following. For a fixed λ, $V_{1,\beta}(\pi, \lambda)$ is linear in π and $V_{0,\beta}(\pi, \lambda)$ is convex in π. Also, $V_{1,\beta}(\pi, \lambda) - V_{0,\beta}(\pi, \lambda)$ is decreasing in π. Thus there is at most one threshold. Furthermore, $V_{1,\beta}(\pi, \lambda)$ and $V_{0,\beta}(\pi, \lambda)$ intersect at least once for $\lambda_{L,\beta} \leq \lambda \leq \lambda_H$, $\pi \in [0,1]$. This completes the proof. □

Remark 2.

1. The threshold policy implies that whenever belief at time step t, π_t is greater than π_T, then the optimal action is to not play the item.
2. For type-A arm, the belief about the state 0 evolves to $(1-p)\pi_t$ when arm is not played. Thus, π_{t+1} decreases whenever the item is not played and after some time steps, the optimal action will be to play the item. Once item is played, then π_{t+1} reaches the state 0 with probability 1. Let K denotes the number of time steps to wait to play that item again and it depends on π_T, π and p. It is defined as follows.

$$K(\pi, \pi_T) := \min\{k \geq 0 : (1-p)^k \pi < \pi_T\}.$$

Then,

$$K(\pi, \pi_T) = \begin{cases} 0 & \text{if } \pi < \pi_T, \\ \left\lfloor \frac{\log(\frac{\pi_T}{\pi})}{\log(1-p)} \right\rfloor + 1 & \text{if } \pi \geq \pi_T. \end{cases} \tag{5}$$

Using a threshold policy result and $K(\pi, \pi_T)$, we can derive the value function expressions as follows.

$$V_{1,\beta}(\pi, \lambda) = \pi\rho_0 + (1-\pi)\rho_1 + \beta V_{0,\beta}(1, \lambda),$$

$$V_{0,\beta}(\pi, \lambda) = \frac{\lambda\left(1 - \beta^{K(\pi,\pi_T)}\right)}{1-\beta} + \beta^{K(\pi,\pi_T)+1} V_{0,\beta}(1, \lambda) + \beta^{K(\pi,\pi_T)} \times$$

$$\left(\rho_1 + (\rho_0 - \rho_1)(1-p)^{K(\pi,\pi_T)}\pi\right),$$

$$V_{0,\beta}(1, \lambda) = \frac{\lambda(1 - \beta^{K(1,\pi_T)})}{\left(1 - \beta^{K(1,\pi_T)+1}\right)(1-\beta)} + \beta^{K(1,\pi_T)} \frac{\left(\rho_1 + (\rho_0 - \rho_1)(1-p)^{K(1,\pi_T)}\right)}{\left(1 - \beta^{K(1,\pi_T)+1}\right)}.$$

$$\tag{6}$$

3. For type-B arm, the belief about the state 0 evolves to $\pi_t + p(1 - \pi_t)$ when arm is not played. Observe that π_{t+1} is increases whenever arm is not played. Define $T(\pi) := \pi + p(1 - \pi)$, $T^k(\pi) = T^{k-1}(T(\pi))$ and $\lim_{k \to \infty} T^k(\pi) = 1$. When a threshold $\pi_T \in (0, 1]$, note that $V_\beta(0, \lambda) = V_{1,\beta}(0, \lambda) = \frac{\rho_1}{1-\beta}$. Also, following holds.

$$V_\beta(T(\pi), \lambda) = \begin{cases} V_{1,\beta}(T(\pi), \lambda) & \text{if } T(\pi) < \pi_T, \\ V_{0,\beta}(T(\pi), \lambda) & \text{if } T(\pi) \geq \pi_T. \end{cases}$$

This discussion suggests that once that item is played, the user keeps liking that item. If the item is not played to the user, i.e. $\pi_t \geq \pi_T$, then the state of the item π_t is always greater than π_T for all t and that means, that item is not played to the user at all. Thus the value function expressions are described below.

$$V_{1,\beta}(\pi, \lambda) = \pi \rho_0 + (1 - \pi)\rho_1 + \beta \frac{\rho_1}{1 - \beta},$$

$$V_{0,\beta}(\pi, \lambda) = \begin{cases} \lambda + \beta(\rho_0 T(\pi) + (1 - T(\pi))\rho_1) + \beta \frac{\rho_1}{1-\beta} & \text{if } T(\pi) < \pi_T, \\ \frac{\lambda}{1-\beta} & \text{if } T(\pi) \geq \pi_T, \end{cases} \tag{7}$$

for $\pi_T \in (0, 1]$. When $\pi_T = 0$, we have

$$V_{1,\beta}(\pi, \lambda) = \pi \rho_0 + (1 - \pi)\rho_1 + \beta \frac{\lambda}{1 - \beta},$$

$$V_{0,\beta}(\pi, \lambda) = \frac{\lambda}{1 - \beta}.$$

From Theorem 1 and Remark 2, we can show the following.

Lemma 4. *For fixed π and β, $V_{1,\beta}(\pi, \lambda) - V_{0,\beta}(\pi, \lambda)$ is a decreasing in λ.*

The proof is given in Appendix A.3. We first define indexability and later show that type-A and type-B arms are indexable. Define,

$$\mathcal{P}(\lambda) := \{\pi \in [0, 1] : V_{1,\beta}(\pi, \lambda) \leq V_{0,\beta}(\pi, \lambda)\}$$

$\mathcal{P}(\lambda)$ is a set of all π for which the optimal action is to not play the arm.

Definition 1 (Whittle indexability, [29]). *An arm is Whittle indexable if $\mathcal{P}(\lambda)$ monotonically increases from $\emptyset$ to the entire state space $[0, 1]$ as λ increases from $-\infty$ to ∞, i.e., $\mathcal{P}(\lambda_1) \setminus \mathcal{P}(\lambda_2) = \emptyset$ whenever $\lambda_1 < \lambda_2$. Further, a multi-armed bandit with N arms is indexable if all arms are indexable.*

We require the following result from [22, Lemma 4] to prove Whittle indexability.

Lemma 5. *Let $\pi_T(\lambda) = \inf\{0 \leq \pi \leq 1 : V_{S,\beta}(\pi, \lambda) = V_{NS,\beta}(\pi, \lambda)\} \in [0, 1]$. If*

$$\left. \frac{\partial V_{1,\beta}(\pi, \lambda)}{\partial \lambda} \right|_{\pi = \pi_T(\lambda)} < \left. \frac{\partial V_{0,\beta}(\pi, \lambda)}{\partial \lambda} \right|_{\pi = \pi_T(\lambda)}, \tag{8}$$

then $\pi_T(\lambda)$ is a monotonically decreasing function of λ.

We next present our second main result.

Theorem 2 (Whittle indexable). *The single-armed bandit is indexable for $0 < \beta < 1$ and $\lambda_{L,\beta} \leq \lambda \leq \lambda_H$.*

Proof. From Definition 1, it is clear that we have to show $\mathcal{P}(\lambda_1) \subseteq \mathcal{P}(\lambda_2)$ whenever $\lambda_2 > \lambda_1$. From Lemma 4, we note that $V_{1,\beta}(\pi, \lambda) - V_{0,\beta}(\pi, \lambda)$ is decreasing in λ for fixed π and β. Therefore, (8) holds true. Using Lemma 5, $\lambda_2 > \lambda_1$ implies $\pi_T(\lambda_2) < \pi_T(\lambda_1)$ for fixed β. Hence, from the definition of the set $\mathcal{P}(\lambda)$, we get $\mathcal{P}(\lambda_1) \subseteq \mathcal{P}(\lambda_2)$ whenever $\lambda_2 > \lambda_1$. This completes the proof. □

We are now ready to define the Whittle index for an arm and provide an explicit formula for Whittle index in case of both type A and type B arms.

Definition 2 (Whittle index). *If an arm is indexable and is in state π, then its Whittle index, $W(\pi)$, is*

$$W(\pi) := \inf_{\lambda} \{\lambda : V_{1,\beta}(\pi, \lambda) = V_{0,\beta}(\pi, \lambda)\}.$$

$W(\pi)$ is the minimum subsidy λ such that the optimal action is to not play the are at the given π. To compute the Whittle index, we have to obtain the expressions of $V_{1,\beta}(\pi, \lambda)$ and $V_{0,\beta}(\pi, \lambda)$, equate them and solve it for λ. After simplification, the Whittle index for type-A arm is as follows.

$$W(\pi) = \rho_1 + \beta^{(K+1)}(\rho_0 - \rho_1)(1-p)^K + \frac{(\rho_0 - \rho_1)}{(1-\beta)}\left(1 - \beta^{(K+1)}\right) \times [(1 - \beta(1-p))\pi].$$

$$(9)$$

Here, $K = K(1, \pi)$ is waiting time before playing that arm again. Similarly, we can obtain the Whittle index formula for type-B arm, and it is

$$W(\pi) = \begin{cases} \rho_1 + (1-\beta)(\rho_0 - \rho_1)\pi & \text{if } \pi \in (0,1], \\ \rho_1 + (\rho_0 - \rho_1)\pi & \text{if } \pi = 0. \end{cases}$$

$$(10)$$

Remark 3. Note that the Whittle index of an arm depends on model parameters p, ρ_0, ρ_1, discount parameter β, and belief π.

3.2 Average Reward Problem

We rewrite the average reward problem (2) in the view of subsidy λ as follows.

$$V_{T,\phi}(\pi) := \mathsf{E}\left(\sum_{t=1}^{T} A_t^{\phi}\left(\pi_t \rho_0 + (1-\pi_t)\rho_1\right) + \lambda(1 - A_t^{\phi})\right),$$

$$V_{\phi}(\pi) = \max_{\phi} \lim_{T \to \infty} \frac{1}{T} V_{T,\phi}(\pi).$$

$$(11)$$

Here, $A^\phi(t) = i$ if $\phi(t) = i$, $i \in \{0,1\}$, $\pi_1 = \pi$. It is solved by the vanishing discount approach [3,26]—by first considering a discounted reward system and then taking limits as the discount approaches to 1. Define

$$\overline{V}_\beta(\pi, \lambda) := \begin{cases} V_\beta(\pi, \lambda) - V_\beta(1, \lambda) & \text{for type-A arm,} \\ V_\beta(\pi, \lambda) - V_\beta(0, \lambda) & \text{for type-B arm,} \end{cases}$$

for $\pi \in [0,1]$. Using Eq. (4), we can obtain for type-A arm

$$\overline{V}_\beta(\pi, \lambda) + (1-\beta)V_\beta(1, \lambda) = \max\left\{\lambda + \beta\overline{V}_\beta((1-p)\pi, \lambda), \pi\rho_0 + (1-\pi)\rho_1\right\}, \quad (12)$$

and for type-B arm

$$\overline{V}_\beta(\pi, \lambda) + (1-\beta)V_\beta(0, \lambda) = \max\left\{\lambda + \beta\overline{V}_\beta(\pi + p(1-\pi), \lambda), \pi\rho_0 + (1-\pi)\rho_1\right\}. \quad (13)$$

From Lemma 1, $\overline{V}_\beta(\pi, \lambda)$ is a convex monotone function in π for fixed λ and β. By definition of $\overline{V}_\beta(\pi, \lambda)$ we have $\overline{V}_\beta(1, \lambda) = 0$ for type-A and $\overline{V}_\beta(0, \lambda) = 0$ for type-B arm. Further, from Lemma 2, we know that there is a constant $C < \infty$ such that $\left|V_\beta(\pi, \lambda) - V_\beta(1, \lambda)\right| < C$ for fixed β and $\lambda \in [-\rho_1, \rho_1]$. This implies that $\overline{V}_\beta(\pi, \lambda)$ is bounded and Lipschitz-continuous. Finally, $(1-\beta)V_\beta(\pi, \lambda)$ is also bounded. Hence we can apply the Arzela-Ascoli theorem [28], to find a subsequence $(\overline{V}_{\beta_k}(\pi, \lambda), (1-\beta_k)V_{\beta_k}(\pi, \lambda))$ that converges uniformly to $(V(\pi, \lambda), g)$ as $\beta_k \to 1$. Thus, as $\beta_k \to 1$, along an appropriate subsequence, (12) reduces to

$$V(\pi, \lambda) + g = \max\left\{\lambda + V((1-p)\pi, \lambda), \pi\rho_0 + (1-\pi)\rho_1\right\}, \quad (14)$$

and (13) reduces to

$$V(\pi, \lambda) + g = \max\left\{\lambda + V(\pi + p(1-\pi), \lambda), \pi\rho_0 + (1-\pi)\rho_1\right\}. \quad (15)$$

Equations (14) and (15) are the dynamic programming equations for type-A and type-B arm in case of average reward system. Hence it is the optimal solution of (11).

Also, note that $V(\pi, \lambda)$ inherits the structural properties of $V_\beta(\pi, \lambda)$. From Lemma 1 and Theorem 1, we obtain next result.

Lemma 6.

1. For fixed λ, $V(\pi, \lambda)$ is a monotone non-increasing and convex in π.
2. The optimal policy is a single threshold type for $\lambda \in [\lambda_L, \lambda_H]$, where $\lambda_H = \rho_1$ and

$$\lambda_L = \begin{cases} \rho_0 + p(\rho_0 - \rho_1) & \text{for type A,} \\ \rho_1 & \text{for type B.} \end{cases}$$

This in turn leads us to the following theorem which is a direct analog of Theorem 6.17 in [26].

Theorem 3. *If there exists a bounded function $V(\pi, \lambda)$ for $\pi \in [0, 1]$, $\lambda \in [\lambda_L, \lambda_H]$ and a constant g that satisfies Eq. (14), (15) then there exists a stationary policy ϕ^* such that*

$$g = \max_\phi \lim_{T \to \infty} \frac{1}{T} V_{T,\phi}(\pi, \lambda) \tag{16}$$

$$\phi^* = \arg \max_\phi \lim_{T \to \infty} \frac{1}{T} V_{T,\phi}(\pi, \lambda). \tag{17}$$

for all $\pi \in [0, 1]$, fixed λ, and moreover, ϕ^* is the policy for which the RHS of (14), (15) is maximized.

We next derive the Whittle index formula. From Lemma 5, recall that to claim indexability, we have shown that $\pi_T(\lambda)$ is a monotonically decreasing in λ for discounted reward case. Similarly, in average reward case, we require to show this claim. From Arzela-Ascoli theorem, we know that $V(\pi, \lambda)$ inherits the properties of $V_\beta(\pi, \lambda)$. Thus, $\pi_T(\lambda)$ is a monotonically decreasing in λ for $\beta = 1$. Then we can show that an arm is indexable. Further, the index can be evaluated by letting $\beta \to 1$ in the Whittle index formula of discounted case. Hence from Eqs. (9) and (10), we obtain the Whittle index formula.

- For type-A arm:

$$W(\pi) = \rho_1 + (\rho_0 - \rho_1)(1 - p)^K + K(\rho_0 - \rho_1)\left[(1 - (1 - p))\pi\right]. \tag{18}$$

  Here, $K = K(1, \pi)$ is waiting time before playing that arm again.
- For type-B arm:

$$W(\pi) = \rho_1. \tag{19}$$

4   Numerical Results: Whittle Index and Myopic Algorithm

In this section we present some numerical results to illustrate the performance of the Whittle index based recommendation algorithm. The simulations use Algorithm 1. We compare the performance of Whittle index based algorithm against that of a myopic algorithm that plays the arm that has the highest expected reward in the step. We consider small size ($N = 5, 10$), medium size ($N = 20$), and large size ($N = 100$) systems. For all the cases we use $\beta = 0.99$.

In Fig. 3, we present numerical examples when there are a small number of arms, i.e., $N = 5$. In this case, arms 1–4 are of type A and arm 5 is of type B arm. The system is simulated for parameter sets which are also shown in the figure. In all the cases, the initial belief used is $\pi = [0.4, 0.4, 0.4, 0.4, 0.4]$. In the

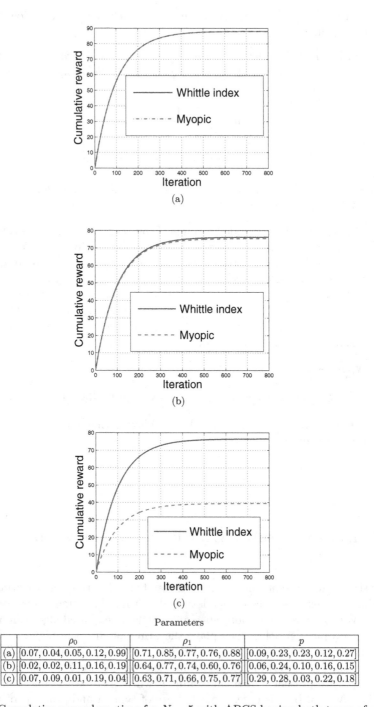

Fig. 3. Cumulative reward vs. time for $N = 5$ with APCS having both types of arms.

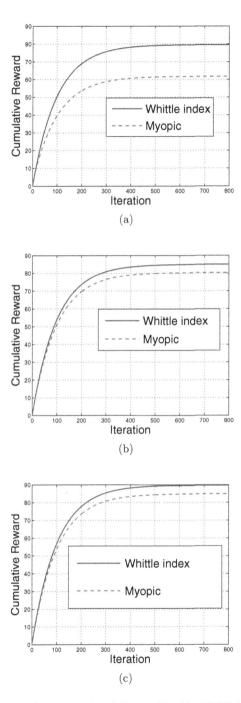

Fig. 4. Cumulative reward vs. time for different N with APCS having both types of arms.

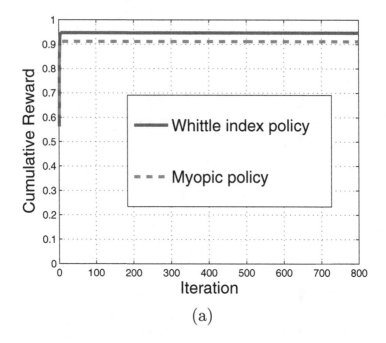

(a)

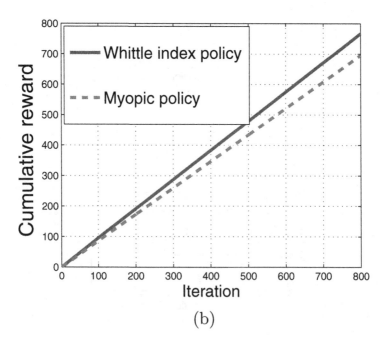

(b)

Fig. 5. Cumulative reward vs. time for $\beta = 0.3, 1$ and $N = 200$ with APCS having both types of arms. Figure 5a $\beta = 0.3$ and Fig. 5b $\beta = 1$.

Algorithm 1: Whittle index algorithm for APCS with type A and type B arms.

Input: N arms, initial belief $\pi = [\pi(1), \cdots, \pi(N)]$, $\pi_1 = \pi$,
repeat
  for $n = 1, \ldots, N$ **do**
    Compute $W(\pi(n))$
  end for
  Evaluate $i = \arg\max_{1 \leq n \leq N} W(\pi(n))$.
  Play arm i
  if i is Type A **then**
    $\pi_{t+1}(i) = 1$
  end if
  if I is Type B **then**
    $\pi_{t+1}(i) = 0$
  end if
  for $n = 1, \ldots, M, n \neq i$ **do**
    $\pi_{t+1}(n) = (1 - p_n)\pi_t(n)$,
  end for
  for $n = M + 1, \ldots, N, n \neq i$ **do**
    $\pi_{t+1}(n) = (1 - p_n)\pi_t(n) + p_n$,
  end for
until forever

---

first system ρ_0 and ρ_1 for the type B arm are close to one and both policies almost always choose that arm. Hence their performances are also comparable. This is seen in Fig. 3(a). The behavior is similar even when the ρ_1s of all the arms are comparable as in the second system with performance shown in Fig. 3(b). In this system, in the 800 plays, the type B arm was played 28 and 75 times in the Whittle index and the myopic systems respectively. In the third small system, the Whittle index system plays the type B arms significantly more frequently than the myopic system and has a significantly better performance; this is shown in Fig. 3c.

Figure 4 shows the performance of the two systems for larger systems. These are obtained as follows. For $N = 10$, we have nine type A arms and one type B arm. For $N = 50$, we use 48 type A arms and 2 type B arms. The system with $N = 200$, has 190 type A arms and 10 type B arms. We generate reward and transition probabilities randomly using the formula $\rho_0 = 0.01 + 0.19 * \text{rand}(1, N)$, $\rho_1 = 0.6 + 0.3 * \text{rand}(1, N)$, $p = 0.01 + 0.29 * \text{rand}(1, N)$. The initial belief $\pi = 0.4 * \text{ones}(1, N)$. We observe that the Whittle index algorithm some gain the over myopic algorithm but the gain decreases with increasing N. The decrease is due because with large N, the waiting time for each item is large and this causes many arms to be in state 1 with high probability.

In Fig. 5, we compare the performance of two systems for different values of discount parameter $\beta = 0.3, 1$ and $N = 200$. We notice that even for small $\beta = 0.3$, the Whittle index algorithm gains over myopic algorithm.

5   Variants of Type A and Type B Arms

Here, we mention few extensions of a hidden RMAB. By considering different structure on transition probabilities, we can obtain different type of arms and models.

- We consider few variants of type A and type B arms that generalized our current model. The transition probabilities for this model are as follows.

$$P_{01}^n(0) = p_n, \quad P_{10}^n(0) = q_n \text{ for both type arm,}$$

$$P_{01}^n(1) = \begin{cases} \epsilon P_{01}^n(0) & \text{if arm is type A,} \\ (1 - \epsilon) + \epsilon P_{01}^n(0) & \text{if arm is type B,} \end{cases}$$

$$P_{10}^n(1) = \begin{cases} (1 - \epsilon) + \epsilon P_{10}^n(0) & \text{if arm is type A,} \\ \epsilon P_{10}^n(0) & \text{if arm is type B,} \end{cases}$$

for $\epsilon \in [0, 1)$. This may be thought as the arm evolving with different speeds under actions 1 and 0. This is referred to dual speed restless bandit in [10, Chap. 6, Sect. 6.2].
- Notice that for $\epsilon = 0$, current model leads to a simple variant of type A and type B arm. For this model, we can derive all properties of value functions as in Sect. 3 using similar approach. Also, the Whittle index formula can be obtained. This is given in next subsection.
- For $\epsilon \in (0, 1)$, difficulty level of problem increases significantly because the current belief about state, $\pi_{t+1}(n)$ becomes non linear function of previous belief $\pi_t(n)$ when arm n is played. Thus, it is hard to show that the arm is Whittle-indexable. But the approximate Whittle-indexability is proved in [22] under restriction on discount parameter β.

5.1   A Simple Variant of the Current Model

In this, we suppose $\epsilon = 0$, and derive the value function expressions, and Whittle index expression. To obtain these, we consider a single arm restless bandit. In such setting, we have transition probabilities as follows. $P_{01}(0) = p$, $P_{10}(0) = q$ for both type arm, and

$$P_{01}^n(1) = \begin{cases} 0 & \text{if arm is type A,} \\ 1 & \text{if arm is type B,} \end{cases}$$

$$P_{10}^n(1) = \begin{cases} 1 & \text{if arm is type A,} \\ 0 & \text{if arm is type B.} \end{cases}$$

We first provide analysis for type A arm and then for type B arm.

1. Type A arm: The dynamic programming equation for discounted reward system is

$$V_\beta(\pi, \lambda) = \max\{V_{0,\beta}(\pi, \lambda), V_{1,\beta}(\pi, \lambda)\},$$
$$V_{0,\beta}(\pi, \lambda) = \lambda + \beta V_\beta(\gamma(\pi), \lambda),$$
$$V_{1,\beta}(\pi, \lambda) = \pi\rho_0 + (1 - \pi)\rho_1 + \beta V_\beta(1, \lambda)),$$

where $\gamma(\pi) = \pi(1 - p) + (1 - \pi)q$. We also assume that $p + q \leq 1$. Define $\gamma^k(\pi) := \gamma^{k-1}(\gamma(\pi))$. Note that as $\lim_{k \to \infty} \gamma^k(\pi) = \gamma_\infty$, where $\gamma_\infty = \frac{q}{q+p}$. Also observe that as $\pi > \gamma_\infty$, then $\gamma^k(\pi)$ is decreases to γ_∞ with k and if $\pi < \gamma_\infty$ then $\gamma^k(\pi)$ is increases to γ_∞ with k.

Mimicking the proof technique in Sect. 3, we can show that the optimal policy is of a threshold type and arm is Whittle indexable. Now using threshold policy result, we can derive the closed form expressions for value functions.

$$K(\pi, \pi_T) := \min\{k \geq 0 : \gamma^k(\pi) < \pi_T\}.$$

Then

$$K(\pi, \pi_T) = \begin{cases} 0 & \text{if } \pi < \pi_T, \\ \left\lfloor \frac{\log(\pi_T)}{\log(\gamma(\pi))} \right\rfloor + 1 & \text{if } \pi \geq \pi_T. \end{cases}$$

To obtain value function expressions, we consider two cases.

- When $\pi_T \in [0, \gamma_\infty)$, $K(1, \pi_T) = \infty$ because $\gamma^k(\pi)$ is decreasing to γ_∞ and this will never cross a threshold π_T for finite k. Also, from Theorem 1, we can have

$$V_{0,\beta}(1, \lambda) = \lambda + \beta V_{0,\beta}(\gamma(1), \lambda)$$
$$= \lambda + \beta\lambda + \beta^2 V_{0,\beta}(\gamma^2(1), \lambda).$$

And $\lim_{k \to \infty} \gamma^k(1) = \gamma_\infty$. Expanding recursion of $V_{0,\beta}(\gamma^k(1), \lambda)$ we obtain

$$V_{0,\beta}(1, \lambda) = \frac{\lambda}{1 - \beta}.$$
$$V_{1,\beta}(\pi, \lambda) = \pi\rho_0 + (1 - \pi)\rho_1 + \beta\frac{\lambda}{1 - \beta}.$$

Note that $\pi \geq \pi_T$, $\gamma^k(\pi) \geq \pi_T$ for any $k \geq 1$. Thus

$$V_{0,\beta}(\pi, \lambda) = \begin{cases} \lambda + \beta\left(\gamma(\pi)\rho_0 + (1 - \gamma(\pi))\rho_1\right) + \beta^2\frac{\lambda}{1-\beta} & \text{if } \gamma(\pi) < \pi_T, \\ \frac{\lambda}{1-\beta} & \text{if } \gamma(\pi) \geq \pi_T. \end{cases}$$

- When $\pi_T \in [\gamma_\infty, 1]$, we have $K(1, \pi_T) < \infty$. Using a threshold policy result and after simplification we get

$$V_{0,\beta}(1, \lambda) = \frac{\lambda \left(1 - \beta^{K(1,\pi_T)}\right)}{\left(1 - \beta^{(K(1,\pi_T)+1)}\right)(1 - \beta)} + \beta^{K(1,\pi_T)} \frac{\rho(\gamma^{K(1,\pi_T)}(1))}{\left(1 - \beta^{(K(1,\pi_T)+1)}\right)},$$

$$V_{0,\beta}(\pi, \lambda) = \frac{\lambda \left(1 - \beta^{K(\pi,\pi_T)}\right)}{(1 - \beta)} + \beta^{K(\pi,\pi_T)} \rho\left(\gamma^{K(\pi,\pi_T)}(\pi)\right) + \beta^{(K(\pi,\pi_T)+1)} V_{0,\beta}(1, \lambda)$$

$$V_{1,\beta}(\pi, \lambda) = \rho(\pi) + \beta V_{0,\beta}(1, \lambda).$$

where $\rho(\pi) = \pi\rho_0 + (1 - \pi)\rho_1$.
We now derive expressions for the Whittle index. When $\pi \in [0, \gamma_\infty)$, the Whittle index is

$$W(\pi) = \pi\rho_0 + (1 - \pi)\rho_1.$$

When $\pi \in [\gamma_\infty, 1]$ the Whittle index is

$$W(\pi) = \rho_1 + \beta^{(K(1,\pi)+1)}(\rho_0 - \rho_1)\gamma^{K(1,\pi)}(1) + \frac{(\rho_0 - \rho_1)}{(1 - \beta)}\left(1 - \beta^{(K(1,\pi)+1)}\right)(\pi - \beta\gamma(\pi)).$$

Using the vanishing discounted approach, we can analyse average reward problem and for that we can obtain the Whittle index expression by letting discount parameter β approach 1. Hence

$$W(\pi) = \begin{cases} \pi\rho_0 + (1 - \pi)\rho_1 & \text{if } \pi \in [0, \gamma_\infty) \\ \rho_1 + (\rho_0 - \rho_1)\gamma^K(1) + K(\rho_0 - \rho_1)(\pi - \beta\gamma(\pi)) & \text{if } \pi \in [\gamma_\infty, 1] \end{cases}$$

where $K = K(1, \pi)$.

2. Type B arm: The dynamic programming equation for discounted reward is as follows.

$$V_\beta(\pi, \lambda) = \max\{V_{1,\beta}(\pi, \lambda), V_{0,\beta}(\pi, \lambda)\},$$
$$V_{1,\beta}(\pi, \lambda) = \pi\rho_0 + (1 - \pi)\rho_1 + \beta V_\beta(0, \lambda),$$
$$V_{0,\beta}(\pi, \lambda) = \lambda + \beta V_\beta(\gamma(\pi), \lambda).$$

We now obtain the value function expressions. For $\pi_T \in (0, 1]$, we can get

$$V_{1,\beta}(0, \lambda) = \rho_1 + \beta V_{1,\beta}(0, \lambda)$$

Hence after simplification we have

$$V_{1,\beta}(0, \lambda) = \frac{\rho_1}{1 - \beta},$$

$$V_{1,\beta}(\pi, \lambda) = \pi\rho_0 + (1 - \pi)\rho_1 + \beta\frac{\rho_1}{1 - \beta}.$$

If $\pi_T \in (0, \gamma_\infty)$ then

$$V_{0,\beta}(\pi, \lambda) = \begin{cases} \lambda + \beta\rho(\gamma(\pi)) + \beta^2 \frac{\rho_1}{1-\beta} & \text{if } \pi < \pi_T, \\ \frac{\lambda}{1-\beta} & \text{if } \pi \geq \pi_T. \end{cases}$$

If $\pi_T \in [\gamma_\infty, 1]$, then

$$V_{0,\beta}(\pi, \lambda) = \begin{cases} \frac{\lambda(1-\beta^{K(\pi,\pi_T)})}{1-\beta} + \beta^{K(\pi,\pi_T)}\left(\rho(\gamma^{K(\pi,\pi_T)}(\pi)) + \beta\frac{\rho_1}{1-\beta}\right) & \text{if } \pi < \pi_T, \\ \lambda + \beta\rho(\gamma(\pi)) + \beta^2\frac{\lambda}{1-\beta} & \text{if } \pi > \pi_T, \\ \frac{\lambda}{1-\beta} & \text{if } \pi = \pi_T. \end{cases}$$

For $\pi_T = 0$ we can obtain

$$V_{1,\beta}(\pi, \lambda) = \pi\rho_0 + (1-\pi)\rho_1 + \beta\frac{\lambda}{1-\beta},$$

$$V_{0,\beta}(\pi, \lambda) = \frac{\lambda}{1-\beta}.$$

The Whittle index expression is given as.

$$W(\pi) = \begin{cases} \rho_1 & \text{for } \pi = 0, \\ (1-\beta)(\pi\rho_0 + (1-\pi)\rho_1) + \beta\rho_1 & \text{for } \pi \in (0, 1]. \end{cases}$$

For average reward, the Whittle index in this model is same as (19).

6   Thompson-Sampling Based Learning

The key to a useful use of the model from the preceding sections is the knowledge of the parameters. These are not known a priori in most systems. In this section, we describe an algorithm that learns the parameters from the available feedback. Our scheme is a version of Thompson sampling [27] which has been studied for stochastic multi-armed bandits [1,12], learning in Markov decision processes (MDPs) [11] and in POMDPs [21]. In fact our algorithm is an extension of the scheme for the one-armed bandit, modeled as a POMDP, that was described and analysed in [21]. An important requirement of the learning algorithm is to have a low regret, i.e., the exploration and exploitation sequences should be cleverly mixed to ensure that the difference between the ideal and the realised objective functions are small. In [21] we formally show that the regret is logarithmic for the one-armed case. The algorithm for the multi-armed case is described in Algorithm 2, and we expect that its performance is also good. A formal analysis is being worked out.

The algorithm proceeds as follows. At the beginning, we initialize a prior distribution on the space of all candidate parameters models, which in our case is a subset Θ_i of the unit cube $[0, 1]^3$; Θ_i contains all possible models for the

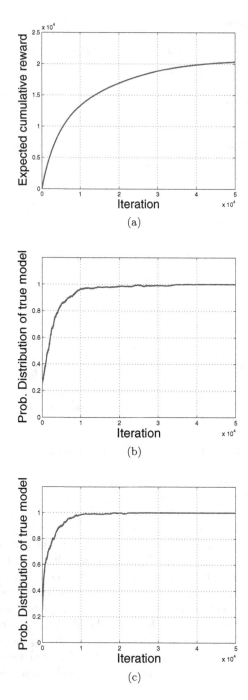

Fig. 6. Expected cumulative regret vs. time horizon and probability mass on true model vs. time horizon for both type of arms.

parameters θ_i of arm i. In each step, assume that the true values of the parameters are θ_i and use the Whittle index (or the myopic) algorithm to choose the arm that is to be played. Recall that the arm with highest index is played in the Whittle index algorithm and the arm with highest expected reward is played in myopic algorithm. The playing of the arm A_t at time t yields a payoff R_t. This is used to update the prior distribution Z_i of the parameter space for that arm. This update is performed using Bayes' rule and the observed reward. The model distribution for the other arms remain unchanged. We explain the update mechanism next. Let $\mathcal{B}(\Theta_i)$ denote the Borel σ-algebra of $\Theta_i \subset [0,1]^3$ for the arms indexed by $i = 1, \ldots, N$. Let $\Pr\left(R = r \mid \theta, A\right)$ denote the likelihood, under the model θ, of observing a reward of $r \in \{0, 1\}$ upon action $A \in \{1, \cdots, N\}$. This likelihood can be seen to be as follows.

$$\Pr\left(R = r \mid \theta, A = i\right) = \begin{cases} f(\theta_i, i) & \text{if } r = 1, \\ 1 - f(\theta_i, i) & \text{if } r = 0. \end{cases}$$

Here $f(\theta_i, i)$ is the probability of observing a reward of 1 after playing arm i when the parameter is θ_i. Letting k_i denote the number of time steps since the last time that arm i was played, we can obtain $f(\theta_i, i)$ as follows.

$$f(\theta_i, i) = \begin{cases} (1 - p_i)^{k_i} \rho_{i,0} + (1 - (1 - p_i)^{k_i}) \rho_{i,1}, & \text{if } i \text{ is type A arm,} \\ (1 - (1 - p_i)^{k_i}) \rho_{i,0} + (1 - p_i)^{k_i} \rho_{i,1}, & \text{if } i \text{ is type B arm.} \end{cases}$$

This likelihood is used to update the prior distribution $Z_{i,t}$ and the parameters of the arm is selected from this distribution. We reiterate that the parameters and the prior distribution on these parameters, of the arms that are not played remain unchanged. The states of the arms, $\pi_{i,t}$ are now updated and the algorithm proceeds as before. The details are described in Algorithm 2.

6.1 Numerical Results

We illustrate performance of Thompson sampling algorithm in Fig. 6 for $N = 5$, where 4 type A items and one type B item. The true model parameters are $p = [0.15, 0.25, 0.25, 0.15, 0.15]$, $\rho_0 = [0.2, 0.2, 0.1, 0.1, 0.1]$, and these are assumed unknown. We assume that $\rho_1 = 0.7$ is known. We simulate it with discrete parameter space into a (2×2) grid of $(0.15, 0.25, 0.1, 0.2)$. At the start of algorithm, we use uniform prior over the 4 points for all the arms. We plot the expected cumulative regret as function of time horizon, see Fig. 6a. The regret incurs whenever sample model different from true model. In Fig. 6b and c, we plot the probability distribution on the true model against time for both types of items. We note that probability distribution of true model is approaching to 1, in Whittle index based algorithm. This suggests that the Thompson sampling strategy indeed learns the true model rather quickly. A more detailed analysis is being performed.

Algorithm 2: Thompson sampling algorithm

Input: Set of arms $\mathcal{N} = \{1, 2, \ldots, N\}$, Action space $\mathcal{A} = \{1, 2, \ldots, N\}$,
Observation space $\mathcal{R} = \{0, 1\}$,
for $i = 1, 2, \cdots, N$ **do**
    Parameter space $\Theta_i \subseteq [0, 1]^3$,
    Prior probability distribution $Z_{i,0}$ over Θ_i
    Sample parameter $\theta_{i,0} \in \Theta_j$ according to $Z_{i,0}$
    $\pi_{i,0} = 1$
end for
for $t = 1, 2, \ldots$ **do**
    $i = $ Best arm determined by Whittle index based policy using $\{\theta_{t-1}, \pi_{t-1}\}$
    Action $A_t = i$
    $R_t = $ Reward from action A_t.
    Update $Z_{i,t}$ to

$$Z_{i,t}(B_i) := \frac{\int_{B_i} \mathsf{Pr}\left(R = R_t \mid \theta_{t-1}, A_t\right) Z_{i,t-1}(\theta_i)d\theta_i}{\int_{\Theta_i} \mathsf{Pr}\left(R = R_t \mid \theta_{t-1}, A_t\right) Z_{i,t-1}(\theta_i)d\theta_i}$$

    Sample parameter $\theta_{i,t} \in \Theta_i$ according to $Z_{i,t}$
    for $j = 1, 2, \cdots, N$ **do**
        Update $\pi_{j,t}$
    end for
end for

---

7   Conclusion

In this paper we studied a restless multi-armed bandit for automated playlist recommendation system with two types of items. We considered infinite horizon discounted and average reward problem. We show that both types arm are indexable and we derived the closed form expression for the Whittle index derived from the state of the belief in the state of the arms and from the model parameters. Our numerical results illustrate that the Whittle index algorithm can perform better than a myopic algorithm. We further discussed the dual speed restless bandit with hidden states and derived Whittle index expression for a variant. We have proposed a Thompson sampling based learning algorithm to learn the true model parameters. Simulation results indicate that the learning is indeed effective. The performance guarantees of the learning algorithm are being investigated.

A   Appendix

A.1   Proof of Lemma 2

The proof is similar for type A and type B arm. It has minor variations due to value function expressions. Here, we present the proof for type A arm. We omit the proof for type B arm. The proof is using induction techniques.

1. Let

$$V_{\beta,1}(\pi,\lambda) = \max\{\lambda, \pi\rho_0 + (1-\pi)\rho_1\}$$
$$V_{\beta,n+1}(\pi,\lambda) = \max\{\lambda + \beta V_{\beta,n}((1-p)\pi,\lambda),$$
$$\pi\rho_0 + (1-\pi)\rho_1 + \beta V_{\beta,n}(1,\lambda)\} \qquad (20)$$

The partial derivative of $V_{\beta,1}(\pi,\lambda)$ w.r.t. π is 0 or $-(\rho_1 - \rho_0)$, depending on π, and λ. Thus the absolute value of slope of $V_{\beta,1}(\pi,\lambda)$ w.r.t. π is bounded above by $(\rho_1 - \rho_0)$. Making the induction hypothesis that the absolute value of slope of $V_{\beta,n}(\pi,\lambda)$ w.r.t. π is bounded above by $(\rho_1 - \rho_0)$. We next want to show that the absolute value of slope of $V_{\beta,n+1}(\pi,\lambda)$ w.r.t. π is bounded above by $(\rho_1 - \rho_0)$.

Note that derivative of the term $\lambda + \beta V_{\beta,n}((1-p)\pi,\lambda)$ w.r.t. π is bounded by $(\rho_0 - \rho_1)$ because first term is constant and second term's derivative is bounded by $\beta(1-p)(\rho_0 - \rho_1)$, this is bounded by $(\rho_1 - \rho_0)$.

Also, the absolute value of slope of $\pi\rho_0 + (1-\pi)\rho_1 + \beta V_{\beta,n}(1,\lambda)$ w.r.t. π is bounded $(\rho_1 - \rho_0)$ because first term's slope is $(\rho_0 - \rho_1)$ and second term is constant. Hence the absolute value of slope of $V_{\beta,n+1}(\pi,\lambda)$ w.r.t. π is bounded above by $(\rho_1 - \rho_0)$.

By induction, it is true for all $n \geq 1$. From [4, Chap. 7], [5, Proposition 2.1, Chap. 2], $V_{\beta,n}(\pi,\lambda) \to V_\beta(\pi,\lambda)$, uniformly. Thus the absolute value of slope of $V_\beta(\pi,\lambda)$ w.r.t. π is bounded above by $(\rho_1 - \rho_0)$.

2. The partial derivative of $V_{\beta,1}(\pi,\lambda)$ in (20) w.r.t. λ is 1 or 0, depending on π, and λ. Thus $\frac{\partial V_{\beta,1}(\pi,\lambda)}{\partial\lambda} < \frac{1}{1-\beta}$ for $0 < \beta < 1$. By induction hypothesis $\frac{\partial V_{\beta,n}(\pi,\lambda)}{\partial\lambda} < \frac{1}{1-\beta}$. The partial derivative of first term in (20) w.r.t. λ is

$$1 + \beta\frac{\partial V_{\beta,n}((1-p)\pi,\lambda)}{\partial\lambda}.$$

It is bounded above by $\frac{1}{1-\beta}$ by our assumption. The partial derivative of second term in (20) w.r.t. λ is

$$\beta\frac{\partial V_{\beta,n}(1,\lambda)}{\partial\lambda}$$

It is also bounded above by $\frac{1}{1-\beta}$. Hence the partial derivative of $V_{\beta,n+1}(\pi,\lambda)$ w.r.t. λ is bounded above by $\frac{1}{1-\beta}$. By induction, it is true for all $n \geq 1$. Using earlier technique, $V_{\beta,n}(\pi,\lambda) \to V_\beta(\pi,\lambda)$, uniformly. Therefore, $\frac{\partial V_\beta(\pi,\lambda)}{\partial\lambda} < \frac{1}{1-\beta}$.

This completes the proof. $\square$

A.2   Proof of Lemma 3

The proof is analogous for both type A and type B arm. Also, it lead to same Lipschitz constant. Here, we detail the proof for only type A arm and omit it for type B arm.

Fix λ, β. Define

$$d_\lambda(\pi) := V_{1,\beta}(\pi, \lambda) - V_{0,\beta}(\pi, \lambda)$$

We have to show that $d_\lambda(\pi_1) > d_\lambda(\pi_2)$ whenever $\pi_2 > \pi_1$, for all $\pi_1, \pi_2 \in [0,1]$. Now

$$d_\lambda(\pi_2) - d_\lambda(\pi_1) = \beta \left(V_\beta((1-p)\pi_1, \lambda) - V_\beta((1-p)\pi_2, \lambda) \right) - (\rho_1 - \rho_0)(\pi_2 - \pi_1).$$

From Lemma 2-1, we obtain

$$V_\beta((1-p)\pi_1, \lambda) - V_\beta((1-p)\pi_2, \lambda) < (1-p)(\rho_1 - \rho_0)|\pi_1 - \pi_2|.$$

Moreover,

$$\beta(1-p)(\rho_1 - \rho_0)|\pi_1 - \pi_2| < (\rho_1 - \rho_0)|\pi_1 - \pi_2|.$$

This implies $d_\lambda(\pi_2) - d_\lambda(\pi_1) < 0$ and our claim follows.   □

A.3   Proof of Lemma 4

– Type A arm:

Fix π, β. It is enough to show that $\frac{\partial d_\lambda(\pi)}{\partial \lambda} = \frac{\partial V_{1,\beta}(\pi,\lambda)}{\partial \lambda} - \frac{\partial V_{0,\beta}(\pi,\lambda)}{\partial \lambda} < 0$. From Eq. (6), taking partial derivative w.r.t. λ, we obtain

$$\frac{\partial V_{1,\beta}(\pi, \lambda)}{\partial \lambda} = \beta \frac{\partial V_{0,\beta}(1, \lambda)}{\partial \lambda},$$

$$\frac{\partial V_{0,\beta}(\pi, \lambda)}{\partial \lambda} = \frac{1 - \beta^{K(\pi,\pi_T)}}{1 - \beta} + \beta^{(K(\pi,\pi_T)+1)} \frac{\partial V_{0,\beta}(1, \lambda)}{\partial \lambda}.$$

Then

$$\frac{\partial V_{1,\beta}(\pi, \lambda)}{\partial \lambda} - \frac{\partial V_{0,\beta}(\pi, \lambda)}{\partial \lambda} = \beta \frac{\partial V_{0,\beta}(1, \lambda)}{\partial \lambda}(1 - \beta^{K(\pi,\pi_T)}) - \frac{(1 - \beta^{K(\pi,\pi_T)})}{(1 - \beta)}.$$

Rewriting, we have

$$\frac{\partial d_\lambda(\pi)}{\partial \lambda} = (1 - \beta^{K(\pi,\pi_T)}) \left[\beta \frac{\partial V_{0,\beta}(1, \lambda)}{\partial \lambda} - \frac{1}{(1 - \beta)} \right].$$

From (6), we can obtain

$$\frac{\partial V_{0,\beta}(\pi, \lambda)}{\partial \lambda} = \frac{(1 - \beta^{\tilde{K}})}{(1 - \beta^{\tilde{K}+1})(1 - \beta)},$$

where $\tilde{K} = K(1, \pi_T)$. After substitution and simplifying expressions, we have

$$\frac{\partial d_\lambda(\pi)}{\partial \lambda} = \frac{(1 - \beta^{K(\pi,\pi_T)})}{(1 - \beta)} \frac{\left(\beta - \beta^{\tilde{K}+1} - 1 + \beta^{\tilde{K}+1} \right)}{(1 - \beta^{\tilde{K}+1})}.$$

Clearly, $\frac{\partial d_\lambda(\pi)}{\partial \lambda} < 0$ for $\beta \in [0, 1)$.

– Type B arm:
  From (7), when $\pi_T \in (0, 1]$ and all $\pi \in [0, 1]$ we can obtain following

$$\frac{\partial V_{1,\beta}(\pi, \lambda)}{\partial \lambda} = 0,$$

$$\frac{\partial V_{0,\beta}(\pi, \lambda)}{\partial \lambda} = \begin{cases} 1 & \text{if } T(\pi) < \pi_T, \\ \frac{1}{1-\beta} & \text{if } T(\pi) \geq \pi_T. \end{cases}$$

Clearly, we have $\frac{\partial d_\eta(\pi)}{\partial \eta} < 0$ for $\pi_T \in (0, 1]$. When $\pi_T = 0$, we can get

$$\frac{\partial V_{1,\beta}(\pi, \lambda)}{\partial \lambda} = \frac{\beta}{1-\beta},$$

$$\frac{\partial V_{0,\beta}(\pi, \lambda)}{\partial \lambda} = \frac{1}{1-\beta}.$$

Hence $\frac{\partial d_\lambda(\pi)}{\partial \lambda} < 0$.

This completes the proof. □

References

1. Agrawal, S., Goyal, N.: Analysis of Thompson sampling for the multi-armed bandit problem. JMLR Workshop Conf. Proc. **23**, 3901–3926 (2012)
2. Auer, P., Cesa-Bianchi, N., Fischer, P.: Finite-time analysis of the multiarmed bandit problem. Mach. Learn. **47**(2–3), 235–256 (2002)
3. Avrachenkov, K., Borkar, V.S.: Whittle index policy for crawling ephemeral content. Technical report, report no. 8702, INRIA (2015). https://hal.archives-ouvertes.fr/
4. Bertsekas, D.P.: Dynamic Programming and Optimal Control, vol. 1, 1st edn. Athena Scientific, Belmont (1995)
5. Bertsekas, D.P.: Dynamic Programming and Optimal Control, vol. 2, 1st edn. Athena Scientific, Belmont (1995)
6. Bubeck, S., Bianchi, N.C.: Regret analysis of stochastic and non-stochastic multi-armed bandit problem. Found. Trends Mach. Learn. **5**(1), 1–122 (2012)
7. Candes, E., Tao, T.: The power of convex relaxation: near optimal matrix completion. IEEE Trans. Inf. Theory **56**(5), 2053–2080 (2010)
8. Caron, S., Kveton, B., Lelarge, M., Bhagat, S.: Leveraging side observations in stochastic bandits. Arxiv (2012)
9. Chapelle, O., Li, L.: An empirical evaluation of Thompson sampling. In: Proceedings of NIPS (2011)
10. Gittins, J., Glazebrook, K., Weber, R.: Multi-armed Bandit Allocation Indices, 2nd edn. Wiley, New York (2011)
11. Gopalan, A., Mannor, S.: Thompson sampling for learning parameterized Markov decision processes. In: Proceedings of COLT (2015)
12. Gopalan, A., Mannor, S., Mansour, Y.: Thompson sampling for complex online problems. In: Proceedings of ICML (2014)

13. Hariri, N., Mobasher, B., Burke, R.: Context-aware music recommendation based on latent topic sequential patterns. In: Proceedings of ACM RecSys (2012)
14. Lai, T.L., Robbins, H.: Asymptotically efficient adaptive allocation rules. Adv. Appl. Math. **6**(1), 4–22 (1985)
15. Langford, J., Zhang, T.: The epoch-greedy algorithm for contextual multi-armed bandits. In: Proceedings of NIPS (2007)
16. Li, L., Chu, W., Langford, J., Schapire, R.E.: A contextual-bandit approach to personalized news article recommendation. In: Proceedings of ACM WWW (2010)
17. Liu, H., Liu, K., Zhao, Q.: Learning in a changing world: restless multiarmed bandit with unknown dynamics. IEEE Trans. Inf. Theory **59**(3), 1902–1916 (2013)
18. Liu, K., Zhao, Q.: Indexability of restless bandit problems and optimality of Whittle index for dynamic multichannel access. IEEE Trans. Inf. Theory **56**(11), 5557–5567 (2010)
19. Meshram, R., Manjunath, D., Gopalan, A.: A restless bandit with no observable states for recommendation systems and communication link scheduling. In: Proceedings of IEEE CDC (2015)
20. Meshram, R., Gopalan, A., Manjunath, D.: Optimal recommendation to users that react: online learning for a class of POMDPs. In: Proceedings of IEEE CDC (2016)
21. Meshram, R., Gopalan, A., Manjunath, D.: Optimal recommendation to users that react: online learning for a class of POMDPs. Arxiv (2016)
22. Meshram, R., Manjunath, D., Gopalan, A.: On the whittle index for restless multi-armed hidden Markov bandits. Arxiv (2016)
23. Meshram, R., Gopalan, A., Manjunath, D.: Restless bandits that hide their hand and recommendation systems. In: Proceedings of IEEE COMSNETS (2017)
24. Papadimitriou, C.H., Tsitsiklis, J.H.: The complexity of optimal queueing network control. Math. Oper. Res. **24**(2), 293–305 (1999)
25. Ross, S.M.: Quality control under Markovian deterioration. Manag. Sci. **17**(9), 587–596 (1971)
26. Ross, S.M.: Applied Probability Models with Optimization Applications. Dover Publications, New York (1993)
27. Thompson, W.R.: On the likelihood that one unknown probability exceeds another in view of the evidence of two samples. Biometrika **24**(3–4), 285–294 (1933)
28. Walter, R.: Principles of Mathematical Analysis, 3rd edn. McGraw-Hill Book Co., New York (1976)
29. Whittle, P.: Restless bandits: activity allocation in a changing world. J. Appl. Probab. **25**(1), 287–298 (1988)

Author Index

Printed in the United States
By Bookmasters